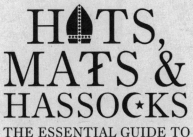

HATS, MATS & HASSOCKS

THE ESSENTIAL GUIDE TO RELIGIOUS ETIQUETTE

EDITED BY STUART M. MATLINS,
ARTHUR J. MAGIDA AND
DAVID MOLONEY

HATS, MATS & HASSOCKS

THE ESSENTIAL GUIDE TO RELIGIOUS ETIQUETTE

EDITED BY STUART M. MATLINS,
ARTHUR J. MAGIDA AND
DAVID MOLONEY

H
HODDER

Hats, Mats and Hassocks is based on the award-winning fourth edition of
How to Be a Perfect Stranger: The Essential Religious Etiquette Handbook
(SkyLight Paths Publishing, 2006) and is a revised and updated edition for the UK.

First published in Great Britain in 2010 by Hodder & Stoughton
An Hachette UK company

This paperback edition first published in 2011

1

A CIP catalogue record for this title is available from the British Library

ISBN 978 0 340 97941 9

Typeset in Sabon MT by Ellipsis Digital Limited, Glasgow

Printed and bound in the UK by Clays Ltd, St Ives plc

Hodder & Stoughton policy is to use papers that are natural, renewable and
recyclable products and made from wood grown in sustainable forests.
The logging and manufacturing processes are expected to conform to the
environmental regulations of the country of origin.

Hodder & Stoughton Ltd
338 Euston Road
London NW1 3BH

www.hodderfaith.com

Contents

Acknowledgements

A book such as this is the product of many contributions by many people. It could be no other way given the broad tapestry of religions in the UK. This essential handbook on religious etiquette is based on the award-winning fourth edition of *How to Be a Perfect Stranger: The Essential Religious Etiquette Handbook* (SkyLight Paths Publishing, 2006), which surveys the North American tapestry.

Instrumental in the evolution of the original edition were Richard A. Siegel and William Shanken, who developed the original concept and helped get the first volume into gear. Stuart M. Matlins, publisher of SkyLight Paths, developed the methodology for obtaining the information, and with Arthur J. Magida oversaw the research and writing and provided the impetus for the project. Sandra Korinchak, editor, shepherded the project from start to finish with the help of Jennifer Goneau, editorial assistant. Research assistant Susan Parks helped ensure that certain denominations responded promptly to our requests. And Jordan D. Wood generously assumed an initiative that delighted us all. Michael Schwartzentruber, series editor of Northstone Publishing, helped in compiling the Canadian data.

Wendy Grisham, publishing director of Hodder Faith in London, spotted the potential for a British edition of the book, and oversaw its acquisition, editing and subsequent production. David Moloney conducted the research, writing and anglicisation.

Many of the chapters in this British edition have been prepared from scratch, namely: Anglican, Christadelphian, Free Presbyterian, Pentecostal, Salvation Army, Spiritualist and United Reformed Church.

Each of the other chapters has been revised, often substantially, from the North American edition, with the help of representatives from the British body of that particular religion or denomination.

Without the help of the following, this book would never have become a reality:

BRITISH EDITION

Anglican

Reverend Peter Moger, National Worship Development Officer, Church of England, London

Reverend Gwynn ap Gwilym, Bishops' Advisor on Church Affairs, Church in Wales, Cardiff, Wales

Reverend Darren McFarland, Convener, Liturgy Committee, Scottish Episcopal Church, Edinburgh, Scotland

Bahá'í

Robert Weinberg, Wellingborough, Northamptonshire

Baptist

Reverend Doctor Paul Goodliff, Head of Ministry, Baptist Union of Great Britain, Didcot, Oxfordshire

Buddhist

Louise Marchant, Registrar, The Buddhist Society, London

Christadelphian

Michael Ashton, Editor, *The Christadelphian*, Birmingham, West Midlands

Christian Science

Rosie Castle, Tony Lobl, Christian Science Committee on Publication, London

Free Presbyterian

Reverend George G. Hutton, Minister, Free Presbyterian Church of Scotland, Inverness, Scotland

Acknowledgements

Hindu

Doctor Prabhu Shastry, Hounslow, Middlesex

Jehovah's Witness

Ian Turvill, General Information Desk, Watch Tower Bible and Tract Society of Britain, London

Jewish

David Frei, Registrar, London Beth Din, London

Lutheran

Very Reverend Thomas Bruch, General Secretary, The Lutheran Council of Great Britain, London

Methodist

Reverend Doctor Martin Wellings, Minister, Wesley Memorial Methodist Church, Oxford, Oxfordshire

Mormon

Malcolm Adcock, Assistant Area Director, Public Affairs Europe, The Church of Jesus Christ of Latter-day Saints, Solihull, West Midlands

Muslim

Ayesha Stout, The Muslim Council of Britain, London

Orthodox

Jessica Rose, Jenny Gerrard, Oxford, Oxfordshire
Father Ian Graham, Rector, Greek Orthodox Church of the Holy Trinity and Annunciation, Oxford, Oxfordshire

Pentecostal

Reverend Bruce Hunter, Cath Symons, Elim International Centre, West Malvern, Worcestershire

Quaker

Anne van Staveren, Tom Harris, John Capper, Friends House, London

Roman Catholic

Father Peter Harris, Dean of Tower Hamlets, London
Clare Ward, Team Leader, CASE, London

Salvation Army

Major Linda Govier, The Salvation Army UK Territorial Headquarters, London

Seventh-day Adventist

Victor Hulbert, Communication Director, British Union Conference of Seventh-day Adventists, Watford, Hertfordshire

Sikh

Bahadur Singh, Sikh Missionary Society UK, Southall, Middlesex

Spiritualist

Vi Kipling, Darlington
Minister Steven Upton, Communications Director, Spiritualists' National Union, Stansted, Essex

Unitarian

Howard Hague, General Assembly of Unitarian and Free Unitarian Churches, London

United Reformed Church

Reverend Elizabeth Welch, Former Moderator of General Assembly,
Stuart Dew, National Press Officer, United Reformed Church, London

NORTH AMERICAN EDITION

Doctor Satyendra Banerjee, Priest and Past President, Bengali Cultural Society of British Columbia

Rabbi Gary M. Bretton-Granatoor, Director of Interreligious Affairs, Union of American Hebrew Congregations (Reform), New York

Ellen K. Campbell, Executive Director, Canadian Unitarian Council, Toronto, Ontario

Archpriest George Corey, Vicar, Antiochian Orthodox Archdiocese, New York

Acknowledgements

Scott Dickson, Public Affairs (Canada), Jehovah's Witnesses, Watch Tower Bible and Tract Society of Canada

Rabbi Moshe Edelman, Director of Programs and Leadership Development, United Synagogue of Conservative Judaism, New York

Eugene J. Fisher, Associate Director of the Secretariat for Ecumenical and Interreligious Affairs of the National Conference of Catholic Bishops, Washington, DC

Ted George, Librarian, Greek Orthodox Cathedral of the Annunciation, Baltimore, Maryland

James S. Golding, Editor, *The [Greek] Orthodox Observer*, New York

Steven D. Goodman, Professor of Indian and Tibetan Buddhism, Institute of Buddhist Studies, Berkeley, California

Father Gregory Havrilak, Director of Communications, Orthodox Church in North America, New York

Hoyt Hickman, now retired from the General Board of Discipleship, United Methodist Church, Nashville, Tennessee

Ibrahim Hooper, Council on American-Islamic Relations, Washington, DC

Bede Hubbard, Assistant General Secretary, Canadian Conference of Catholic Bishops, Ottawa, Ontario

John Hurley, Archivist and Public Relations Officer, Unitarian Universalist Association of Congregations, Boston, Massachusetts

Ralph Janes, Communications Director, Seventh-day Adventist Church in Canada

Hari Dharam Kaur Khalsa, The Mukhia Sardarni Sahiba, Sikh Dharma of New Mexico, Española, New Mexico

Don LeFevre, Manager of Public Affairs Department, The Church of Jesus Christ of Latter-day Saints, Salt Lake City, Utah

Reverend David Mahsman, Director of News and Information, The Lutheran Church-Missouri Synod, St Louis, Missouri

The Very Reverend Protopresbyter Frank P. Miloro, The American

Carpatho-Russian Orthodox Greek Catholic Diocese of the USA, Johnstown, Pennsylvania

Ronald R. Minor, General Secretary, The Pentecostal Church of God, Joplin, Missouri

Dana Mullen, Clerk-Representative Meeting, Canadian Yearly Meeting, Ottawa, Ontario

Doctor Paul Nelson, Director for Worship, Evangelical Lutheran Church in America, Chicago, Illinois

Father Louis Noplos, Assistant Pastor, Greek Orthodox Cathedral of the Annunciation, Baltimore, Maryland

Reverend Doctor David Ocea, The Romanian Orthodox Episcopate of North America, Grass Lake, Minnesota

Sara Palmer, Program Secretary, The Wider Quaker Fellowship, Philadelphia, Pennsylvania

Mark Parent, PhD, Pereaux United Baptist Church, Pereaux, Nova Scotia

Richard Payne, Dean, Institute of Buddhist Studies, Berkeley, California

Pal S. Purewal, former President, Sikh Society of Alberta, Edmonton, Alberta

Reverend Frank Reid, Senior Pastor, Bethel African Methodist Episcopal Church, Baltimore, Maryland

Doctor George W. Reid, Director of the Biblical Research Institute, Seventh-day Adventists, Silver Spring, Maryland

Raymond Richardson, Writing Department, Jehovah's Witnesses, Brooklyn, New York

Reverend John Roberts, Pastor, Woodbrook Baptist Church, Baltimore, Maryland

Michael R. Rothaar, Acting Director for Worship, Evangelical Lutheran Church in America, Chicago, Illinois

John Schlenck, Librarian and Music Director, Vedanta Society of New York

Acknowledgements

Bhante Seelawimala, Professor of Theravada Buddhism, Institute of Buddhist Studies, Berkeley, California

Bruce Smith, Public Affairs, The Church of Jesus Christ of Latter-day Saints, North York, Ontario

Rabbi David Sulomm Stein, Beit Tikvah Congregation (Reconstructionist), Baltimore, Maryland

Doctor Suwanda Sugunasiri, President, Buddhist Council of Canada; Teaching Staff and Research Associate in Buddhist Studies, Trinity College, University of Toronto

Trish Swanson, Former Director, Office of Public Information, Bahá'ís of the United States, New York

Imam Michael Abdur Rashid Taylor, Islamic Chaplaincy Services Canada, Bancroft, Ontario

Doctor David A. Teutsch, President, Reconstructionist Rabbinical College, Wyncote, Pennsylvania

Jerry Van Marter, Mission Interpreter and International News, Presbyterian Church (USA), Louisville, Kentucky

Reverend Kenn Ward, Editor, *Canada Lutheran*, Winnipeg, Manitoba

Deborah Weiner, Director, Public Relations, Unitarian Universalist Association of Congregations, Boston, Massachusetts

Rabbi Tzvi Hersh Weinreb, Shomrei Emunah Congregation (Orthodox), Baltimore, Maryland

Pamela Zivari, Director, Office of Public Information, Bahá'ís of the United States, New York

Introduction

A few notes on the way in which *Hats, Mats and Hassocks* was compiled and structured:

Each chapter is devoted to a particular religion or denomination; each is organised around that religion's life cycle events, religious calendar and home celebrations.

Basic research was conducted through an extensive questionnaire that was completed in almost all cases by the national office of each religion and denomination. For those denominations whose national office did not respond to the questionnaire, we obtained responses from clergy of that particular faith. For the British edition, an adapted version of the American questionnaire was used, except for a small number of cases in which the British representative of the religion or denomination was asked to provide amendments to the American chapter.

Hats, Mats and Hassocks is not intended as a substitute for the social common sense that should prevail at social or religious events. For example, if a chapter advises readers that 'casual dress' is acceptable at a religious service, this is not to suggest that it is appropriate to show up in Bermuda shorts. Or if a certain denomination allows visitors to use a flash or video recording equipment, the equipment should not be used in such a way that it disrupts the religious ceremony or disturbs worshippers or other visitors.

The guidelines in this book are just that. They should not be mistaken for firm and unbendable rules. Religious customs, traditions and rituals are strongly influenced by where people live and the part of the world from which their ancestors originated. As a result, there may be a variety of practices within a single denomination. This book is a general guide to religious practice, and it is important to remember that particulars may sometimes vary broadly within individual denominations.

Terms within each chapter are those used by that religion. For example, the terms 'New Testament' and 'Old Testament' appear in almost every chapter about various Christian denominations. Some Jewish people may find this disconcerting, since they recognise only one testament. The purpose is not to offend, but to portray these religions as they portray themselves. The goal of this book, one must remember, is to enable us to be 'a perfect stranger'. And 'perfection' might well begin with recognising that when we join others in celebrating events in their religion's vernacular, we are obliged, as guests, to know the customs, rituals and language of the event.

For future editions of *Hats, Mats and Hassocks*, we encourage readers to write to us and suggest ways in which this book could be made more useful to them and to others. Are there additional subjects that future editions should cover? Have important subtleties been missed? We see this book as an ongoing work-in-progress, and we welcome your comments. Please write to:

Editor, *Hats, Mats and Hassocks*
Hodder Faith
Hachette UK
338 Euston Road
London
NW1 3BH
www.hodderfaith.com

The 'Everything You Need to Know Before You Go' Checklist

The Essentials

Review the appropriate chapter(s) to answer at least these basic questions:

How should I be dressed?

What will happen during the service?

What will happen after the service?

Should I bring a gift?

Will I be expected to participate in any way?

1

Anglican

Including
Church of England, Church of Ireland,
Scottish Episcopal Church, Church in Wales

1. HISTORY AND BELIEFS

The Church of England, the Church of Ireland, the Scottish Episcopal Church and the Church in Wales are all members of the Anglican Communion, a worldwide network of churches and Christian communities which exist autonomously but in communion with the Church of England and its primate, the Archbishop of Canterbury. While there is significant diversity in the cultures and traditions of churches within the Anglican Communion – indeed, even within each of the national churches of the British Isles – there is mutual agreement on most essential doctrines, and confirmed Anglicans are permitted to partake in the *sacraments* (sacred rituals and practices, of which baptism and Holy Communion are the most important) of any church within the Anglican Communion.

The Church of England traces its history to the Roman Catholic mission to Britain of 597, and the church established by Augustine of Canterbury. In 1534 it separated from the authority of the Pope in Rome, consolidating as the Church of England under the headship of the British monarch.

Henry VIII declared himself head of the Church in Ireland in 1537, although the majority of its members initially stayed loyal to Rome. In 1871 the Church of Ireland was disestablished from the English state and throne, although it remained outwith the jurisdiction of the Pope. It comprises churches from both Northern Ireland and the Republic of Ireland.

In Scotland, the national Church was split from Rome in 1560 and the Scottish Episcopal Church was formed in 1582, as a separate body from the Church of Scotland, which rejected the governance of bishops.

Christianity in Wales traces its history back to the days of Roman occupation, and documents record a Synod in Wales in the year 569, nearly thirty years before Augustine arrived in England. The Church in Wales was formed as an autonomous body in 1920 as the Welsh dioceses were disestablished from the Church of England.

Although they exist in their current form as a direct result of the Reformation, many Anglicans prefer not to describe themselves as 'Protestant', seeing themselves instead as 'Catholic' (descended from the original, first-century church) and 'Reformed' (denying the authority of the Pope). Within all the Anglican bodies in the British Isles, there are Christians of different traditions: Anglo-Catholics, whose traditional worship style is sometimes described as 'high church' and who stress the mystery of God; evangelicals, whose less ceremonial style is sometimes described as 'low church' and who stress the fundamental importance of Bible-based teaching; and liberals, who are characterised by an openness to the questioning of tradition in response to the changing culture and challenges of the world.

Anglicans believe in God's plan for the availability of personal salvation to all people through faith in his Son, Jesus Christ, and the proclamation of this good news (the *gospel*) to all creation. Two of the most important sacraments are *baptism*, by which a person is made one with Christ and welcomed into the fellowship of the Church, and the *Eucharist* (or *Holy Communion*), by which the life, death and sacrifice of Christ are celebrated by the sharing of bread and wine representing his body and his blood.

Such are the cultural differences between individual Anglican churches in the British Isles, even within the autonomous church networks of each country, that it is difficult to provide a guide to worship etiquette that applies to every single church. What follows is a general guide; most regular churchgoers are sensitive to the fact that a visitor will be unaware of some of their traditions and it is unlikely that a breach of etiquette would be frowned upon!

Church of England churches: over 16,000
Church of England membership: approximately 25 million
Church of England weekly attendance: approximately 1.6 million

Church of Ireland churches: over 450
Church of Ireland membership: 390,000

Scottish Episcopal Church churches: 322
Scottish Episcopal Church membership: over 38,000

Church in Wales churches: 1,418
Church in Wales membership: over 37,000

For more information, contact:

The Church of England
Church House
Great Smith Street
London
SW1P 3AZ
020 7898 1000
www.cofe.anglican.org

The Church of Ireland
Church of Ireland House
Church Avenue
Rathmines
Dublin 6
+353 (0)1 4978 422
www.ireland.anglican.org

General Synod of the Scottish Episcopal Church
21 Grosvenor Crescent
Edinburgh
Scotland
EH12 5EE
0131 225 6357
www.scotland.anglican.org

The Church in Wales
39 Cathedral Road

Cardiff
CF11 9XF
029 2034 8200
www.churchinwales.org.uk

2. THE BASIC SERVICE

The basic service in Anglican churches generally takes place on a Sunday morning, and sometimes also on a Sunday evening, and is known by a number of different names depending on the individual church, the most common names being Holy Communion, the Eucharist, Sung Eucharist, the Mass, the Lord's Supper or, in Wales, *Cymun Bendigaid*. Its purpose is to respond to Christ's command at the Last Supper to take bread and wine 'in remembrance of him'.

In it, the people of God gather; hear and reflect on the Christian Scriptures; pray for the Church, the world and those in need; give thanks for Christ's death and resurrection; share bread and wine together; and depart to continue their part in Christ's mission to the world.

Anybody is welcome to attend such a service, regardless of your own faith or whether or not you have an invitation. The service will normally last about an hour, or a bit longer in some churches.

Appropriate Attire

There is no official dress code for men or women, although it is worth asking in advance whether the particular church you are visiting has a preference. In some churches, t-shirts and jeans are as acceptable as smart suits or dresses. Some women choose to wear hats to church, but this is not normally a prerequisite. Men generally do not wear hats in church.

The Sanctuary

What are the major sections of the church?
The main sanctuary: The part of the church where the altar is

located and where ministers lead congregants in prayer. It is set off from the body of the church by a distinctive structural feature, such as an elevation above the floor level or by ornamentation. It is usually at the front of the church.

The pulpit or lectern: The stand at which scriptural lessons and psalm responses are read and the word of God is preached.

The nave: Where the congregation is seated.

The chancel: Where the organ and choir (if there is one) are situated.

Seating for congregants: Pews and/or seats, usually in front and/or to the side of the altar.

Side chapel: A smaller arrangement of altar and pews or seats to one side of the main body of the church, where services are sometimes held for smaller congregations.

※

The Service

When should guests arrive and where should they sit? It is customary to arrive early or at the time called. Some congregations are better at turning up on time than others! There are usually no restrictions on where to sit, although in some churches some of the regular congregants like to sit in the front one or two pews or rows of seats. It is advisable not to sit too near the front if you are a guest; if you sit behind some of the regular congregants, it will be easier to notice when to sit and when to stand.

If arriving late, are there times when a guest should not enter the service? No.

Are there times when a guest should not leave the service? There are no strict rules about this, although it would be preferable to not leave during the prayer of consecration (when the priest prays over the bread and wine at the altar), or in a way that would be noisy or disruptive to other congregants during times of prayer or silent reflection.

Who are the major officiants, leaders or participants and what do they do?

A priest, or president, who presides over the whole service, prays over the bread and wine at the altar and may also preach.

A deacon (in some churches), who assists the president, reads the
Gospel, takes other designated liturgical roles, such as setting up
the altar and dismissing the people, and may also preach.

A preacher, other than the priest or deacon, may occasionally preach.

A lesson reader, who reads out loud from the Bible.

An intercessor, who leads the congregation in prayer.

A server, who helps with the ceremonial aspects of the service.

A communion assistant, who helps with the distribution of the
Holy Communion.

A sidesperson, who welcomes visitors and may direct them to a seat.

Musicians, such as an organist, choir members, instrumentalists,
singers and members of a worship group, who are responsible for
the musical aspects of the service.

An audio-visual technician, who is responsible for the screen projection (if available) and sound management.

The number of officiants and participants varies between
churches. Some may have only a priest, a server/sidesperson and
an organist.

What are the major ritual objects of the service?

Bread and wine, which are consecrated to be received as the body
and blood of Jesus Christ.

The chalice and paten, which contain the wine and the bread.

The altar, or table where the bread and wine are consecrated.

The Bible, from which the Gospel, which records the life and ministry
of Jesus, and other scriptural readings are read.

What books are used? A service book containing the order of service,
prayers and responses and a book of hymns or songs, or a printed
sheet containing both. Increasing numbers of churches include this
material on a projected screen display. In some churches, a Bible will
be provided for each member of the congregation.

To indicate the order of the service: A printed order of service will
be provided in the majority of churches. Increasing numbers of churches
will have a projected screen display. The president or deacon will
make periodic announcements.

❦

Guest Behaviour during the Service

Will a guest who is not an Anglican be expected to do anything other than sit? No. It is acceptable to stand and kneel with the congregation, read prayers aloud and sing with congregants, if this does not compromise your personal beliefs. If you do not wish to kneel, sit when congregants do so.

It is preferable not to talk during the service unless absolutely necessary and, if you do, to keep it to a whisper.

Are there any parts of the service in which a guest who is not an Anglican should not participate? Yes. Do not receive Communion (only baptised Anglicans may receive Communion) or join in any of the prayers if you feel unable to do so.

If you wish to approach the altar for a prayer of blessing from the priest during the time of Communion, process forward with other members of the congregation during Communion and kneel alongside them at the altar rail but keep your hands at your side. The priest will know the baptised Anglicans because they will hold their hands in front of them to receive the bread; if you keep your hands by your side the priest will stop and say a short prayer over you. Wait quietly and then rise and return to your seat at the same time as the other congregants.

The Church in Wales usually invites all baptised Christians to take Communion.

If not disruptive to the service, is it OK to:

Take pictures? No.
Use a flash? No.
Use video recording equipment? No, other than by special, prior arrangement.
Use audio recording equipment? Possibly, by arrangement.

Will contributions to the church be collected at the service? Usually, yes. The offertory takes place about midway through the service. During a hymn, servers usually pass a plate or pouch among the congregants in which cash offerings (sometimes in an envelope) are placed. Some people pay by standing order and put nothing in the plate during the service. Gift-aiding is encouraged.

How much is it customary to contribute? Anglican churches give no guidance on this, but expect members to commit to 5 per cent of disposable income. For guests, there is no expectation that an offering will be made, nor a particular amount.

⁓

After the Service

Is there usually a reception after the ceremony? There is usually an informal reception after the service, held in the church itself or an adjoining room or hall. It will be announced during or at the end of the service. Coffee and biscuits are usually served (or, in some prestigious churches or cathedrals, sherry!), and it will usually last less than half an hour.

Would it be considered impolite to neither eat nor drink? No.

Is there a ritual before eating or drinking? No.

Is there a grace or benediction after eating or drinking? No.

Is there a traditional form of address for clergy who may be at the reception? This varies between churches and, while there is no harm in enquiring what form of address is appropriate, it is unlikely that you would cause offence by using the wrong one. In churches of 'higher', Catholic tradition, the clergy may be addressed as 'Father', while in churches of 'lower', evangelical tradition it is common to address the clergy by their first name. Some older people use the title 'Vicar' or 'Rector'.

Is it OK to leave early? Yes. People tend to leave when they have drunk their coffee and had a small chat.

⁓

Special Vocabulary

Key words or phrases that it might be helpful for a visitor to know:

Gospel: As used during worship, this means a reading from one of the accounts of the life of Jesus as written in the New Testament by four of his apostles.

Sermon: A talk, based on the Gospel text that is read during the service.

Communion or Eucharist: The service in which bread and wine are shared in memory of Christ.

Morning (or Evening) Prayer: A worship service that includes prayer and possibly a sermon, but not Communion.

Some Basic Beliefs

Some basic books to which a guest can refer to learn more about the Anglican faith:

Worship Changes Lives, edited by Paul Bradshaw and Peter Moger (Church House Publishing, 2007).

3. HOLY DAYS AND FESTIVALS

Christmas: Always falls on 25 December. Celebrates the birth of Jesus Christ. The traditional greeting is 'Merry Christmas'.

Easter: Always falls on the Sunday after the first full moon that occurs on or after the spring equinox of 21 March. Celebrates the resurrection of Jesus. The traditional greeting is 'Happy Easter'.

Pentecost: Occurs fifty days after Easter, because this is when the Holy Spirit descended on Jesus' apostles. Celebrates the power of the Holy Spirit and its manifestation in the early Christian church. There is no traditional greeting for this holiday.

Ash Wednesday: Occurs forty days before Easter. Commemorates the beginning of Lent, which is a season for preparation and penitence before Easter itself. There is no traditional greeting for this holiday.

Maundy Thursday: Falls four days before Easter. Commemorates the institution of the Eucharist (also known as Communion) and Jesus' subsequent arrest and trial. There is no traditional greeting.

Good Friday: Three days before Easter. Commemorates the cruci-fixion, death and burial of Jesus.

Christmas, Easter and Pentecost are joyful celebrations. Ash Wednesday, Maundy Thursday and Good Friday are sombre, peni-tential commemorations. During the services for these latter three holidays, decorum and discretion are of great importance.

4. LIFE CYCLE EVENTS

Birth Ceremony

Baptism – the first part of the Anglican Church's two-stage initia-tion practice – is administered once to each person, usually as an infant. However, it is not only a birth rite but also a rite of joining the Christian community, and so is also applicable to adult converts. During the ceremony, which is usually an additional element of a larger Sunday morning Communion service but is occasionally a shorter ceremony in its own right, a priest pours water on the head of the baptismal candidate. This symbolises the washing away of sins. The Holy Spirit is also called upon to strengthen the new church member.

Baptism is a pledge of repentance and obedience to the divine will. It initiates the individual into the Christian community and into the larger family of the children of a loving God.

Before the ceremony

Are guests usually invited by a formal invitation? Yes, except regular congregation members who will be at the service anyway.

If not stated explicitly, should one assume that children are invited? Yes.

If one cannot attend, what should one do? This is at the discretion of the individual. A polite and prompt reply, expressing regret, is recommended.

Appropriate attire

Smart clothes are recommended, especially for family members of the baptismal candidate, but there is no official dress code for men or women (see 'Appropriate Attire' in 'The Basic Service' section).

Gifts

Is a gift customarily expected? If the baptismal candidate is a child, it is normal for invited guests to bring a gift for the child. If the candidate is an adult, close family members may be expected to bring a gift, but it is not necessarily expected from other guests. The gift is up to the individual; for children, a gift that will last a long period of time as a memento of the day is common. In the Scottish Episcopal Church, money for the parents (between £10 and £50) is recommended as a suitable gift.

Should gifts be brought to the ceremony? They are normally given at a reception following the ceremony.

The ceremony

Where will the ceremony take place? In the main sanctuary of the church. The baptism part of the service will take place around the font (which holds the water for baptism).

When should guests arrive and where should they sit? It is customary to arrive early or at the time called. There are usually no restrictions on where to sit, although in some churches some of the regular congregants like to sit in the front one or two pews or rows of seats. It may be wise to take note of where the font is positioned and try to sit somewhere that will allow you a good view during the baptism part of the service, especially if you have children.

If arriving late, are there times when a guest should not enter the service? No.

Are there times when a guest should not leave the service? There are no strict rules about this, although it would be preferable not to leave during the prayer of consecration (when the priest prays over the bread and wine at the altar), which is part of the Communion service, or in a way that would be noisy or disruptive to other congregants during times of prayer or silent reflection.

Who are the major officiants, leaders or participants in the ceremony and what do they do?

A priest, who will baptise the child. This may be a different priest from the one presiding over the main service.

The child's parents.

Godparents, who will agree to aid in the candidate's upbringing as a Christian. (Other regular participants are listed under The Basic Service.)

What are the major ritual objects of the service?

The font, a receptacle (normally made of stone or glass) containing the water for administering the baptism. Some churches have fonts adjoining or near their entrance. This position indicates that through baptism one is initiated, or 'enters', the church.

Oil stock, contains holy oil for anointing.

Paschal candle, a candle lit as a reminder of the presence of the risen Christ, and the new life available to us through him.

What books are used? A service book containing the order of service, prayers and responses and a book of hymns or songs, or a printed sheet containing both. Increasing numbers of churches include this material on a projected screen display. In some churches, a Bible will be provided for each member of the congregation.

To indicate the order of the service: A printed order of service will be provided in the majority of churches. Increasing numbers of churches will have a projected screen display. The president or deacon will make periodic announcements.

Will a guest who is not an Anglican be expected to do anything other than sit? No. It is acceptable to stand and kneel with the congregation, read prayers aloud and sing with congregants, if this does not compromise your personal beliefs. If you do not wish to kneel, sit when congregants do so.

If you are a parent or godparent of the baptismal candidate, you should receive instructions beforehand on where to stand and what to say during the baptism part of the ceremony. You will not be expected to do or say anything else during the rest of the service, apart from that expected of the rest of the congregation.

Are there any parts of the service in which a guest who is not an Anglican should not participate? Yes. Do not receive Communion (only baptised Anglicans may receive Communion) or join in any of the prayers if you feel unable to do so.

If you wish to approach the altar for a prayer of blessing from the priest during the time of Communion, process forward with other members of the congregation during Communion and kneel alongside them at the altar rail but keep your hands at your side. The priest will know the baptised Anglicans because they will hold their hands in front of them to receive the bread; if you keep your hands by your side the priest will stop and say a short prayer over you. Wait quietly and then rise and return to your seat at the same time as the other congregants.

The Church in Wales usually invites all baptised Christians to take Communion.

If not disruptive to the service, is it OK to:

Take pictures? No.

Use a flash? No.

Use video recording equipment? No, other than by special, prior arrangement.

Use audio recording equipment? Possibly, by arrangement.

Will contributions to the church be collected at the service? Usually, yes. The offertory takes place about midway through the service. Servers usually pass a plate or pouch amongst the congregants in which cash offerings (sometimes in an envelope) are placed. Some people pay by standing order and put nothing in the plate during the service. Gift-aiding is encouraged.

How much is it customary to contribute? Anglican churches give no guidance on this, but expect members to commit to 5 per cent of disposable income. For guests, there is no expectation that an offering will be made, nor a particular amount.

After the ceremony

Is there usually a reception after the ceremony? A private reception will normally be organised by the family, and the format of this will be at their discretion. There is usually a short informal reception organised by the church after the service, held in the church itself or an adjoining room or hall. It will be announced during or at the end of the service. Coffee and biscuits are usually served, and it will usually last less than half an hour.

Would it be considered impolite to neither eat nor drink? No.

Is there a ritual before eating or drinking? No.

Is there a grace or benediction after eating or drinking? No.

Is there a traditional form of address for clergy who may be at the reception? This varies between churches and, while there is no harm in enquiring what form of address is appropriate, it is unlikely that you would cause offence by using the wrong one. In churches of 'higher', Catholic tradition the clergy may be addressed as 'Father', while in churches of 'lower', evangelical tradition it is common to address the clergy by their first name. Some older people use the title 'Vicar' or 'Rector'.

Is it OK to leave early? Yes. People tend to leave when they have drunk their coffee and had a small chat.

Some basic beliefs

A basic resource to which a guest can refer to learn more about baptism in Anglican churches:

The website www.cofe.anglican.org/lifeevents/baptism1.html provides a detailed guide to the baptism ceremony.

❧

Initiation Ceremony

Confirmation, or First Communion, is the second part of the Anglican Church's two-stage initiation practice, and is most commonly undertaken by young people around the ages of twelve to fifteen years. The confirmation candidate will affirm for themselves the faith into which they were earlier baptised and their intention to live a life of responsible and committed discipleship, and a bishop will be present to confirm this decision before God and in the presence of God's people.

The confirmation ceremony will normally take place as part of a regular Sunday morning or evening service of Holy Communion and will be attended by a bishop. There will usually be more than one candidate being confirmed – all candidates having completed a series of preparation classes during the preceding weeks. The service is likely to last between one and one and a half hours.

Before the ceremony

Are guests usually invited by a formal invitation? Yes, except regular congregation members who will be at the service anyway.

If not stated explicitly, should one assume that children are invited? No.

If one cannot attend, what should one do? This is at the discretion of the individual. A polite and prompt reply, expressing regret, is recommended.

Appropriate attire

Smart clothes are recommended, especially for family members of the confirmation candidate, but there is no official dress code for men or women (see 'Appropriate Attire' in 'The Basic Service' section).

Gifts

Is a gift customarily expected? Close family members may be expected to bring a gift, but it is not necessarily expected from other guests.

Should gifts be brought to the ceremony? They are normally given at a reception following the ceremony.

The ceremony

Where will the ceremony take place? In the main sanctuary of the church. The confirmation candidates will be called forward to the front of the altar at the appropriate time.

When should guests arrive and where should they sit? It is customary to arrive early or at the time called. There are usually no restrictions on where to sit, although in some churches some of the regular congregants like to sit in the front one or two pews or rows of seats.

If arriving late, are there times when a guest should not enter the service? No.

Are there times when a guest should not leave the service? There are no strict rules about this, although it would be preferable not to leave during the prayer of consecration (when the priest prays over the bread and wine at the altar), or in a way that would be noisy or disruptive to other congregants during times of prayer or silent reflection.

Who are the major officiants, leaders or participants in the ceremony and what do they do?

A *bishop*, who will normally assume the role of president at the service, and will usually also preach.
(Other regular participants are listed under 'The Basic Service'.)

What books are used? A service book containing the order of service, prayers and responses and a book of hymns or songs, or a printed sheet containing both. Increasing numbers of churches include this material on a projected screen display. In some churches, a Bible will be provided for each member of the congregation.

To indicate the order of the service: A printed order of service will be provided in the majority of churches. Increasing numbers of churches will have a projected screen display. The president or deacon will make periodic announcements.

Will a guest who is not an Anglican be expected to do anything other than sit? No. It is acceptable to stand and kneel with the congregation, read prayers aloud and sing with congregants, if this does not compromise your personal beliefs. If you do not wish to kneel, sit when congregants do so.

Are there any parts of the service in which a guest who is not an Anglican should not participate? Yes. Do not receive Communion (only baptised Anglicans may receive Communion) or join in any of the prayers if you feel unable to do so.

If you wish to approach the altar for a prayer of blessing from the priest during the time of Communion, process forward with other members of the congregation during Communion and kneel alongside them at the altar rail but keep your hands at your side. The priest will know the baptised Anglicans because they will hold their hands in front of them to receive the bread; if you keep your hands by your side the priest will stop and say a short prayer over you. Wait quietly and then rise and return to your seat at the same time as the other congregants.

The Church in Wales usually invites all baptised Christians to take Communion.

If not disruptive to the service, is it OK to:

Take pictures? No.
Use a flash? No.
Use video recording equipment? No, other than by special, prior arrangement.
Use audio recording equipment? Possibly, by arrangement.

Will contributions to the church be collected at the service? Usually, yes. The offertory takes place about midway through the service. Servers usually pass a plate or pouch amongst the congregants in which cash offerings (sometimes in an envelope) are placed. Some people pay by standing order and put nothing in the plate during the service. Gift-aiding is encouraged.

How much is it customary to contribute? Anglican churches give no guidance on this, but expect members to commit to 5 per cent of disposable income. For guests, there is no expectation that an offering will be made, nor a particular amount.

After the ceremony

Is there usually a reception after the ceremony? A private reception may be organised by the confirmation candidate or their family, and the format of this will be at their discretion. There is usually a short informal reception organised by the church after the service, held in the church itself or an adjoining room or hall. It will be announced during or at the end of the service. Coffee and biscuits are usually served, and it will usually last less than half an hour.

Would it be considered impolite to neither eat nor drink? No.

Is there a ritual before eating or drinking? No.

Is there a grace or benediction after eating or drinking? No.

Is there a traditional form of address for clergy who may be at the reception? This varies between churches and, while there is no harm in enquiring what form of address is appropriate, it is unlikely that you would cause offence by using the wrong one. In churches of 'higher', Catholic tradition the bishop may be addressed as 'Your Worship', and other clergy as 'Father', while in churches of 'lower', evangelical tradition it is common to address the clergy by their first name, and the bishop as 'Bishop [first name]'.

Is it OK to leave early? Yes. People tend to leave when they have drunk their coffee and had a small chat.

Some basic beliefs

A basic resource to which a guest can refer to learn more about confirmation in Anglican churches:

The website www.cofe.anglican.org/lifeevents/baptismconfirm provides a detailed guide to the confirmation ceremony.

Marriage Ceremony

Anglicans believe that, through the sacrament of marriage, God joins together man and woman in physical and spiritual union.

The marriage ceremony is most commonly a ceremony in itself lasting between thirty and sixty minutes, but occasionally will be a part of a regular Sunday morning service of Holy Communion, in which case it will probably last over an hour.

Before the ceremony

Are guests usually invited by a formal invitation? Yes.

If not stated explicitly, should one assume that children are invited? No.

If one cannot attend, what should one do? Send a polite and prompt reply, and send a gift if possible.

Appropriate attire

Men: Jacket and tie or more casual clothing (depending on the style of the wedding – this may be indicated in the invitation).

Women: Dress or a skirt and blouse or a trouser suit. Open-toed shoes and jewellery are permissible. A hat is acceptable, but it is preferable that this is not worn in church.

There are no rules regarding colours of clothing.

Gifts

Is a gift customarily expected? Yes. Details of a gift list are often included with the wedding invitation. If not, then the nature of the gift is at the discretion of the individual.

Should gifts be brought to the ceremony? They are generally better taken to the reception or sent to the home.

The ceremony

Where will the ceremony take place? In the main sanctuary of the church. The wedding couple will be at the front of the congregation throughout the service.

When should guests arrive and where should they sit? Arrive early. Ushers will be on hand to show guests where to sit.

If arriving late, are there times when a guest should not enter the ceremony? No.

Are there times when a guest should not leave the ceremony? There are no strict rules about this, although it would be preferable not to leave during the prayer of consecration (when the priest prays over the bread and wine at the altar), if Communion is involved, or during the wedding vows, or in a way that would be noisy or disruptive to other congregants during times of prayer or silent reflection.

Who are the major officiants, leaders or participants at the ceremony and what do they do?

A *priest*, who will conduct the service, marry the couple, preach and celebrate Communion.
(Other regular participants are listed under 'The Basic Service'.)

What books are used? A specially printed order of service containing the prayers, readings and the words of the hymns or songs is usually provided by the wedding couple.

Will a guest who is not an Anglican be expected to do anything other than sit? It is expected that you will stand at the same time as the rest of the congregation, if you are able, and you are also free to kneel with the congregation, read prayers aloud and sing with congregants if this does not compromise your personal beliefs. If you do not wish to kneel, sit when congregants do so.

Are there any parts of the ceremony in which a guest who is not an Anglican should not participate? Do not receive Communion or say any prayers contradictory to the beliefs of your own faith. Only baptised Anglicans may receive Communion.

If you wish to approach the altar for a prayer of blessing from the priest during the time of Communion, process forward with other members of the congregation during Communion and kneel alongside them at the altar rail but keep your hands at your side. The priest will know the baptised Anglicans because they will hold their hands in front of them to receive the bread; if you keep your hands by your side the priest will stop and say a short prayer over you. Wait quietly and then rise and return to your seat at the same time as the other congregants.

The Church in Wales usually invites all baptised Christians to take Communion.

If not disruptive to the ceremony, is it OK to:

Take pictures? No.
Use a flash? No.
Use video recording equipment? Possibly, by special arrangement.
Use audio recording equipment? Possibly, by special arrangement.
(Photos and videos are usually taken after the ceremony.)

Will contributions to the church be collected at the service? Not usually.

After the ceremony

Is there usually a reception after the ceremony? There will usually be a private reception after the service, which will be organised by the wedding couple, and details will be provided with the wedding invitation. It will take place at a private venue, and could last through the rest of the day and evening. Depending on the wishes of the wedding couple, food and drink may be served and there may be speeches, the cutting of a wedding cake, dancing and music.

Would it be considered impolite to neither eat nor drink? Yes, unless there are special circumstances, and it is advisable to inform the wedding couple of any special dietary requirements before the day.

Is there a ritual before eating or drinking? After all the guests are seated, it is common for everyone to wait for the official entry of the bride and groom to the dining hall. There may be a grace said before people start to eat.

Is there a ritual after eating or drinking? There may be an official departure of the bride and groom from the dining hall.

Is there a traditional greeting for the family? It is common for the wedding couple, their parents, best man and bridesmaids to meet all guests in an official line before the meal. Offer your congratulations and best wishes.

Is there a traditional form of address for clergy who may be at the reception? This varies between churches and, while there is no harm in enquiring what form of address is appropriate, it is unlikely that you would cause offence by using the wrong one. In churches of 'higher', Catholic tradition the clergy may be addressed as 'Father', while in churches of 'lower', evangelical tradition it is common to address the clergy by their first name. Some older people use the title 'Vicar' or 'Rector'.

Is it OK to leave early? Yes, but ideally only after toasts have been made and the wedding cake is cut and served.

Some basic beliefs

A basic resource to which a guest can refer to learn more about marriage in Anglican churches:

The website www.cofe.anglican.org/lifeevents/weddings provides a detailed guide to the marriage ceremony.

Funerals and Mourning

In Anglican churches, a funeral service is most commonly a ceremony in itself which can last anywhere between fifteen and sixty minutes, but occasionally will be a part of a regular Sunday morning service of Holy Communion.

Anglicans believe that the resurrection of Jesus Christ was a victory for good over evil, and life over death, making eternal life available to us all. Those who are believers will, following death, proceed to an afterlife in the nearer presence of God.

Occasionally, the format of a funeral service may differ from the following if the deceased has made special requests for how they would like their life to be remembered.

Before the ceremony

How soon after the death does the funeral usually take place? It can be within a week of the death, but may take longer for a number of reasons (such as the need for a post-mortem, or if the funeral is to take place at a crematorium which may have a waiting list).

What should someone who is not an Anglican do upon hearing of the death of a member of that faith? Telephone or visit the bereaved, or send a letter expressing your sympathy.

Gifts

Is it appropriate to send flowers or make a contribution? Obituary notices will often indicate if flowers are appropriate and may list specific charities to which contributions can be made in memory of the deceased. If nothing has been indicated, it is usually appropriate to send flowers to the funeral, and this can be arranged via the undertaker.

Appropriate attire

Men: Jacket and tie. In some cases, a black tie is expected. No head covering is required.

Women: A dress, skirt and blouse or trouser suit. Clothing should be modest, with hems below the knee. Open-toed shoes and modest jewellery are permissible. No head covering is required.

Sombre colours are recommended, although the bereaved family sometimes request against this.

The ceremony

Where will the ceremony take place? At a church – both within the main sanctuary and at the graveside – or the chapel of a crematorium or cemetery.

When should guests arrive and where should they sit? Arrive early. There will sometimes be an usher to guide you where to sit. If not, sit wherever you choose.

If arriving late, are there times when a guest should not enter the ceremony? No.

Will the bereaved family be present at the church or funeral home before the service? Usually.

Is there a traditional greeting for the family? No.

Will there be an open coffin? Rarely.

Is a guest expected to view the body? This is optional.

What is appropriate behaviour upon viewing the body? This is at the individual's discretion, although a moment of silent prayer or reflection is common.

Who are the major officiants at the ceremony and what do they do?
A minister, either an ordained priest or a lay minister, conducts the service and will preach and commit the dead person into God's care.
(Other regular participants are listed under 'The Basic Service'.)

What are the major ritual objects of the service?

The coffin, a receptacle for the dead person's body.
Aspergillium, an instrument used for sprinkling the coffin with the water of baptism.
Pall, a cloth that covers the coffin.

What books are used? A hymn book or service book may occasionally be used.

To indicate the order of the ceremony: An order of service will normally be provided.

Will a guest who is not an Anglican be expected to do anything other than sit? It is expected that you will stand at the same time as the rest of the congregation, if you are able, and you are also free to kneel with the congregation, read prayers aloud and sing with congregants if this does not compromise your personal beliefs. If you do not wish to kneel, sit when congregants do so.

Are there any parts of the ceremony in which a guest who is not an Anglican should not participate? Do not receive Communion or say any prayers contradictory to the beliefs of your own faith. Only baptised Christians may receive Communion.

If you wish to approach the altar for a prayer of blessing from the priest during the time of Communion, process forward with other members of the congregation during Communion and kneel alongside them at the altar rail but keep your hands at your side. The priest will know the baptised Anglicans because they will hold their hands in front of them to receive the bread; if you keep your hands by your side the priest will stop and say a short prayer over you. Wait quietly and then rise and return to your seat at the same time as the other congregants.

The Church in Wales usually invites all baptised Christians to take Communion.

If not disruptive to the ceremony, is it OK to:

Take pictures? No.
Use a flash? No.
Use video recording equipment? No.
Use audio recording equipment? No.

Will contributions to the church be collected at the service? Usually, yes. The collection may be for a charity specified by the deceased or their family. The offertory takes place about midway through the service. Servers usually pass a plate or pouch amongst the congregants in which cash offerings (sometimes in an envelope) are placed. Some people pay by standing order and put nothing in the plate during the service. Gift-aiding is encouraged.

How much is it customary to contribute? Anglican churches give no guidance on this, but expect members to commit to 5 per cent of disposable income. For guests, there is no expectation that an offering will be made, nor a particular amount.

The interment

Should guests attend the interment? Yes, if the deceased was a close friend or family member.

Whom should one ask for directions? The undertaker or another guest.

What happens at the graveside of a burial? There will be a recitation of Scripture, after which the coffin will be lowered into the ground and a prayer will be said. Guests are required simply to be present. Sometimes, guests will be invited to throw earth onto the coffin once it has been placed in the ground.

What happens at a cremation? There will be a recitation of Scripture, after which the coffin will be removed (often being transported behind a curtain) to be burned and a prayer will be said. Guests are required simply to be present.

Comforting the bereaved

Is it appropriate to visit the home of the bereaved after the funeral? This is at your personal discretion. There is no specific ritual or tradition governing this.

How soon after the funeral will a mourner usually return to a normal work schedule? This varies, depending on the individual.

How soon after the funeral will a mourner usually return to a normal social schedule? This is entirely at the discretion of the individual.

Some basic beliefs

A basic resource to which a guest can refer to learn more about funerals in Anglican churches:

The website www.cofe.anglican.org/lifeevents/funerals provides a detailed guide to the funeral ceremony.

5. HOME CELEBRATIONS

Not applicable for Anglican churches.

2
Bahá'í

1. HISTORY AND BELIEFS

The Bahá'í faith emerged from the Bábí faith, which was founded in the mid-nineteenth century in Persia (now Iran) by a young merchant, Mírzá 'Alí-Muhammad, a direct descendant of the Prophet Muhammad. Against a background of moral breakdown in Persia, his message aroused excitement and hope among all classes, rapidly attracting thousands of followers. He took the name 'Báb', meaning 'Gate' in Arabic. The Báb announced that his mission was to prepare the way for the coming of a second Messenger, greater than himself, who would usher in an age of justice and peace promised in Islam, Judaism, Christianity and all the other world religions.

In 1850 the Báb was killed by a firing squad in Tabriz, Persia, on the order of the grand vizier of the new Shah of Iran. The grand vizier was acting on behalf of traditional Islamic clergy in his country, who were alarmed at what they perceived to be the heretical doctrine being taught by the Báb and also by the fact that he was gaining followers.

In 1863 one of the Báb's most socially prominent followers, Bahá'u'lláh, made his public declaration, while he was in exile in Iraq, that he was 'He Whom God Shall Manifest', the messianic figure whom the Báb had predicted. He was soon banished by the Iraqi government to Istanbul and then to Adrianople, where he stayed for five years.

Agitation from opponents caused the Turkish government to send the exiles to Acre, Palestine, where Bahá'u'lláh spent his last years.

Upon his death his eldest son, 'Abdu'l-Bahá, 'The Servant of Baha', led the faith, as had been determined in his father's will. With his death in 1921 leadership fell, as stipulated in 'Abdu'l-Bahá's will, to his eldest grandson, Shoghi Effendi, 'The Guardian of the Cause of God', who devoted himself to expanding the worldwide Bahá'í community, establishing its central administrative offices in Haifa, and translating the writings of his great-grandfather, Bahá'u'lláh.

Central to Bahá'í beliefs is the unity of all religions and of all humanity. God, Bahá'ís teach, may be unknowable, but the divine presence manifests itself in various ways. Among these are the creation of the world and the prophets, beginning with Adam, and continuing through the Jewish prophets, Buddha, Krishna, Zoroaster, Jesus and Muhammad, who was succeeded by Bahá'u'lláh. Each prophet represents a divine message that was appropriate for the era in which he appeared. Bahá'ís believe that other prophets may come in the future, and that there is no last revelation or final prophet.

Members are elected to Bahá'í's approximately 11,740 local spiritual assemblies, and to 175 national spiritual assemblies throughout the world (the national spiritual assembly for the UK is based in London). The head of the faith is the Universal House of Justice, an elected nine-member council, which has administrative, judicial and legislative functions and the authority to frame new rules for situations not provided for in the writings of Bahá'u'lláh.

There are now more than 5 million Bahá'ís in 235 countries and territories. Throughout the world, the Bahá'í faith has only seven houses of worship, one on each continent. The house of worship in Europe is in Langenhain, near Frankfurt, Germany. Locally, Bahá'ís may meet for worship or for communal activities in homes or Bahá'í centres. The minimum number of Bahá'ís that can comprise a local community is two, but nine are required for a local spiritual assembly.

UK communities: approximately 150
UK membership: approximately 6,000

For more information, contact:

Office of Public Information
National Spiritual Assembly of the Bahá'ís of the UK
27 Rutland Gate
London
SW7 1PD
Tel: 020 7584 2566
Email: opi@bahai.org.uk

2. THE BASIC SERVICE

The centrepiece of the Bahá'í community is the Nineteen Day Feast, which is held every nineteen days and is the local community's regular worship gathering – and more. The feast day is held on the first day of each of the nineteen months in the Bahá'í calendar.

The Nineteen Day Feast helps sustain the unity of the local Bahá'í community. While Bahá'í feasts around the world adapt to local cultural and social needs, they always contain spiritual devotions, administrative consultation and fellowship.

The word *feast* is used to imply not that a large meal will be served, but that a 'spiritual feast' – worship, companionship and unity – will be available.

During devotions, selections from the writings of the Bahá'í faith and, sometimes, other faiths will be read aloud. This is followed by a general discussion, which allows every member of the community to have a voice in community affairs.

In addition to the Nineteen Day Feast, all Bahá'í communities host communal worship gatherings known as 'Devotional Meetings', open to all people. In a friendly and relaxed atmosphere, attendees read prayers and other inspirational texts and take time to reflect. Such meetings are often accompanied by efforts to beautify the room where they are held, with flowers, lit candles or other decoration. Meetings usually end with light refreshments.

Appropriate Attire

Men: Personal preference for attire, plus one's own sense of reverence, are the only criteria. This may range from jacket and tie to slacks or jeans. No head covering is required.

Women: Personal preference for attire, plus one's own sense of reverence, are the only criteria. This may range from a dress or skirt to slacks or jeans. Clothing need not cover the arms or reach below the knees. No head covering is required. Women may wear open-toed shoes and/or modest jewellery.

There are no rules regarding colours of clothing.

The Sanctuary

What are the major sections of the house of worship? The only Bahá'í house of worship in Europe is in Langenhain, near Frankfurt, Germany. It has no 'sanctuary'. Instead, it has an entirely open, domed interior with a podium at the front. Elsewhere, Bahá'ís may meet in homes or in Bahá'í community centres.

The Meeting

When should guests arrive and where should they sit? Arrive at the time for which the meeting has been called. Guests may sit wherever they wish. There are no ushers to guide them to their seats.

If arriving late, are there times when a guest should not enter the meeting? Yes. Do not enter during prayers.

Are there times when a guest should not leave the meeting? No.

Who are the major officiants, leaders or participants and what do they do?

The chairperson or host, who will conduct the flow of activities during the meeting. There are no clergy in the Bahá'í faith. The method of selecting the host varies among local Bahá'í communities. They usually either are invited or simply volunteer for the position. Often, the person in whose home a Nineteen Day Feast is held is the host for that occasion.

What are the major ritual objects of the meeting? There are no ritual objects in the Bahá'í faith.

What books are used? Programmes draw on many published anthologies of Bahá'í sacred writings. Most Bahá'ís would make use of a Bahá'í prayer book, in which are collected prayers by the Báb, Bahá'u'lláh and 'Abdu'l-Bahá. Readings may often be taken from *Gleanings from the Writings of Bahá'u'lláh* (Bahá'í Publishing Trust, 1976) and other sacred texts.

Guest Behaviour during the Meeting

Will a guest who is not a Bahá'í be expected to do anything other than sit? No, although it is optional for guests to sing with the congregation.

Are there any parts of the meeting in which a guest who is not a Bahá'í should not participate? Bahá'í devotional meetings are open to all visitors and everyone is welcome for the duration of the meeting. In the Nineteen Day Feast, the middle portion is set aside to discuss matters mainly of interest to the local Bahá'í community, including the group's financial accounts and plans for activities. Bahá'ís often take this opportunity to ask questions of the members of their local spiritual assembly, and are free to make recommendations about any aspect of the work of the community. Generally speaking, visitors who are not registered members of the Bahá'í community would not be much interested in this portion of the meeting and are free to absent themselves during this time. Communities are careful, however, not to make a visitor feel uncomfortable or unwanted and, if a visitor is present, the Bahá'ís would limit their discussions to items which would be of broader or more general interest.

If not disruptive to the meeting, is it OK to:

Take pictures? Yes.
Use a flash? Yes.
Use video recording equipment? Yes.
Use audio recording equipment? Yes.

Will contributions to the church be collected at the meeting? No.
But even if there were collections, only Bahá'ís may contribute to the
Bahá'í faith. The primary reason for this is to make Bahá'ís solely
responsible for their faith. Also, contributing to the faith is consid-
ered a sacred privilege that rests on recognising Bahá'u'lláh as the
Messenger of God for this day.

After the Service

Is there usually a reception after the meeting? There may be a
reception, depending on the customs of the individual community,
each of which sets its own policy. If there is a reception, which is
called the 'social portion', it may last about thirty minutes to several
hours. Food will definitely be served at a reception, but not alcoholic
drinks, since alcohol is forbidden to Bahá'ís.

*Is there a traditional form of address for clergy who may be at
the reception?* No, since there are no clergy in the Bahá'í faith.

Is it OK to leave early? Yes.

Special Vocabulary

Key words or phrases that it might be helpful for a visitor to know:

Bahá'u'lláh ('Bah-HAH-oo-LAH'): Prophet. The founder of the Bahá'í
    faith, whose name means 'Glory of God'.
'Abdu'l-Bahá ('Ab-DOOL-bah-HAH'): Son of Bahá'u'lláh, whose name
    means 'Servant of Baha'.
Shoghi Effendi ('SHOW-gey Eh-FEN-dee'): Grandson of 'Abdu'l-
    Bahá, also called 'The Guardian'.
Allah'u'Abhá ('Ah-lah-oo-ab-HAH'): 'God is most glorious'.
Bahá'í ('Ba-HIGH'): A follower of Bahá'u'lláh.

꿿

Some Basic Beliefs

Bahá'ís believe:

Humanity is one.

Men and women are equal.

Any apparent inequality between the capacities of men and women is due solely to the lack of educational opportunities currently available to women.

Prejudice, religious intolerance and the extremes between wealth and poverty must be eliminated.

In addition to the Ten Commandments, behaviour should be guided by avoiding such activities as gambling, drinking alcohol, drug abuse, gossip and backbiting.

Ethical work is a form of worship.

In establishing a world federation and a world language.

In universal education for all.

Science and religion are in fundamental agreement about the cosmos, since God would not have given humanity two systems that attempt to explain existence that are in conflict.

Some basic books to which a guest can refer to learn more about the Bahá'í faith:

The Bahá'í Faith – An Introduction by Gloria Faizi (Bahá'í Publications Trust, 2002).

Bahá'u'lláh and the New Era by J. E. Esselmont (Bahá'í Publishing Trust, 2002).

The Proofs of Bahá'u'lláh's Mission: A Compilation from Bahá'í Sacred Writings (Palabra Publications, 1994).

The above books may be obtained from:

Bahá'í Books UK
5 Station Approach
Oakham
Rutland
LE15 6QW
Telephone 01572 722780
Email: bpt.sales@bahai.org.uk

3. HOLY DAYS AND FESTIVALS

Ayyám-i-Há ('Ah-yah-mee-HAH') or 'Days of Ha': Celebrated from 26 February to 1 March. The holiday is devoted to hospitality, charity and gift-giving and to spiritually preparing oneself for the annual fast for the entire length of the last month in the Bahá'í calendar. The fast continues from sunrise to sundown for nineteen days. Ayyám-i-Há is celebrated during the four days (five in a leap year) before the last month of the Bahá'í year. There is no traditional greeting for this holiday.

Naw-Rúz ('Naw-ROOZ'): The Bahá'í New Year's Day, which occurs on 21 March. The day is astronomically fixed to commence the year on the first day of spring. Bahá'ís attend neither work nor school on this day. While there are no set rituals for observing the holiday, it is often marked by prayers, feasts and possible festive communal field trips. There is no traditional greeting for this holiday.

Festival of Ridván ('RIZ-von'): Celebrated from 21 April to 2 May. This twelve-day holiday commemorates the twelve days from 21 April to 2 May 1863, when Bahá'u'lláh, the prophet-founder of the Bahá'í faith, publicly proclaimed in a garden in Baghdad his mission as God's messenger for this age. The garden was called 'Ridván'. Three days during the Festival of Ridván are holy days during which work and school are suspended: the first day (21 April), the ninth day (29 April) and the twelfth day (2 May). There is no traditional greeting for this holiday.

The Declaration of the Báb: Occurs on 23 May. Commemorates the date in 1844 when the Báb, the prophet-herald of the Bahá'í faith, announced in Shiraz, Persia, that he was the herald of a new messenger of God. Work and school are suspended on this day, for which there is no traditional greeting.

The Martyrdom of the Báb: Occurs on 9 July, and commemorates the anniversary of the execution by a firing squad in Tabriz, Persia, of Mírzá 'Alí-Muhammad, the Báb, the prophet-herald of the Bahá'í faith. The martyrdom is marked with prayers at noon, which is when the Báb was executed. There is no traditional greeting for this holiday.

The Birth of the Báb: Celebrated on 20 October. Commemorates the anniversary of the birth of the Báb, which means 'the Gate', who was the prophet-herald of the Bahá'í faith. The Báb was born with the name Siyyid 'Alí-Muhammad in 1819. Work and school are suspended on this holiday. While there are no set rituals for observing the holiday, it is often marked by prayers, feasts and possibly festive communal field trips. There is no traditional greeting for this holiday.

The Birth of Bahá'u'lláh ('Bah-HAH-oo-LAH'): Celebrated on 12 November. Commemorates the birth of Bahá'u'lláh, who was born Mírzá Husayn Ali in 1817 in Nur, Persia. Bahá'u'lláh, which means 'Glory of God', was the prophet-founder of the Bahá'í faith. Work and school are suspended on this holiday. While there are no set rituals for observing the holiday, it is often marked by prayers, feasts and possibly festive communal field trips. There is no traditional greeting for this holiday.

The Day of the Covenant: Occurs on 26 November. Commemorates Bahá'u'lláh's appointing of his son 'Abdu'l-Bahá as the Centre of his Covenant. While there are no set rituals for observing the holiday, it is often marked by prayers, feasts and possibly festive communal field trips. There is no traditional greeting for this holiday.

4. LIFE CYCLE EVENTS

Birth Ceremony

Not applicable to the Bahá'í faith.

Initiation Ceremony

Not applicable to the Bahá'í faith.

Marriage Ceremony

The Bahá'í faith teaches that the family is the basic unit of society and that monogamous marriage is the foundation of family life. Also, preparation for marriage is essential for ensuring a happy marriage. Preparation includes parental approval for the choice of a spouse. This does not mean that Bahá'í marriages are arranged, since Bahá'ís marry the person of their choice. But once the choice is made, parents have the right and the obligation to weigh carefully whether to give their consent and, thus, to guide their offspring in one of life's most important decisions.

Bahá'ís encourage interracial marriages, since these stress humanity's essential oneness. The faith also does not discourage interfaith marriages.

The Bahá'í faith allows divorce, although it strongly discourages it. If a Bahá'í couple decide to seek a divorce, they must live apart from each other for at least one year – the 'year of patience' – while they attempt to reconcile. If they still desire a divorce after those twelve months, it is granted.

The Bahá'í faith does not have a standard wedding meeting. Its only stipulation for a wedding is that the bride and groom must exchange vows in front of two witnesses designated by the local Bahá'í spiritual assembly. The vow repeated by the bride and groom is, 'We will all verily abide by the Will of God.' For a Bahá'í, that Will implies all of the commitments associated with marriage, including to love, honour and cherish; to care for each other, regardless of health or wealth; and to share with and serve each other.

Other than meeting the criteria regarding witnesses and the bride and groom reciting the vows, a Bahá'í wedding may be as simple or elaborate as a couple wishes. The length of the wedding varies, depending on its content.

Before the ceremony

Are guests usually invited by a formal invitation? Either by a written invitation or by a telephone call.

If not stated explicitly, should one assume that children are invited? Yes.

If one cannot attend, what should one do? Depending on your personal preference, you may send flowers or a gift to the couple along with writing or telephoning your regrets that you cannot attend.

Appropriate attire

Men: A jacket and tie. No head covering is required.

Women: Personal preference for attire, and one's own sense of reverence, are the only criteria. This may range from a dress or skirt to slacks or jeans. Clothing need not cover the arms or reach below the knees. No head covering is required. Women may wear open-toed shoes and/or modest jewellery.

There are no rules regarding colours of clothing.

Gifts

Is a gift customarily expected? Yes. Appropriate gifts are whatever is the norm in one's culture.

Should gifts be brought to the ceremony? They may be brought to the ceremony or the reception or sent to the home of the newlyweds.

The ceremony

Where will the ceremony take place? Bahá'í weddings may be held wherever the bride and groom desire.

When should guests arrive and where should they sit? Arrive at the time for which the meeting has been called. At some weddings, there may be ushers to advise guests on where to sit.

If arriving late, are there times when a guest should not enter the ceremony? No.

Are there times when a guest should not leave the ceremony? No.

Who are the major officiants, leaders or participants at the ceremony and what do they do? The bride, the groom and two witnesses approved by the local spiritual assembly and who need not be Bahá'ís.

What books are used? There are no standard readings at Bahá'í weddings. Whatever is read is chosen by the bride and groom and usually includes writings from Bahá'í and other faiths, and other poetry and prose.

To indicate the order of the ceremony: There may be a programme or periodic announcements.

Will a guest who is not a Bahá'í be expected to do anything other than sit? No.

Are there any parts of the ceremony in which a guest who is not a Bahá'í should not participate? No.

If not disruptive to the ceremony, is it OK to:

Take pictures? Yes.
Use a flash? Yes.
Use video recording equipment? Yes.
Use audio recording equipment? Yes.

Will contributions to the house of worship be collected at the ceremony? No.

After the ceremony

Is there usually a reception after the ceremony? Possibly, depending on personal preference. If there is a reception, there will probably be food. It is not common for alcoholic drinks to be served at a Bahá'í wedding. However, alcohol may be served if either the bride or the groom is not a Bahá'í, or if the couple feel it appropriate for their non-Bahá'í guests. There may also be music and dancing at the reception.

Would it be considered impolite to neither eat nor drink? No.

Is there a grace or benediction before eating or drinking? No.

Is there a grace or benediction after eating or drinking? No.

Is there a traditional greeting for the family? No.

Is there a traditional form of address for clergy who may be at the reception? No, since there are no clergy in the Bahá'í faith.

Is it OK to leave early? Yes.

❈

Funerals and Mourning

The Bahá'í faith teaches that there is a separate, rational soul for every human. It provides the underlying animation for the body and is our real self. Upon the death of the body, the soul is freed from its ties with the physical body and the surrounding physical world, and begins its journey through the spiritual world. Bahá'ís understand the spiritual world to be a timeless, placeless extension of our own universe, and not a physically remote or removed place.

Heaven is envisioned partly as a state of nearness to God; hell is a state of remoteness from God. Each state is a natural consequence of the efforts of an individual – or the lack of them – to develop spiritually. The key to spiritual progress is to follow the path outlined by the various prophets of God, who include Adam, Moses, Buddha, Krishna, Zoroaster, Jesus and Muhammad, and Bahá'u'lláh.

Beyond this, the exact nature of afterlife remains a mystery.

While the Bahá'í faith is relatively free of teachings regarding the actual rituals of funerals, it does advise that the deceased should not be embalmed, unless it is required by state law. Also the deceased should be buried within one hour's travel time from the place of death.

Before the ceremony

How soon after the death does the funeral usually take place? Usually within two or three days.

What should a non-Bahá'í do upon hearing of the death of a member of that faith? Convey your condolences to the bereaved either by telephone or by a visit to their home.

Appropriate attire

Men: Personal preference for attire, and one's own sense of reverence, are the only criteria. This may range from jacket and tie to slacks or jeans. No head covering is required.

Women: Personal preference for attire, and one's own sense of reverence, are the only criteria. This may range from a dress or skirt to slacks or jeans. Clothing need not cover the arms or reach below the knees. No head covering is required. Women may wear open-toed shoes and/or modest jewellery.

There are no rules regarding colours of clothing, but these should conform to social and cultural custom.

Gifts

Is it appropriate to send flowers or make a contribution? Yes. Flowers may be sent either to the home of the bereaved before or after the funeral or to the funeral itself. Contributions may be made to a fund or charity designated by the bereaved or before death by the deceased, but non-Bahá'ís cannot contribute to a Bahá'í fund.

Is it appropriate to send food? Food may be sent to the home of the bereaved before or after the funeral. No specific types of food are best to send or are prohibited.

The ceremony

Where will the ceremony take place? At the local house of worship or at a funeral home.

When should guests arrive and where should they sit? Arrive early or at the time for which the meeting has been called. Ushers may be available to advise guests on where to sit.

If arriving late, are there times when a guest should not enter the ceremony? No.

Will the bereaved family be present before the ceremony? Possibly.

Is there a traditional greeting for the family? No. Simply express your condolences.

Will there be an open coffin? Rarely, since the Bahá'í faith does not allow embalming.

Is a guest expected to view the body? This is entirely optional.

What is appropriate behaviour upon viewing the body? The Bahá'í faith does not ordain certain behaviour at such moments, since open coffins are so rare.

Who are the major officiants at the ceremony and what do they do? Whoever the family asks to officiate. They will see that the meeting is carried out according to the family's wishes.

What books are used? Funeral programmes may draw on many published anthologies of Bahá'í sacred writings. Most would make use of prayers for the departed from a Bahá'í prayer book, in which are collected prayers by the Báb, Bahá'u'lláh and 'Abdu'l-Bahá.

To indicate the order of the ceremony: There may be periodic announcements or a programme may be distributed.

Will a guest who is not a Bahá'í be expected to do anything other than sit? No.

Are there any parts of the ceremony in which a guest who is not a Bahá'í should not participate? No.

If not disruptive to the ceremony, is it OK to:

Take pictures? Possibly, depending on the preference of the family members.

Use a flash? Possibly, depending on the preference of the family members.

Use video recording equipment? Possibly, depending on the preference of the family members.

Use audio recording equipment? Possibly, depending on the preference of the family members.

Will contributions to the Bahá'í Faith's fund be collected at the ceremony? No.

The interment

Should guests attend the interment? Yes, if the family of the deceased desire it.

Whom should one ask for directions? Family members or the funeral director.

What happens at the graveside? A particular Bahá'í prayer for the deceased may be recited at the graveside.

Do guests who are not Bahá'ís participate at the graveside ceremony? Depending on a guest's relationship with the deceased, the bereaved family may possibly ask a guest to read aloud some prayers to those gathered at the funeral.

Comforting the bereaved

Is it appropriate to visit the home of the bereaved after the funeral? Yes. The timing of the visit entirely depends on the personal preference of the visitor and the bereaved.

Will there be a religious meeting at the home of the bereaved? No.

Will food be served? Probably.

How soon after the funeral will a mourner usually return to a normal work schedule? The Bahá'í faith ordains no particular mourning period. The length of a mourner's absence from work depends entirely on the individual mourner.

How soon after the funeral will a mourner usually return to a normal social schedule? The Bahá'í faith ordains no particular mourning period. The length of a mourner's absence from social events depends entirely on the individual mourner.

Are there mourning customs to which a friend who is not a Bahá'í should be sensitive? No, since the Bahá'í faith ordains no particular mourning customs.

Are there rituals for observing the anniversary of the death? No.

5. HOME CELEBRATIONS

Not applicable to the Bahá'í faith.

3

Baptist

1. HISTORY AND BELIEFS

The Baptist churches descend from the spiritual ferment generated by seventeenth-century English Puritanism. Essentially, Baptists believe in the authority of the Bible, the right to interpret it privately, baptising only those old enough to profess belief for themselves, and strict separation of church and state.

The movement began in England in the early seventeenth century. Its founders, John Smyth and Thomas Helwys, sought to purify the Church of England of all traces of Roman Catholicism, but faced persecution for their activities and eventually fled to Holland, seeking religious liberty. It was there that Smyth baptised himself, Helwys and other congregation memebers by pouring water on their heads – a radical and contentious act for a Church of England minister. The belief in baptism through immersion in water became a practice characteristic of these new reformers, and it was their opponents who first coined the phrase 'Baptists', although adherents themselves initially rejected the name.

In 1612 Smyth and Helwys returned to England and established the first Baptist church, in Spitalfields, London. Helwys published *A Short Declaration of the Mystery of Iniquity*, one of the first books to call for religious liberty. In the seventeenth century Baptists refused to conform and be members of the Church of England, arguing that Christ and not the King (or Queen) was head of the church, and they continued to be persecuted for their beliefs. They were known variously as 'Nonconformists' and 'Dissenters'. The Act of Toleration in 1689 allowed Baptists freedom of worship for the first time.

The nineteenth century saw significant growth in the size and influence of the Baptist Church in the UK. Charles Spurgeon, one of modern Christianity's greatest preachers, began his ministry at this time. The Baptist Union of Great Britain was formed in 1891, as two previously distinct streams of Baptist theology were united: the General Baptists (who believed that when Christ died on the cross he died for everyone) and the Particular Baptists (who believed that Christ died for an elect).

UK churches: 2,150
UK membership: approximately 150,000

For more information, contact:

The Baptist Union of Great Britain
Baptist House
PO BOX 44
129 Broadway
Didcot
OX11 8RT
Telephone: 01235 517700
Email: info@baptist.org.uk

2. THE BASIC SERVICE

At the heart of the Baptist service is the sermon, which usually flows from that day's Scripture lesson, as do the hymns chosen for that service. The sermon is followed by 'the invitation', which asks those present either to become members of the church or to rededicate themselves to Christ. One or more hymns are sung as congregants or guests come forward to accept 'the invitation'. The service lasts about one hour.

✵

Appropriate Attire

Men: Generally casual clothing is worn, although some churches might expect a more formal appearance. No head covering is required.

Women: Generally casual, although some modesty would be expected (i.e. not too alluring). Sleeveless tops and above-the-knee skirts or shorts are permitted. Open-toed shoes and modest jewellery are allowed. No head covering is required.

There are no rules regarding colours of clothing.

✵

The Sanctuary

What are the major sections of the church?

The sanctuary: The part of the church where the Lord's Table is located and where ministers lead congregants in prayer. It is usually elevated above the floor level and is invariably at the front of the church.

The pulpit or lectern: The stand at which scriptural lessons and psalm responses are read and the word of God is preached.

Seating for congregants: Seats and sometimes kneeling benches, usually in front and/or to the side of the altar or Communion table.

Communion table: The place from which the Lord's Supper is served.

Baptistery: The place for administering baptism.

✵

The Service

When should guests arrive and where should they sit? Arrive at the time for which the service has been called. There are no special rules governing where you should sit.

If arriving late, are there times when a guest should not enter the service? Do not enter while prayers are being recited or while announcements are being made.

Are there times when a guest should not leave the service? Do not leave during the sermon or during the benediction.

Who are the major officiants, leaders or participants and what do they do?

The pastor, who presides during the service and preaches.

The church secretary, who gives the notices.

The worship band leader, who leads the singing, or the organist who plays for the hymns.

What are the major ritual objects of the service?

Bread and grape juice (wine is rarely served), which compose the Communion (or the Lord's Supper) and are considered a memorial to the body and blood of Jesus Christ, as well as a reminder of his second coming.

The Communion table, from which the bread and grape juice are offered to congregants. On it may be a crucifix, candles or flowers.

What books are used? Several translations of the Bible may be used, in particular the New International Version and the New Revised Standard Version. Hymn books are sometimes used, although digital projection onto screens of songs and other items is becoming commonplace.

To indicate the order of the service: A programme or bulletin will be distributed.

Guest Behaviour during the Service

Will a guest who is not a Baptist be expected to do anything other than sit? Guests of other faiths are expected to stand, kneel, read prayers aloud and sing with those present, unless this violates their own religious beliefs. If you would prefer to neither kneel nor stand, it is acceptable to remain seated.

Are there any parts of the service in which a guest who is not a Baptist should not participate? In some churches, Communion (or the Lord's Supper) is offered only to members of that congregation.

If not disruptive to the service, is it OK to:

Take pictures? Yes, but only with prior permission of the pastor.
Use a flash? Yes, but only with prior permission of the pastor.
Use video recording equipment? Yes, but only with prior permission of the pastor.
Use audio recording equipment? Yes, but only with prior permission of the pastor.

Will contributions to the church be collected at the service? Yes.

How much is it customary to contribute? It is not expected that guests will contribute.

After the Service

Is there usually a reception after the service? Generally, light refreshments such as tea and coffee are offered after the morning service.

Is there a traditional form of address for clergy whom a guest may meet? 'Pastor' is the more formal address, but most would be happy being called 'Mr' or 'Mrs' followed by their surname, or even just by their Christian name.

Is it OK to leave early? Yes.

Some Basic Beliefs

Baptists believe:

That our Lord and Saviour Jesus Christ, God manifest in the flesh, is the sole and absolute authority in all matters pertaining to faith and practice, as revealed in the Holy Scriptures, and that each church has liberty, under the guidance of the Holy Spirit, to interpret and administer his laws.

That Christian baptism is the immersion in water into the Name of the Father, the Son and the Holy Ghost, of those who have professed repentance towards God and faith in our Lord Jesus Christ who 'died for our sins according to the Scriptures; was buried, and rose again the third day'.

That it is the duty of every disciple to bear personal witness to the gospel of Jesus Christ, and to take part in the evangelisation of the world.

Some basic books to which a guest can refer to learn more about the Baptist faith:

Baptist Basics, New Series by Dr Nigel Wright (a series of leaflets published by the Baptist Union of Great Britain).

3. HOLY DAYS AND FESTIVALS

Christmas: Always falls on 25 December. Celebrates the birth of Christ. The traditional greeting is 'Merry Christmas'.

Easter: Always falls on the Sunday after the first full moon that occurs on or after the spring equinox of 21 March. Commemorates the death and resurrection of Jesus. The traditional greeting is 'Happy Easter'.

Pentecost: Occurs fifty days after Easter because this is when the Holy Ghost (the Spirit of Jesus) descended on his apostles. Celebrates the power of the Holy Spirit and its manifestation in the early Christian church. There is no traditional greeting for this holiday.

Ash Wednesday: Occurs forty days before Easter. Commemorates the beginning of Lent, which is a season of preparation and penitence before Easter itself. There is no traditional greeting for this holiday.

Maundy Thursday: Falls four days before Easter. Commemorates the institution of the Lord's Supper (also known as Communion) and Jesus' subsequent arrest and trial. There is no traditional greeting.

Good Friday: Three days before Easter. Commemorates the crucifixion, death and burial of Jesus.

Christmas, Easter and Pentecost are joyful celebrations. Ash Wednesday, Maundy Thursday and Good Friday are sombre, penitential commemorations. During the services for these latter three holidays, decorum and discretion are of great importance.

4. LIFE CYCLE EVENTS

Birth Ceremony

Baptists practise a child dedication service in which parents present their child and themselves to God in dedication. The congregation is also asked at this time to help the parents nurture their child in the Christian faith. This service usually takes place within the child's first year of life.

Initiation Ceremony

During this ceremony, which is called a baptism, an individual is completely immersed into the baptismal waters. The ceremony represents an active, volitional, public declaration of one's commitment to the Church. One's downward movement into the baptismal waters symbolises the death of Jesus; the upward movement symbolises his resurrection.

Baptism occurs at the 'age of accountability', which the Church has not defined, but which is assumed to occur usually between the ages of nine and twelve years. The actual baptism takes about five to ten minutes, although the larger basic service of which it is a part lasts about one hour.

Before the ceremony

Are guests usually invited by a formal invitation? Guests are usually invited orally, either by telephone or in person.

If not stated explicitly, should one assume that children are invited? Yes.

If one cannot attend, what should one do? RSVP with regrets. Gifts are not expected.

Appropriate attire

Men: Generally casual clothing is worn, although some churches might expect a more formal appearance. No head covering is required.

Women: Generally casual, although some modesty would be expected (i.e. not too alluring). Sleeveless tops and above-the-knee skirts or shorts are permitted. Open-toed shoes and modest jewellery are allowed. No head covering is required.

There are no rules regarding colours of clothing.

Gifts

Is a gift customarily expected? No.

The ceremony

When should guests arrive and where should they sit? Arrive at the time for which the service has been called. There are no special rules governing where you should sit.

If arriving late, are there times when a guest should not enter the service? Do not enter while prayers are being recited or while announcements are being made.

Are there times when a guest should not leave the service? Do not leave during the sermon or during the benediction.

Who are the major officiants, leaders or participants and what do they do?

The pastor, who presides during the service and preaches.
The church secretary, who gives the notices.
The worship band leader, who leads the singing, or the organist who plays for the hymns.

What books are used? Several translations of the Bible may be used, in particular the New International Version and the New Revised Standard Version. Hymn books are sometimes used, although digital projection onto screens of songs and other items is becoming commonplace.

To indicate the order of the service: A programme or bulletin will be distributed.

Will a guest who is not a Baptist be expected to do anything other than sit? Guests of other faiths are expected to stand, kneel, read prayers aloud and sing with those present, unless this violates their own religious beliefs. If you would prefer to neither kneel nor stand, it is acceptable to remain seated.

Are there any parts of the service in which a guest who is not a Baptist should not participate? In some churches, Communion (or the Lord's Supper) is offered only to members of that congregation.

If not disruptive to the service, is it OK to:

Take pictures? Yes, but only with prior permission of the pastor.
Use a flash? Yes, but only with prior permission of the pastor.
Use video recording equipment? Yes, but only with prior permission of the pastor.
Use audio recording equipment? Yes, but only with prior permission of the pastor.

Will contributions to the church be collected at the service? Yes.

How much is it customary to contribute? It is not expected that guests will contribute.

After the ceremony

Is there usually a reception after the ceremony? There may possibly be a reception. If so, it is usually held in the fellowship hall of the church or at the home of the individual who has been baptised. Light food, such as sandwiches and cake, may be served. The reception may last up to two hours.

Would it be considered impolite to neither eat nor drink? No.

Is there a grace or benediction before eating or drinking? Yes.

Is there a grace or benediction after eating or drinking? No.

Is there a traditional greeting for the family? Just offer your congratulations.

Is there a traditional form of address for clergy who may be at the reception? 'Pastor' is the more formal address, but most would be happy being called 'Mr' or 'Mrs' followed by their surname, or even just by their Christian name.

Is it OK to leave early? Yes.

Marriage Ceremony

Marriage is considered to be a three-way covenant between a woman, a man and God, who is represented at the marriage ceremony by the pastor, the congregation and the Holy Spirit (the empowering Spirit of God). The service takes about thirty to sixty minutes and is a ceremony in itself.

Before the ceremony

Are guests usually invited by a formal invitation? Yes.

If not stated explicitly, should one assume that children are invited? No.

If one cannot attend, what should one do? RSVP with regrets and send a gift.

Appropriate attire

Men: A suit or a jacket and tie. No head covering is required.

Women: A dress or skirt. Clothing should cover the arms, and hems should reach below the knees. Open-toed shoes and modest jewellery are allowed. No head covering is required.

There are no rules regarding colours of clothing.

Gifts

Is a gift customarily expected? Yes. Often appropriate are such house-hold items as sheets, kitchenware or small household appliances.

Should gifts be brought to the ceremony? Send gifts to the home of the newlyweds, or bring them to the reception.

The ceremony

Where will the ceremony take place? In either a church or a home.

When should guests arrive and where should they sit? Arrive about ten minutes before the time for which the ceremony has been called. Ushers will advise guests where to sit.

If arriving late, are there times when a guest should not enter the ceremony? Do not enter during the procession or recession of the wedding party.

Are there times when a guest should not leave the ceremony? Do not leave before the ceremony has ended.

Who are the major officiants, leaders or participants at the ceremony and what do they do?
The pastor, who performs the ceremony.
The bride and groom.
Musicians, who provide music before, during and after the ceremony.

What books are used? Several translations of the Bible may be used, in particular the New International Version and the New Revised Standard Version. Hymn books are sometimes used, although digital projection onto screens of songs and other items is becoming common-place.

To indicate the order of the ceremony: No such guidance is needed for those present, since the ceremony is relatively brief and there is no participation by guests.

Will a guest who is not a Baptist be expected to do anything other than sit? No.

Are there any parts of the ceremony in which a guest who is not a Baptist should not participate? No.

If not disruptive to the ceremony, is it OK to:

Take pictures? Yes, but only with prior permission of the pastor.

Use a flash? Yes, but only with prior permission of the pastor.

Use video recording equipment? Yes, but only with prior permission of the pastor.

Use audio recording equipment? Yes, but only with prior permission of the pastor.

Will contributions to the church be collected at the ceremony? No.

After the ceremony

Is there usually a reception after the ceremony? Yes. It may be held at the church where the ceremony is conducted or in a home, hotel or other hired venue. Depending on the choice of the couple and of the bride's family, a full-course meal may be served. Alcoholic drinks are rarely served. There may be music and dancing. The reception may last more than two hours.

Would it be considered impolite to neither eat nor drink? Yes.

Is there a grace or benediction before eating or drinking? Possibly.

Is there a grace or benediction after eating or drinking? Possibly. If guests arrive and start eating at different times, grace may be said after the meal.

Is there a traditional greeting for the family? Offer your congratulations when you meet the family in the reception line after the service.

Is there a traditional form of address for clergy who may be at the reception? 'Pastor' is the more formal address, but most would be happy being called 'Mr' or 'Mrs' followed by their surname, or even just by their Christian name.

Is it OK to leave early? Yes.

❀

Funerals and Mourning

There are two schools of belief in the Baptist faith about afterlife. One maintains that one enters paradise immediately after death. This is based on Jesus' words on the cross to the penitent thief, 'This day thou shalt be with me in Paradise' (Luke 23:43). The other school maintains that upon Jesus' second coming, a trumpet will sound and the dead will be raised to paradise. This is based on Paul's writings in 1 Corinthians 15:32. The funeral service, which is a ceremony in itself, lasts about thirty to sixty minutes.

Before the ceremony

How soon after the death does the funeral usually take place? Within one week.

What should a non-Baptist do upon hearing of the death of a member of that faith? Telephone or visit the bereaved to offer condolences and sympathies.

Appropriate attire

Men: A suit or a jacket and tie. No head covering is required.

Women: A dress or skirt. Clothing should cover the arms, and hems should reach below the knees. Open-toed shoes and modest jewellery are allowed. No head covering is required.

Dark, sombre colours are advised.

Gifts

Is it appropriate to send flowers or make a contribution? Flowers may be sent to the home of the bereaved before the funeral, or to the church or funeral home where the funeral will take place. Contributions to a particular charity may be sent to the home of the bereaved before or after the funeral. The amount of the contribution is at the discretion of the donor. Such gifts should be presented to the spouse or adult children of the deceased.

Is it appropriate to send food? Not unless requested.

The ceremony

Where will the ceremony take place? In either a church or a funeral home.

When should guests arrive and where should they sit? Arrive about ten minutes before the time for which the ceremony has been called. Ushers will advise guests where to sit.

If arriving late, are there times when a guest should not enter the ceremony? Do not enter when the bereaved family is entering or during prayers.

Will the bereaved family be present at the church or funeral home before the ceremony? No.

Is there a traditional greeting for the family? No. Just offer your condolences.

Will there be an open coffin? Not usually, except for some West Indian funerals.

Is a guest expected to view the body? This is optional.

What is appropriate behaviour upon viewing the body? Join the line of viewers and view the body silently and sombrely.

Who are the major officiants at the ceremony and what do they do?
The pastor, who performs the service.
Musicians, who provide music before, during and after the service.

What books are used? Several translations of the Bible may be used, in particular the New International Version and the New Revised Standard Version.

To indicate the order of the ceremony: A printed order of service will be distributed.

Will a guest who is not a Baptist be expected to do anything other than sit? Guests of other faiths are expected to stand, kneel, read prayers aloud and sing with those present, unless this violates their own religious beliefs. If you would prefer to neither kneel nor stand, it is acceptable to remain seated.

Are there any parts of the ceremony in which a guest who is not a Baptist should not participate? No, although, very rarely, Communion (or the Lord's Supper) is offered at funeral ceremonies. In some churches, Communion is offered only to members of that congregation. In such cases, follow the cues of those present, ask a fellow guest for guidance or ask a pastor for advice before the service begins.

If not disruptive to the ceremony, is it OK to:

Take pictures? No.
Use a flash? No.
Use video recording equipment? No.
Use audio recording equipment? No.

Will contributions to the church be collected at the ceremony? No.

The interment

Should guests attend the interment? Yes.

Whom should one ask for directions? Either ask the funeral director or follow the funeral procession to the cemetery.

What happens at the graveside? During a brief service, Scriptures are read, prayers are recited and the coffin is committed to the ground.

Do guests who are not Baptists participate at the graveside ceremony? No. They are simply present.

Comforting the bereaved

Is it appropriate to visit the home of the bereaved after the funeral? Yes. It is appropriate to do so after the burial. During such visits, happy times during the life of the deceased are recalled and spoken about. A visit of no more than thirty minutes is fitting.

Will there be a religious service at the home of the bereaved? No.

Will food be served? Yes, but no alcoholic drinks. It would be considered impolite for a visitor not to eat. No grace or benediction will be recited before or after eating or drinking.

How soon after the funeral will a mourner usually return to a normal work schedule? Possibly in one week, although there are no doctrinal prescriptions.

How soon after the funeral will a mourner usually return to a normal social schedule? Possibly two months, although there are no doctrinal prescriptions.

Are there mourning customs to which a friend who is not a Baptist should be sensitive? No.

Are there rituals for observing the anniversary of the death? There is usually no formal remembrance in a church, but there are often quiet commemorations of the death within the family of the deceased.

5. HOME CELEBRATIONS

Not applicable to Baptists.

4

Buddhist

1. HISTORY AND BELIEFS

Buddhism was founded in the sixth century BC in northern India by Siddhartha Gautama, who was born the son of a king in what is now southern Nepal. Warned by a sage that his son would become either an ascetic or a universal monarch, the king confined his son to home. A few years after marrying and having a child of his own, Siddhartha escaped from his father's palace at around the age of twenty-nine. Since he had been sheltered for his entire life from the pains of life, he was shocked when he beheld three men. The first was old and weak; the second was ill and diseased; the last was dead. Each represented different aspects of the impermanence inherent in all forms of earthly existence. He also saw a religious ascetic, who represented the possibility of a solution to these frailties.

Wandering in search of peace, Siddhartha tried many disciplines, including severe asceticism, until he came to the Bodhi tree (the Tree of Enlightenment). He sat there in meditation until, at the age of thirty-five, he became a Buddha, or one who is enlightened.

In his first sermon after achieving enlightenment, the Buddha spoke of the Four Noble Truths and the Noble Eightfold Path. These succinctly comprise the Buddha's insights into the essential ways of life and how to achieve spiritual liberation. The Buddha died at the age of eighty. His last words were for his disciples to depend not on him, but on the *dharma*, or Buddhist teachings.

In subsequent centuries, Buddhism flowered in Asia. Interest in Buddhism began to develop in the UK in the mid-to-late nineteenth century as various texts – including the *Pali Canon*, or *Tipitaka* – were translated into English, and has grown significantly in popularity since the 1960s, partly due to the arrival of Tibetan teachers (*Lamas*) in the West, having been forced out of Tibet by the Chinese.

UK temples: over 650
UK practitioners: over 150,000

For more information, contact:

The Buddhist Society
58 Eccleston Square
London
SW1V 1PH
Tel: 020 7834 5858
Email: info@thebuddhistsociety.org

The Buddhist Society publishes *The Buddhist Directory* (Tenth Edition), containing listings of over 649 Buddhist centres and resources from many traditions throughout the UK. Available by post or from their bookshop.

2. THE BASIC GATHERING

There are many varieties of Buddhist gathering. Some are almost entirely devoted to silent meditation; others include *puja* (offering) ceremonies, talks and teachings by a teacher, who might be an ordained monk or nun, or a lay person, and announcements by the leader of the Buddhist temple. Elements most common to Buddhist gatherings are chanting, an incense offering, silent meditation, readings of Buddhist *sutras* (texts) and stories and a sermon or talk by a teacher.

Gatherings can last one to two hours or – if it is described as a retreat – a whole day, weekend or even longer.

Appropriate Attire

There are no strict rules regarding clothing, although smart casual and modest (keeping arms, legs and chest covered) is preferred. Your clothing should be comfortable. You will need to remove your shoes in Shrine rooms, so it is a good idea to bring socks to cover your feet. In some places it will be recommended that you sit in a cross-legged lotus position on a meditation cushion, so consider this when choosing appropriate clothing. Wearing jewellery is fine.

There are no rules regarding colours of clothing, although extremely bright or fluorescent colours are discouraged.

The Sanctuary

What are the major sections of the Buddhist centre or temple? The architecture of Buddhist centres and temples varies widely. These elements will be found in many, but not all:

The Shrine: Contains statues of one or more Buddhas, or sometimes the Buddha Gautama (Shakamuni) with disciples. This is at the front of the sanctuary.

Side Shrine: Contains statues or pictures of the founder of the particular lineage/tradition/school adhered to by a temple. A lineage is a line of teachers and their students who, in turn, also become teachers.

Meditation cushions: Where both practitioners and visitors sit. Most centres, temples and organisations will have chairs for people to sit on, and a few will also have meditation benches.

The Ceremony

When should guests arrive and where should they sit? It is customary to arrive early, in good time to compose yourself and be ready to listen and meditate. Where one sits depends on the particular school or tradition of that temple. If there is a seated meditation, a visitor will probably be directed to a meditation cushion. Ensure that your feet are never pointed at the Shrine or any Buddhist image.

If arriving late, are there times when a guest should not enter the ceremony? Do not enter during meditation unless you are told to do so. Try to cause the minimum disruption as you find somewhere to sit, preferably towards the back of the room.

Are there times when a guest should not leave the ceremony? Do not leave during the meditation session, unless you are feeling unwell.

Who are the major officiants, leaders or participants and what do they do?
A Lama, Ajahn, Venerable, monk or nun, who leads the ceremony, including chanting. In some traditions this role is filled by a *senior lay practitioner or teacher*.

What are the major objects used?

A picture or image of the Buddha.

Incense, which is usually at the front of the shrine. The incense is used as an offering, and is lit by a designated person belonging to the particular centre or temple.

Flowers and other offerings.

Mala, a string of beads (usually seeds from a Bodhi tree but could be made from precious stones) that is used to count recitations of a mantra. Malas are used by Buddhist practitioners in some traditions, but not all.

What books are used? There will usually be Buddhist chanting sheets or books distributed (although some regular practitioners may bring their own). These texts should be treated with care, and never placed on the floor where they could be damaged.

There are three collections of texts considered central to Buddhist teaching, sometimes known as the *Tipitaka* ('the Three Baskets'): the *Sutta Pitaka* – the Buddha's teachings; *Abhidhamma Pitaka* – a philosophical analysis of his teachings; and *Vinaya Pitaka* – which prescribes the monastic training and disciplines.

To indicate the order of the ceremony: Periodic announcements may be made or instructions given. If in doubt, follow what other people are doing or just sit quietly.

✼

Guest Behaviour during the Ceremony

Will a guest who is not a Buddhist be expected to do anything other than sit? It is entirely optional for a guest from another faith to chant with the Buddhist practitioners or stand when they do so.

Are there any parts of the ceremony in which a guest who is not a Buddhist should not participate? No.

If not disruptive to the ceremony, is it OK to:

Take pictures? Only with prior approval of the person in charge.
Use a flash? Only with prior approval of the person in charge.
Use video recording equipment? Only with prior approval of the person in charge.
Use audio recording equipment? Only with prior approval of the person in charge.

Will contributions to the temple be collected at the ceremony? Possibly. In some centres or temples, there may be a donations box, plate or bowl near the front door. Occasionally there will be a bowl of fruit on the shrine, into which money can be placed.

How much is it customary to contribute? Students of Buddhist teaching and meditation are encouraged to give *Dana* (a contribution, or donation) based purely on what they can afford, which can even be nothing if your circumstances do not allow you to contribute. In non-Western Buddhist cultures, Dana can sometimes be something useful to the temple, like flowers, food or incense, but in the West it is most normal to contribute money.

✼

After the Ceremony

Is there usually a reception after the ceremony? There may be a reception in the temple's reception area at which light food may be served. Usually there would be no alcohol or meat served. The reception may last between half an hour and an hour. It may be considered impolite to neither eat nor drink something (as in Eastern cultures it is considered impolite not to at least have a little). Some temples have a form of spoken dedication before or after eating or drinking.

Is there a traditional form of address for clergy who may be at the reception? There are many different conventions followed in the various Buddhist traditions. Best to ask at the time.

Is it OK to leave early? Yes, but do so respectfully and causing minimum disruption.

⚜

General Guidelines and Advice

You would not generally be expected to participate in meditations or practices, other than the response to public teaching (for which you will be informed or given chanting sheets to follow), unless specifically requested by the Buddhist teacher. It is fine not to participate in rituals or meditations if one is uncomfortable about them. Guests who do not participate should sit quietly and still.

A typical mistake that guests should avoid is talking or restless behaviour during the ceremony. Remember to turn off mobile phones, music players or other equipment which might distract other people.

Food and drink are usually not allowed in the Shrine room, unless provided by the centre or temple as part of the particular event or practice.

Remember to remove your hats and shoes before entering the Shrine or practice room.

It is important to show particular respect to Buddhist teachers (generally anybody dressed in robes). You should never touch a person in robes unless initiated by them (if they offer their hand to shake, for example). Do not use bad language or behave in a disrespectful manner in front of a person in robes. Food and drink should always be offered first to a person in robes; as a rule, they do not ask for themselves.

꙳

Some Basic Beliefs

Buddhists believe:

The Four Noble Truths, originally enunciated by the Buddha, comprise the essence of Buddhist teaching and practice:

1. All life (birth, ageing, death) is suffering.
2. Suffering is caused by craving or desire.
3. Cessation of suffering is possible.
4. The Noble Eightfold Path can lead to the extinction of suffering.

The Noble Eightfold Path consists of:

1. Right understanding of the nature of reality.
2. Right thought, which is free from sensuous desire, ill will and cruelty.
3. Right speech, which should be absent of falsehoods, harsh words and idle chatter.
4. Right action, which includes refraining from killing, stealing and wrong conduct in matters of bodily pleasure, intoxicants and gambling.
5. Right livelihood, which forbids any conduct contrary to right speech and right action and any trickery or fraud in the ceremony of commerce or one's trade.
6. Right effort, which seeks to avoid generating new, unwholesome actions and encourages purifying the mind (by avoiding and overcoming unwholesome states of mind, while developing and maintaining wholesome states).
7. Right mindfulness, or meditative practices that encourage greater alertness and awareness of one's self.
8. Right concentration, or striving for mental 'one-pointedness'. Right effort and right mindfulness together develop right concentration – and vice versa.

Basic books to which a guest can refer to learn more about Buddhism:

What the Buddha Taught, by Walpola Rahula (Oneworld Publications, 1997).

The Buddhist Handbook, by John Snelling (Inner Traditions International, 1999).

3. HOLY DAYS AND FESTIVALS

Many Buddhists consider participation in festivals and celebrations an important aspect of Buddhist practice. Since the celebrations have developed in different countries, and over long periods of time, there are variations. There are numerous festivals, and those mentioned here are the more important national festivals in Mahayana (M), Theravada (Th) and Tibetan (T) Buddhism.

Nehan-e: Observed on 15 February (or the nearest weekend day) and commemorates Buddha's passing away (M).

Cho Trul Duchen: A fifteen-day celebration in March, remembering Buddha's display of miracles in order to bolster the devotion of disciples (T).

Higan-e: Observed on 21 March and 21 September (or nearest weekend days) and is a reminder of our impermanence (M).

Hanamatsuri: Observed on 8 April (or the nearest weekend day) to celebrate the birth of Buddha (M).

Vesak, Buddha Day: Celebrates in May Buddha's birth, enlightenment and passing away (Th).

Saka Dawa: Celebrates in June Buddha's birth, enlightenment and passing away (T).

Dhammacakka Day (Th) and Chor Khor Duchen (T): Both remember in July Buddha's first proclamation of his doctrine to the world.

Kathina: In October or November, this is the largest alms-giving ceremony of the Buddhist year (Th).

Lha Bab Duchen: Celebrates in November Buddha's descent from the heavenly realm to the earth (T).

Jodo-e: Remembers on 8 December (or nearest weekend day) Buddha's enlightenment (M).

4. LIFE CYCLE EVENTS

Birth Ceremony

Not applicable to Buddhism, although people often hold blessing ceremonies for babies and children. This might include the lighting of candles and incense, the ringing of a sacred bell, and chanting (for which you would be given a chant sheet). There may be prayers for a baby's health, welfare, wisdom and long life, and a talk by a Buddhist teacher. Other conventions of the blessing ceremony are covered under 'The Basic Gathering', above.

Marriage Ceremony

There is no standard Buddhist marriage ceremony in the Western cultures. In some cases, the ceremony may be modelled after a standard Christian wedding ceremony in which the marriage is blessed. Regardless of the structure of the ceremony, the overall purpose is to remind those present of Buddhist principles. For a marriage to become legal, it will need to be conducted as a civil ceremony by a registrar. The ceremony may last from fifteen to thirty minutes.

Before the ceremony

Are guests usually invited by a formal invitation? Guests will be invited orally, either in person or on the telephone, or through a written invitation.

If not stated explicitly, should one assume that children are invited? The broad variables of Buddhist practice make this impossible to answer. Ask the couple or family members.

If one cannot attend, what should one do? RSVP with regrets. Ordinarily, no present is expected.

Appropriate attire

There are no strict rules regarding clothing, although smart casual and modest (keeping arms, legs and chest covered) is preferred. Your clothing should be comfortable. You will need to remove your shoes in Shrine rooms, so it is a good idea to bring socks to cover your feet. In some places it will be recommended that you sit in a cross-legged lotus position on a meditation cushion, so consider this when choosing appropriate clothing. Wearing jewellery is fine.

There are no rules regarding colours of clothing, although extremely bright or fluorescent colours are discouraged.

Gifts

Is a gift customarily expected? A gift is not necessarily expected, but would be warmly received. Some couples might have a wedding gift list, but if not something simple and attractive for the home or related to their beliefs would be appropriate.

Should gifts be brought to the ceremony? Yes, unless otherwise indicated.

The ceremony

Where will the ceremony take place? In a temple, hired room or outdoors.

When should guests arrive and where should they sit? It is customary to arrive early. Where one sits depends on the particular tradition of that temple. Guests should be aware that a temple may have meditation cushions on the floor and not pews in which to sit. Chairs are usually provided.

If arriving late, are there times when a guest should not enter the ceremony? Do not enter during meditation.

Are there times when a guest should not leave the ceremony? No.

Who are the major officiants, leaders or participants at the ceremony and what do they do?

A Lama, Ajahn, Venerable or senior teacher.
The bride and groom.

What books are used? There are no standard texts for Buddhist wedding ceremonies, although any readings will usually refer to Buddhist principles and include words on kindness and compassion for one another.

To indicate the order of the ceremony: The Lama, Ajahn, Venerable or senior teacher would normally indicate if guests are required to join in chanting, or if there will be a period of meditation.

Will a guest who is not a Buddhist be expected to do anything other than sit? Perhaps only to stand when others do.

Are there any parts of the ceremony in which a guest who is not a Buddhist should not participate? No.

If not disruptive to the ceremony, is it OK to:

Take pictures? Only with prior approval of the person in charge.
Use a flash? Only with prior approval of the person in charge.
Use video recording equipment? Only with prior approval of the person in charge.
Use audio recording equipment? Only with prior approval of the person in charge.

Will contributions to the temple be collected at the ceremony? No.

After the ceremony

Is there usually a reception after the ceremony? There may be a reception in the temple's reception area or at another site chosen by the newlyweds, at which light food may be served. Usually there would be no alcohol or meat served. It may be considered impolite to neither eat nor drink something (as in Eastern cultures it is considered impolite not to at least have a little). Some temples have a form of spoken dedication before or after eating or drinking. The reception may last sixty minutes or longer.

Is there a grace or benediction before eating or drinking? Possibly, depending on the particular Buddhist denomination or tradition.

Is there a grace or benediction after eating or drinking? Possibly, depending on the particular Buddhist denomination or tradition.

Is there a traditional greeting for the family? Just offer your congratulations.

Is there a traditional form of address for the person leading the ceremony who may be at the reception? Depending on the particular Buddhist denomination, the form of address may be 'Reverend', 'Lama' or 'Roshi'. It is always best to ask in advance.

Is it OK to leave early? Yes.

A basic resource to which a guest can refer to learn more about Buddhist weddings:

There is a useful article on Buddhist weddings in the 'Information and Advice' section of the website www.confetti.co.uk.

Funerals and Mourning

According to Buddhist belief, when people die they are reborn as another kind of being, and not necessarily as a human. All beings are subject to death and rebirth, and Buddhist funeral rituals are designed to help the deceased move on to a beneficial rebirth.

The main components of any Buddhist funeral ceremony involve producing positive energy through reciting Buddhist prayers and meditation, and then transferring this for the benefit of the deceased, and all beings who suffer.

Buddhists are generally cremated. A funeral ceremony in most Buddhist traditions resembles a Christian ceremony in the West, with a eulogy and prayers at a funeral home, crematorium or sometimes a church when permitted. There may be chanting and periods of meditation. Often, members of the family and friends will give a reading from a Buddhist text or say a poem or something about the person. It may last one hour or longer.

Before the ceremony

How soon after the death does the funeral usually take place?
This varies, depending on the specific Buddhist tradition of the
bereaved. In certain Japanese traditions, the funeral is usually within
one week. In the Buddhist traditions of Myanmar, Cambodia, Sri
Lanka and Thailand, there are three ceremonies. In the first, which
is held within two days after death, monks hold a ceremony at the
home of the bereaved. In the second, which is held within two to five
days after death, monks conduct a ceremony at a funeral home. In
the third, which is held seven days after the cremation, monks lead
a ceremony either at the home of the bereaved or at a temple. This
last ceremony, called a 'merit transference', seeks to generate good
energy for the deceased in his or her new incarnation.

*What should a non-Buddhist do upon hearing of the death of a
member of that faith?* Whatever seems appropriate, according to the
level of acquaintance.

Appropriate attire

There are no strict rules regarding clothing, although smart casual
and modest (keeping arms, legs and chest covered) is preferred. Your
clothing should be comfortable. You will need to remove your shoes
in Shrine rooms, so it is a good idea to bring socks to cover your feet.
In some places it will be recommended that you sit in a cross-legged
lotus position on a meditation cushion, so consider this when choosing
appropriate clothing. Wearing jewellery is fine.

Gifts

Is it appropriate to send flowers or make a contribution? It is
appropriate to send flowers to the funeral or to make a donation of
money, depending on one's relation to the deceased. Typically, the
bereaved family recommends a specific charity or cause as the recip-
ient of donations.

The ceremony

Where will the ceremony take place? The ceremony is usually held at a funeral home, crematorium or sometimes a church when permitted.

When should guests arrive and where should they sit? Arrive at the time for which the ceremony has been called. Sit wherever you wish. If the ceremony is in a funeral home, crematorium or church there will be pews for sitting. If held at the home or the temple, sitting will probably be on the floor on meditation cushions. Chairs would be provided for those unable to sit on meditation cushions.

If arriving late, are there times when a guest should not enter the ceremony? No.

Will the bereaved family be present at the temple or funeral home before the ceremony? Yes.

Is there a traditional greeting for the family? Just offer your condolences.

Will there be an open coffin? Not usually.

Who are the major officiants at the ceremony?
A Lama, Ajahn, Venerable or senior teacher.

What books are used? There will usually be Buddhist chanting sheets or books distributed (although some regular practitioners may bring their own). These texts should be treated with care, and never placed on the floor where they could be damaged. Specific texts (plus translations of the original languages) may have been prepared and bound for people to follow the chants and readings.

To indicate the order of the ceremony: Periodic announcements may be made or instructions given. If in doubt, follow what other people are doing or just sit quietly.

Will a guest who is not a Buddhist be expected to do anything other than sit? Stand when others do so.

Are there any parts of the ceremony in which a guest who is not a Buddhist should not participate? No.

If not disruptive to the ceremony, is it OK to:

Take pictures? No.
Use a flash? No.
Use video recording equipment? No.
Use audio recording equipment? No.

Will contributions to the temple be collected at the ceremony? No.

The interment

Should guests attend the cremation? If invited.

Whom should one ask for directions? If the directions are not provided on the invitation, ask a member of the family or the funeral director.

What happens at the crematorium? Prayers are recited and the body is removed for cremation. Periodic announcements may be made or instructions given. If in doubt, follow what other people are doing or just sit quietly.

Comforting the bereaved

Is it appropriate to visit the home of the bereaved after the funeral? Yes.

Will food be served? Yes.

How soon after the funeral will a mourner usually return to a normal work schedule? This totally depends on the individual mourner. There are no religious prescriptions regarding refraining from work.

How soon after the funeral will a mourner usually return to a normal social schedule? This totally depends on the individual mourner. There are no religious prescriptions regarding refraining from social life.

Are there mourning customs to which a friend who is not a Buddhist should be sensitive? No.

Are there rituals for observing the anniversary of the death? This varies between traditions.

5. HOME CELEBRATIONS

Not applicable to Buddhism.

5

Christadelphian

1. HISTORY AND BELIEFS

The Christadelphians pursue a life and faith based on the teaching of the Bible, which they believe is the inspired word of God – infallible and the only reliable source of knowledge about God and his plans for humankind – and on the worship practices of the early church. Some of their doctrine is similar to that of other Christian traditions, although significant points of difference are the Christadelphians' rejection of the concepts of the Trinity and the immortality of the soul.

The group, which has an estimated worldwide membership of more than 50,000 people, has its origins in the research and thinking of Dr John Thomas, an Englishman who moved to America in 1832 having become disillusioned with the sectarianism of established churches in England. Convinced that the Christianity practised in his day did not truly represent the teaching of Jesus Christ and his apostles, Thomas studied the Scriptures for a more authentic way of faith.

His findings, published in a series of books and self-founded magazines, and expounded through speaking tours of both America and the UK, attracted the sympathies of many people in both countries and congregations of adherents to his views began to grow. One of the group's tenets was a refusal to fight or go to war; when, in 1864, members wished to be conscientious objectors during the American Civil War, their only legal recourse was to form a recognised religious group opposed to the war. And so the Christadelphians were officially formed, the name meaning 'brothers in Christ'. The group was given structure and organisation in the latter half of the nineteenth century largely through the efforts of a Scot, Robert Roberts.

The Christadelphians do not have a single, centralised leadership or hierarchy. Every local group of like-minded believers – or *ecclesia*, meaning 'assembly of those summoned' – is autonomous, while sharing association and fellowship with other ecclesias. Members are appointed to manage various aspects of each ecclesia's affairs and to preside at meetings, but there are no paid ministers or leaders, ecclesiastical robes or elaborate ceremonies. Practices and minor differences in belief may vary between ecclesias, most of which have their own constitution and a Statement of Faith, which lists the Bible teachings believed by all Christadelphians within that ecclesia. Membership is restricted to adults who have been baptised, although the children of members are encouraged to attend Sunday schools and youth groups.

Regular Bible reading is integral to the Christadelphians' faith, and members are encouraged to follow a reading plan which enables them to read the Old Testament once and the New Testament twice through the course of each year.

UK ecclesias: approximately 300
UK membership: approximately 20,000

For more information, contact:

The Christadelphians
Freepost MID 30912
Birmingham
B27 6BR
www.godsaves.co.uk

The Christadelphian
404 Shaftmoor Lane
Hall Green
Birmingham
B28 8SZ
www.thechristadelphian.com

2. THE BASIC SERVICE

Christadelphians model their regular meetings for worship and fellow-ship on the example set by the earliest Christians, as recorded in the New Testament. They meet for the 'Breaking of the Bread' (or 'Memorial Service') – remembering the sacrifice made for all people by Jesus Christ – every Sunday (morning or afternoon), and this meeting will usually include hymns, prayers, readings from the Bible and a sermon based on the Bible.

Appropriate Attire

Men: Smart clothing such as jacket and tie or smart casual is preferred. No head covering is required.

Women: Smart, modest clothing such as a dress, skirt and blouse or smart trousers is preferred. Open-toed shoes and jewellery are fine. No head covering is required of non-Christadelphian women.

There are no rules regarding colours of clothing.

The Setting

The meeting will take place at the local Christadelphian meeting hall unless otherwise notified.

The Service

When should guests arrive and where should they sit? It would be helpful to arrive in good time (at least ten minutes) before the meeting is due to start. Unless you are the guest of a member of the ecclesia, sit towards the rear of the hall.

If arriving late, are there times when a guest should not enter the service? Yes, during hymns, prayers or Bible readings. Wait until a suitable pause before entering and finding a seat.

Are there times when a guest should not leave the service? Yes, while the bread and wine are circulating, or during a prayer.

Who are the major officials, leaders or participants and what do they do?

The **president**, who chairs the service.
The **speaker**, who presents a Bible-based talk.
The **servers**, who pass the bread and wine among baptised believers.

What books are used? A Bible and hymn book.

To indicate the order of the service: Periodic announcements will be made by the president.

How long will the service last? Normally about an hour.

Guest Behaviour during the Service

Will a guest who is not a Christadelphian be expected to do anything other than sit? Stand at the same time as the rest of the congregation if you are able. Singing the hymns is optional; you are welcome to participate if it does not compromise your personal beliefs.

Are there any parts of the service in which a guest who is not a Christadelphian should not participate? Yes. The sharing of the bread and wine is intended for believers who have been baptised according to Christadelphian beliefs.

If not disruptive to the service, is it OK to:

Take pictures? Yes.
Use a flash? No.
Use video recording equipment? Yes.
Use audio recording equipment? Yes.

Will contributions to the church be collected at the service? Yes. Contributions are voluntary, and all money is put towards meeting the costs of the meeting and the running of the local ecclesia.

❦

After the Service

There is not usually any sort of reception after the meeting has finished.

❦

Some Basic Beliefs

Christadelphians believe:

The Bible is the inspired word of God, and can only be understood within its whole context (Old and New Testaments together).

Jesus Christ was the Son of God, whose death atoned for our sin and who now sits with God in heaven, but he is *not* one aspect of a three-personed God. Similarly, the Holy Spirit is the power by which God achieves his ends, but is *not* one aspect of a three-personed God. These beliefs distinguish Christadelphians from many other Christian traditions which believe in a trinitarian God.

The 'devil' is not a biblical concept; the real enemy of God and threat to humankind is our own self-indulgent and sinful nature.

After we die, we will rest in a state of non-existence until the second coming of Jesus Christ, when we will be judged and rewarded according to our deeds, and a new kingdom of God will be established on earth.

A basic booklet to which a guest can refer to learn more about the Christadelphian Church:

Who Are the Christadelphians? by Fred Pearce (Christadelphian Publishing Office).

3. HOLY DAYS AND FESTIVALS

The only event which Christadelphians believe it is important to celebrate collectively is the sacrifice of Jesus Christ, which is remembered on a weekly basis through the Breaking of the Bread. Otherwise there are no particular holy days or festivals.

4. LIFE CYCLE EVENTS

Baptism Ceremony

Christadelphians hold that baptism – by full immersion in water – is a requirement for all sincere believers, following the example of the earliest believers in Christ. The immersion under water signifies being 'buried with Christ', and the rising up out of the water indicates 'newness of life', just as Christ was raised from death to immortal life. We are all alienated from God by our sin, but baptism marks a believer's change in attitude and willingness to confess their sins, request God's forgiveness and live according to the teachings of Christ, and so God forgives the sins of those who have been baptised and brings them into fellowship with himself.

The service of baptism is a ceremony in its own right, distinct from the regular Sunday meeting, and will normally last between thirty minutes and an hour. It will centre around one or multiple candidates professing and accepting the doctrines and precepts of Christ as defined in the ecclesia's Statement of Faith and each candidate being fully immersed in a baptismal bath or pool. Candidates are always adults.

Before the ceremony

Are guests usually invited by a formal invitation? Guests are normally invited by personal, informal request of one of the candidates.

If not stated explicitly, should one assume that children are invited? No.

If one cannot attend, what should one do? Decline either by telephone or a short written message.

Appropriate attire

Men: Smart clothing such as jacket and tie or smart casual is preferred. No head covering is required.

Women: Smart, modest clothing such as a dress, skirt and blouse or smart trousers is preferred. Open-toed shoes and jewellery are fine. No head covering is required of non-Christadelphian women.

There are no rules regarding colours of clothing.

The setting

The meeting will take place at the local Christadelphian meeting hall if it has suitable facilities; if not, then another venue will be arranged and you will be notified.

Gifts

Is a gift customarily expected? No.

The ceremony

Where will the ceremony take place? At the local Christadelphian meeting hall if it has suitable facilities; if not, then another venue will be arranged and you will be notified.

When should guests arrive and where should they sit? It would be helpful to arrive in good time (at least ten minutes) before the service is due to start. Unless you are the guest of a member of the ecclesia, sit towards the rear of the hall.

If arriving late, are there times when a guest should not enter the ceremony? Yes, during hymns, prayers or Bible readings. Wait until a suitable pause before entering and finding a seat.

Are there times when a guest should not leave the ceremony? Yes, during a prayer.

Who are the major officials, leaders or participants at the ceremony and what do they do?
The president, who chairs the service.
The speaker, who presents a Bible-based talk.
The baptist, who baptises the candidate.
The candidate(s), who is/are being baptised.

What books are used? A Bible and hymn book.

To indicate the order of the ceremony: Periodic announcements will be made by the president.

Will a guest who is not a Christadelphian be expected to do anything other than sit? Stand at the same time as the rest of the congregation if you are able. Singing the hymns is optional; you are welcome to participate if it does not compromise your personal beliefs.

Are there any parts of the ceremony in which a guest who is not a Christadelphian should not participate? No, unless there is a sharing of bread and wine (see 'The Basic Service' above).

If not disruptive to the ceremony, is it OK to:

Take pictures? Yes.
Use a flash? No.
Use video recording equipment? Yes.
Use audio recording equipment? Yes.

Will contributions to the church be collected at the ceremony? No.

After the ceremony

There is not usually any sort of reception after the ceremony has finished.

❦

Marriage Ceremony

Marriage is extremely important to Christadelphians, marking the joining together 'as one flesh' of husband and wife for the purpose of working in partnership to the glory of God. The marriage service is a ceremony in its own right, distinct from the regular Sunday meeting, and will normally last between thirty minutes and an hour.

Before the ceremony

Are guests usually invited by a formal invitation? Yes.

If not stated explicitly, should one assume that children are invited? No.

If one cannot attend, what should one do? Send a card or written message to decline.

Appropriate attire

Men: Smart clothing such as jacket and tie or smart casual is preferred. No head covering is required.

Women: Smart, modest clothing such as a dress, skirt and blouse or smart trousers is preferred. Open-toed shoes and jewellery are fine. No head covering is required of non-Christadelphian women.

There are no rules regarding colours of clothing.

Gifts

Is a gift ordinarily expected? Yes. Small household decorative items or appliances are preferred, but there is no required type of gift – the nature of gift and level of generosity really depends on the relationship you have with the bride or groom.

Should gifts be brought to the ceremony? They can be brought to the ceremony or reception or sent to the home.

The ceremony

Where will the ceremony take place? Usually in the local Christadelphian meeting hall, or rented premises.

When should guests arrive and where should they sit? Arrive early. An usher or attendant will tell you where to sit.

If arriving late, are there times when a guest should not enter the ceremony? Yes, during hymns, prayers or Bible readings. Wait until a suitable pause, when an usher should direct you to your seat.

Are there times when a guest should not leave the ceremony? Yes, during prayers.

Who are the major officiants, leaders or participants at the ceremony and what do they do?

The president or marriage celebrant, who will lead the service, including the vows and the Bible-based talk.
The bride and groom.

To indicate the order of the ceremony: An order of service will usually be provided, and periodic announcements will be made by the president.

What books are used? A Bible and hymn book may be used, or some or all of the hymns and readings may be printed on the order of service.

Will a guest who is not a Christadelphian be expected to do anything other than sit? Stand at the same time as the rest of the congregation if you are able. Singing the hymns is optional; you are welcome to participate if it does not compromise your personal beliefs.

Are there any parts of the ceremony in which a guest who is not a Christadelphian should not participate? No.

If not disruptive to the ceremony, is it OK to:

Take pictures? Yes.
Use a flash? No.
Use video recording equipment? Yes.
Use audio recording equipment? Yes.

Will contributions to the church be collected at the ceremony? No.

After the ceremony

Is there usually a reception after the ceremony? Yes, there is normally a reception held at a venue other than the place of the marriage, such as a hotel. This will provide an opportunity to greet the bride and groom and meet other members of the bridal party. Food will be served and there will be speeches and toasts, and possibly dancing. Alcoholic drinks may be available at some receptions depending on the wishes of the bride and groom (Christadelphians do not prohibit drinking of alcohol, but advise against overindulgence). Receptions are of variable length, but most will last for at least two hours, probably longer.

Would it be considered impolite to neither eat nor drink? No. If you have dietary restrictions, advise the bride or groom before the day of the ceremony.

Is there a grace or benediction before eating or drinking? Yes, a prayer of thanks will be said.

Is there a grace or benediction after eating or drinking? No.

Is there a traditional greeting for the family? No. Just offer your congratulations.

Is there a traditional form of address for clergy who may be at the reception? No.

Is it OK to leave early? Yes, but usually only after toasts have been made.

Funerals and Mourning

Christadelphians believe that we do not proceed from death to any sort of afterlife. However, those who believe and have been baptised will be resurrected from the grave upon the second coming of Jesus Christ. The bodies of those who are not resurrected will perish. The funeral service is a ceremony in its own right, distinct from the regular Sunday meeting, and will normally last between twenty and forty-five minutes.

Before the ceremony

How soon after the death will the funeral usually take place? There is no set time, but it is usually dependent on the availability of an undertaker.

What should a non-Christadelphian do upon hearing of the death of a member of that faith? Send a card or message expressing condolences.

Gifts

Is it appropriate to send flowers or make a contribution? Yes. Flowers are sometimes restricted to close family members, so it is worth enquiring about this in advance. If they are appropriate, they should be sent to the funeral venue. A contribution of money is not expected, but is at your own discretion. Provision for a contribution, including details of a charity which might be nominated to receive the donation, would usually be made at the funeral.

Is it appropriate to send food? Not unless specifically requested.

Appropriate attire

Men: Smart clothing such as jacket and tie or smart casual is preferred. No head covering is required.

Women: Smart, modest clothing such as a dress, skirt and blouse or smart trousers is preferred. Open-toed shoes and jewellery are fine. No head covering is required of non-Christadelphian women.

There are no rules regarding colours of clothing.

The ceremony

Where will the ceremony take place? At the local Christadelphian meeting hall or a funeral parlour.

Should a guest visit the bereaved family before the ceremony? No.

When should guests arrive and where should they sit? It would be helpful to arrive in good time (at least ten minutes) before the service is due to start. Unless you are the guest of a member of the ecclesia, sit towards the rear of the hall.

If arriving late, are there times when a guest should not enter the ceremony? Yes, during hymns, prayers or Bible readings. Wait until a suitable pause before entering and finding a seat.

Are there times when a guest should not leave the ceremony? Yes, during prayers.

Will the bereaved family be present at the church or funeral home before the ceremony? No.

Is there a traditional greeting for the family? No.

Will there be an open coffin? Rarely.

Is a guest expected to view the body? If there is an open coffin, this is optional.

What is appropriate behaviour upon viewing the body? Bow your head.

Who are the major officiants at the ceremony and what do they do?

The president, who leads the service and presents the obituary and Bible-based talk.

To indicate the order of the ceremony: An order of service will usually be provided, and periodic announcements will be made by the president.

What books are used? A Bible and hymn book may be used, or some or all of the hymns and readings may be printed on the order of service.

Will a guest who is not a Christadelphian be expected to do anything other than sit? Stand at the same time as the rest of the congregation if you are able. Singing the hymns is optional; you are welcome to participate if it does not compromise your personal beliefs.

Are there any parts of the ceremony in which a guest who is not a Christadelphian should not participate? No.

If not disruptive to the ceremony, is it OK to:

Take pictures? No.
Use a flash? No.
Use video recording equipment? No.
Use audio recording equipment? No.

Will contributions to the church be collected at the ceremony?
No.

The interment

Should guests attend the interment? This is optional.

Whom should one ask for directions? They will be provided at the end of the funeral service.

What happens at the burial or cremation? There may be brief comments made by the president, and a Bible reading and prayer, before the interment.

Do guests who are not Christadelphians participate at the interment ceremony? No. They are simply present.

Comforting the bereaved

Is it appropriate to visit the home of the bereaved after the funeral? This is optional.

Will there be a religious service at the home of the bereaved? No.

Will food be served? Possibly, depending on the individual. However, it would not be impolite to decline to eat. A prayer of thanks would normally be said before food is eaten.

How soon after the funeral will a mourner usually return to a normal work schedule? This is entirely at the discretion of the bereaved.

How soon after the funeral will a mourner usually return to a normal social schedule? This is entirely at the discretion of the bereaved.

Are there mourning customs to which a friend who is not a Christadelphian should be sensitive? No.

Are there rituals for observing the anniversary of the death? No.

5. HOME CELEBRATIONS

Not applicable to Christadelphians.

6

Christian Science

The Church of Christ, Scientist

1. HISTORY AND BELIEFS

Christian Science was founded in 1879 by Mary Baker Eddy, who was healed of a serious injury in 1866 while reading an account in the New Testament of Jesus' healings. Thirteen years later she established the Church of Christ, Scientist, in Boston. Mrs Eddy died in 1910.

The Church consists of the Mother Church – The First Church of Christ, Scientist – in Boston, USA, and over two thousand branch churches in about seventy-five countries around the world.

Christian Science theology holds that God created man in his image and likeness. Christian Scientists also believe that God is good and that his creation is all that is real and eternal. This belief is based on the first chapter of Genesis, which states, 'So God created man in His own image, in the image of God created He him; male and female created He them . . . And God saw everything that He had made, and, behold, it was good.'

Therefore, Christian Scientists believe that sin, disease and death do not originate in God. Rather, they are considered to be distortions of the human mind.

The Church is grounded in the teachings of the King James Bible and relies on spiritual means for healing. According to the Church, its spiritual healing:

is not popular faith healing or human mind cure. It is not self-hypnosis, mere positive thinking, autosuggestion, or spontaneous remission. Nor is it to be confused with Scientology or New Age thinking . . .

Christian Scientists find the Christian healing they experience is the reinstatement of the healing method practised by Jesus 2,000 years ago. It is based on understanding the laws of God revealed in the Bible, and conforming to them. These laws are available for all mankind to practise and, thereby, obtain full salvation from sickness as well as sin.

Christian Science healing involves more than healing sick bodies. It heals broken hearts and minds as well as broken homes, and is directly applicable to all of society's ills.

UK churches: 120
UK membership: not available

For more information, contact:

Christian Science Committee on Publication
10 Tideway Yard
125 Mortlake High Street
London
SW14 8SN
Tel: 0208 150 0245
Email: LondonCS@csps.com
www.churchofchristscientist.org

2. THE BASIC SERVICE

Christian Science's basic religious service is held on Sunday morning in a Christian Science church. The sixty-minute service includes congregational singing, silent and audible prayer, and reading a Lesson-Sermon consisting of passages from the King James Version of the Bible and *Science and Health with Key to the Scriptures*, written by the founder of Christian Science, Mary Baker Eddy.

Communion is held twice a year: on the second Sunday in January and the second Sunday in July, when the congregation kneels for a moment of silent prayer followed by the audible repetition of the Lord's Prayer. No bread or wine is given.

Each church holds a Wednesday evening testimony meeting, in which the First Reader chooses a subject, prepares readings from the King James Bible and Mary Baker Eddy's *Science and Health*, and selects the hymns. The meeting also includes spontaneous sharing of testimonies of healing and remarks on Christian Science by individuals in the congregation.

The public is welcome to attend Sunday and Wednesday services.

※

Appropriate Attire

Men: Jacket and tie are not expected. Casual or formal attire is acceptable. No head covering is required.

Women: Casual or formal attire is acceptable. Arms do not have to be covered by clothing, nor do hems need to reach below the knees. Jewellery and open-toed shoes are permissible. No head covering is required.

There are no rules regarding colours of clothing.

※

The Sanctuary

What are the major sections of the church? A Christian Science church has no altar. The service is conducted from a platform that has no ritual significance, or at floor level, in an auditorium or service room with no sections.

※

The Service

When should guests arrive and where should they sit? People are welcome whenever they arrive. Usually an usher will greet latecomers at the door and seat them if required. If not, guests may sit wherever they wish.

If arriving late, are there times when a guest should not enter the service? No, but usually ushers will help you determine when to enter.

Are there times when a guest should not leave the service? No.

Who are the major officiants, leaders or participants and what do they do?

The 'pastor' in a Christian Science church is the King James Version of the Bible and *Science and Health with Key to the Scriptures* by Mary Baker Eddy. Other than that, there are two primary participants in the service:

The First Reader, elected for a term of one to three years by congregants. He or she conducts the service, reading mainly from *Science and Health* on Sundays and equally from the King James Bible and *Science and Health* on Wednesdays.

The Second Reader, elected by members to read from the Bible at the Sunday service. He or she shares the platform with the First Reader and presides over the service in the absence of the First Reader.

What are the major ritual objects of the service? Simplicity is the mark of a Christian Science service. There are no ritual objects – and few rituals.

What books are used? The King James Version of the Bible (with some additional use of other translations), *Science and Health with Key to the Scriptures*, the *Christian Science Quarterly* and the *Christian Science Hymnal*.

To indicate the order of service: Refer to the second page of the *Christian Science Quarterly*, which is provided by ushers. The First Reader may give cues to the service by saying 'Let us sing' or 'Let us pray'.

❧

Guest Behaviour during the Service

Will a guest who is not a Christian Scientist be expected to do anything other than sit? No. The following behaviour is optional: standing, kneeling or singing with the congregation; saying or repeating the Lord's Prayer, which is the only prayer said orally; contributing to collections; and giving testimony at Wednesday services.

Are there any parts of the service in which a guest who is not a Christian Scientist should not participate? No.

If not disruptive to the service, is it OK to:

Take pictures? Only with prior permission.
Use a flash? Only with prior permission.
Use video recording equipment? Only with prior permission.
Use audio recording equipment? Only with prior permission.

Will contributions to the church be collected at the service? Only on Sundays. Collection is taken by ushers after the Lesson-Sermon is read. No one is required to contribute.

How much is it customary to contribute? Whatever congregants and guests wish to give.

After the Service

Is there usually a reception after the service? No.

Is there a traditional form of address for clergy whom a guest might meet? No. Christian Science has no clergy.

General Guidelines and Advice

The congregation stands only while singing hymns. At the end of the third hymn, congregants remain standing while the First Reader reads the 'Scientific Statement of Being' (from *Science and Health with Key to the Scriptures*), passages from 1 John, and the benediction. After the 'Amen', worshippers may leave.

After the second hymn at the Wednesday testimony meeting, worshippers are invited to give testimonies of healing, or just expressions of gratitude to God and Christian Science. Guests are not expected to do this, but may if they wish.

༄

Special Vocabulary

Key words or phrases that it might be helpful for a visitor to know:

Mind, Spirit, Soul, Principle, Life, Truth, Love: When capitalised, these are interchangeable names for God.

Prayer: Desire for good; a total turning to and trusting in God; searching to understand the relationship between God and man.

Healing: A realisation of God's goodness and the perfection of man made in his image; regeneration of thought reflected on the body.

Error: Mary Baker Eddy's word for 'evil'; the opposite of God and good; defined in *Science and Health* as something that 'seemeth to be and is not'.

Mortal Mind: Another name for error or evil; the belief in a mind or life separate from God.

Matter: That which appears 'real' to the five senses.

Mortal: A concept of each person as born and dying. The opposite of the 'real', or spiritual, person.

༄

Some Basic Beliefs

This summary of Christian Science's religious tenets appears in Science and Health:

1. As adherents of Truth, we take the inspired Word of the Bible as our sufficient guide to eternal Life.

2. We acknowledge and adore one supreme and infinite God. We acknowledge his Son, one Christ; the Holy Ghost or divine Comforter; and man in God's image and likeness.

3. We acknowledge God's forgiveness of sin in the destruction of sin and the spiritual understanding that casts out evil as unreal. But the belief in sin is punished so long as the belief lasts.

4. We acknowledge Jesus' atonement as the evidence of divine, efficacious Love, unfolding man's unity with God through Christ Jesus the Way-shower; and we acknowledge that man is saved

through Christ, through Truth, Life and Love as demonstrated by the Galilean Prophet in healing the sick and overcoming sin and death.

5. We acknowledge that the crucifixion of Jesus and his resurrection served to uplift faith to understand eternal Life, even the allness of Soul, Spirit and the nothingness of matter.

6. And we solemnly promise to watch, and pray for that Mind to be in us which was also in Christ Jesus; to do unto others as we would have them do unto us; and to be merciful, just and pure.

Some basic books or resources to which a guest can refer to learn more about Christian Science:

Science and Health with Key to the Scriptures, by Mary Baker Eddy (Christian Science Publishing Society).

Two magazines, the weekly *Christian Science Sentinel* and the monthly *Christian Science Journal*. These may be obtained in any Christian Science Reading Room.

A website where people may visit for background or write and ask for more information is www.churchofchristscientist.org.

Ask a librarian in a Christian Science Reading Room to help you find appropriate materials. The addresses of these reading rooms can usually be found in your local telephone yellow pages.

3. HOLY DAYS AND FESTIVALS

Christian Science has no special holidays or festivals.

While services at Christmas and Easter focus on the birth, resurrection and ascension of Jesus respectively, there are no special holy days or festivals at these times, since the emphasis is on the timeless spiritual significance of these historical events, contemplated and drawn upon throughout the year.

In the UK, a special Thanksgiving service is held on the evening of that US holiday, or on another appropriate occasion such as New Year's Day. This reflects Mary Baker Eddy's emphasis on gratitude. Similar to a Wednesday testimony meeting, it includes a Bible Lesson-

Sermon, silent and audible prayer, and a period for expressions of gratitude. No collection is taken at this service.

4. LIFE CYCLE EVENTS

Birth Ceremony

There is no special ceremony for the birth or naming of a child.

Initiation Ceremony

There is no initiation ceremony. A participant may apply to join the Mother Church and his or her local church as early as the age of twelve. But one is not required to do so and may apply to join whenever one feels it is appropriate.

At the age of twenty, students graduate from Sunday school and may be informally presented with a copy of *The Mother Church Manual*. Again, there is no formal ceremony.

Marriage Ceremony

There is no set marriage ceremony. Since Christian Science has no ordained clergy, it has no one who can legally perform a marriage in church. In accordance with the laws where they reside, Christian Scientists may be married by the clergy of another faith.

Funerals and Mourning

The church does not designate special arrangements or rituals for funerals or mourning. A funeral service is optional.

Before the ceremony

How soon after the death does the funeral usually take place?
There is no set time frame.

What should someone who is not a Christian Scientist do upon hearing of the death of a member of that faith? Telephone or visit the bereaved or send a condolence card or personal letter.

Appropriate attire

Men: No special attire is required.

Women: No special attire is required.

Guests should be guided by their knowledge of the deceased's family as to the level of formality. There are no rules regarding colours of clothing.

Gifts

Is it appropriate to send flowers or make a contribution? If no guidance is given by the family beforehand, flowers are usually appropriate and are normally sent beforehand to the funeral directors.

Is it appropriate to send food? Only if indicated by the family.

The ceremony

Where will the ceremony take place? Christian Science churches are used only for public worship services. Private funeral or memorial services are arranged by the families concerned and are usually held in crematoria.

When should guests arrive and where should they sit? Arrive early. Sit wherever you wish.

If arriving late, are there times when a guest should not enter the ceremony? No.

Will the bereaved family be present at the church or crematorium before the ceremony? This depends on the family's wishes.

Is there a traditional greeting for the family? No.

Will there be an open coffin? Rarely. While most Christian Scientists do not have open viewing at the memorial service, this is done at the discretion of the individual.

Who are the major officiants at the ceremony and what do they do? Since the Christian Science Church has no clergy, the service is conducted by a Christian Scientist who might be a Reader or a Christian Science practitioner or teacher, or a friend of the deceased.

(A 'practitioner' is an experienced Christian Scientist who, on a professional basis, devotes full time to the healing ministry. Individuals enter the public practice of Christian Science as a life work only after demonstrating a consistent ability to heal others through Christian Scientific prayer.)

What books are used? The format and content of a Christian Science funeral service are determined by the family or whoever conducts the service. However, the service typically consists of readings from the King James Bible and from *Science and Health with Key to the Scriptures* or some other writing by Mrs Eddy. Silent prayer, followed by those attending repeating the Lord's Prayer, may also be included. If music is desired, the *Christian Science Hymnal* contains hymns suitable for funerals.

The service usually includes personal remarks or a eulogy, but the family's wishes are taken into account. If they request, a poem or solo hymn that is not in the *Christian Science Hymnal* may be read or sung.

Will a guest who is not a Christian Scientist be expected to do anything other than sit? No.

Are there any parts of the ceremony in which a guest who is not a Christian Scientist should not participate? No.

If not disruptive to the ceremony, is it OK to:

Take pictures? No.
Use a flash? No.

Use video recording equipment? No.
Use audio recording equipment? No.

Will contributions to the church be collected at the ceremony?
No.

The interment

Cremation or burial is solely the bereaved family's decision.

Comforting the bereaved

Is it appropriate to visit the home of the bereaved after the funeral?
A reception is usually, but not always, held afterwards at a venue of
the family's choice, which may be their home.

Will there be a religious service at the home of the bereaved? No.

Will food be served? Refreshments including food, but not alcoholic
drinks, are usually provided at the reception.

*How soon after the funeral will a mourner usually return to a
normal work schedule?* This is solely an individual decision. Christian Scientists do not have a prescribed period of mourning or specific
customs of mourning.

Are there rituals for observing the anniversary of the death? No.

5. HOME CELEBRATIONS

Not applicable to Christian Science.

7

Free Presbyterian

1. HISTORY AND BELIEFS

The Presbyterian Church was founded on the ideals of the Protestant Reformation and based on the concept of democratic rule under the authority of God. John Calvin (1509–64) is the father of Presbyterianism.

All Presbyterians are required to trust in Christ as their forgiving Saviour, promise to follow Christ and his example for living, and commit themselves to attend church and to become involved in its work. They believe in the Holy Spirit (the empowering presence of God) speaking through the Bible, and in the sanctity of life.

Presbyterian theology emphasises the majesty of God, who is conceived not just as truth or beauty, but also as intention, purpose, energy and will. The human counterpart of this is understanding the Christian life as the embodiment of the purposes of God and the working out of these purposes in one's life. Because of this, Presbyterians include many social activists, and those who try to shape and influence culture and history.

The Free Presbyterian Church in Scotland was formed in 1893, of several congregations formerly belonging to the Free Church of Scotland. It is distinct from the Free Presbyterian Church of Ulster, a separate denomination founded in Northern Ireland in 1951. This chapter is based on research conducted through members of the Scottish Free Presbyterian Church.

Free Presbyterian Church of Scotland churches: 42

Free Presbyterian Church of Scotland membership: Information not available

Free Presbyterian Church of Ulster churches: approximately 60

Free Presbyterian Church of Ulster membership: approximately 12,000

For more information, contact:

Reverend Donald A. Ross
Free Presbyterian Manse
Laide
Ross-shire
IV22 2NB
Scotland
www.fpchurch.co.uk

2. THE BASIC SERVICE

The basic service of Public Worship, which will normally last for about an hour, is generally held on Sunday mornings and evenings. Sundays are known as the Christian Sabbath.

The purpose of Public Worship is to meet together as a Christian community to worship God according to the instructions he has given in his Word, the Bible. Free Presbyterian worship aims to be plain and simple, with as little ritual embellishment as possible.

Appropriate Attire

Men: Jacket and tie or, at the discretion of the individual, smart casual clothing. No head covering is required.

Women: Ideally a dress or a skirt and blouse. Open-toed shoes and modest jewellery are permitted. It is preferred in some churches that women wear a head covering.

There are no rules regarding colours of clothing.

~*~

The Sanctuary

What are the major sections of the church?

There is generally just one single open meeting place to accommodate all worshippers.

~*~

The Service

When should guests arrive and where should they sit? It is customary to arrive a little bit before the start of the service. Sit wherever you like.

If arriving late, are there times when a guest should not enter the service? When the minister is engaged in public prayer.

Are there times when a guest should not leave the service? When the minister is engaged in public prayer.

Who are the major officiants, leaders or participants and what do they do?

The minister, who conducts the worship and preaches the sermon. The precentor, who leads the singing by the congregation.

What are the major ritual objects of the service?

A Bible and a Psalter are the only ritual objects used in the service. The Bible will often be left sitting open, symbolising that the Old and New Testaments are the primary source of Scripture and of faith for Free Presbyterians.

What books are used? A Bible and a Metrical Psalter, a book containing the words of the book of Psalms set in verse form suitable for singing.

To indicate the order of the service: The minister will make periodic announcements.

✳

Guest Behaviour during the Service

Will a guest who is not a Free Presbyterian be expected to do anything other than sit? Nothing is 'expected' of guests. If they wish, they may stand, sing and pray with the congregation if this does not compromise their own religious beliefs.

Are there any parts of the service in which a guest who is not a Free Presbyterian should not participate? No.

If not disruptive to the service, is it OK to:

Take pictures? No.

Use a flash? No.

Use video recording equipment? No.

Use audio recording equipment? Possibly, although worth asking permission first.

Will contributions to the church be collected at the service? There may be a collection plate at the entrance of the building, for worshippers to make free-will contributions if they wish.

How much is it customary to contribute? This is down to individual discretion.

✳

After the Service

Is there usually a reception after the service? No.

Is there a traditional form of address for clergy whom a guest may meet? 'Mr' or 'Sir'.

✳

General Guidelines

No particular behaviour is 'expected' of guests, but it is hoped that all will respect the general solemnity and quietness of the service.

ﻬ

Some Basic Beliefs

Free Presbyterians believe:

There is one God, who created the whole universe.

This one God exists in three Persons: Father, Son and Holy Spirit.

Man's main duty in life is to know, love and glorify God.

Everyone is guilty of sin and deserves to be punished in hell for ever.

God in his mercy has sent his Son, Jesus Christ, who is both God and man, to be the Saviour of sinners.

Jesus was crucified for sinners, rose from the dead, and ascended into heaven.

Those who trust in Christ are accepted by God and will go to heaven.

Only the Holy Spirit can bring people to faith.

Jesus will return at the Day of Judgement.

Some basic books to which a guest can refer to learn more about Free Presbyterianism:

The Westminster Confession of Faith. Several editions of this seventeenth-century document are available. Drawn up at the request of the English Parliament, it contains a doctrine of faith in the Calvinist theological tradition, and has been used ever since as a blueprint of Christian worship and practice by Reformed churches around the world.

3. HOLY DAYS AND FESTIVALS

Advent: Occurs four weeks before Christmas. Its purpose is to begin preparing for Christmas and to focus on Christ. There is no traditional greeting for this holiday.

Christmas: Occurs on the evening of 24 December and the day of 25 December. Marks the birth and the incarnation of God as a man. The traditional greeting is 'Merry Christmas'.

Lent: Begins on Ash Wednesday, which occurs six weeks before Easter. The purpose is to prepare for Easter. There is no traditional greeting for Lent. Between Lent and Easter, abstention from entertainment is encouraged, as is increased giving to the poor. Often, there are midweek worship services. Very few Free Presbyterians fast during Lent.

Easter: Always falls on the Sunday after the first full moon that occurs on or after the spring equinox on 21 March. Celebrates the resurrection of Jesus Christ. The traditional greeting is 'Happy Easter!' In worship services, the pastor may greet congregants with the words, 'He is risen!' Congregants respond with, 'He is risen indeed!'

Pentecost Sunday: The seventh Sunday after Easter. Celebrates the coming of the Holy Spirit, which is the empowering Spirit of God in human life. This is often considered the birth of the Christian Church. There is no traditional greeting for this holiday.

4. LIFE CYCLE EVENTS

Birth Ceremony

Baptism is usually the celebration of the birth of an infant into the Church, although it can occur any time from birth onward through adulthood. The ceremony is usually integrated into a regular church service.

In the Free Presbyterian Church, baptism is administered only once.

The Church teaches that baptism 'initiates us into the Church, bestows the promise of God's grace upon us, assures us that God forgives our sins, calls us to a life of Christian service and fulfilment'.

A Free Presbyterian baptism has five parts:

'Presentation', in which the parents or guardian of the child bring the child forward for baptism. This happens immediately after the sermon.

'Profession of Faith and Promise', in which parents and the entire congregation promise to love and care for the newly baptised.

'Thanksgiving and Prayer', in which the congregation stands and offers God a prayer of praise and thanks.

The actual 'Washing with Water', in which the minister addresses the infant by his or her new official name and says, 'I baptise you in the name of the Father, and of the Son, and of the Holy Spirit.' The minister then pours or sprinkles water over the child's head, or dips or immerses him or her in water.

The newly baptised infant is then welcomed into the congregation and proclaimed a member of God's family.

Before the ceremony

Are guests usually invited by a formal invitation? Yes, normally an invitation from the family of the baptismal candidate.

If not stated explicitly, should one assume that children are invited? Yes.

If one cannot attend, what should one do? RSVP with regrets.

Appropriate attire

Men: Jacket and tie or, at the discretion of the individual, smart casual clothing. No head covering is required.

Women: Ideally a dress or a skirt and blouse. Open-toed shoes and modest jewellery are permitted. It is preferred in some churches that women wear a head covering.

There are no rules regarding colours of clothing.

Gifts

Is a gift customarily expected? No.

The ceremony

Where will the ceremony take place? In the main building for public worship.

When should guests arrive and where should they sit? It is customary to arrive a little bit before the start of the service. Sit wherever you like.

If arriving late, are there times when a guest should not enter the service? When the minister is engaged in public prayer.

Are there times when a guest should not leave the service? When the minister is engaged in public prayer.

Who are the major officiants, leaders or participants and what do they do?

The minister, who conducts the worship and preaches the sermon. The precentor, who leads the singing by the congregation.

What are the major ritual objects of the service?

A Bible and a Psalter are the only ritual objects used in the service. The Bible will often be left sitting open, symbolising that the Old and New Testaments are the primary source of Scripture and of faith for Free Presbyterians.

Water will be used in the process of baptism. It symbolises the spiritual cleansing of sin.

What books are used? A Bible and a Metrical Psalter, a book containing the words of the book of Psalms set in verse form suitable for singing.

To indicate the order of the service: The minister will make periodic announcements.

Will a guest who is not a Free Presbyterian be expected to do anything other than sit? Nothing is 'expected' of guests. If they wish, they may stand, sing and pray with the congregation if this does not compromise their own religious beliefs.

Are there any parts of the service in which a guest who is not a Free Presbyterian should not participate? No.

If not disruptive to the service, is it OK to:

Take pictures? No.
Use a flash? No.
Use video recording equipment? No.
Use audio recording equipment? Possibly, although worth asking permission first.

Will contributions to the church be collected at the service? There may be a collection plate at the entrance of the building, for worshippers to make free-will contributions if they wish.

How much is it customary to contribute? This is down to individual discretion.

After the service

Is there usually a reception after the service? No.

Is there a traditional form of address for clergy whom a guest may meet? 'Mr' or 'Sir'.

Marriage Ceremony

Free Presbyterians consider the marital relationship to be sacred, but the wedding ceremony is not a sacrament in itself.

The wedding ceremony is a service unto itself and varies widely, but generally follows the order of worship used by the church during Public Worship, with the addition of exchanging rings and vows. The wedding ceremony normally takes thirty to sixty minutes.

Before the ceremony

Are guests usually invited by a formal invitation? Yes.

If not stated explicitly, should one assume that children are invited? No.

If one cannot attend, what should one do? RSVP with regrets and send a gift or card.

Appropriate attire

Men: Jacket and tie or, at the discretion of the individual, smart casual clothing. No head covering is required.

Women: Ideally a dress or a skirt and blouse. Open-toed shoes and modest jewellery are permitted. It is preferred in some churches that women wear a head covering.

There are no rules regarding colours of clothing.

Gifts

Is a gift customarily expected? Yes, usually such gifts as household items are appropriate.

Should gifts be brought to the ceremony? Gifts should be sent to the home of the newlyweds or brought to the reception.

The ceremony

Where will the ceremony take place? In the main building for public worship.

When should guests arrive and where should they sit? It is customary to arrive a little bit before the start of the service. An usher will normally be on hand to direct you where to sit.

If arriving late, are there times when a guest should not enter the service? When the minister is engaged in public prayer.

Are there times when a guest should not leave the service? When the minister is engaged in public prayer.

Who are the major officiants, leaders or participants and what do they do?

The minister, who will perform the marriage ceremony and pronounce the couple as husband and wife.

What are the major ritual objects of the service?

A Bible and a Psalter are the only ritual objects used in the service. The Bible will often be left sitting open, symbolising that the Old and New Testaments are the primary source of Scripture and of faith for Free Presbyterians.

What books are used? A Bible and a Metrical Psalter, a book containing the words of the book of Psalms set in verse form suitable for singing.

To indicate the order of the service: A printed programme or order of service will be provided.

Will a guest who is not a Free Presbyterian be expected to do anything other than sit? Nothing is 'expected' of guests. If they wish, they may stand, sing and pray with the congregation if this does not compromise their own religious beliefs.

Are there any parts of the service in which a guest who is not a Free Presbyterian should not participate? No.

If not disruptive to the service, is it OK to:

Take pictures? No.
Use a flash? No.
Use video recording equipment? No.
Use audio recording equipment? Possibly, although worth asking permission first.

Will contributions to the church be collected at the service? No.

After the ceremony

Is there usually a reception after the ceremony? There will probably be a reception held by the married couple at a hotel or public hall. The reception will comprise a banquet meal for all invited guests, and speeches by members of the couple's families. A large meal will be served and there will usually be alcoholic drinks available.

Would it be considered impolite to neither eat nor drink? Yes, unless there are particular circumstances which prevent you from doing so.

Is there a grace or benediction before eating or drinking? Yes, somebody will ask God for his blessing upon the food.

Is there a grace or benediction after eating or drinking? Yes, someone will say a Returning Thanks.

Is there a traditional greeting for the family? Just offer your congratulations to the bride and groom and their immediate family.

Is there a traditional form of address for clergy who may be at the reception? 'Mr' or 'Sir'.

Is it OK to leave early? Yes, although it would be polite to wait until after the meal.

※

Funerals and Mourning

Free Presbyterians believe that in heaven the souls of the faithful are reunited with God in a warm and loving relationship. They also believe that it is not for humans to judge the fate of the unfaithful.

The funeral will consist of prayers, singing and reading of Scripture texts that are used to convey assurances of eternal life. It will usually last between fifteen and thirty minutes. The body of the deceased will then be buried.

Before the ceremony

How soon after the death does the funeral usually take place? Usually within one week.

What should a non-Free Presbyterian do upon hearing of the death of a member of that faith? Telephone the bereaved to express your sympathy and offer comfort, or visit them if you feel it is appropriate. Sometimes a time of family worship may be held at the bereaved family's residence, conducted by the minister and church elders.

Appropriate attire

Dress smartly and sombrely, avoiding gaudy or extreme bright colours. Members of the deceased's immediate family will usually wear black or dark clothing.

Gifts

Is it appropriate to send flowers or make a contribution? A contribution to a favourite or designated charity of the deceased would be most appropriate. Collections may be made at the funeral parlour or at the entrance of the church.

The ceremony

Where will the ceremony take place? At the main building of public worship, or a funeral parlour.

When should guests arrive and where should they sit? It is customary to arrive a little bit before the start of the service. Sit wherever you like.

If arriving late, are there times when a guest should not enter the service? When the minister is engaged in public prayer.

Are there times when a guest should not leave the service? When the minister is engaged in public prayer.

Will the bereaved family be present at the church or the funeral home before the ceremony? Usually.

Is there a traditional greeting for the family? Just offer your condolences.

Will there be an open coffin? No.

Who are the major officiants at the ceremony and what do they do?
The minister, who conducts the worship and preaches the sermon.
The precentor, who leads the singing by the congregation.
A church officer, who will lead mourners to their seats.

What books are used? A Bible and a Metrical Psalter, a book containing the words of the book of Psalms set in verse form suitable for singing.

To indicate the order of the service: The minister will make periodic announcements. A printed order of service may also be provided.

Will a guest who is not a Free Presbyterian be expected to do anything other than sit? Nothing is 'expected' of guests. If they wish, they may stand, sing and pray with the congregation if this does not compromise their own religious beliefs.

Are there any parts of the service in which a guest who is not a Free Presbyterian should not participate? No.

If not disruptive to the service, is it OK to:

Take pictures? No.
Use a flash? No.
Use video recording equipment? No.
Use audio recording equipment? No.

Will contributions to the church be collected at the service? No.

The interment

Should guests attend the interment? Yes.

Whom should one ask for directions? The funeral director, or members of the family.

What happens at the graveside? The coffin will be lowered by cords into the grave, by appointed friends or family. The minister will then make a short address. The graveside service may last ten to fifteen minutes.

Do guests who are not Free Presbyterians participate at the graveside service? No. They are simply present.

Comforting the bereaved

Is it appropriate to visit the home of the bereaved after the funeral? This depends on the preferences of the bereaved. There is no set tradition, but one, or even several, visits are normally appreciated.

Will there be a religious service at the home of the bereaved? No.

Will food be served? Possibly. Light refreshments may be provided at the discretion of the hosts.

How soon after the funeral will a mourner usually return to a normal work schedule? This is left to the discretion of the mourner, but is usually about a week.

How soon after the funeral will a mourner usually return to a normal social schedule? This is left to the discretion of the mourner, but is usually about a week.

Are there mourning customs to which a friend who is not Free Presbyterian should be sensitive? No.

Are there rituals for observing the anniversary of the death? No.

5. HOME CELEBRATIONS

Not applicable to Free Presbyterians.

8
Hindu

1. HISTORY AND BELIEFS

There are extraordinary differences between Hindu culture and beliefs and the prevailing Judeo-Christian religions and cultures in the UK. Yet, from the transcendentalists of the early nineteenth century through the beatniks of the 1950s to the spiritual seekers of today, Hinduism has held a fascination for many thousands of Westerners. Most of these were either influenced tangentially by Hinduism or became actual practitioners of certain aspects of it for a while. But today, the vast majority of Hindus in the UK are immigrants from Asia.

Unlike other religions, Hinduism has no founder and no common creed or doctrine. Generally, it teaches that God is within every being and object in the universe and transcends every being and object, that the essence of each soul is divine, and that the purpose of life is to become aware of that divine essence. The many forms of worship ritual and meditation in Hinduism are intended to lead the soul towards direct experience of God or Self.

In general, the different gods and goddesses in Hinduism are different ways of conceiving and approaching the one God beyond name and form. Different forms of worship through images, symbols and rituals are helpful to different kinds of persons. Some do not need external worship. The goal is to transcend these forms and the world as it is ordinarily perceived and to realise the divine presence everywhere.

UK temples: approximately 135
UK membership: estimated between 0.5 and 1.5 million

For more information, contact:

The Hindu Literature Centre
46–48 Loughborough Road
Leicester
LE4 5LD
Tel: 0116 261 1303
Email: admin@hss-leic.demon.co.uk

2. THE BASIC CEREMONY

Hindu temples are understood to be the residence of a particular god or goddess, or many gods and goddesses. At their centre is a small room where a main image of that deity is kept. Hindu worship also takes place in family homes, most of which will contain their own shrine and image or statue of a deity.

During the typical *pooja* or *vidhi* – the ritual worship that is held before a specific deity, the god is treated as a 'guest' and the devotee is its 'host'. Prayers are directed to it, flowers are draped around or near it and incense is lit near it. It may even be bathed in special oils. The intention is to offer the best things to the 'guest', to gain its blessing and for the removal of evil.

During the ceremony, sacramental food called *prasad* may be served to those present. It is usually vegetarian food cooked in an Indian style. Guests who wish to abstain may do so without offending congregants. During the ritual called *bhog*, which is performed prior to eating, the food is blessed. No alcoholic drinks or non-vegetarian dishes are served as part of *prasad*.

The day on which a *pooja* is held is usually fixed in consultation with solar and lunar astrological almanacs, rather than a particular day of the week. Ceremonies are flexible in length, but can last between one and two hours.

Appropriate Attire

Men: Dress casually. Some men choose to wear the *dhoti* (cloth wrapped around waist and legs) and *kurta* (long, loose shirt) of their family tradition.

Women: Dress casually. Some women choose to wear a colourful sari and blouse.

Wear shoes that can be easily removed, as this is a requirement in some temples.

❧

The Sanctuary

What are the major sections of the temple? There are many variables in Hindu temple architecture. But generally, there is a large room called a *natmandir*, where worshippers sit or stand. This faces a smaller section where the deity of the temple resides and where rituals honouring it are performed.

❧

The Ceremony

When should guests arrive and where should they sit? Arrive at the time for which the ceremony is called. Sit wherever you wish on seats provided or the floor, as other worshippers.

If arriving late, are there times when a guest should not enter the ceremony? No.

Are there times when a guest should not leave the ceremony? No, although it is appreciated if you stay for the duration.

Who are the major officiants, leaders or participants and what do they do?

The priest, who officiates.

What are the major ritual objects of the ceremony?

Statues or pictures that represent any of the thousands of Hindu deities. Narayana shalagram, a black round stone that symbolises totality. Flowers, fruits and other food, which may be placed in front of a picture or statue of the temple's deity.

Incense, which is usually burned near the deity to perfume the air.
Water from the Ganges River, the river in India that is holy to Hindus.
Lamps with five wicks dipped in clarified butter, and rotated near
the deity by the worshippers.

What books are used? A *pooja* manual is sometimes used by worshippers, assisted by the priest.

To indicate the order of the ceremony: Periodic announcements will
be made by a priest.

Guest Behaviour during the Ceremony

*Will a guest who is not a Hindu be expected to do anything other
than sit?* No.

*Are there any parts of the ceremony in which a guest who is not
a Hindu should not participate?* Guests of other faiths are welcome
to participate in any aspects of the ceremony if these do not compromise or violate their own religious beliefs. Otherwise they are welcome
to watch the ceremony.

If not disruptive to the ceremony, is it OK to:

Take pictures? Yes, with permission of the priest.
Use a flash? Yes, with permission of the priest.
Use video recording equipment? Yes, with permission of the priest.
Use audio recording equipment? Yes, with permission of the priest.

Will contributions to the temple be collected at the ceremony? No.

*Is there a traditional form of address for clergy whom a guest may
meet?* 'Swamiji' if a monk, 'Panditji' if a priest.

Is there usually a reception after the ceremony? No.

General Guidelines and Advice

Ask before entering the venue of the ceremony whether you should
remove your shoes.

Silence is expected from all present during the ceremony, except during chanting.

Do not touch any worship materials with your left hand.

❧

Special Vocabulary

Key words or phrases that it might be helpful for a visitor to know:

Pooja: The name of the worship ceremony.

Prasad: Sacramental food.

Prarthana, mantras, stotra: Repeated prayers.

Murti, pratma: A statue or picture representing a deity.

Ghanta: A bell used in the ceremony.

Deepa, diya: A lamp used in the ceremony.

Agar batti, dhoop: Incense used in the ceremony.

Deva, Devi, Ishuar, Bhagwan, Paramatma: Names for god or goddess.

❧

Some Basic Beliefs

Hindus believe:

Humans are cast in a recurring cycle of birth and rebirth called *samsara*. *Karma*, the consequences of one's actions, determines one's lot in a future reincarnation from one lifetime to another.

The Path of Desire, or the attractions of worldly success, is ephemeral and seductive.

The Path of Renunciation, which comes after one realises the short-comings of the Path of Desire, can lead to exhilaration and confidence in life's higher calling. The path includes discipline (of every form) and preferring difficult, time-consuming accomplishments to those that are easy and quick.

Four yogas, or disciplines, comprise four paths to enlightenment, or discerning the true nature of reality:

Jnana yoga, marshalling the powers of the intellect to cut through the veils of illusion. Includes meditative practices.

Bhakti yoga, directing one's love towards God.

Karma yoga, selfless ceremony towards others.

Raja yoga, which incorporates the above yogas into a unified discipline that addresses the body, mind and emotions. Included in *raja yoga* is *hatha yoga*, which disciplines and subdues the body.

Some basic books to which a guest can refer to learn more about Hinduism:

Explaining Hindu Dharma, by Nawal K. Prinja (Vishwa Hindu Parishad, 1999).

Hinduism: The Eternal Tradition, by David Frawley (Voice of India, 2009).

The Upanishads and the *Bhagavad Gita*, both of which are available in numerous translations from several publishers.

Am I a Hindu?, by Ed Viswanathan (RUPA, 1996).

Hindu Culture: An Introduction, by Swami Tejomayananda (Chinmaya Publications West, 1993).

The Complete Idiot's Guide to Hinduism, by Linda Johnsen (Alpha Books, 2009).

3. HOLY DAYS AND FESTIVALS

The specific dates of Hindu holidays vary from year to year in relation to the Western secular calendar because the Hindu calendar is lunar based.

Shiva Ratri: An all-night worship of God as the god Shiva. Shiva's primary qualities are creation and destruction, and compassion and renunciation. This holiday usually occurs in late winter. There is no traditional greeting for this holiday.

Duhsehra/Durga Puja: Celebrates the triumph of good over evil. Usually occurs in early autumn. There is no traditional greeting for this holiday.

Rama Navami: Worship of Rama, who (along with the god Krishna) is regarded as God incarnate. This usually occurs in the spring. There is no traditional greeting for this holiday.

Krishna Janmashtami: The birthday celebration of Krishna, who (along with Rama) is regarded as God incarnate. Krishna is perhaps the most widely worshipped Hindu deity. This holiday occurs in the late summer. There is no traditional greeting for this holiday.

4. LIFE CYCLE EVENTS

Birth Ceremony

The naming ceremony, known variously as *Naama Sanskaar*, *Naama Grahana* and *Naama Karana*, occurs when a newborn is six to eight months old. It is sometimes also known as the 'rice-eating ceremony' because it marks the first time the child has eaten solid food. It is a ceremony in itself, and may be held at a temple, in the family's home or in a hired public hall.

Before the ceremony

Are guests usually invited by a formal invitation? Yes.

If not stated explicitly, should one assume that children are invited? Yes. In fact an invitation is generally extended to the entire household and any guests staying with you at that time.

If one cannot attend, what should one do? Telephone with regrets.

Appropriate attire

Men: Dress in a smart casual style. Some family members of the child will wear traditional dress.

Women: Dress in a smart casual style. Some family members of the child will wear traditional dress.

Wear shoes that can be easily removed, as this is a requirement in some temples. There are no special colours that should be worn, but try to avoid wearing black in recognition that this is a happy occasion.

Gifts

Is a gift customarily expected? There is no expectation, but a small gift such as clothes or a toy for the baby would always be gratefully received.

Should gifts be brought to the ceremony? Bring gifts to the ceremony itself.

The ceremony

When should guests arrive and where should they sit? Arrive at the time called for the ceremony to begin, and sit with other guests.

If arriving late, are there times when a guest should not enter the ceremony? No.

Are there times when a guest should not leave the ceremony? No.

Who are the major officiants, leaders or participants at the ceremony and what do they do?

The priest (Pandit, Purohit, Maharaj), who will officiate over the naming ceremony.

The parents of the child, or the eldest male in the family (*Yajaman-Grhini*) and his wife, who will represent the family in the ceremony. The child's grandparents, uncles and aunts and other family members will probably all be present.

What books are used? Hindu prayer books and a manual of priesthood services may be used.

To indicate the order of the ceremony: A printed programme may be provided.

Will a guest who is not a Hindu be expected to do anything other than sit? No.

Are there any parts of the ceremony in which a guest who is not a Hindu should not participate? Guests of other faiths are welcome to participate in any aspects of the ceremony if these do not compromise or violate their own religious beliefs.

If not disruptive to the ceremony, is it OK to:

Take pictures? Yes, with permission of the priest.
Use a flash? Yes, with permission of the priest.
Use video recording equipment? Yes, with permission of the priest.
Use audio recording equipment? Yes, with permission of the priest.

Will contributions to the temple be collected at the ceremony? No.

After the ceremony

Is there usually a reception after the ceremony? Occasionally, a reception may be held after the ceremony, often in the same place as the ceremony itself. Traditional Indian food would be served. No alcoholic drinks would usually be served. There will possibly be singing and dancing.

Would it be considered impolite to neither eat nor drink? No.

Is there a grace or benediction before eating or drinking? No.

Is there a grace or benediction after eating or drinking? No.

Is there a traditional greeting for the family? Just offer your congratulations.

Is there a traditional form of address for clergy who may be at the reception? 'Swamiji' if a monk, 'Panditji' if a priest.

General guidelines and advice

Ask before entering the venue of the ceremony whether you should remove your shoes.

Do not touch any worship materials with your left hand.

Special vocabulary

Key words or phrases that it might be helpful for a visitor to know:

Ashirwad: Blessings which may be said at the end of the ceremony.
Bhajan: A melodious song in praise of deities.
Arati: A lamp which is lit while singing a Bhajan.

꧁

Initiation Ceremony

There is a sacred Hindu ceremony, *Janoi*, by which young people celebrate their coming into adulthood, sometimes known as *Upanayana* for males and *Gayatri Upadesh* for females. It is sometimes also known as the 'sacred thread ceremony' for boys, as they are given a sacred thread which will hang over their left shoulder, with the intention that it will be worn for their whole lifetime as a support for regular chanting of sacred mantras. It is a ceremony in itself, and may be held at a temple, in the family's home or in a hired public hall.

Before the ceremony

Are guests usually invited by a formal invitation? Yes.

If not stated explicitly, should one assume that children are invited? Yes. In fact an invitation is generally extended to the entire household and any guests staying with you at that time.

If one cannot attend, what should one do? Telephone with regrets.

Appropriate attire

Men: Dress in a smart casual style. Some family members of the initiation candidate will wear traditional dress.

Women: Dress in smart casual style. Some family members of the initiation candidate will wear traditional dress.

Wear shoes that can be easily removed, as this is a requirement in some temples. There are no special colours that should be worn, but try to avoid wearing black in recognition that this is a happy occasion.

Gifts

Is a gift customarily expected? There is no expectation, but a small gift suitable for the initiation candidate would always be gratefully received.

Should gifts be brought to the ceremony? Bring gifts to the ceremony itself.

The ceremony

When should guests arrive and where should they sit? Arrive at the time called for the ceremony to begin, and sit with other guests.

If arriving late, are there times when a guest should not enter the ceremony? No.

Are there times when a guest should not leave the ceremony? No.

Who are the major officiants, leaders or participants at the ceremony and what do they do?

The priest (Pandit, Purohit, Maharaj), who will officiate over the ceremony.

The parents of the young person, or the eldest male in the family (*Yajaman-Grhini*) and his wife, who will represent the family in the ceremony. The candidate's grandparents, uncles and aunts and other family members will probably all be present.

What books are used? Hindu prayer books and a manual of priesthood services may be used.

To indicate the order of the ceremony: A printed programme may be provided.

Will a guest who is not a Hindu be expected to do anything other than sit? No.

Are there any parts of the ceremony in which a guest who is not a Hindu should not participate? Guests of other faiths are welcome to participate in any aspects of the ceremony if these do not compromise or violate their own religious beliefs.

If not disruptive to the ceremony, is it OK to:

Take pictures? Yes, with permission of the priest.
Use a flash? Yes, with permission of the priest.
Use video recording equipment? Yes, with permission of the priest.

Use audio recording equipment? Yes, with permission of the priest.

Will contributions to the temple be collected at the ceremony? No.

After the ceremony

Is there usually a reception after the ceremony? Occasionally, a reception may be held after the ceremony, often in the same place as the ceremony itself. Traditional Indian food would be served. No alcoholic drinks would usually be served. There will possibly be singing and dancing.

Would it be considered impolite to neither eat nor drink? No.

Is there a grace or benediction before eating or drinking? No.

Is there a grace or benediction after eating or drinking? No.

Is there a traditional greeting for the family? Just offer your congratulations.

Is there a traditional form of address for clergy who may be at the reception? 'Swamiji' if a monk, 'Panditji' if a priest.

General guidelines and advice

Ask before entering the venue of the ceremony whether you should remove your shoes.

Do not touch any worship materials with your left hand.

Marriage Ceremony

While, traditionally, Hindu marriages have often been arranged by the parents or guardians of the bride and groom, this practice is now considered outdated among the majority of Hindus in the UK. Most young Hindus now choose their own marriage partner, and there is an increasing trend for interfaith marriages.

A Hindu marriage has seven major ceremonies:

Vagdana, the verbal contract about the marriage between the fathers or guardians of the bride and groom.

Kanya Sampradana, the giving away of the daughter to the groom by her father or guardian.

Varana, welcoming the bride and groom.

Panigrahana, ritualistic holding of each other's hands by the bride and groom.

Saptapadi, a seven-step walking ritual by the bride and groom.

Laj homa, creation of the holy fire that symbolises the formless divinity. The bride and groom circle it four times and offer a parched paddy as oblation.

Sindur dam, the groom puts red vermilion on the forehead and the furrow of the parted hair of the bride.

A marriage ceremony is usually held after sunset and before sunrise. It is a ceremony in itself, and may be held at a temple, in the family's home or in a hired public hall.

Before the ceremony

Are guests usually invited by a formal invitation? Yes.

If not stated explicitly, should one assume that children are invited? Yes. In fact an invitation is generally extended to the entire household and any guests staying with you at that time.

If one cannot attend, what should one do? Telephone with regrets.

Appropriate attire

Men: Dress in a smart casual style. Some family members of the bride and groom will wear traditional dress.

Women: Dress in smart casual style. Some family members of the bride and groom will wear traditional dress.

Wear shoes that can be easily removed, as this is a requirement in some temples. There are no special colours that should be worn, but try to dress in a manner that reflects the happiness of the occasion.

Gifts

Is a gift customarily expected? There is no expectation, but a small gift suitable for the marrying couple would always be gratefully received.

Should gifts be brought to the ceremony? Bring gifts to the ceremony itself.

The ceremony

When should guests arrive and where should they sit? Arrive at the time called for the ceremony to begin, and sit with other guests.

If arriving late, are there times when a guest should not enter the ceremony? No.

Are there times when a guest should not leave the ceremony? No.

Who are the major officiants, leaders or participants at the ceremony and what do they do?

The priest (Pandit, Purohit, Maharaj), who will officiate over the marriage ceremony, conducting most of the rituals and chanting.

The parents and grandparents of the wedding couple all have specific roles in the ceremony.

The best friends of the wedding couple stay close to them for support and to be involved in various parts of the ceremony as instructed by the priest.

What books are used? Hindu prayer books and a manual of priesthood services may be used.

To indicate the order of the ceremony: A printed programme may be provided and the priest will usually make announcements of the various rituals.

Will a guest who is not a Hindu be expected to do anything other than sit? No.

Are there any parts of the ceremony in which a guest who is not a Hindu should not participate? Guests of other faiths are welcome to participate in any aspects of the ceremony if these do not compromise or violate their own religious beliefs.

If not disruptive to the ceremony, is it OK to:

Take pictures? Yes, with permission of the priest.
Use a flash? Yes, with permission of the priest.
Use video recording equipment? Yes, with permission of the priest.
Use audio recording equipment? Yes, with permission of the priest.

Will contributions to the temple be collected at the ceremony? No.

After the ceremony

Is there usually a reception after the ceremony? A reception will usually be held after the ceremony, often in the same place as the ceremony itself. Traditional Indian food would be served. No alcoholic drinks would usually be served. There will be singing and dancing.

Would it be considered impolite to neither eat nor drink? No.

Is there a grace or benediction before eating or drinking? No.

Is there a grace or benediction after eating or drinking? No.

Is there a traditional greeting for the family? Just offer your congratulations.

Is there a traditional form of address for clergy who may be at the reception? 'Swamiji' if a monk, 'Panditji' if a priest.

Funerals and Mourning

Although the physical body dies, the individual soul or spirit – *atma* or *jeeva* – has no beginning and no end. It may, upon death, pass into another reincarnation, the condition of which depends on the *karma*, or consequences of one's actions, reaped during the life that just ended, as well as during previous lifetimes.

But if, over many lifetimes, the deceased has realised the true nature of reality, the individuality of the soul will be lost upon death and it will become one with Brahman, the One, All-Encompassing Soul.

The body of the deceased is usually cremated, and the funeral ceremony will be a part of a thirteen-day period of mourning.

Before the ceremony

How soon after the death does the funeral usually take place? As soon as possible, subject to medical and legal requirements.

What should a non-Hindu do upon hearing of the death of a member of that faith? Telephone, visit the bereaved or send a card offering your condolences.

Appropriate attire

Men: Dress in a smart casual style. Some family members of the deceased will wear traditional dress.

Women: Dress in smart casual style. Some family members of the deceased will wear traditional dress.

Wear shoes that can be easily removed, as this is a requirement in some temples. Strong and vibrant colours are discouraged. Some Hindu families prefer all mourners to wear white, so it is worth enquiring about this in advance.

Gifts

Is it appropriate to send flowers or make a contribution? Flowers for the funeral are usually arranged by specific family members. Some bereaved families request that donations be made to a favoured charity, and a collection box is sometimes placed outside the doors of the crematorium for this purpose. A written message of condolence would also be an appropriate gift.

Is it appropriate to send food? No.

The ceremony

Where will the ceremony take place? At the place of cremation.

When should guests arrive and where should they sit? Arrive at the time for which the ceremony has been called. Sit with other guests rather than with the family and household of the deceased.

If arriving late, are there times when a guest should not enter the ceremony? No.

Will the bereaved family be present at the place of cremation before the ceremony? Yes.

Is there a traditional greeting for the family? No. Just offer your condolences.

Will there be an open coffin? Sometimes.

Is a guest expected to view the body? Yes.

What is appropriate behaviour upon viewing the body? Look reverently and sympathetically upon the body and do not touch it.

Who are the major officiants at the ceremony?

Priest and members of the immediate family.

What are the major ritual objects of the service?

Photographs of the dead person.
Lamps and incense.
Food, groceries and containers of water are sometimes placed around the dead body.

What books are used? Special books containing Vedic mantras and verses from the *Bhagavad Gita* for funeral ceremonies will be used by the priest.

To indicate the order of the ceremony: A printed programme may be provided, or sometimes the ceremony just proceeds without one.

Will a guest who is not a Hindu be expected to do anything other than sit? No, unless requested to say something as a close friend of the deceased.

Are there any parts of the ceremony in which a guest who is not a Hindu should not participate? Guests of other faiths are welcome to participate in any aspects of the ceremony if these do not compromise or violate their own religious beliefs.

If not disruptive to the ceremony, is it OK to:
Take pictures? No.
Use a flash? No.
Use video recording equipment? No.
Use audio recording equipment? No.

The cremation

Should guests attend the cremation? If they wish to. It is not normal for children to be present at the cremation.

Whom should one ask for directions? Ask family members.

What happens at the cremation? The cremation ceremony is called *mukhagni*. Short prayers and speeches will usually be said, and members of the deceased's family will conduct various rituals. The last food offering will be symbolically made to the deceased and then the body is cremated.

Do guests who are not Hindus participate at the cremation ceremony? No. They are simply present.

Comforting the bereaved

Is it appropriate to visit the home of the bereaved after the funeral? Yes, soon after they have received the ashes of the deceased.

Will there be a religious ceremony at the home of the bereaved? The *shraddha* ceremony is performed at home. Guests are usually invited to it by phone.

Will food be served? Sometimes simple food or the favourite food of the deceased person will be provided.

How soon after the funeral will a mourner usually return to a normal work schedule? About thirteen days.

How soon after the funeral will a mourner usually return to a normal social schedule? About a month.

Are there rituals for observing the anniversary of the death? Yes. The *shraddha* ceremony is observed by the family once a month during the first year after the death, and thereafter once a year.

Special vocabulary

Key words or phrases that it might be helpful for a visitor to know:

Shava: The dead body.
Agni: Fire, used in cremation of the body.
Bali, pinda: Food offered to the spirit of the dead person.

5. HOME CELEBRATIONS

Worship in the home is a paramount aspect of Hindu ritual. Most ceremonies will centre around the small shrine for a god and goddess found in most Hindu homes.

Some of those to which a guest might be invited are:

Seemanta: A ceremony for the blessing of an unborn child in a mother's womb.
Janma Divasjaata Karma: A ceremony for a newborn baby, in which its body and soul are purified and the new member of a family blessed.
Janma Nakshatra or Janma Divas: An annual celebration of a child's birth, the date of which is calculated according to astronomical almanacs. The child will be blessed for longevity, prosperity and happiness, leading to contentment.
Grha Pravesh: A house-warming ceremony, involving worship and feasting. The deities and planetary bodies which influence lives on earth are invoked for their blessing upon all in the household.
Shraddha: A ceremony expressing respect and gratitude to, and seeking guidance from, deceased family members and ancestors.

9

Jehovah's Witness

1. HISTORY AND BELIEFS

The Jehovah's Witnesses are a worldwide faith known for their assertive proselytising and expectations of an imminent apocalypse. They have drawn attention because of their refusal to celebrate Christmas, by their dedicated missionary work and by using Jehovah as the sole name of God.

Jehovah's Witnesses derive their name from the forty-third chapter of the book of Isaiah, in which the gods of the nations are invited to bring forth their witnesses to prove their claimed cases of righteousness or to hear the witnesses for Jehovah's side and acknowledge the truth: 'Ye are my witnesses, saith Jehovah, and my servants whom I have chosen; that ye may know and believe me, and understand that I am he; before me there was no God formed, neither shall there be after me. I, even I, am Jehovah; and besides me there is no saviour' (Isaiah 43:10–11, American Standard Version of the Bible).

In the Bible, all faithful worshippers, such as Abel, Noah, Abraham and Jesus, were called 'witnesses of God' (Hebrews 11:1–12; Revelation 3:14).

The faith was founded in western Pennsylvania in the early 1870s by Charles Taze Russell, who had organised a Bible study group to promote the basic teachings of the Bible. It was his desire to return to the teachings of first-century Christianity.

Jehovah's Witnesses believe that God demands unconditional obedience and that the infallible source of truth is the Bible, which is true in every detail. Jesus, who was the Son of God and was his first creation, was responsible for all the rest of God's creation on earth. While residing on earth, Jesus was entirely a man. After his death, he was raised by God to heaven and restored to a place second only to that of his Father, Jehovah.

The fulfilment of God's kingdom will occur through the battle of Armageddon, the appearance of the Lord in the air, the thousand-year rule on earth of Christ (during which resurrection and judgement take place). This process began in 1914 and its completion will soon occur.

Members of the Church are expected to devote their primary loyalty and time to the movement, and not participate in politics or inter-faith movements. They believe that all human laws that do not conflict with God's law should be obeyed. They also do not vote in secular elections or serve in the military. They respect each country's flag (or other national symbols), but do not salute it, since they believe this would be idolatry.

UK churches: 1,519
UK membership: 132,000

For more information, contact:

Jehovah's Witnesses
Watch Tower House
The Ridgeway
London
NW7 1RN
Tel: 0208 906 2211
www.watchtower.org

2. THE BASIC SERVICE

Congregational meetings are highly instructional and primarily deal with Bible teachings, prophecy or counsel on Christian living. Some of these meetings are conducted as Bible studies with audience participation, usually using a magazine (such as *The Watchtower*) or a book published by the Jehovah's Witnesses' publishing house, the Watchtower Society. The person conducting the study may pose questions based on a paragraph that has been read aloud to the group.

Meetings last slightly more than one hour and are held on Sundays, with the times varying among congregations, and on one other day each week.

❧

Appropriate Attire

Men: Jacket and tie are usually worn, although they are not required. No head covering is required.

Women: A dress or a skirt and blouse. Dress 'modestly' and 'sensibly'. Hems need not reach below the knees, nor need clothing cover the arms. Open-toed shoes and modest jewellery are permissible. No head covering is required.

There are no rules regarding colours of clothing.

❧

The Sanctuary

What are the major sections of the meeting hall?

Kingdom Halls, the name of Jehovah's Witnesses' meeting halls, are usually plain structures, inside and out. They resemble auditoriums more than churches or synagogues.

❧

The Service

When should guests arrive and where should they sit? Arrive early. Sit wherever you wish.

If arriving late, are there times when a guest should not enter the service? No, but latecomers will be assisted by attendants to find an appropriate seat.

Are there times when a guest should not leave the service? No.

Who are the major officiants, leaders or participants and what do they do?

The Congregation Elders, who deliver talks on the Bible and lead Bible discussions with the congregants.

What are the major ritual objects of the service? None.

What books are used? The Old and New Testaments, primarily the New World Translation (The Watchtower Bible and Tract Society of New York, 1961); *The Watchtower*, a semi-monthly journal published by Jehovah's Witnesses headquarters in New York, USA; and a hymnal, *Sing Praises to Jehovah* (The Watchtower Bible and Tract Society of New York, 1984).

To indicate the order of the service: Periodic announcements will be made by an elder in the congregation.

Guest Behaviour during the Service

Will a guest who is not a Jehovah's Witness be expected to do anything other than sit? It is entirely optional for a guest of another faith to stand and sing with the congregation and to answer questions during a discussion of the Bible. During prayer, guests may bow their head reverently. Jehovah's Witnesses do not kneel during their congregational meetings.

Are there any parts of the service in which a guest who is not a Jehovah's Witness should not participate? No.

If not disruptive to the service, is it OK to:

Take pictures? Yes.
Use a flash? Yes.
Use video recording equipment? Yes.
Use audio recording equipment? Yes.

(Note: Do not use the above equipment during prayer. Using a flash during the Bible talk would also be inappropriate.)

Will contributions to the church be collected at the service? No.

✻

After the Service

Is there usually a reception after the service? No.

Is there a traditional form of address for clergy whom a guest may meet? Either 'Brother' or 'Mr', followed by last name.

✻

Special Vocabulary

Key words or phrases that it might be helpful for a visitor to know:

Jehovah: The personal name of the one true God. From the book of Psalms (83:18) in the King James Version of the Bible: 'That men may know that Thou, whose name alone is Jehovah, art the most high over all the earth.' Also from the New World Translation of Isaiah (42:8): 'I am Jehovah. That is My name.'

Hebrew Scriptures and Christian Greek Scriptures: The terms used, respectively, for the Old and New Testaments.

✻

Some Basic Beliefs

Jehovah's Witnesses believe:

The books of the Bible's Old and New Testaments are divinely inspired and historically accurate.

Jehovah created earth for humanity and settled the first human pair, Adam and Eve, in the Garden of Eden. If obedient to God, they had the prospect of living for ever and expanding the paradise earthwide. With their sin, humanity lost this paradise. Yet God's purpose for the earth will not fail. The means by which Jehovah will fulfil his purpose for earth is through the kingdom of God with Jesus as King. This heavenly government will soon remove wickedness from the earth and convert it into a paradise wherein true worshippers will live for ever. There will also be a resurrection of the dead into that paradise.

The kingdom of God began to rule invisibly in heaven in 1914 and after the wicked are destroyed will usher in the thousand-year Reign of Christ (the Millennium) during which the earth and humanity will be helped to reach perfection and to live endlessly on earth.

Some basic pamphlets to which a guest can refer to learn more about Jehovah's Witnesses:

Does God Really Care About Us? (The Watchtower Bible and Tract Society of New York, 1992).

Jehovah's Witnesses – Who Are They? What Do They Believe? (The Watchtower Bible and Tract Society of New York, 1989).

Jehovah's Witnesses Unitedly Doing God's Will Worldwide (The Watchtower Bible and Tract Society of New York, 1986).

3. HOLY DAYS AND FESTIVALS

The Memorial of Christ's Death, also called the Lord's Evening Meal: This special congregational meeting is held in each Kingdom Hall after sundown of the first evening of the Jewish holiday of Passover, which occurs in either March or April. (The date varies because the Hebrew calendar is lunar based.) There is no traditional greeting for this one holiday observed by Jehovah's Witnesses.

4. LIFE CYCLE EVENTS

Birth Ceremony

Not applicable to Jehovah's Witnesses.

Initiation Ceremony

Not applicable to Jehovah's Witnesses.

Marriage Ceremony

Jehovah's Witnesses view marriage as a sacred vow made before God. It seals a permanent union that can be broken only by infidelity or death. The marriage ceremony, which may last about thirty minutes, is a ceremony in itself.

Before the ceremony

Are guests usually invited by a formal invitation? Yes. An announcement is made in a Kingdom Hall issuing a general invitation to all members of the congregation. Guests who are not members of the congregation usually receive a written invitation.

If not stated explicitly, should one assume that children are invited? Yes.

If one cannot attend, what should one do? Nothing is required if one is a member who has heard the invitation in a Kingdom Hall. If one has received a written invitation, RSVP with regrets.

Appropriate attire

Men: A jacket and tie. No head covering is required.

Women: A dress or a skirt and blouse. Dress 'modestly' and 'sensibly'. Hems need not reach below the knees, nor need clothing cover the arms. Open-toed shoes and modest jewellery are permissible. No head covering is required.

There are no rules regarding colours of clothing.

Gifts

Is a gift customarily expected? While gifts are not required, they are certainly appropriate. Gifts of money or such household items as sheets, kitchenware or small appliances are customary.

Should gifts be brought to the ceremony? Either to the ceremony or to the reception afterwards.

The ceremony

Where will the ceremony take place? In the main auditorium of a Kingdom Hall where Bible lectures are normally given.

When should guests arrive and where should they sit? Arrive early to avoid causing a distraction. Attendants will seat guests. The front few rows are reserved for family.

If arriving late, are there times when a guest should not enter the ceremony? No, but usually attendants will seat late-arriving guests in such a way as not to create a disturbance.

Are there times when a guest should not leave the ceremony? No.

Who are the major officiants, leaders or participants at the ceremony and what do they do?

The Congregation Elder, who gives a Bible talk to the bride and groom and solemnises the marriage.

What books are used? The Old and New Testaments, primarily the New World Translation (The Watchtower Bible and Tract Society of New York, 1961).

To indicate the order of the ceremony: The officiating elder will make periodic announcements.

Will a guest who is not a Jehovah's Witness be expected to do anything other than sit? No.

Are there any parts of the ceremony in which a guest who is not a Jehovah's Witness should not participate? No.

If not disruptive to the ceremony, is it OK to:

Take pictures? Yes.
Use a flash? Yes.
Use video recording equipment? Yes.
Use audio recording equipment? Yes.

(Note: Do not use the above equipment during prayer. Flash pictures should not be taken during the Bible talk, since this can be very distracting.)

Will contributions to the church be collected at the ceremony? No.

After the ceremony

Is there usually a reception after the ceremony? Yes. It may be held in the home or a catering hall. It is never held in the Kingdom Hall where the wedding took place. Usually, refreshments are served. The reception may last more than two hours.

Would it be considered impolite to neither eat nor drink? No.

Is there a grace or benediction before eating or drinking? Yes.

Is there a grace or benediction after eating or drinking? No.

Is there a traditional greeting for the family? Just offer your congratulations.

Is there a traditional form of address for clergy who may be at the reception? Either 'Brother' or 'Mr', followed by last name.

Is it OK to leave early? Yes.

Funerals and Mourning

Jehovah's Witnesses believe that the dead are 'conscious of nothing at all' and are asleep in the grave awaiting resurrection to life. While the majority will be raised to life in an earthly paradise, a small number – 144,000 – will be raised as immortal spirit creatures to rule with Christ in the heavenly kingdom of God.

The funeral service, which is a ceremony in itself, may last about fifteen to thirty minutes.

Before the ceremony

How soon after the death does the funeral usually take place? Usually within one week.

What should a non-Jehovah's Witness do upon hearing of the death of a member of that faith? Telephone or visit the bereaved to offer your condolences.

Appropriate attire

Men: A jacket and tie. No head covering is required.

Women: A dress or a skirt and blouse. Dress 'modestly' and 'sensibly'. Hems need not reach below the knees, nor need clothing cover the arms. Open-toed shoes and modest jewellery are permissible. No head covering is required.

There are no rules regarding colours of clothing, but what is worn should respect the sobriety of the occasion.

Gifts

Is it appropriate to send flowers or make a contribution? Yes. Flowers may be sent to the home of the bereaved before or after the funeral or to the funeral home. Notice that contributions to a charity in memory of the deceased can be sent to the mourners' home before or after the funeral.

Is it appropriate to send food? Yes. This can be sent to the home of the bereaved before or after the funeral.

The ceremony

Where will the ceremony take place? Either at a Kingdom Hall or in a funeral home.

When should guests arrive and where should they sit? Arrive early to avoid causing a distraction. Attendants will seat guests. The front few rows are reserved for family.

If arriving late, are there times when a guest should not enter the ceremony? No, but attendants will direct latecomers to seats.

Will the bereaved family be present at the Kingdom Hall or funeral home before the ceremony? Possibly.

Is there a traditional greeting for the family? No. Just offer your condolences.

Will there be an open coffin? Possibly. This depends on the preference of the immediate family.

Is a guest expected to view the body? There are no such expectations.

What is appropriate behaviour upon viewing the body? Look upon it sombrely for a few moments.

Who are the major officiants at the ceremony and what do they do?

The Congregation Elder, who will deliver a talk from the Bible designed to comfort the bereaved.

What books are used? Usually no books are used by the audience. Occasionally a Bible, such as the New World Translation (The Watchtower Bible and Tract Society of New York, 1961), or a songbook, such as *Sing Praises to Jehovah* (The Watchtower Bible and Tract Society of New York, 1984), may be used.

To indicate the order of the ceremony: Directions are not necessary because of the brevity of the service, which is led entirely by the Congregation Elder.

Will a guest who is not a Jehovah's Witness be expected to do anything other than sit? No.

Are there any parts of the ceremony in which a guest who is not a Jehovah's Witness should not participate? No.

If not disruptive to the ceremony, is it OK to:

Take pictures? No.

Use a flash? No.
Use video recording equipment? No.
Use audio recording equipment? Yes.

Will contributions to the church be collected at the ceremony?
No.

The interment

Should guests attend the interment? Such attendance is done at the discretion of the guest.

Whom should one ask for directions? The funeral director or his or her assistants.

What happens at the graveside? Brief comments on the Scriptures are followed by prayer.

Do guests who are not Jehovah's Witnesses participate at the graveside ceremony? No, they are simply present.

Comforting the bereaved

Is it appropriate to visit the home of the bereaved after the funeral? Yes. The length of the visit depends on the circumstances. Discussing with the bereaved what you appreciated about the deceased is helpful.

Will there be a religious service at the home of the bereaved? No.

Will food be served? Possibly. This depends on the preference of the mourners.

How soon after the funeral will a mourner usually return to a normal work schedule? This depends on the preferences and the circumstances of the mourners. There is no set time for remaining away from work, although mourners are usually absent from work for at least a few days.

How soon after the funeral will a mourner usually return to a normal social schedule? This is entirely an individual matter and depends on the preferences and the circumstances of the mourners. There is no set time for abstaining from social activities.

Are there mourning customs to which a friend who is not a Jehovah's Witness should be sensitive? No.

Are there rituals for observing the anniversary of the death? No.

5. HOME CELEBRATIONS

Not applicable to Jehovah's Witnesses.

10
Jewish

1. HISTORY AND BELIEFS

Judaism includes religious rituals and beliefs along with a code of ethical behaviour. It also incorporates and reflects the ancient history of the Jews as a nation in its rituals, ceremonies and celebrations. Today, its adherents include people of every race and most nations.

The foundation of Judaism is the Torah, the first five books of the Bible (Genesis, Exodus, Leviticus, Numbers and Deuteronomy). According to the Torah, God made a covenant with the Jews, beginning with the three patriarchs – Abraham, his son Isaac, and his grandson Jacob, whose name God changed to 'Israel'. At a time when people worshipped many gods, the Jewish people, through this covenant, accepted the 'One God' as the only God.

Central to this covenant is the concept of being 'chosen' as a people, for as Moses tells his people in the Bible, 'The Lord has chosen you to be a people for his own possession, out of all the peoples that are on the face of the earth' (Deuteronomy 14:2). Being 'chosen' does not confer special privilege. It means that the Jewish people are obliged to bring God's message to the world.

As part of God's covenant with Abraham, his descendants were promised the area now known as Israel – the Promised Land – as their homeland. They took possession of it in approximately 1200 BC. The conquering Romans destroyed Jerusalem and its temple, which was the centre of Jewish religious life, and drove the Jewish people from their land to end repeated rebellions. This began the period known as 'the Diaspora', when the Jewish people were without a homeland. Many drifted to the northern and southern rim of the Mediterranean, while others emigrated eastwards.

Before the Diaspora, Judaism as a religion evolved under a hereditary priesthood that officiated at the temple in Jerusalem, and through the ethical and moral teachings of a series of prophets. Following the temple's destruction, religious leadership passed from priests to *rabbis* – teachers and scholars. Today, the rabbinate includes both men and women in all movements except the Orthodox.

It is believed that Jewish people have lived in Britain since Roman times, although the population remained relatively small until the late nineteenth century.

There are now four major Jewish religious movements in the UK. In terms of theology, Liberal Judaism and Reform Judaism are, as the former's name suggests, at the most liberal end, while Masorti Judaism occupies the centre ground and Orthodox Judaism is the more traditional form of Judaism (although it includes different subgroupings, some of which, such as Modern Orthodox, are more centrist and others, such as Hasidism, more fundamentalist).

Hebrew, the traditional language of Jewish worship, is used to varying degrees in the services or celebrations of each movement. Each also has its own version of the prayer book, and almost all include translations of the Hebrew material.

Liberal Judaism in the UK is commonly dated back to the founding of the Jewish Religious Union in 1902, which sought to hold Sabbath afternoon services in which English was used as well as Hebrew. The movement has grown with the aims of reverencing Judaism's religious and cultural traditions within a framework of modern thinking and morality.

Reform Judaism, which began in the early nineteenth century in Germany but developed independently in Britain with the establishment of the West London Synagogue in 1842, regards Judaism as an ongoing process resulting from the relationship between God and the Jewish people over its history. It considers Torah divinely inspired and subject to individual interpretation based on study, and emphasises the ethical and moral messages of the prophets to help create a just society.

Masorti Judaism (known as Conservative Judaism in North America) was established in the UK in 1964, with the founding of the New London Synagogue. It teaches that while the Torah as a whole is binding and much of Jewish law remains authoritative, nonetheless new ideas and practices have always influenced Jewish beliefs and rituals and this should continue today as well.

Orthodox Judaism teaches that the Torah was divinely revealed to Moses at Mount Sinai and that the *halachah* ('hah-lah-KHAH'), the interpretative process of that law, is both divinely guided and authoritative. Thus no law stemming from the Torah can be tampered with even if it displeases modern sensibilities. Orthodoxy often rejects more modern forms of Judaism as deviations from divine truths and authentic modes of Jewish life.

Houses of worship are typically called 'synagogues', or sometimes 'temples'.

UK synagogues/temples: approximately 175
UK membership: approximately 250,000

For more information, contact:

The Board of Deputies of British Jews
6 Bloomsbury Square
London
WC1A 2LP
Tel: 0207 543 5400
Email: info@bod.org.uk

2. THE BASIC SERVICE

According to Jewish tradition, communal prayer requires a *minyan* ('MIN-yahn'), a quorum of at least ten persons over the age of thirteen. It takes place three times daily: in the early morning, at midday, and at sunset. Each communal prayer service takes about fifteen to thirty minutes. If a Jewish person cannot join the communal prayer, he or she may pray alone, omitting from the service certain prayers that are said only when there is a *minyan*. Orthodox and some Masorti congregations only count males in the number of persons in the *minyan*.

Each service contains many common elements and some minor variations according to the time of day and the time of the month. The fullest Jewish service takes place on the Jewish Sabbath, or *Shabbat* ('shah-BAHT'), which begins at sunset on Friday and ends at nightfall on Saturday. All Orthodox and Masorti congregations have services on Friday evenings and Saturday mornings, as do most Reform and Liberal congregations.

The major units of the service are the *Amidah* ('ah-mee-DAH'), a series of praises, thanks and petitions to God; and the *Sh'ma*, whose central phrase, 'Hear O Israel, the Lord is our God, the Lord is One', is a declaration of faith, a pledge of allegiance and an affirmation of Judaism. Another key element is the public reading from the Torah scroll, the first five books of the Bible.

The Friday evening service may last between thirty and ninety minutes and the Saturday morning service may last from ninety minutes to over three hours, depending on the congregation. Services are usually longer in Orthodox and Masorti congregations than in Reform or Liberal. The amount of Hebrew used during the service varies with each congregation, but Reform congregations will use the least and Orthodox the most. Prayer books normally include translations or interpretations of the Hebrew material.

Appropriate Attire

Men: A jacket and tie are never inappropriate. In some Reform and Liberal congregations, more informal attire may be appropriate on occasion.

A small head covering called a *yarmulke* ('YAHR-mihl-kah') or *kippah* ('keep-AH') is required in all Orthodox and Masorti congregations and in some Reform and Liberal congregations. They will be available just before one enters the main sanctuary. If required in Reform congregations, a sign is usually posted to that effect.

Women: A dress, skirt and blouse, or a trouser suit. In general, clothing should be modest, depending on the fashion and the locale.

In some Masorti synagogues, a hat or another head covering may be required. Open-toed shoes and modest jewellery are appropriate. A skirt is usually preferable to trousers in some Orthodox synagogues, while clothing should cover the arms, hems should reach below the knees and heads should be covered with a hat or veil.

On the Sabbath, do not carry a purse or similar accessory, since Jewish law prohibits labour, including carrying objects, on Shabbat.

Note: The *tallit* ('tah-LEET'), or prayer shawl, is worn by all Orthodox men, Masorti men and some women, and by some men and women in Reform and Liberal congregations. Non-Jews should not wear the *tallit*.

Do not openly wear symbols of other faiths, such as a cross.

There are no rules regarding colours of clothing.

The Sanctuary

What are the major sections of the synagogue/temple?

The bimah ('BEE-mah'): The part of the sanctuary from where the service is led and where the rabbi and cantor stand and sit. Also called the pulpit. It is usually raised above the level where congregants sit and is at the front or in the middle of the sanctuary.

The ark: The cabinet on the pulpit where the Torah is kept.

The Torah reading table: The table on which the Torah is opened and read.

The rabbi's pulpit: Where the rabbi stands when delivering his or her sermon or when teaching and commenting on the service.

The eternal light: A lamp, either gas or electric, that burns continuously above and in front of the ark where the Torah is kept.

The mehitsah ('meh-HEET-sah'): A partition used in Orthodox congregations to separate the seating sections for men and women. In more traditional congregations, women are seated to the rear of the men or in a balcony above them. In others, they are seated in a section parallel to the men's. Some 'modern' Orthodox congregations have eliminated the *mehitsah*, but men and women still sit separately.

✿

The Service

When should guests arrive and where should they sit? At events occurring on Saturday morning it is customary for guests who are not Jews to arrive at the scheduled time at Reform and Liberal services. For Orthodox or Masorti services, which tend to be longer, unless you want to participate in the entire service, ask your host the time you should arrive so you can be present for the specific event within the service for which you have been invited.

Sit wherever you wish, while respecting any separation of men and women, which occurs in all Orthodox congregations.

If arriving late, are there times when a guest should not enter the service? Do not enter when the congregation is standing or during the rabbi's sermon. In most congregations, an usher will advise latecomers when to enter.

Are there times when a guest should not leave the service? Do not leave when the congregation is standing, when the Torah is being taken out or returned to the ark, when the rabbi is speaking or when the specific ceremony during the service for which you have been invited is taking place.

Who are the major officiants, leaders or participants and what do they do?

The rabbi, who directs the service and teaches and preaches. (Any Jewish person over the age of thirteen may lead a service; in an Orthodox congregation, this can only be a male.) In larger congregations, there may be a senior rabbi and one or more rabbis who are his or her assistants.

The cantor, who chants and sings parts of the service and leads the congregation in song.

The Torah reader, who reads or chants from the Torah.

The gabbai ('gab-BYE'), a lay person who oversees the honours of reading from the Torah and of saying blessings for the Torah reading.

The congregation's president, or his or her representative, who may welcome congregants and visitors from the *bimah* and make announcements about upcoming events and programmes.

Note: In smaller congregations, the same person may have more than one role. For instance, the rabbi may also be the cantor.

What are the major ritual objects of the service?

The tallit, or prayer shawl, which is worn by all Orthodox men, Masorti men and some women, and by some men and women in Reform and Liberal congregations. Non-Jews should not wear the *tallit*.

The Torah ('TOH-rah'), a scroll on which are handwritten the first five books of the Bible: Genesis, Exodus, Leviticus, Numbers and Deuteronomy.

The yad ('yahd'), a metal pointer used when reading the Torah because one is not supposed to touch the handwritten letters.

The menorah ('min-OHR-ah'), a seven-branched candelabra, which was part of the ancient temple in Jerusalem and which is often placed on the *bimah* as an ornament.

The ark, the place in which a Torah scroll(s) is kept on the *bimah*.

Torah ornaments, such as a cover of fabric, a breastplate and crown of silver, which adorn the outside of the closed scroll.

Tefillin ('teh-FILL-in'), or phylacteries, two small black leather boxes containing four biblical passages which a male Jew from the age of thirteen wears on the left arm and the head during morning services on weekdays. They are held in place with leather straps. They are not worn for Shabbat services or festivals.

What books are used? The *siddur* ('SEE-door'), or prayerbook, which varies among (and sometimes within) the various religious movements; and the *chumash* ('KOOH-mahsh'), which contains the first five books of the Bible (Genesis, Exodus, Leviticus, Numbers and Deuteronomy), and the traditional section from Prophets that is associated with each weekly Torah portion and is read after the public Torah reading (called the *haftarah*, 'hahf-TOH-rah'). It may also contain editorial commentaries on the text.

To indicate the order of the service: In most congregations, the rabbi or another leader of the service will make periodic announcements. In some Orthodox congregations, it is generally assumed that those present know the order of the service and no announcements are made. In many Orthodox and Masorti congregations major portions of the service are read individually, often aloud, at the individual's own pace. As a result, the service may appear to be unorganised.

Guest Behaviour during the Service

Will a guest who is not Jewish be expected to do anything other than sit? They are expected to stand with the congregation. It is optional for them to read prayers aloud and sing with congregants if this would not violate their religious beliefs. Kneeling is not part of any Jewish service.

Are there any parts of the service in which a guest who is not Jewish should not participate? In all Orthodox, Masorti and most Reform and Liberal congregations, non-Jews will not be called to read from the Torah or participate in any honours involving the Torah.

If not disruptive to the service, is it OK to:

Take pictures? No.
Use a flash? No.
Use video recording equipment? No.
Use audio recording equipment? No.

Will contributions to the synagogue/temple be collected at the service? No.

After the Service

Is there usually a reception after the service? Yes. This is called a *kiddush* ('kee-DOOSH') or an *oneg Shabbat* ('OH-neg shah-BAHT'). It may last thirty to sixty minutes. Usually served is such light food as coffee, tea, fruit or pastries. Sometimes appetiser-type foods are served. Wait for a blessing to be said before eating or drinking. Wine and grape juice are provided in almost all congregations for the ceremonial blessing before drinking the 'fruit of the vine'. A blessing called *ha'motzi* ('hah-MOH-tsee') is recited before eating bread. In all Orthodox and some Masorti congregations, ritual handwashing is done before eating or drinking.

In most Reform and Liberal congregations, no blessing is recited after meals. All Orthodox and many Masorti congregations have a grace after meals. This is called *birkat hamazon* ('beer-KAHT hah-mah-ZONE').

Is there a traditional form of address for clergy who may be at the reception? 'Rabbi' or 'Cantor'.

Is it OK to leave early? Yes.

General Guidelines and Advice

In Orthodox congregations, decorum in synagogue calls for no public display of physical affection between the sexes. Often, Orthodox men and women do not even shake each other's hands. On Shabbat, most Orthodox Jews do not drive, smoke, write, use the telephone, turn electricity on or off, cook, handle money or do work of any kind. Many Masorti and some Reform and Liberal Jews will abstain from some of these activities.

Special Vocabulary

Key words or phrases that it might be helpful for a visitor to know:

Torah ('TOH-rah'): Most commonly used to refer to the scroll of the Five Books of Moses (Genesis, Exodus, Leviticus, Numbers and Deuteronomy).

Aliyah ('ah-lee-YAH'): Literally 'going up', it is the honour of being called to the *bimah* to participate in reading the Torah.

Sh'ma ('shih-MAH'): A central prayer of the worship service. Essentially a statement of faith that is derived from Deuteronomy 6:

'Hear O Israel, the Lord is our God, the Lord is One.'

Amidah ('ah-mee-DAH'): A series of praises, thanks and petitions to God. Recited by the entire congregation while standing, they are the central part of the prayer service.

Simcha ('SIHM-khah'): Means 'to rejoice'. May be used during a service to refer to a special happy event, such as a birth, a bar or bat mitzvah or a wedding.

Mazal tov ('MAH-zahl tohv'): Literally 'good luck', but used as 'congratulations'. Especially used at the occasion of a *simcha*.

Some Basic Beliefs

There is no single official creed that all Jews accept.

Jews believe:

There is only one God, to whom prayer is directed, and with whom each person has a personal and direct relationship.

Congregational prayer and community are a cornerstone of faith.

The Torah is a guide to righteous living, as a continual source of revelation, although not all accept it literally.

Study of Torah is equivalent to prayer.

God is supreme over all and possesses absolute sovereignty.

People have free will and there is no original sin.

Righteousness is not limited to members of the Jewish faith.

They share a sense of community with and responsibility for Jews throughout the world.

Some basic books to which a guest can refer to learn more about Judaism:

Conservative Judaism: The New Century, by Neil Gillman (Behrman House, Inc., 1993).

Jewish Spirituality: A Brief Introduction for Christians, by Lawrence Kushner (Jewish Lights Publishing, 2001).

The Rituals and Practices of a Jewish Life: A Handbook for Personal Spiritual Renewal, by Rabbi Kerry M. Olitzky and Rabbi Daniel Judson (Jewish Lights Publishing, 2002).

This Is My God: The Jewish Way of Life, by Herman Wouk (Little, Brown, 1974).

What Is a Jew?, by Morris N. Kertzer, revised by Lawrence A. Hoffman (Simon & Schuster, 1996).

What You Will See Inside a Synagogue, by Rabbi Lawrence A. Hoffman and Dr Ron Wolfson, with photographs by Bill Aron (SkyLight Paths Publishing, 2008).

3. HOLY DAYS AND FESTIVALS

Jewish holy days and festivals celebrate historical events in the life of the Jewish people or are times that the Torah specifically sets aside for religious services. Noted below for each major holiday are those times when observant Jews are required to abstain from 'work' on their days of observance. The definition of activities that constitute 'work' varies, but all include transacting business.

A lunar-based religious calendar is used, so each new day starts at sunset. Sunday is the first day of the week. The Sabbath, the weekly seventh day of rest, begins at sunset on Friday and is observed until nightfall on Saturday. The coincidence of Jewish holidays with the solar-based Christian calendar varies as much as a month from year to year.

Rosh Hashanah ('rohsh hah-SHAH-nah'): The Jewish religious New Year, which also commemorates the creation of the world, traditionally counted as being approximately 5,800 years ago. Occurs on the first and second days of the Hebrew month of Tishrei and is observed on both days in Orthodox and Masorti congregations and on the first day only in Reform and Liberal congregations. Usually occurs mid-September to mid-October. The greeting for Rosh Hashanah is 'Happy New Year', in Hebrew *'Shana Tovah'* ('shah-NAH toh-VAH'). Almost all Jews abstain from work on their days of observance.

Yom Kippur ('yohm kee-POOR'): The Day of Atonement, on which one engages in reflection and prayer and formally repents for sins committed during the previous Hebrew year. Occurs on the tenth day of the Hebrew month of Tishrei, which usually falls in late

September to mid-October. The greetings for Yom Kippur are 'Have an easy fast' or 'Happy New Year', in Hebrew '*Shana Tovah*' ('shah-NAH toh-VAH'). Male Jews of thirteen or older, and female Jews of twelve or older, are required to abstain from work and fast (no liquids or food) from the sundown when Yom Kippur begins until nightfall of the following day.

Sukkot ('soo-KOTE'): The Feast of Booths. A seven-day harvest holiday. This usually occurs in early or mid-October. A traditional greeting is 'Happy holiday', or, in Hebrew, '*Chag samayach*' ('hahg sah-MAY-ahk'). Orthodox Jews in particular abstain from work during the first two days of the holiday, as do many Masorti Jews, while Liberal and Reform Jews may abstain from work on the first day only. Following directly after Sukkot, a two-day festival known as *Simchat Torah* begins; this is when the annual cycle of reading the Torah is completed. This is a very joyous occasion when all Torah scrolls are withdrawn from the ark and congregants dance with them.

Chanukah ('HAH-noo-kah'): The Festival of Lights. Commemorates the victory in about 163 BC of the Maccabees over the Syrians who tried to eradicate Judaism. It is observed for the eight days beginning with the twenty-fifth day of the Hebrew month of Kislev. This is usually in early to mid-December. The traditional greeting is 'Happy Chanukah', or, in Hebrew, '*Chanukah samayach*' ('HAH-noo-kah sah-MAY-ahk'). There are no requirements to abstain from work during Chanukah.

Purim ('POO-rim'): A celebration of deliverance from destruction. Marked by reading the Purim story from a *megillah* ('m'gee-LAH'), a scroll of the book of Esther, and merry-making. Usually occurs in late February or early March. The traditional greeting is 'Happy Holiday', in Hebrew, '*Chag samayach*' ('hahg sah-MAY-ack'), or 'Happy Purim'. There are no requirements to abstain from work on Purim.

Pesach ('PAY-sakh'): Passover. Celebrates the Jewish people's freedom from slavery in Egypt. Beginning with the fifteenth day of the Hebrew month of Nisan, it is observed for eight days by Orthodox and Masorti Jews and for seven days by Reform and Liberal Jews. Almost all Jews abstain from eating bread and other foods made with yeast. Usually occurs in late March or early to mid-April. A traditional greeting is 'Happy holiday', in Hebrew, '*Chag samayach*' ('hahg sah-MAY-ack'), or 'Happy Passover'. Orthodox Jews in particular abstain from work during the first two days and the last two days of the holiday, as do many Masorti Jews. Liberal and Reform Jews may abstain from work on the first and last days only.

Shavuot ('shah-voo-OTE'): The Festival of Weeks. Commemorates the giving of the Torah at Mount Sinai, as well as the first fruits of the spring harvest. Occurs on the sixth and seventh of the Hebrew month of Sivan, which usually occurs in May or June. A traditional greeting is 'Happy holiday', or in Hebrew, '*Chag samayach*' ('hahg sah-MAY-ahk'). Orthodox Jews in particular abstain from work during both days of this holiday, as do many Masorti Jews, while Liberal and Reform Jews observe it for only one day.

4. LIFE CYCLE EVENTS

Birth Ceremony

In Hebrew, the ceremony is called a *brit* ('breet'), which literally means 'covenant', and can apply to newborn males and females.

For boys, the *brit milah* ('breet mee-LAH'), or the 'covenant of circumcision', occurs on the eighth day of a male child's life. This is a sign of the covenant between God and the Jewish people. The biblical roots of circumcision are in Genesis, which states that God told Abraham, 'Every male among you shall be circumcised . . . and that shall be the sign of the covenant between Me and you throughout the generations' (Genesis 17:10).

The circumcision may be performed at home, in a synagogue/temple or in a hospital. It requires removing the entire foreskin of the penis, a simple surgical technique that takes only a few seconds. The entire ceremony, including giving the child his Hebrew name, may take fifteen to sixty minutes.

For girls, the naming ceremony is the *brit bat* ('breet baht'), the 'covenant of the daughter', or the *brit hayyim* ('breet hy-YEEM'), the 'covenant of life'. It is held at home or at the synagogue/temple, usually during the Torah reading portion of the Sabbath or weekday service.

If a more creative or non-traditional baby-naming ceremony is held at home, it may take about twenty minutes.

Before the ceremony

Are guests usually invited by a formal invitation? They are usually invited by telephone or by written invitation.

If not stated explicitly, should one assume that children are invited? Yes.

If one cannot attend, what should one do? RSVP with regrets and send a small gift appropriate for the child, such as clothing, a toy or baby equipment.

Appropriate attire

Men: If the ceremony is at home, dress casually, although a jacket and tie may be appropriate. If at a synagogue/temple, a jacket and tie is appropriate.

A small head covering called a *yarmulke* ('YAHR-mihl-kah') or *kippah* ('keep-AH') is required in all Orthodox and Masorti congregations and in some Reform and Liberal congregations. They will be available just before one enters the main sanctuary. If required in Reform congregations, a sign is usually posted to that effect.

Women: A dress, skirt and blouse, or a trouser suit. In general, clothing should be modest, depending on the fashion and the locale. In some Masorti synagogues, a hat or another head covering may be required. Open-toed shoes and modest jewellery are appropriate. A skirt is usually preferable to trousers in some Orthodox synagogues, while clothing should cover the arms, hems should reach below the knees and heads should be covered with a hat or veil.

On the Sabbath, do not carry a purse or similar accessory, since Jewish law prohibits labour, including carrying objects, on Shabbat.

Note: The *tallit* ('tah-LEET'), or prayer shawl, is worn by all Orthodox men, Masorti men and some women, and by some men and women in Reform and Liberal congregations. Non-Jews should not wear the *tallit*.

Do not openly wear symbols of other faiths, such as a cross.

There are no rules regarding colours of clothing, but this is a festive time.

Gifts

Is a gift customarily expected? Yes, often cash, toys or children's clothing or baby equipment.

Should gifts be brought to the ceremony? Either to the synagogue/temple (if the ceremony is not on the Sabbath) or to the home.

The ceremony

Where will the ceremony take place? At the child's home, or at a synagogue/temple.

When should guests arrive and where should they sit? Arrive early. Sit anywhere, except in the front row, which is usually reserved for close family members.

If arriving late, are there times when a guest should not enter the ceremony? Not for a *brit* at home. If the *brit* is at a synagogue/temple, ushers usually will tell latecomers when they can enter.

Are there times when a guest should not leave the ceremony? Not if the ceremony is at home. If at a synagogue/temple, do not leave when the congregation is standing, when the Torah is being taken out or returned to the ark, when the rabbi is speaking, or when the specific ceremony during the service for which you have been invited is taking place.

Who are the major officiants, leaders or participants at the ceremony and what do they do?

For a male's *brit milah*:

A mohel ('MOH-hail'), or specially trained ritual circumciser, who may also be a rabbi or physician.

A rabbi, who may also be the *mohel*.

The child's parents, who recite blessings and may hold the child during the ceremony.

The child's grandparents, who bring the child into the room where the ceremony is held. At an Orthodox synagogue, the child will be brought in by a young couple who have not yet had children.

The child's godparents, who hold the child during the actual circumcision and who must be members of the Jewish faith.

For a girl's naming ceremony:

A rabbi.

The child's parents, who recite blessings and may hold the child during the ceremony.

The child's grandparents, who bring the child into the room where the ceremony is held.

The child's godparents.

A cantor (if the ceremony is in a synagogue), who leads the congregation in song.

The Torah reader (if the ceremony is in a synagogue), who chants from the Torah.

The gabbai ('gab-BYE') (if the ceremony is in a synagogue), who oversees the honours of reading from the Torah.

What books are used? The *siddur* ('SEE-door'), or prayer book, or a ceremony specially prepared by the parents.

To indicate the order of the ceremony: The rabbi or another leader of the service will make periodic announcements.

Will a guest who is not Jewish be expected to do anything other than sit? They are expected to stand with the congregation. It is optional for them to read prayers aloud and sing with other guests if this would not violate their religious beliefs.

Are there any parts of the ceremony in which a guest who is not

Jewish should not participate? In Orthodox and Masorti and in most Reform and Liberal congregations, non-Jews will not be called to read from the Torah or participate in any honours involving the Torah.

If not disruptive to the ceremony, is it OK to:

Take pictures? Ask the rabbi and ask permission of the host.

Use a flash? Ask the rabbi and ask permission of the host.

Use video recording equipment? Ask the rabbi and ask permission of the host.

Use audio recording equipment? Ask the rabbi and ask permission of the host.

Will contributions to the synagogue/temple be collected at the ceremony? No.

After the ceremony

Is there usually a reception after the ceremony? There is almost always a reception called a *kiddush* ('kee-DOOSH'). Usually served is such light food as coffee, tea, fruit and pastries. Sometimes appetiser-type foods are served. Wine and grape juice are provided in almost all congregations for the ceremonial blessing before drinking the 'fruit of the vine'. There is no music or dancing.

If in the home, the reception may last up to two hours. If in a synagogue/temple, it may last thirty to sixty minutes.

Among Orthodox Jews, the reception may include a meal and possibly a brief sermon or discourse by the father, or some distinguished family member, guest or the rabbi. At the home of the infant's parents, a catering hall or the site of the *brit*, the reception may last one hour.

Would it be considered impolite to neither eat nor drink? No.

Is there a grace or benediction before eating or drinking? Yes. Wait for a blessing to be said before eating or drinking. A blessing is said before drinking wine or grape juice. A blessing called *ha'motzi* ('hah-MOH-tsee') is recited before eating bread. In all Orthodox and some

Masorti congregations, ritual handwashing is done before eating or drinking.

Is there a grace or benediction after eating or drinking? In most Reform and Liberal congregations, no blessing is recited after meals. All Orthodox and many Masorti congregations have a grace after meals. This is called *birkat hamazon* ('beer-KAHT hah-mah-ZONE').

Is there a traditional greeting for the family? 'Congratulations', or, in Hebrew, '*Mazal tov*' ('MAH-zahl tohv').

Is there a traditional form of address for clergy who may be at the reception? 'Rabbi' or 'Cantor'. There is no special form of address for the *mohel*.

Is it OK to leave early? Yes.

Initiation Ceremony

These ceremonies mark an adolescent's entry into religious adulthood and responsibility, after which they are included in the *minyan* ('MIN-yahn') or quorum of ten Jewish people (men or women in Reform, Liberal and Masorti congregations; only men in Orthodox) needed to hold congregational prayers.

For a boy, *bar mitzvah* ('bahr MITS-vah'), or 'son of the commandment', occurs upon reaching the age of thirteen, when, according to Jewish tradition, males are liable for their own transgressions and their fathers no longer bear this responsibility.

A *bat mitzvah* ('baht MITS-vah'), or 'daughter of the commandment', is held at the age of twelve or thirteen. According to Jewish law, females attain religious adulthood and responsibility upon reaching twelve years and one day. There are no specific legal requirements in Judaism for a girl to participate in a ceremony marking this occasion, and bat mitzvah ceremonies began only in the twentieth century.

In Orthodox and Masorti congregations, a boy publicly reads from the Torah for the first time at a bar mitzvah. In a Reform or Liberal congregation, both boys and girls publicly read from the Torah. In those Reform or Liberal congregations where the *haftarah* (a reading from Prophets) is read, boys and girls also read from this text. He or she may also lead other parts of the service, and usually deliver a speech to the congregation on the significance of attaining religious adulthood.

A bar or bat mitzvah service is always part of a larger, basic service and is almost always on a Saturday morning.

Bar or bat mitzvah services usually last about one hour in Reform and Liberal congregations and about two hours in Orthodox and Masorti congregations. The balance of the basic Sabbath service will add about an hour (or more) to the entire service.

Before the ceremony

Are guests usually invited by a formal invitation? Yes.

If not stated explicitly, should one assume that children are invited? No.

If one cannot attend, what should one do? RSVP with your regrets and send a small gift for the bar/bat mitzvah boy or girl.

Appropriate attire

Men: If the ceremony is at home, dress casually, although a jacket and tie may be appropriate. If at a synagogue/temple, a jacket and tie is appropriate.

A small head covering called a *yarmulke* ('YAHR-mihl-kah') or *kippah* ('keep-AH') is required in all Orthodox and Masorti congregations and in some Reform and Liberal congregations. They will be available just before one enters the main sanctuary. If required in Reform congregations, a sign is usually posted to that effect.

Women: A dress, skirt and blouse, or a trouser suit. In general, clothing should be modest, depending on the fashion and the locale. In some Masorti synagogues, a hat or another head covering may be required. Open-toed shoes and modest jewellery are appropriate. A skirt is usually preferable to trousers in some Orthodox synagogues, while clothing should cover the arms, hems should reach below the knees and heads should be covered with a hat or veil.

On the Sabbath, do not carry a purse or similar accessory, since Jewish law prohibits labour, including carrying objects, on Shabbat.

Note: The *tallit* ('tah-LEET'), or prayer shawl, is worn by all Orthodox men, Masorti men and some women, and by some men and women in Reform and Liberal congregations. Non-Jews should not wear the *tallit*.

Do not openly wear symbols of other faiths, such as a cross.

There are no rules regarding colours of clothing, but this is a festive time.

Gifts

Is a gift customarily expected? Yes. Customary gifts are cash, books or ritual items of Judaica.

Should gifts be brought to the ceremony? Gifts should be sent to the child's home.

The ceremony

Where will the ceremony take place? In the sanctuary of the synagogue/temple.

When should guests arrive and where should they sit? It is more customary for guests who are not Jews to arrive at the time called at Reform and Liberal Saturday morning services than at Masorti and Orthodox services, which tend to be longer. Unless you want to participate in the entire service, ask your host the time you should arrive so you can be present for the specific event within the service for which you have been invited. Sit wherever you wish, while respecting any separation of men and women, which occurs in all Orthodox congregations.

If arriving late, are there times when a guest should not enter the ceremony? Do not enter when the congregation is standing or during the rabbi's sermon. In most congregations, an usher will advise latecomers when they can enter.

Are there times when a guest should not leave the ceremony? Yes, when the congregation is standing, when the Torah is being taken out or returned to the ark, when the rabbi is speaking, or when the specific ceremony during the service for which you have been invited is taking place.

Who are the major officiants, leaders or participants at the ceremony and what do they do?

The bar or bat mitzvah boy or girl.

The child's parents.

The rabbi, who directs the service and teaches and preaches. (Any Jewish person over the age of thirteen may lead a service; in an Orthodox congregation, this can only be a male.) In larger congregations, there may be a senior rabbi and one or more rabbis who are his or her assistants.

The cantor, who chants and sings parts of the service and leads the congregation in song.

The Torah reader, who chants from the Torah.

The gabbai ('gab-BYE'), a lay person who oversees the honours of reading from the Torah and of saying blessings for the Torah reading.

The congregation's president, or his or her representative, who may welcome congregants and visitors from the *bimah* ('BEE-mah') and make announcements about upcoming events and programmes.

Note: In smaller congregations, the same person may have more than one role. For instance, the rabbi may also be the cantor.

What books are used? The *siddur* ('SEE-door'), or prayerbook, which varies among (and sometimes within) the various religious movements; and the *chumash* ('KOOH-mahsh'), which contains the first five books of the Torah, also known as the Five Books of Moses: Genesis, Exodus, Leviticus, Numbers and Deuteronomy. It also contains a traditional section from Prophets that is associated with each Torah section and that is read after the Torah reading (which is called the *haftarah*, pronounced 'hahf-TOH-rah') and may contain editorial commentaries on the text.

To indicate the order of the ceremony: In most congregations, the rabbi or another leader of the service will make periodic announcements. In some Orthodox congregations, it is generally assumed that those present know the order of the service and no announcements are made. In many Orthodox congregations major portions of the service are read individually, often aloud, at the individual's own pace. As a result, the service may appear to be unorganised.

Will a guest who is not Jewish be expected to do anything other than sit? They are expected to stand with the congregation. It is optional for them to read prayers aloud and to sing with congregants, if this would not violate their religious beliefs.

Are there any parts of the ceremony in which a guest who is not Jewish should not participate? In Orthodox and Masorti and in most Reform and Liberal congregations, non-Jews are not called to read from the Torah or participate in any honours involving the Torah.

If not disruptive to the ceremony, is it OK to:

Take pictures? Not on Saturdays; possibly on other days. Ask your host.

Use a flash? Not on Saturdays; possibly on other days. Ask your host.

Use video recording equipment? Not on Saturdays; possibly on other days. Ask your host.

Use audio recording equipment? Not on Saturdays; possibly on other days. Ask your host.

Will contributions to the synagogue/temple be collected at the ceremony? No.

After the ceremony

Is there usually a reception after the ceremony? There is usually a small, relatively brief (fifteen to thirty minutes) reception for the entire congregation and invited guests. This is called a *kiddush* ('kee-DOOSH') and is almost always held in a reception area of the synagogue/temple. Usually served are coffee, tea, fruit, pastries or punch.

Sometimes appetiser-type foods are served. There may be wine and, in some congregations, whisky.

For invited guests only, there may be a larger reception and celebration after the kiddush at which a full meal is served and at which there is music and dancing. This may be held in a reception room of the synagogue/temple, in a separate catering hall/hotel or at the home of the bar or bat mitzvah child. This meal and celebration may last three hours or more.

Would it be considered impolite to neither eat nor drink? No. In general, guests should not expect non-kosher food, such as pork or shellfish, or expect to mix dairy and meat products at the reception if it is kosher (i.e. observes the traditional Jewish dietary laws). All Orthodox receptions, most Masorti and some Reform and Liberal receptions are kosher.

Is there a grace or benediction before eating or drinking? Yes. Wait for a blessing to be said before eating or drinking. A blessing is said before drinking wine or grape juice. A blessing called *ha'motzi* ('hah-MOH-tsee') is recited before eating. It might be led by a rabbi, cantor or lay person who is an honoured guest. In all Orthodox and some Masorti congregations, ritual handwashing is done before eating or drinking.

Is there a grace or benediction after eating or drinking? Not in most Reform and Liberal congregations or households. All Orthodox and many Masorti congregations or households have a grace after meals called *birkat hamazon* ('beer-KAHT hah-mah-ZONE').

Is there a traditional greeting for the family? 'Congratulations' or, in Hebrew, *'Mazal tov'* ('MAH-zahl tohv').

Is there a traditional form of address for clergy who may be at the reception? 'Rabbi' or 'Cantor'.

Is it OK to leave early? Yes, but usually only after the main course has been served.

Marriage Ceremony

Judaism considers marriage a divine command, a sacred bond and a means of personal fulfilment. Marriage is deemed the natural and desirable state of every adult. The Hebrew word for marriage is *kiddushin* ('kee-doo-SHEEN'), which means 'sanctification'.

The *huppah* ('hoo-PAH'), or wedding canopy, under which the ceremony takes place, symbolises the canopy of the heavens under which all life transpires. A glass, which the groom breaks underfoot after he and the bride have said their wedding vows, is an ancient tradition that has been interpreted in many ways, including commemorating at this time of great joy a moment of great sadness: the destruction of the temple in Jerusalem in AD 70.

The wedding ceremony is always a service in itself. It may take about fifteen to thirty minutes.

Before the ceremony

Are guests usually invited by a formal invitation? Yes.

If not stated explicitly, should one assume that children are invited? No.

If one cannot attend, what should one do? RSVP with regrets and send a gift.

Appropriate attire

Men: Attire depends on the social formality of the event. A small head covering called a *yarmulke* ('YAHR-mihl-kah') or *kippah* ('keep-AH') is required in all Orthodox and Masorti congregations and in some Reform and Liberal congregations. They will be available just before one enters the main sanctuary. If required in Reform congregations, a sign is usually posted to that effect.

Women: Attire depends on the social formality of the event. A dress, skirt and blouse, or a trouser suit are usually appropriate. In some Masorti synagogues, a hat or another head covering may be required.

Open-toed shoes and modest jewellery are appropriate. A skirt is usually preferable to trousers in some Orthodox synagogues, while clothing should cover the arms, hems should reach below the knees and heads should be covered with a hat or veil.

Do not openly wear symbols of other faiths, such as a cross.

There are no rules regarding colours of clothing, but this is a festive time.

Gifts

Is a gift customarily expected? Yes. Appropriate are such household items as small appliances or sheets or towels. The couple often have a gift list at a local department store.

Should gifts be brought to the ceremony? No. Send them to the bride's home or to the reception.

The ceremony

Where will the ceremony take place? Depending on the desires of the couple, it may be at a synagogue/temple, at a hotel, at home or at any other location chosen by them.

When should guests arrive and where should they sit? It is customary to arrive at the time called. Ushers usually will be present to seat you. Otherwise, sit wherever you wish.

If arriving late, are there times when a guest should not enter the ceremony? Do not enter during the processional or recessional.

Are there times when a guest should not leave the ceremony? Not during the processional or recessional or while the officiant is blessing or addressing the couple.

Who are the major officiants, leaders or participants at the ceremony and what do they do?

The rabbi, who leads the ceremony.
The cantor, who sings during the ceremony or who may lead it instead of a rabbi.

The bride and groom.

Parents of the bride and groom and other members of the wedding party.

What books are used? None. There may be special material prepared by the bridal couple.

To indicate the order of the ceremony: There may be a programme.

Will a guest who is not Jewish be expected to do anything other than sit? No.

Are there any parts of the ceremony in which a guest who is not Jewish should not participate? No.

If not disruptive to the ceremony, is it OK to:

Take pictures? Possibly. Ask your host.

Use a flash? Possibly. Ask your host.

Use video recording equipment? Possibly. Ask your host.

Use audio recording equipment? Possibly. Ask your host.

Will contributions to the synagogue/temple be collected at the ceremony? No.

After the ceremony

Is there usually a reception after the ceremony? Weddings are times of great celebration. Often, a full meal is served at which there is music and dancing. This may be held in a reception room of the synagogue/temple, in a separate hall, at a hotel, or at another site. There may also be a light smorgasbord before the ceremony itself.

Guests should not expect to mix dairy and meat products at the reception if it is kosher (i.e. observes the traditional Jewish dietary laws). All Orthodox receptions, most Masorti and some Reform and Liberal receptions are kosher.

Would it be considered impolite to neither eat nor drink? No.

Is there a grace or benediction before eating or drinking? Yes. Wait for a blessing to be said before eating or drinking. A benediction called *ha'motzi* ('hah-MOH-tsee') is recited before eating bread. It might be said by a rabbi, cantor or a lay person who is an honoured guest.

Is there a grace or benediction after eating or drinking? All Orthodox and many Masorti ceremonies have a grace after meals called *birkat hamazon* ('beer-KAHT hah-mah-ZONE'). This is increasingly common in Reform and Liberal ceremonies.

Is there a traditional greeting for the family? 'Congratulations' or, in Hebrew, '*Mazal tov*' ('MAH-zal tohv').

Is there a traditional form of address for clergy who may be at the reception? 'Rabbi' or 'cantor'.

Is it OK to leave early? Yes, but usually only after the main course has been served.

Funerals and Mourning

A Jewish funeral will last between fifteen and sixty minutes. It is a time of intense mourning and public grieving. It is a service in itself and is not part of a larger service.

The Reform and Liberal movements reject all notions of bodily resurrection and of a physical life after death. Instead, they believe in the immortality of every soul, which will eventually return to God. True immortality resides in memories treasured in this world by those who knew and loved the deceased.

The Masorti movement talks about the resurrection of the dead, but does not specify whether this will be a physical or a spiritual resurrection. The former would occur upon the coming of the Messiah; the latter would occur by those remaining on earth sensing and remembering the deceased.

Orthodox Jews believe in bodily resurrection and a physical life after death. This would occur upon the coming of the Messiah. In the meantime, there are rough equivalents to heaven and hell, with righteous souls enjoying the pleasures of *olam ha'bah* ('oh-LAHM hah-BAH'), 'the world to come', which has a Garden of Eden-like quality; and the wicked suffering in the fiery pits of Gehenna ('geh-HEN-ah').

Traditional Jewish law forbids cremation, but cremation is allowed among Reform and Liberal Jews.

Before the ceremony

How soon after the death does the funeral usually take place?
Generally the day after the death, unless there are extraordinary circumstances. Some Orthodox funerals take place on the same day as the death. In some Reform and Liberal families, it can be up to two or three days after the death.

What should a non-Jew do upon hearing of the death of a member of that faith? Telephone or visit the bereaved at home and offer condolences and to help out in any way. Possibly bring food to their home. Especially for Orthodox families, make certain the food is kosher (i.e. conforms with traditional Jewish dietary laws). If particularly close to the bereaved, offer to take them to the funeral home to arrange details for the funeral.

Appropriate attire

Men: A jacket and tie. A small head covering called a *yarmulke* ('YAHR-mihl-kah') or *kippah* ('keep-AH') is required at Orthodox and Masorti funerals and at some Reform and Liberal funerals. They will be available at the funeral home or synagogue/temple.

Women: A dress or a skirt and blouse. Clothing should be modest. At some Masorti funerals, a hat or another form of head covering may be required. Open-toed shoes and modest jewellery are appropriate. For Orthodox funerals, clothing should cover the arms, hems should reach below the knees and heads should be covered with a hat or veil.

Do not openly wear symbols of other faiths, such as a cross.

Sombre colours for clothing are recommended.

Gifts

Is it appropriate to send flowers or make a contribution? Flowers are never appropriate for Orthodox or Masorti funerals, but are sometimes appropriate for Reform or Liberal funerals. Contributions in memory of the deceased are customary. Small contributions are often given to a charity or cause favoured by the deceased that may be listed in an obituary in a local newspaper, or to a special fund established by the bereaved family.

Is it appropriate to send food? Yes, to the home of the bereaved after the funeral. Even if the family is not ritually observant, it is best if the food is kosher (i.e. conforms with traditional Jewish dietary laws) to avoid even the possibility of offending them.

The ceremony

Where will the ceremony take place? Either at a synagogue/temple or at a funeral home.

When should guests arrive and where should they sit? Arrive on time. Ushers may be available to direct guests to seating.

If arriving late, are there times when a guest should not enter the ceremony? Do not enter during the processional or recessional, if they take place, or while eulogies are being delivered.

Will the bereaved family be present at the synagogue/ temple or the funeral home before the ceremony? Yes, usually for no longer than one hour.

Is there a traditional greeting for the family? Offer condolences, such as 'I'm sorry for your loss'.

Will there be an open coffin? Never.

Who are the major officiants at the ceremony and what do they do?

A rabbi, who officiates and delivers a eulogy.
A cantor, who sings.

Family members or friends, who may also deliver a eulogy or memorial.

What books are used? None. The service is led entirely by the rabbi, with no lay participation other than eulogies or memorials by relatives or friends.

To indicate the order of the ceremony: The officiating rabbi will make occasional announcements.

Will a guest who is not Jewish be expected to do anything other than sit? Guests are expected to stand with the other mourners.

Are there any parts of the ceremony in which a guest who is not Jewish should not participate? No.

If not disruptive to the ceremony, is it OK to:

Take pictures? No.
Use a flash? No.
Use video recording equipment? No.
Use audio recording equipment? Possibly. Ask permission from a member of the deceased's immediate family.

Will contributions to the synagogue/temple be collected at the ceremony? No.

The interment

Should guests attend the interment? It is expected only of family and close friends, not acquaintances.

Whom should one ask for directions? The funeral director.

What happens at the graveside? The service will vary, depending as much on the family's background as on its religious affiliation. At the simplest graveside service, the rabbi recites prayers and leads the family in the mourners' *kaddish* ('KAH-dish'), the prayer for the deceased. At a traditional service, once the mourners have arrived at the cemetery, there is a slow procession to the grave itself, with several pauses along the way. After prayers and kaddish have been recited, all present participate in filling in the grave by each putting one spadeful of earth into it. As the closest family members leave the gravesite, they pass between two rows of relatives and friends.

Do guests who are not Jews participate at the graveside ceremony? They participate in filling in the grave, if this custom is followed. Otherwise, they are simply present.

Comforting the bereaved

Is it appropriate to visit the home of the bereaved after the funeral? Yes. The family sits in mourning for seven days after the funeral. This is called the *shiva* period ('SHIH-vah'). Visits should last about thirty minutes. They are usually made during the daytime or early evening hours. After expressing your condolences, it is customary to sit quietly or talk to other callers, and wait to be spoken to by the principal mourners.

There are no ritual objects at the home of the bereaved, but some home traditions during the mourning period may include:

Covering mirrors in the home to concentrate on mourning and not on vanity.

Burning a special memorial candle for seven days in memory of the deceased.

Immediate members of the family sitting on small chairs or boxes; wearing jackets or sweaters that have been cut and slippers or just socks rather than shoes; and, for men, not shaving.

All these symbolise mourners' lack of interest in their comfort or how they appear to others.

Will there be a religious service at the home of the bereaved? Yes. Twice a day, morning and evening. These usually last about ten to twenty minutes. Non-Jews should take a prayer book when these are offered and may silently read the English, if this does not violate their religious beliefs. They should stand when those present stand during the brief service.

Will food be served? In most cases, yes, although it is rare at an Orthodox shiva (unless the mourners are *Sefardi* – Eastern Jews).

Guests should not wait for a grace or benediction before eating. Guests will eat as they arrive, after expressing their condolences to the bereaved.

How soon after the funeral will a mourner usually return to a normal work schedule? One week.

How soon after the funeral will a mourner usually return to a normal social schedule? One month to one year, depending on the deceased's relation to the person as well as personal inclination.

Are there mourning customs to which a friend who is not Jewish should be sensitive? For eleven months after the death of their parent or child, thirty days for other relatives, mourners who follow traditional practice will attend daily morning and/or evening services at the synagogue/temple, where he (or she, too, in a more 'modern' Orthodox household) participates in the service and, in particular, recites the mourners' *kaddish* ('KAH-dish'), the special prayer for the deceased.

Are there rituals for observing the anniversary of the death? The anniversary of the death is called a *yahrzeit* ('YAHR-tzite'), upon which the bereaved attends a service at a synagogue/temple and lights at home a *yahrzeit* candle that burns for twenty-four hours. An 'unveiling' of the tombstone usually takes place on approximately the first anniversary of the death and involves a simple ceremony at the gravesite. Attendance is by specific invitation only.

5. HOME CELEBRATIONS

Passover Seder

What is its significance? Passover commemorates the Jewish people's liberation from slavery in Egypt.

When does it occur? In the springtime.

What is the proper greeting to the celebrants? 'Happy Passover' or 'Happy holiday', which in Hebrew is '*Chag samayach*' ('hahg sah-MAY-ahk').

Before the ceremony

Are guests usually invited by a formal invitation? Yes. They may receive a phone call, or be invited face to face.

If not stated explicitly, should one assume children are invited? No. Clarify this with your host.

If one cannot attend, what should one do? Express regrets. Send flowers or special Passover candy.

Appropriate attire

Men: Ask your host about attire. Some may prefer jacket and tie; others may request more informal attire. A small head covering called a *yarmulke* ('YAHR-mihl-kah') or *kippah* ('keep-AH') is required at all Orthodox and most Masorti seders and at some Reform and Liberal seders. If required, your host will provide them for you.

Women: Ask your host about attire. Some may prefer a dress or a skirt and blouse or a trouser suit. Open-toed shoes and modest jewellery are appropriate.

Do not openly wear symbols of other faiths, such as a cross.

There are no rules regarding colours of clothing, but this is a festive occasion.

Gifts

Is a gift customarily expected? This is entirely optional.

If one decides to give a gift, is a certain type of gift appropriate? Flowers for the seder table or special Passover candy are welcome.

Jewish

The ceremony

The Passover *seder* ('SAY-dihr') is a festive dinner at home at which the story of the Jewish people's liberation from slavery in Egypt, the Exodus, is told. Rituals precede and follow the meal. A seder is usually led by the head of the household, although everyone present participates.

Seders (including the meal) may take from ninety minutes to more than three hours, depending upon the detail in which the story is told and family customs. It is customary to arrive at the time called; this is a dinner, as well as a religious celebration.

What are the major ritual objects of the ceremony?

A seder plate, on which are symbols of various aspects of the Passover story.

Matzah ('MAH-tzah'), or flat, unleavened bread, similar to the bread made by the Jewish people as they fled Egypt.

What books are used? A *Haggadah* ('hah-GAH-dah'), a text in Hebrew and English that tells the Passover story and its meaning for each generation. There are hundreds of different versions of the Haggadah. Many focus on different elements of the holiday or interpret it from their own particular perspective, such as feminism or ecology, but all tell the basic story of the Exodus.

Will a guest who is not Jewish be expected to do anything other than sit? If asked to do so by the leader, they should read aloud English portions of the Haggadah.

Are there any parts of the ceremony in which a non-Jewish guest should not participate? No.

If not disruptive to the ceremony, is it OK to:

Take pictures? Not in Orthodox homes; possibly in others. Ask your host.

Use a flash? Not in Orthodox homes; possibly in others. Ask your host.

Use video recording equipment? Not in Orthodox homes; possibly in others. Ask your host.

Use audio recording equipment? Not in Orthodox homes; possibly in others. Ask your host.

Eating and drinking

Is a meal part of the celebration? Yes. It is usually served after the first part of the ritual portion of the seder.

Will there be alcoholic drinks? Wine is an integral part of the seder. Other alcoholic drinks may be served prior to or after the seder, depending upon the family's customs.

Would it be considered impolite not to eat? Yes, since the meal is central to the celebration.

Is there a grace or benediction before eating or drinking? Yes. Wait for a blessing before eating or drinking. There are usually several blessings over wine and different types of food. There is also a ritual washing of the hands.

Is there a grace or benediction after eating or drinking? Yes. This is called *birkat hamazon* ('beer-KAHT hah-mah-ZONE').

At the meal, will a guest be asked to say or do anything? If asked to do so by the leader, they should read aloud English portions of the Haggadah.

Will there be:

Dancing? No.

Music? Usually there is just singing. Guitar or piano may accompany the singing. There will not be any musical instruments at an Orthodox seder.

General guidelines and advice

Listen to the seder leader for instructions about the meaning and the order of the seder and for what to do.

❦

Shabbat Dinner

What is its significance? *Shabbat* ('shah-BAHT'), or the Sabbath, commemorates the day on which God rested after creating the world during the previous six days. The Jewish Sabbath begins at sunset on Friday and ends at nightfall on Saturday. The Shabbat dinner, which is held at home on Friday evening, is a family-oriented celebration of the Sabbath.

When does it occur? Friday evenings. Among the Orthodox, there are Shabbat dinners both in the evening and at lunchtime after synagogue.

What is the proper greeting to the celebrants? '*Shabbat shalom*' ('shah-BAHT shah-LOME'), Hebrew for 'Peaceful Sabbath'.

Before the ceremony

Are guests usually invited by a formal invitation? Yes. They may receive a phone call or be invited face to face.

If not stated explicitly, should one assume that children are invited? Yes.

If one cannot attend, what should one do? Express regrets.

Appropriate attire

Men: Ask your hosts about attire. Some may prefer jacket and tie; others may prefer more informal attire. A small head covering called a *yarmulke* ('YAHR-mihl-kah') or *kippah* ('keep-AH') is required during all Orthodox and most Masorti Shabbat dinners and at some Reform and Liberal Shabbat dinners. If required, they will be provided.

Women: Ask your hosts about attire. Some may prefer a dress or a skirt and blouse or a trouser suit. Open-toed shoes and modest jewellery are appropriate. In Orthodox homes, clothing should cover the arms, hems should reach below the knees. Do not carry a purse or similar accessory, since Jewish law prohibits labour, including carrying objects, on Shabbat.

Do not openly wear symbols of other faiths, such as a cross.

There are no rules regarding colours of clothing, but in Orthodox homes, such bright colours as red or hot pink are not appropriate.

Gifts

Is a gift customarily expected? This is entirely optional.

If one decides to give a gift, is a certain type of gift appropriate? Flowers or sweets would be welcome.

The ceremony

Welcoming the Sabbath is a joyous event and may include the following, although some may be done before guests arrive: lighting the Sabbath candles and reciting the blessing over them; reciting *kiddush* ('kee-DOOSH'), a prayer accompanied by wine or grape juice before dinner; reciting *ha'motzi* ('hah-MOH-tsee'), the blessing over bread; parents blessing their children; songs to celebrate and welcome the Sabbath.

Depending on how many rituals are observed, they may take about five to fifteen minutes.

The ceremony is usually led by the head of the household, although everyone present may participate. The Sabbath dinner is a celebration in itself and is not part of a larger service. Its duration will be that of a social dinner. Arrive at the time called, since this is a social dinner as well as a religious celebration.

What are the major ritual objects of the ceremony?

A kippah ('keep-AH'), or small head covering.

Sabbath candlesticks (two), for the ceremonial lighting of candles to welcome Shabbat and mark its beginning.

A kiddush ('kee-DOOSH') cup, for the ritual blessing over wine.

A loaf of challah ('HAH-lah'), specially prepared, braided Sabbath bread.

What books are used? A *siddur* ('SEE-door'), or prayer book, or an abbreviated version of it that is just for this purpose.

Will a guest who is not Jewish be expected to do anything other than sit? Stand when other participants stand. If asked to do so by the leader, guests should read aloud English portions of the prayer book if these do not violate their religious beliefs.

Are there any parts of the ceremony in which a non-Jewish guest should not participate? No.

If not disruptive to the ceremony, is it OK to:

Take pictures? Not in Orthodox homes; possibly in others. Ask your host.

Use a flash? Not in Orthodox homes; possibly in others. Ask your host.

Use video recording equipment? Not in Orthodox homes; possibly in others. Ask your host.

Use audio recording equipment? Not in Orthodox homes; possibly in others. Ask your host.

Eating and drinking

Is a meal part of the celebration? Yes, an integral part.

Will there be alcoholic drinks? Wine is part of the Shabbat ritual. Other alcoholic drinks may be served, depending on the family's social customs.

Would it be considered impolite to neither eat nor drink? Yes, since the meal is central to the celebration.

Is there a grace or benediction before eating or drinking? Yes. Wait for a blessing to be said before eating or drinking. The blessing over bread is called *ha'motzi* ('hah-MOH-tsee'). In some homes, there is also a ritual washing of the hands.

Is there a grace or benediction after eating or drinking? Yes. This is called *birkat hamazon* ('beer-KAHT hah-mah-ZONE'). It will be said in all Orthodox homes and in some other Jewish homes.

At the meal, will a guest be asked to say or do anything? Stand when other participants stand. If asked to do so by the leader, guests should read aloud English portions of the prayer book and join in any singing, if these do not violate their religious beliefs.

Will there be:

Dancing? No.

Music? Usually there is just singing. Guitar or piano may accompany the singing. There will not be any musical instruments at an Orthodox Shabbat dinner.

General guidelines and advice

On Shabbat, most Orthodox Jews do not drive, smoke, write, use the telephone, turn electricity on or off, cook or handle money. It is expected that guests observe the same customs while visiting an Orthodox home.

Do not expect such foods as pork or shellfish or expect to mix dairy and meat products, since Orthodox and many other Jewish households 'keep kosher' (i.e. observe the traditional Jewish dietary laws).

Orthodox men ordinarily do not shake the hands of women to whom they are not married, and Orthodox women ordinarily do not shake the hands of men to whom they are not married; nor is there public display of physical affection (such as kissing or hugging) between men and women who are not married to each other.

11

Lutheran

HISTORY AND BELIEFS

Lutherans trace their convictions back to the German monk and theologian Martin Luther (1483–1546), who sought to reform many of the doctrines and practices of the Roman Catholic Church. Objecting to the Church's teachings that one is saved by faith and by doing good works, he maintained that, according to the Bible, one is made just in God's eyes only by trusting in Jesus' accomplishments for humanity. This is distinct from any good that one does.

Luther also objected to corruption among the clergy and advocated worship in the language of the people rather than in Latin. He favoured a married, rather than a celibate, clergy.

Although the Church of Rome considered Luther disloyal and drove him out, later many priests and laity, especially in northern Germany and the Nordic countries, eventually agreed with Luther's teachings and revamped already existing churches around them.

Lutherans have worshipped in England for several centuries. The first official congregation was established in London in 1669, used by Germans and Scandinavians. By the end of the seventeenth century, two further congregations (one German and one Scandinavian) had been established.

In recent years, the number of Lutherans in Britain has been augmented by the opening of borders within the European Union, as well as the arrival of many Africans, particularly from East Africa and the Horn. Now there are Lutheran parishes and congregations in all parts of the country and Lutheran worship is conducted in a wide range of languages in Britain, reflecting Lutheranism's international character – Amharic, Cantonese, Danish, English, Estonian, Faroese, Finnish, German, Hungarian, Icelandic, Latvian, Mandarin, Norwegian, Oromo, Polish, Swahili, Swedish and Tigrinya. Taking these nationalities together, there are about 180,000 Lutherans in Britain, mainly from the Nordic countries.

UK churches: information not available
UK membership: approximately 180,000

For more information, contact:

The Lutheran Council of Great Britain
30 Thanet Street
London
WC1H 9QH
Tel: 0207 554 2900
www.lutheran.org.uk

2. THE BASIC SERVICE

The basic worship service is normally a formal liturgy that retains the traditional form of the mass, with an emphasis on the preaching of God's word and the celebration of the Lord's Supper (the ritual commemorating the Lord's Supper is known as Holy Communion or the Mass). The service includes the liturgy with hymns, psalms, Bible readings, a sermon and, in most services, Holy Communion.

Lutherans believe that the Lord's Supper is a direct encounter with God, and that Jesus Christ's body and blood are really present through the bread and wine of the Holy Communion.

The service usually lasts about one hour.

Appropriate Attire

Because the Lutheran churches in Britain include worshippers from a wide range of nationalities and cultural groups, the styles of dress can vary markedly from congregation to congregation. Sometimes national dress is worn by both women and men, particularly in the African congregations or, more generally, for special national occasions. A worshipper should not feel out of place, however, if the following basic principles are observed.

Men: Jacket and tie or smart casual clothing. Varies from congregation to congregation. No head covering is required.

Women: Dress, skirt and blouse or trousers are acceptable. Open-toed shoes and modest jewellery are fine. Hems need not reach below the knees. No head covering is required.

There are no rules regarding colours of clothing.

❧

The Sanctuary

What are the major sections of the church? The architecture of Lutheran churches varies from the most traditional gothic to avant-garde modern styles. These are the key areas in every church:

The narthex: The vestibule or entrance hall. This is at the end of the nave (see below) and opposite the altar area. Usually, the main outside door enters into the narthex.

The nave: Where congregants sit.

The choir loft: Where the choir sits.

The chancel: Includes the altar and pulpit and seating for clergy. The pastor conducts the worship from this area.

❧

The Service

When should guests arrive and where should they sit? Although this standard varies by culture and community, it is generally appropriate to arrive a few minutes early to be seated, since services typically begin at the hour called. Usually, ushers will be available to assist you in finding a seat.

If arriving late, are there times when a guest should not enter the service? Do not enter during prayers or the spoken part of the service. Entry during music is fine.

Are there times when a guest should not leave the service? Do not exit while any prayers are being recited or the sermon is being delivered. Leaving during hymns is fine. Almost everyone remains until the end. If you plan to leave by a certain time, sit near the rear of the church and leave quietly.

Who are the major officiants, leaders or participants and what do they do?

The pastor or priest, who preaches, oversees others and administers sacraments.

Assisting ministers, who aid with prayers and administering certain sacraments.

The lector, who reads the Scripture lessons.

An acolyte, who lights candles and assists with Communion and other tasks.

The choir, which leads singing.

Ushers and greeters, who welcome guests, seat them and distribute books.

The music leader, who plays an organ and directs the choir.

What are the major ritual objects of the service?

The altar, which symbolises the presence of God and at which the bread and wine of Holy Communion are consecrated.

The pulpit, which the pastor uses for preaching.

The lectern, where Scripture is read.

The baptismal font, which is used for baptising. It is usually near the front of the church.

A cross or a crucifix (a cross with a representation of the body of Jesus Christ on it).

What books are used? Bibles and hymn books will be found in the pews or chair racks, or will be handed out by the ushers.

To indicate the order of the service: There might be a separate leaflet or the pastor/priest or assisting minister will make periodic announcements.

ᘑ

Guest Behaviour during the Service

Will a guest who is not a Lutheran be expected to do anything other than sit? The level of participation depends on whether or not the guest is Christian. Christians will generally be expected to stand, kneel and sing with the congregation and read prayers aloud. Non-Christians are expected to stand with congregants, but not necessarily to kneel, sing or pray with them. Remaining seated when others are kneeling is fine.

Are there any parts of the service in which a non-Lutheran guest should not participate? Who is welcome to receive Holy Communion varies among Lutheran churches. The worship bulletin will usually state the policy for visitors.

If not disruptive to the service, is it OK to:

Take pictures? Only with prior permission from the pastor.
Use a flash? Only with prior permission from the pastor.
Use video recording equipment? Only with prior permission from the pastor.
Use audio recording equipment? Only with prior permission from the pastor.

Will contributions to the church be collected at the service? Generally, contributions are collected by ushers passing an offering plate or basket among the seated congregation. It is the guest's choice whether or not to contribute.

How much is it customary to contribute? A donation of £1 to £5 is appropriate.

ᘑ

After the Service

Is there usually a reception after the service? This will vary by location. Coffee and snacks may be served in a reception area or in the church hall. The reception may last about half an hour.

Is there a traditional form of address for clergy? The titles and greetings vary from language to language. When speaking English, usually 'Pastor' followed by the last name is appropriate; occasionally, clergy prefer being called 'Father', but this is quite unusual.

Is it OK to leave early? Yes.

✺

General Guidelines and Advice

Guests are welcome in most congregations. You may be invited to sign a guest book or to introduce yourself.

Respect the dignity of the service. Although you need not stand when the congregation does, you may feel more comfortable doing so.

Feel free to ask a worshipper in your pew for assistance in following the liturgy, should you have any difficulty.

Most Lutheran churches invite baptised Christians who receive Holy Communion in their own churches to come forward with the other communicants and receive the bread and wine. Those who are not in that category are generally welcome to come forward to receive a blessing from the pastor. Some Lutheran churches, however, admit only Lutherans who are members of churches with whom they are in fellowship to receive Holy Communion. If in doubt, ask the pastor or an usher.

✺

Special Vocabulary

Key words or phrases that it might be helpful for a visitor to know:

Holy Communion: A rite through which Lutherans believe they receive Christ's body and blood as assurance that God has forgiven their sins, and for their spiritual nourishment.

Grace: The loving mercy that God shows us in Jesus Christ.

Alleluia (Hallelujah): From the Hebrew, 'Praise ye the Lord!'

Lessons: Readings from the Bible (or Scripture), including the Old Testament, the Epistles (generally from one of the letters of St Paul or another New Testament writer) and the Gospel (a reading from Matthew, Mark, Luke or John, the 'biographers' of Jesus).

Creed: Statement of belief. Generally, one of the early Christian creeds is used, either the Apostles' Creed or the Nicene Creed.

Some Basic Beliefs

Lutherans believe:

The Law of God, as found, for example, in the Ten Commandments, tells what God expects of us and how we are to live. The Law also shows us that we fall short of God's expectations and that we are disobedient to God.

The gospel is the good news that God, in his love and mercy, does not want to see any of us punished or separated from him because of our sin.

The good news (which is what 'gospel' means) is the liberating and consoling assurance that God saves humanity and all creation through Christ, who is the eternal Son of God and is himself fully God. God acted in Christ to give us the free gift of salvation, which we receive by faith in his promises.

Some books to which a guest can refer to learn more about the Lutheran faith:

Principles of Lutheran Theology, by Carl E. Braaten (Augsburg Fortress Press, 1983).

Grace that Frees: The Lutheran Tradition, by Bradley C. Hanson (Darton, Longman and Todd, 2004).

3. HOLY DAYS AND FESTIVALS

Advent: Occurs four weeks before Christmas. The purpose is to begin preparing for Christmas and to focus on Christ. There is no traditional greeting to Lutherans for this holiday. Additional services are sometimes added to the church schedule.

Christmas: Occurs on the evening of 24 December and the day of 25 December. Marks the birth and the incarnation of God as a man. The traditional greeting to Lutherans is 'Happy Christmas' or 'Blessed Christmas'.

Lent: Begins on Ash Wednesday, which occurs six weeks before Easter. The purpose is to prepare for Easter. There is no traditional greeting to Lutherans for Lent. Between Lent and Easter, abstention from entertainment is encouraged, as is increased giving to the poor. Often, there are midweek worship services. Some churches sponsor a light soup supper once a week, with proceeds going towards combating world hunger and encouraging global peace. While traditionally, among many Christian denominations, Lent is a time of fasting or abstaining from certain foods, relatively few contemporary Lutherans now do this and such fasting is given little prominence by the Church.

Easter: Always falls on the Sunday after the first full moon that occurs on or after 21 March. Celebrates the resurrection of Jesus Christ. The traditional greeting to Lutherans is 'Happy Easter'. In worship services, the pastor may greet congregants with the words, 'He is risen!' Congregants respond with, 'He is risen, indeed!'

Pentecost Sunday: The seventh Sunday after Easter. Celebrates the coming of the Holy Spirit, which is the empowering Spirit of God in human life. This is often considered the birth of the Christian Church. There is no traditional greeting for this holiday.

Reformation Day: Occurs on 31 October. Reformation Sunday, the day on which Reformation Day is celebrated, is the Sunday before Reformation Day. Commemorates 31 October 1517, the day on which Martin Luther is said to have nailed 95 statements of belief (called the '95 Theses') on the door of the Castle Church in Wittenberg, Germany. This was then the practice for inviting scholarly debate. There is no traditional greeting for this holiday.

4. LIFE CYCLE EVENTS

Birth Ceremony

Baptism is the one-time sacrament of initiation into the family of God, the Holy Christian Church. In the Lutheran Church, infants are baptised. (Also baptised are previously unbaptised youths or adults when they confess faith in Jesus Christ and ask to join the Church.)

As a sacrament, baptism is a means by which God creates and strengthens faith and through which he assures the forgiveness of sins and the promise of eternal life with him. Baptism is done with water applied to the head of the person being initiated and in the name of the Father, the Son and the Holy Spirit (the three persons of God). It marks entry into Christian faith, not simply the birth of a child.

Typically, the baptism is part of a Sunday service. When this occurs, the service will be slightly longer than the 'basic service' described above.

Before the ceremony

Are guests usually invited by a formal invitation? Guests are usually invited by a note or phone call.

If not stated explicitly, should one assume that children are invited? Yes.

If one cannot attend, what should one do? Call the family to express congratulations or send a baptism card. These are available at most card shops.

Appropriate attire

Because the Lutheran churches in Britain include worshippers from a wide range of nationalities and cultural groups, the styles of dress can vary markedly from congregation to congregation. Sometimes national dress is worn by both women and men, particularly in the African congregations or, more generally, for special national occasions. A worshipper should not feel out of place, however, if the following basic principles are observed.

Men: Jacket and tie or smart casual clothing. Varies from congregation to congregation. No head covering is required.

Women: Dress, skirt and blouse or trousers are acceptable. Open-toed shoes and modest jewellery are fine. Hems need not reach below the knees. No head covering is required.

There are no rules regarding colours of clothing.

Gifts

Is a gift customarily expected? Yes, clothing or toys for a newborn are most frequently given. Money is not appropriate.

Should gifts be brought to the ceremony? It is customary to bring a gift to the home following the ceremony.

The ceremony

Where will the ceremony take place? Partly at the baptismal font in the main sanctuary of the church, and partly near the altar.

When should guests arrive and where should they sit? Arrive a few minutes early to be seated, since services typically begin at the hour called. Ushers will help you find a seat.

If arriving late, are there times when a guest should not enter the ceremony? Do not enter during prayers or the spoken part of the service. Entry during music is fine.

Are there times when a guest should not leave the service? Do not exit while any prayers are being recited or the sermon is being delivered. Leaving during hymns is fine. Almost everyone remains until the end. If you plan to leave by a certain time, sit near the rear of the church and leave quietly.

Who are the major officiants, leaders or participants at the ceremony and what do they do?

The pastor or priest, who presides and baptises.

An assisting minister, who leads prayers and assists the pastor.

Ushers, who greet congregants and guests and assist in seating.

The sponsors or godparents, who answer questions and confess to the Christian faith on behalf of the infant being baptised. (Parents may also serve this function.) Sponsors are not used at youth or adult baptisms, since those being baptised can speak for themselves.

What books are used? Bibles and hymn books will be found in the pews or chair racks, or will be handed out by the ushers.

To indicate the order of the service: There might be a separate leaflet or the pastor/priest or assisting minister will make periodic announcements.

Will a guest who is not a Lutheran be expected to do anything other than sit? The level of participation depends on whether or not the guest is Christian. Christians will generally be expected to stand, kneel and sing with the congregation and read prayers aloud. Non-Christians are expected to stand with congregants, but not necessarily to kneel, sing or pray with them. Remaining seated when others are kneeling is fine.

Are there any parts of the service in which a non-Lutheran guest should not participate? Who is welcome to receive Holy Communion varies among Lutheran churches. The worship bulletin will usually state the policy for visitors.

If not disruptive to the service, is it OK to:

Take pictures? Only with prior permission from the pastor.
Use a flash? Only with prior permission from the pastor.
Use video recording equipment? Only with prior permission from the pastor.
Use audio recording equipment? Only with prior permission from the pastor.

Will contributions to the church be collected at the service? Generally, contributions are collected by ushers passing an offering plate or basket among the seated congregation. It is the guest's choice whether or not to contribute.

How much is it customary to contribute? A donation of £1 to £5 is appropriate.

After the ceremony

Is there usually a reception after the ceremony? There may be a reception after the ceremony at the home of the infant's parents. This may include a meal or refreshments and presenting gifts to the baptised. Since this is generally a family affair, you should behave as you would as a guest in someone's home.

Would it be considered impolite to neither eat nor drink? No.

Is there a grace or benediction before eating or drinking? No.

Is there a grace or benediction after eating or drinking? No.

Is there a traditional greeting for the family? Offer your congratulations.

Is there a traditional form of address for clergy who may be at the reception? 'Pastor' followed by last name.

Is it OK to leave early? Yes.

Initiation Ceremony

Confirmation is a church rite in which one who was previously baptised expresses his or her faith in Jesus Christ. The ceremony is an additional liturgy added to the 'Basic Service'. In it, confirmation candidates come forward individually as their names are called and the pastor places his or her hands on the confirmation candidate's head and prays God's blessing on that person. Generally, a special verse of Scripture, selected especially for that confirmation candidate, is read.

Confirmation usually takes place in early adolescence and often in a group.

Before the ceremony

Are guests usually invited by a formal invitation? Yes.

If not stated explicitly, should one assume that children are invited? Yes.

If one cannot attend, what should one do? Send a gift or call the family to express congratulations.

Appropriate attire

Because the Lutheran churches in Britain include worshippers from a wide range of nationalities and cultural groups, the styles of dress can vary markedly from congregation to congregation. Sometimes national dress is worn by both women and men, particularly in the African congregations or, more generally, for special national occasions. A worshipper should not feel out of place, however, if the following basic principles are observed.

Men: Jacket and tie or smart casual clothing. Varies from congregation to congregation. No head covering is required.

Women: Dress, skirt and blouse or trousers are acceptable. Open-toed shoes and modest jewellery are fine. Hems need not reach below the knees. No head covering is required.

There are no rules regarding colours of clothing.

Gifts

Is a gift customarily expected? It is customary to present a gift at the confirmation of youths. In some cultures (for example the Nordic countries), confirmation is a very important social and family occasion as well as a religious rite. It is best to consult a member of the particular congregation for advice on appropriate gifts.

Should gifts be brought to the ceremony? The gift should be brought to the home after the service.

The ceremony

Where will the ceremony take place? In the main sanctuary of the church.

When should guests arrive and where should they sit? Although this standard varies by culture and community, it is generally appropriate to arrive a few minutes early to be seated, since services typically begin at the hour called.

If arriving late, are there times when a guest should not enter the ceremony? Do not enter during prayers. Usually, ushers will help you find a seat.

Are there times when a guest should not leave the ceremony? Almost everyone remains until the end. If you plan to leave by a certain time, sit near the rear of the church and leave quietly. Do not leave while any prayers are being recited or the sermon is being delivered. Departure during songs is advised.

Who are the major officiants, leaders or participants at the ceremony and what do they do?

The pastor or priest, who preaches, oversees others and administers sacraments.

The assisting ministers, who aid with prayers and certain sacraments.

Ushers and greeters, who welcome guests, seat them and distribute books.

The music leader, who plays an organ, directs the choir and leads singing.

The readers, who read lessons from Scripture.

What books are used? Bibles and hymn books will be found in the pews or chair racks, or will be handed out by the ushers.

To indicate the order of the service: There might be a separate leaflet or the pastor/priest or assisting minister will make periodic announcements.

Will a guest who is not a Lutheran be expected to do anything other than sit? The level of participation depends on whether or not the guest is Christian. Christians will generally be expected to stand, kneel and sing with the congregation and read prayers aloud. Non-Christians are expected to stand with congregants, but not necessarily to kneel, sing or pray with them. Remaining seated when others are kneeling is fine.

Are there any parts of the service in which a non-Lutheran guest should not participate? Who is welcome to receive Holy Communion varies among Lutheran churches. The worship bulletin will usually state the policy for visitors.

If not disruptive to the service, is it OK to:

Take pictures? Only with prior permission from the pastor.

Use a flash? Only with prior permission from the pastor.

Use video recording equipment? Only with prior permission from the pastor.

Use audio recording equipment? Only with prior permission from the pastor.

Will contributions to the church be collected at the service? Generally, contributions are collected by ushers passing an offering plate or basket among the seated congregation. It is the guest's choice whether or not to contribute.

How much is it customary to contribute? A donation of £1 to £5 is appropriate.

After the ceremony

Is there usually a reception after the ceremony? There may be a reception at the church in the fellowship hall. Generally, individual families plan receptions in their homes for invited guests. There will probably be light refreshments or a meal. If at home, alcoholic drinks may be served.

If it is held at the church, the reception may last about thirty minutes. If in a home or restaurant, it usually lasts at least two hours.

Would it be considered impolite to neither eat nor drink? No.

Is there a grace or benediction before eating or drinking? Guests should wait for the saying of grace or an invocation before eating.

Is there a grace or benediction after eating or drinking? There may be a benediction after the meal.

Is there a traditional greeting for the family? It is proper to congratulate the confirmation candidate and his or her family.

Is there a traditional form of address for clergy who may be at the reception? 'Pastor' followed by last name.

Is it OK to leave early? Yes.

Marriage Ceremony

A church wedding is an act of worship. In the service, the couple profess their love for and their commitment to each other before God and ask his blessing on their marriage. The same decorum exercised in any worship service should be exercised in the wedding service.

The ceremony may either be a service in itself or be part of the Holy Communion service. The bridal party will proceed in, then the pastor will read appropriate lessons from the Bible and ask the bride and groom about their lifelong commitment to one another. The pastor will deliver a brief homily, wedding vows and rings will be exchanged, and the pastor will pronounce the couple husband and wife.

If the ceremony is a service by itself, it will last fifteen to thirty minutes. If part of the celebration of Holy Communion and also depending on the music selected, it will last around half an hour.

Before the ceremony

Are guests usually invited by a formal invitation? Yes.

If not stated explicitly, should one assume that children are invited? Yes.

If one cannot attend, what should one do? Reply in writing or call and send a gift.

Appropriate attire

Because the Lutheran churches in Britain include worshippers from a wide range of nationalities and cultural groups, the styles of dress can vary markedly from congregation to congregation. Sometimes national dress is worn by both women and men, particularly in the African congregations or, more generally, for special national occasions. A worshipper should not feel out of place, however, if the following basic principles are observed.

Men: Jacket and tie or smart casual clothing. Varies from congregation to congregation. No head covering is required.

Women: Dress, skirt and blouse or trousers are acceptable. Open-toed shoes and modest jewellery are fine. Hems need not reach below the knees. No head covering is required.

There are no rules regarding colours of clothing.

Gifts

Is a gift customarily expected? Yes. Appropriate gifts are such household items as appliances, dishes, towels or blankets. The couple may also have a wish list at a local department store.

Should gifts be brought to the ceremony? If you are also invited to the reception afterwards, gifts are more often brought to the reception and placed on the gift table there.

The ceremony

Where will the ceremony take place? In the main sanctuary of the house of worship. The bridal party will stand near the altar in the chancel, the area in front of the sanctuary, which includes the altar and pulpit and seating for clergy.

When should guests arrive and where should they sit? It is appropriate to arrive before the time called for the ceremony. An usher will tell you where to sit.

If arriving late, are there times when a guest should not enter the ceremony? Do not enter during the processional or recessional or during prayer.

Are there times when a guest should not leave the ceremony? Do not leave during the processional or recessional or during prayer.

Who are the major officiants, leaders or participants at the ceremony and what do they do?

The **pastor**, who presides.

What books are used? A service book and hymnal may be used.

To indicate the order of the ceremony: There will normally be a special leaflet.

Will a guest who is not a Lutheran be expected to do anything other than sit? Guests are not expected to do anything other than sit and enjoy.

Are there any parts of the ceremony in which a guest who is not a Lutheran should not participate? Who is welcome to receive Holy Communion varies among Lutheran churches. The worship bulletin will usually state the policy for visitors.

If not disruptive to the ceremony, is it OK to:

Take pictures? Only with prior permission from the pastor.
Use a flash? Only with prior permission from the pastor.
Use video recording equipment? Only with prior permission from the pastor.
Use audio recording equipment? Only with prior permission from the pastor.

Will contributions to the church be collected at the ceremony? No.

After the ceremony

Is there usually a reception after the ceremony? Customs vary locally and by individual preference. However, there will generally be a reception at home or in a restaurant. Depending on local custom, there may also be music and dancing. The menu will vary from light refreshments and cake to a full meal. Alcoholic drinks may be served.

If at a home or restaurant, it will usually last at least two hours.

Would it be considered impolite to neither eat nor drink? Yes. If you have dietary restrictions, inform your host or hostess in advance.

Is there a grace or benediction before eating or drinking? Guests should wait for the saying of grace or an invocation before eating.

Is there a grace or benediction after eating or drinking? No.

Is there a traditional greeting for the family? Congratulate the new couple and their parents.

Is there a traditional form of address for clergy who may be at the reception? 'Pastor' followed by last name.

Is it OK to leave early? Yes.

Funerals and Mourning

For Lutherans, death is not the end of life, but the beginning of new life. While Lutherans will grieve, they do not mourn as do those who have no hope of ever seeing the deceased again or without the sure hope that those who die in faith in Jesus Christ are assured eternal life with God.

The funeral is usually a service in itself. The pastor presides. Pall-bearers carry the coffin into the funeral chapel or church sanctuary. The service will rarely last more than thirty minutes. All attending are expected to remain to the end.

Before the ceremony

How soon after the death does the funeral usually take place? There is no set period during which the funeral should occur, but it usually takes place within a week after death.

What should a non-Lutheran do upon hearing of the death of a member of that faith? Call the bereaved, visit or send a note to express your sympathy at their loss. Express your care and love for the bereaved.

Appropriate attire

Men: Jacket and tie. No head covering is required.

Women: A dress or skirt and blouse are acceptable. Open-toed shoes and modest jewellery are fine. Hems need not reach the knees. No head covering is required.

Local social customs govern, but conservative clothing and dark, sombre colours are recommended.

Gifts

Is it appropriate to send flowers or make a contribution? It is appropriate to send flowers unless the family expresses otherwise. Send them to the deceased's home or to the place where the funeral will be held.

It is also appropriate to make a donation in the form of a 'memorial' in memory of the deceased. The family will often announce, either through the funeral home or in the funeral worship folder, the preferred charity or church for memorial contributions. Memorials are often mailed or hand-delivered to the funeral home or church office. There is no standard amount to be donated.

Is it appropriate to send food? You may want to send food to the home of the bereaved for the family and their guests.

The ceremony

Where will the ceremony take place? Typically, in the church of the deceased, although it may be at a funeral chapel.

When should guests arrive and where should they sit? It is customary to arrive early enough to be seated when the service begins. Someone will tell you where and when to sit.

If arriving late, are there times when a guest should not enter the ceremony? Do not enter during the procession or prayer.

Will the bereaved family be present at the church or funeral home before the ceremony? If there is a visitation at the funeral home the night before the funeral, you can attend and express your sorrow and regret.

Is there a traditional greeting for the family? Just offer your condolences.

Will there be an open coffin? Possibly.

Is a guest expected to view the body? This is optional.

What is appropriate behaviour upon viewing the body? Stand quietly and then move on.

Who are the major officiants at the ceremony and what do they do?
The pastor, who presides.

What books are used? Bibles and hymn books will be found in the pews or chair racks, or will be handed out by the ushers.

To indicate the order of the service: There might be a separate leaflet or the pastor/priest or assisting minister will make periodic announcements.

Will a guest who is not a Lutheran be expected to do anything other than sit? The level of participation depends on whether or not the guest is Christian. Christians will generally be expected to stand, kneel and sing with the congregation and read prayers aloud. Non-Christians are expected to stand with congregants, but not necessarily to kneel, sing or pray with them. Remaining seated when others are kneeling is fine.

Are there any parts of the service in which a non-Lutheran guest should not participate? Who is welcome to receive Holy Communion varies among Lutheran churches. The worship bulletin will usually state the policy for visitors.

If not disruptive to the service, is it OK to:

Take pictures? Only with prior permission from the pastor.
Use a flash? Only with prior permission from the pastor.
Use video recording equipment? Only with prior permission from the pastor.
Use audio recording equipment? Only with prior permission from the pastor.

Will contributions to the church be collected at the ceremony?
No.

The interment

Should guests attend the interment? Yes.

Whom should one ask for directions? Either join the funeral procession or ask the funeral director for directions.

What happens at the graveside? The coffin is carried to the grave. Prayers and readings are offered. The pastor blesses the earth placed on the coffin and blesses those gathered at the graveside.

Do guests who are not Lutherans participate at the graveside service? If this does not conflict with their own religious beliefs, they recite the Lord's Prayer and join in these responses to other prayers: 'The Lord be with you' and 'And also with you'.

Comforting the bereaved

Is it appropriate to visit the home of the bereaved after the funeral? Yes, more than once is appropriate. Share in the conversation and refreshments.

Will there be a religious service at the home of the bereaved? No.

Will food be served? Possibly. If food is served, wait for the saying of grace before eating. It would be impolite not to eat, unless you have dietary restrictions. (If so, mention these to your host or hostess.) There may be alcoholic drinks, depending on the family's custom.

How soon after the funeral will a mourner usually return to a normal work schedule? Bereaved often stay home from work for several days.

How soon after the funeral will a mourner usually return to a normal social schedule? Not for several weeks after the funeral.

Are there mourning customs to which a friend who is not a Lutheran should be sensitive? No.

Are there rituals for observing the anniversary of the death? While there are no specific rituals, some congregations remember the first-year anniversary in prayers in church.

5. HOME CELEBRATIONS

Not applicable to Lutherans.

12
Methodist

1. HISTORY AND BELIEFS

The Methodist Church grew from a movement of religious renewal which touched eighteenth-century Britain, Europe and North America. Among the leaders were John and Charles Wesley, both Anglican priests, whose itinerant preaching, writing and organising drew one strand of the Evangelical Revival into a 'Connexion' of religious societies which eventually evolved into the Methodist Church.

The Wesleys emphasised the availability of God's love and grace to all. They encouraged people to turn to God for forgiveness and assurance of salvation. They promoted a disciplined and methodical piety, expressed in personal devotion, mutual accountability and social responsibility.

Although the Wesleys remained Anglicans and disavowed attempts to form a new church, Methodism eventually grew apart from the Church of England. In the nineteenth century, the original Wesleyan Connexion split into several separate churches, but most of these reunited in 1932 to form the present Methodist Church of Great Britain. In the meantime, strong missionary programmes helped plant Methodism abroad. Methodist missionaries from America followed their British colleagues to India and Africa, where they founded new churches. British Methodism today includes representatives of many partner churches from around the world.

Local Methodist churches are grouped into 'circuits', each with a team of ordained ministers (presbyters and deacons). The ministers are appointed by the annual conference, and each church elects its own church council, which initiates planning and sets local goals and policies.

UK churches: approximately 6,000
UK membership: approximately 300,000

For more information, contact:

Methodist Church House
25 Marylebone Road
London
NW1 5JR
Tel: 020 7486 5502
Email: helpdesk@methodistchurch.org.uk

2. THE BASIC SERVICE

To Methodists, worship is a congregation's encounter and communion with God and with one another in God's name. It usually includes prayer and praise – congregational singing is an important aspect of Methodist worship – Scripture readings, a sermon and sometimes Holy Communion. Most Methodist services last about one hour.

Appropriate Attire

There is no official dress code for men or women, although it is worth asking in advance whether the particular church you are visiting has a preference. In some churches, casual wear is as acceptable as smart suits or dresses.

There are no rules regarding colours of clothing.

The Sanctuary

What are the major sections of the church?

The platform or chancel: A raised section at the front of the church. This is where the leaders function.
The nave: Where congregants sit on pews or chairs.

The Service

When should guests arrive and where should they sit? Arrive five or ten minutes before the time for which the service has been called. A steward will indicate where to sit. There are usually no restrictions on where to sit.

If arriving late, are there times when a guest should not enter the service? Yes. Stewards should seat you when appropriate.

Are there times when a guest should not leave the service? No.

Who are the major officiants, leaders or participants and what do they do?

The minister, who presides, preaches and celebrates Communion. An authorised lay person may also lead aspects of the service but may not preside over Communion.

The choir or soloists, who may sing an anthem or introit (a short sung prayer performed as the congregants enter the sanctuary). Choirs are increasingly rare in Methodist churches.

What are the major ritual objects of the service?

Bible, the sacred text of Christianity, comprising the Hebrew Scriptures of the Old Testament and the Christian writings now known as the New Testament.

Pulpit or Lectern, from which worship is led, Scriptures read and expounded, and prayers offered.

Font, used for the sacrament of baptism.

Communion table, usually placed at the front centre of the sanctuary and often enclosed by a low rail.

Bread, which is eaten during Holy Communion and signifies the body of Jesus Christ.

Wine (Grape juice), which the minister presents to congregants to drink during Holy Communion and which signifies the blood of Jesus Christ.

What books are used? Hymns and Psalms (Methodist Publishing

House, 1983) and a Bible. Methodists have no official Bible translation, although the New Revised Standard Version, New International Version and Good News Bible are commonly used translations.

To indicate the order of the service: A printed order of service may be provided and periodic announcements will be made by the minister or lay leader.

⁂

Guest Behaviour during the Service

Will a guest who is not a Methodist be expected to do anything other than sit? Standing with the congregation and reading prayers aloud and singing with congregants are all welcome, but optional. Guests are encouraged to participate if this does not compromise their personal beliefs.

Are there any parts of the service in which a guest who is not a Methodist should not participate? No. Methodists invite all to receive Holy Communion, if this is in accordance with the discipline of their own church or faith. However, guests should also feel free to remain seated as others go forward for Communion. Likewise, if Communion bread and cups are passed among the pews, feel free to pass them along without partaking.

If not disruptive to the service, is it OK to:

Take pictures? Possibly. Ask stewards.
Use a flash? Possibly. Ask stewards.
Use video recording equipment? Possibly. Ask stewards.
Use audio recording equipment? Possibly. Ask stewards.

Will contributions to the church be collected at the service? Yes. The offering plate will be passed through the congregation during the service.

How much is it customary to contribute? There is no customary contribution: it is a free-will offering, and entirely voluntary.

꙾

After the Service

Is there usually a reception after the service? Yes, in the church's hall or reception area. It usually lasts less than thirty minutes, and coffee and tea are ordinarily served. It is not considered impolite to neither eat nor drink. There is no grace or benediction before or after eating or drinking.

Is there a traditional form of address for clergy who may be at the reception? 'Reverend' is a formal style of address; clergy will often prefer informality once introduced.

Is it OK to leave early? Yes.

꙾

General Guidelines and Advice

The chief potential for mistake occurs during Holy Communion. Feel free not to partake if you cannot in good conscience do so. But Christian guests should also be aware that the Methodist Church never refuses Communion to anyone.

The cups at Holy Communion always contain grape juice, not wine. Children, as well as adults, are welcome to partake or to receive a blessing.

꙾

Some Basic Beliefs

Methodists believe:

In the common doctrinal heritage of all Christians, expressed in the Scriptures and the Creeds.

In the universality of God's grace, so that the salvation achieved through Jesus Christ is accessible to everyone.

In the presence of God the Holy Spirit in all people, drawing them to faith and helping them to grow in love for God.

In the requirement to put faith into practice in daily living and social responsibility.

A basic book to which a guest can refer to learn more about the Methodist Church:

Called by Name: Being a Member in the Methodist Church (Methodist Publishing House, 2002).

3. HOLY DAYS AND FESTIVALS

Advent: Occurs four weeks before Christmas. The purpose is to focus on the birth of Jesus Christ at Christmas and on the future fulfilment of God's purpose for the world. There is no traditional greeting for this season.

Christmas: Occurs on the evening of 24 December and the day of 25 December. Marks the birth of Jesus, the incarnation of God as a human being. The traditional greeting is 'Merry Christmas'.

Lent: Begins on Ash Wednesday, which occurs six weeks before Easter. The purpose is to prepare for Easter by tracing the life of Jesus, through to his crucifixion on Good Friday. Between Lent and Easter, fasting and abstention from entertainment are encouraged, as is increased giving to the poor. Often there are midweek worship services or devotional meetings. There are no traditional greetings for this season.

Easter: Always falls on the Sunday after the first full moon that occurs on or after 21 March. Celebrates the resurrection of Jesus Christ. The traditional greeting to Methodists is 'Happy Easter'.

Pentecost Sunday: The seventh Sunday after Easter. Celebrates the coming of the Holy Spirit, who is the empowering Spirit of God in human life. This is often considered the birth of the Christian Church. There are no traditional greetings for this holiday.

4. LIFE CYCLE EVENTS

Birth Ceremony

Baptism initiates a person into Christianity. It is administered once to each person, usually during infancy. The major ritual object used during the ceremony is a baptismal font, which holds the baptismal water. The minister sprinkles or pours water on the person's head or immerses the person in water. This signifies the washing away of sins and participation in the death and resurrection of Jesus Christ. God is invoked to strengthen this new Christian, and the congregation, as well as the parents and godparents, pledge to nurture him or her in the Christian faith and life.

Baptism is part of the larger weekly congregational Sunday morning service, which usually lasts about an hour.

Before the ceremony

Are guests usually invited by a formal invitation? Yes.

If not stated explicitly, should one assume that children are invited? Yes.

If one cannot attend, what should one do? Send flowers or a gift, or telephone or email the parents with your congratulations and your regrets that you cannot attend.

Appropriate attire

There is no official dress code for men or women, although smart or smart casual attire would be appropriate for guests at a baptism.

There are no rules regarding colours of clothing.

Gifts

Is a gift customarily expected? No, but it is appropriate. Gifts such as savings bonds or baby clothes or toys are commonly given.

Should gifts be brought to the ceremony? Usually gifts can be brought to the reception.

The ceremony

Where will the ceremony take place? In the parents' church.

When should guests arrive and where should they sit? Arrive about ten minutes before the time for which the service has been called. Stewards will indicate where to sit. There are usually no restrictions on where to sit, but places may have been specially reserved for guests, usually near the front of the congregation.

If arriving late, are there times when a guest should not enter the ceremony? Yes. Stewards will seat you when appropriate.

Are there times when a guest should not leave the ceremony? No.

Who are the major officiants, leaders or participants in the ceremony and what do they do?

The minister, who will baptise the child.

What books are used? Hymns and Psalms (Methodist Publishing House, 1983) and a Bible. Methodists have no official Bible translation, although the New Revised Standard Version, New International Version and Good News Bible are commonly used translations. The liturgy for baptism will usually follow that set out in *The Methodist Worship Book* (Methodist Publishing House, 1999).

To indicate the order of the ceremony: A printed liturgy may be followed and periodic announcements will be made by the minister.

Will a guest who is not a Methodist be expected to do anything other than sit? Standing with the congregation and reading prayers aloud and singing with congregants are all welcome, but optional. Guests are encouraged to participate if this does not compromise their personal beliefs.

Are there any parts of the service in which a guest who is not a Methodist should not participate? No. Methodists invite all to receive Holy Communion, if this is in accordance with the discipline of their own church or faith. However, guests should also feel free to remain seated as others go forward for Communion. Likewise, if Communion bread and cups are passed among the pews, feel free to pass them along without partaking.

If not disruptive to the service, is it OK to:

Take pictures? Possibly. Ask stewards.

Use a flash? Possibly. Ask stewards.
Use video recording equipment? Possibly. Ask stewards.
Use audio recording equipment? Possibly. Ask stewards.

Will contributions to the church be collected at the service? Yes. The offering plate will be passed through the congregation during the service.

How much is it customary to contribute? There is no customary contribution: it is a free-will offering, and entirely voluntary.

After the ceremony

Is there usually a reception after the service? Yes, in the church's hall or reception area. It usually lasts less than thirty minutes, and coffee and tea are ordinarily served.

It is not considered impolite to neither eat nor drink. There is no grace or benediction before or after eating or drinking.

Is there a traditional form of address for clergy who may be at the reception? 'Reverend' is a formal style of address; clergy will often prefer informality once introduced.

Is it OK to leave early? Yes.

Initiation Ceremony

Confirmation is a Methodist's first formal and public profession of faith. The candidates affirm for themselves the Christian faith into which they were baptised (usually as infants) and are received into membership of their local church.

The fifteen-minute ceremony is part of a larger Sunday morning service, which lasts about an hour.

Before the ceremony

Are guests usually invited by a formal invitation? Yes.

If not stated explicitly, should one assume that children are invited?
Yes.

If one cannot attend, what should one do? Send flowers or a gift,
or telephone or email the confirmation candidate with your congratulations and your regrets that you cannot attend.

Appropriate attire

There is no official dress code for men or women, although smart or
smart casual attire would be appropriate for guests at a confirmation.

There are no rules regarding colours of clothing.

Gifts

Is a gift customarily expected? No.

The ceremony

Where will the ceremony take place? In the confirmation candidate's church.

When should guests arrive and where should they sit? Arrive
about ten minutes before the time for which the service has been called.
Stewards will indicate where to sit. There are usually no restrictions
on where to sit, but places may have been specially reserved for guests,
usually near the front of the congregation.

*If arriving late, are there times when a guest should not enter the
ceremony?* Yes. Stewards will seat you when appropriate.

Are there times when a guest should not leave the ceremony? No.

*Who are the major officiants, leaders or participants at the
ceremony and what do they do?*

The minister, who confirms the candidate.

What books are used? Hymns and Psalms (Methodist Publishing House, 1983) and a Bible. Methodists have no official Bible

translation, although the New Revised Standard Version, New International Version and Good News Bible are commonly used translations. The liturgy for confirmation will usually follow that set out in *The Methodist Worship Book* (Methodist Publishing House, 1999).

To indicate the order of the ceremony: A printed liturgy may be followed and periodic announcements will be made by the minister.

Will a guest who is not a Methodist be expected to do anything other than sit? Standing with the congregation and reading prayers aloud and singing with congregants are all welcome, but optional. Guests are encouraged to participate if this does not compromise their personal beliefs.

Are there any parts of the service in which a guest who is not a Methodist should not participate? No. Methodists invite all to receive Holy Communion, if this is in accordance with the discipline of their own church or faith. However, guests should also feel free to remain seated as others go forward for Communion. Likewise, if Communion bread and cups are passed among the pews, feel free to pass them along without partaking.

If not disruptive to the service, is it OK to:

Take pictures? Possibly. Ask stewards.
Use a flash? Possibly. Ask stewards.
Use video recording equipment? Possibly. Ask stewards.
Use audio recording equipment? Possibly. Ask stewards.

Will contributions to the church be collected at the service? Yes. The offering plate will be passed through the congregation during the service.

How much is it customary to contribute? There is no customary contribution: it is a free-will offering, and entirely voluntary.

After the ceremony

Is there usually a reception after the service? Yes, in the church's hall or reception area. It usually lasts less than thirty minutes, and coffee and tea are ordinarily served.

It is not considered impolite to neither eat nor drink. There is no grace or benediction before or after eating or drinking.

Is there a traditional form of address for clergy who may be at the reception? 'Reverend' is a formal style of address; clergy will often prefer informality once introduced.

Is it OK to leave early? Yes.

❦

Marriage Ceremony

Marriage is the uniting of a man and a woman in a union that is intended – and that is pledged – to be lifelong. The marriage ceremony is a service in itself. It may last between thirty and sixty minutes.

Before the ceremony

Are guests usually invited by a formal invitation? Yes.

If not stated explicitly, should one assume that children are invited? No.

If one cannot attend, what should one do? RSVP with your regrets and send a gift.

Appropriate attire

There is no official dress code for men or women, although smart attire would be appropriate for guests at a wedding.

There are no rules regarding colours of clothing.

Gifts

Is a gift ordinarily expected? Yes. Such gifts as small appliances, sheets, towels or other household gifts are appropriate.

Should gifts be brought to the ceremony? They are usually taken to the reception and given to the couple there.

The ceremony

Where will the ceremony take place? Usually in the main sanctuary of a church.

When should guests arrive and where should they sit? Arrive early. Depending on the setting, ushers may show guests where to sit.

If arriving late, are there times when a guest should not enter the ceremony? Ushers will assist latecomers.

Are there times when a guest should not leave the ceremony? No.

Who are the major officiants, leaders or participants at the ceremony and what do they do?

The minister, who officiates.
The bride and groom.
The wedding party.

What books are used? Possibly a hymnal.

To indicate the order of the ceremony: A printed order of service will be provided.

Will a guest who is not a Methodist be expected to do anything other than sit? Standing with the congregation and reading prayers aloud and singing with congregants are all welcome, but optional. Guests are encouraged to participate if this does not compromise their personal beliefs.

Are there any parts of the service in which a guest who is not a Methodist should not participate? No. Methodists invite all to receive Holy Communion, if this is in accordance with the discipline of their own church or faith. However, guests should also feel free to remain seated as others go forward for Communion. Likewise, if Communion bread and cups are passed among the pews, feel free to pass them along without partaking.

If not disruptive to the service, is it OK to:

Take pictures? Possibly. Ask ushers.
Use a flash? Possibly. Ask ushers.

Use video recording equipment? Possibly. Ask ushers.
Use audio recording equipment? Possibly. Ask ushers.

Will contributions to the church be collected at the ceremony?
No.

After the ceremony

Is there usually a reception after the ceremony? There is often a reception that may last at least two hours. It may be at a hotel or other hired venue. Ordinarily, food and drinks are served and there is dancing and music. Alcoholic drinks may be served.

Would it be considered impolite to neither eat nor drink? No.

Is there a grace or benediction before eating or drinking? There will sometimes be a grace said before eating.

Is there a grace or benediction after eating or drinking? No.

Is there a traditional greeting for the family? No. Just offer your congratulations.

Is there a traditional form of address for clergy who may be at the reception? 'Reverend' is a formal style of address; clergy will often prefer informality once introduced.

Is it OK to leave early? Yes, but usually only after toasts have been made and the wedding cake has been served.

Funerals and Mourning

The Methodist Church affirms that the faithful can look forward to life with God after death.

Funerals have as their purposes: (1) expressing grief and comforting one another in our bereavement, (2) celebrating the life of the deceased, and (3) affirming faith in life with God after death. Which of these is most emphasised at the funeral depends on the circumstances of the death and the extent of the faith of the deceased.

Before the ceremony

How soon after the death will the funeral usually take place?
Usually within one to two weeks.

What should a non-Methodist do upon hearing of the death of a member of that faith? Telephone or visit the bereaved, or send a card or letter of sympathy.

Appropriate attire

There is no official dress code for men or women, although smart attire would be appropriate for guests at a wedding.

There are no rules regarding colours of clothing, but sombre, dark colours are recommended, unless the bereaved family has requested otherwise.

Gifts

Is it appropriate to send flowers or make a contribution? Usually, although this can be checked in advance with the funeral director. Send flowers to the home of the bereaved. Contributions are also optional. The recommended charity may be mentioned in the deceased's obituary.

Is it appropriate to send food? No.

The ceremony

Where will the ceremony take place? At a church, cemetery chapel or crematorium.

When should guests arrive and where should they sit? Arrive early. Stewards will advise where to sit.

If arriving late, are there times when a guest should not enter the ceremony? No.

Will the bereaved family be present at the church or funeral home before the ceremony? Possibly.

Is there a traditional greeting for the family? Simply express your condolences.

Will there be an open coffin? Not usually.

Is a guest expected to view the body? This is entirely optional.

What is appropriate behaviour upon viewing the body? Silent prayer.

Who are the major officiants at the ceremony and what do they do?

A minister, who officiates.

To indicate the order of the ceremony: A printed order of service will usually be provided.

Will a guest who is not a Methodist be expected to do anything other than sit? No.

Are there any parts of the service in which a guest who is not a Methodist should not participate? No.

If not disruptive to the ceremony, is it OK to:

Take pictures? No.
Use a flash? No.
Use video recording equipment? No.
Use audio recording equipment? No.

Will contributions to the church be collected at the ceremony? No.

The interment

Should guests attend the interment? Yes.

Whom should one ask for directions? The funeral director.

What happens at the graveside? Prayers are recited by the minister and the body is committed to the ground. If there has been a cremation, which is done privately before the service, the ashes are either buried or put in a vault.

Do guests who are not Methodists participate at the graveside ceremony? No. They are simply present.

Comforting the bereaved

Is it appropriate to visit the home of the bereaved after the funeral? Yes, at any mutually convenient time. How long one stays depends on your closeness to the bereaved. Typically, one stays about thirty to forty-five minutes.

Will there be a religious service at the home of the bereaved? No.

Will food be served? No.

How soon after the funeral will a mourner usually return to a normal work schedule? This is entirely at the discretion of the bereaved.

How soon after the funeral will a mourner usually return to a normal social schedule? This is entirely at the discretion of the bereaved.

Are there mourning customs to which a friend who is not a Methodist should be sensitive? No.

Are there rituals for observing the anniversary of the death? There may be a service commemorating the deceased.

5. HOME CELEBRATIONS

Not applicable to Methodists.

13

Mormon

The Church of Jesus Christ of Latter-day Saints

1. HISTORY AND BELIEFS

The Church of Jesus Christ of Latter-day Saints, the largest indigenous religious group in the USA, was founded by Joseph Smith in the early nineteenth century. Living in upstate New York, Smith had a vision in 1820 in which God and Jesus Christ appeared to him. Three years later, the angel Moroni told him of the location of gold tablets containing God's revelations. In 1830, Smith published a translation of these revelations entitled *The Book of Mormon*. He soon became the 'seer, translator, prophet and apostle' of a group committed to restoring the church established centuries before by Christ.

Latter-day Saints stressed the coming of Christ's kingdom to earth and encouraged others to adhere to the teachings of the Saviour.

Smith's group moved first to Ohio, and then to Missouri, where violence ensued prompted by their polygamy and their anti-slavery stance. Persecution forced the group to move to Illinois, where they built their own city and named it Nauvoo. In 1844, while imprisoned for destroying an opposition printing press, Smith was killed by a mob that attacked the jail.

Schisms erupted amid the subsequent leadership vacuum and concern over polygamy, a practice that Smith had said in 1843 had come to him in a vision and that became church doctrine in 1852. Most Latter-day Saints followed the leadership of Brigham Young, who led them into the Great Salt Lake area of what is now Utah. Latter-day Saints are headquartered there to this day.

While many Latter-day Saints' beliefs are similar to orthodox

Christian ideas, Smith uniquely taught that God, although omniscient, has a material body. He taught that through repentance and baptism by immersion, anyone can gain entrance to Christ's earthly kingdom. Through 'proxies' who receive baptism in a Latter-day Saints' temple, the dead may also share in the highest of post-mortal rewards or blessings.

The Church teaches that men and women are equal in the eyes of the Lord and that they cannot achieve the highest eternal rewards without each other.

The charge given by Jesus to Matthew, 'Go ye unto all the world' to share the teachings of his gospel, motivates the Church's more than 50,000 full-time missionaries around the world. Most are college-age males who serve for two years at their own expense. Their success has led to the Church currently having more than 28,000 congregations in 160 nations and territories around the world.

In addition to churches, where worship services are conducted, temples are located around the world. These are closed on Sundays, but open every other day of the week for marriages and other sacred ordinances. Only faithful members of the Church may enter a temple.

UK churches: 336
UK temples: 2
UK membership: 185,000

For more information, contact:

The Church of Jesus Christ of Latter-day Saints
England London Mission
64–68 Exhibition Road
London
SW7 2PA
Tel: 0207 584 7553

2. THE BASIC SERVICE

The basic service is called a 'sacrament meeting'. It includes an opening song sung by the congregation; an opening prayer assigned in advance and offered from the pulpit by a lay member of the congregation; a 'sacrament hymn' sung by the congregation; 'sacrament prayers' recited by a young (usually sixteen- to eighteen-year-old) lay priest on the bread and the water of Communion and upon their distribution among congregants by teenagers on trays and in individual cups; brief talks by one or more youths of the congregation on a subject of their choice related to the Gospels; a sermon, delivered by a lay member of the congregation; a closing song by the congregation; and a benediction or closing prayer offered by a congregant.

The sacrament represents a reminder of the crucifixion and of the atonement of Jesus for the sins of humanity. It also renews the covenants congregants made when they were baptised into the Church.

The service usually lasts slightly over an hour.

Appropriate Attire

Men: A suit or jacket and tie. No head covering required.

Women: A dress or a skirt and blouse. No head covering required, but the overall fashion statement should be conservative and dignified. Hems should be near the knees. Open-toed shoes and modest jewellery are permissible.

Modest and dignified clothing is appreciated.

The Sanctuary

What are the major sections of the church?

The chapel: Where the worship service is held.
The pulpit: Where the presiding officer and speakers sit.
The sacrament table: Where the lay priests officiate.
The pews: Where congregants sit.

❧

The Service

When should guests arrive and where should they sit? Arrive early and sit where you wish.

If arriving late, are there times when a guest should not enter the service? Do not enter during Communion.

Are there times when a guest should not leave the service? Do not leave during Communion unless absolutely necessary.

Who are the major officiants, leaders or participants and what do they do?

A bishop, who presides over the service.
Two bishop's counsellors, assistants to the bishop. The bishop and his two counsellors take weekly turns conducting the worship service.

What are the major ritual objects of the service? The bread and water of the Sacrament (the Communion), which are passed among congregants on trays and in individual cups.

What books are used? The King James Version of the Bible and *The Book of Mormon, The Doctrine and Covenants, The Hymns of the Church of Jesus Christ of Latter-day Saints*, and *The Pearl of Great Price* (Church of Jesus Christ of Latter-day Saints). The Bible and other scriptures are used only by those conducting the service, but congregants may refer to their personal copies of the scriptures to follow along, if they wish.

To indicate the order of the service: A programme may be distributed.

❧

Guest Behaviour during the Service

Will a guest who is not a Latter-day Saint be expected to do anything other than sit? Guests of other faiths are invited to sing and pray with the congregation, but they are not expected to do so, especially if participating would violate their own religious beliefs. One of the few times the congregation stands during the service is sometimes midway through the service during the singing of the 'Intermediate Hymn'. Again, guests are invited to stand, but are not obligated to do so.

Are there any parts of the service in which a guest who is not a Latter-day Saint should not participate? No, although it is one's personal choice whether to receive the Sacrament.

If not disruptive to the service, is it OK to:

Take pictures? No.
Use a flash? No.
Use video recording equipment? No.
Use audio recording equipment? No.

Will contributions to the church be collected at the service? No.

❧

After the Service

Is there usually a reception after the service? No.

Is there a traditional form of address for clergy whom a guest may meet? The chief officiant is referred to as 'Bishop', followed by his last name. His counsellors are addressed as 'Brother', followed by their last names.

❧

General Guidelines and Advice

There is no kneeling at Latter-day Saint services.

❧

Special Vocabulary

Key words or phrases that it might be helpful for a visitor to know:
Sacrament: The Communion of bread and water.

'Brother' and 'Sister': Terms for fellow members of the Church.

᠅

Some Basic Beliefs

Mormons believe:

The Godhead is composed of God the Father; his Son, Jesus Christ; and the Holy Ghost. They are considered one in purpose, but are separate in being.

Revelation from God did not cease nearly 2,000 years ago with the crucifixion of Jesus Christ. Rather, it has continued through the centuries through various living prophets. The presidents of the Church are considered to be prophets in the same sense that Moses and other biblical leaders were also prophets.

The Book of Mormon is divinely inspired scripture, as is the Holy Bible. They are used side by side in Church curricula.

The Word of Wisdom, a health code divinely revealed in 1833, forbids the use of tobacco, alcoholic drinks, tea and coffee, and emphasises a healthy diet and physical and spiritual fitness.

The biblical principle of tithing, or donating 10 per cent of one's income to the Church, is adhered to by faithful members.

A professional clergy is not needed. Instead, churches are led and staffed by lay members without financial compensation.

Some basic books to which a guest can refer to learn more:

The Book of Mormon (Church of Jesus Christ of Latter-day Saints).
The Doctrine and Covenants (Church of Jesus Christ of Latter-day Saints).
The Pearl of Great Price (Church of Jesus Christ of Latter-day Saints).
Our Search for Happiness, M. Russell Ballard (Deseret Books, 1993).
The Book of Mormon: Annotated and Explained, annotated by Jana Riess (SkyLight Paths Publishing, 2005).

3. HOLY DAYS AND FESTIVALS

Christmas: Always falls on 25 December. Celebrates the birth of Christ. A traditional greeting for this holiday is 'Merry Christmas'.

Easter: Usually occurs in April. Commemorates the death and resurrection of Jesus. Always falls on the Sunday after the first full moon that occurs on or after the spring equinox of 21 March. There is no traditional greeting for this holiday.

4. LIFE CYCLE EVENTS

Birth Ceremony

The ceremony for the blessing and naming of a newborn infant is part of a regular worship service on the first Sunday of the month. The ceremony, which is the same for males and females, consists of a brief blessing. The worship service of which the blessing is a part lasts slightly more than one hour.

Before the ceremony

Are guests usually invited by a formal invitation? Invitations are usually fairly informal and often given verbally.

If not stated explicitly, should one assume that children are invited? Yes.

If one cannot attend, what should one do? RSVP with regrets.

Appropriate attire

Men: A suit or jacket and tie. No head covering required.

Women: A dress or a skirt and blouse. No head covering required, but the overall fashion statement should be conservative and dignified. Hems should be near the knees. Open-toed shoes and modest jewellery are permissible.

Modest and dignified clothing is appreciated.

Gifts

Is a gift customarily expected? No.

Should gifts be brought to the ceremony? See above.

The ceremony

Where will the ceremony take place? In the parents' church.

When should guests arrive and where should they sit? Arrive early and sit wherever you wish.

If arriving late, are there times when a guest should not enter the ceremony? Do not enter during Communion.

Are there times when a guest should not leave the ceremony? Do not leave during Communion.

Who are the major officiants, leaders or participants at the ceremony and what do they do?

The child's father, a lay leader or another designated holder of the priesthood, who blesses the child.
A bishop, who presides over the service.
Two bishop's counsellors, assistants to the bishop.

What books are used? No books are used for the blessing itself. Used for the rest of the worship service, of which the blessing is a part, are the King James Version of the Bible and *The Hymns of the Church of Jesus Christ of Latter-day Saints, The Book of Mormon, The Doctrine of Covenants* and *The Pearl of Great Price* (Church of Jesus Christ of Latter-day Saints). The Bible and other scriptures are used only by those conducting the service, but congregants may refer to their personal copies of the scriptures to follow along, if they wish.

To indicate the order of the ceremony: A programme may be distributed.

Will a guest who is not a Latter-day Saint be expected to do anything other than sit? Guests of other faiths are invited to sing and pray with the congregation, but they are not expected to do so, especially if participating would violate their own religious beliefs. One of the few times the congregation stands during the service is sometimes midway through the service during the singing of the 'Intermediate Hymn'. Again, guests are invited to stand, but are not obligated to do so.

Are there any parts of the ceremony in which a guest who is not a Latter-day Saint should not participate? No, although it is one's personal choice whether to receive the Sacrament.

If not disruptive to the ceremony, is it OK to:

Take pictures? No.
Use a flash? No.
Use video recording equipment? No.
Use audio recording equipment? No.

Will contributions to the church be collected at the ceremony? No.

After the ceremony

Is there usually a reception after the ceremony? No.

Is there a traditional form of address for clergy whom a guest may meet? The chief officiant is referred to as 'Bishop', followed by his last name. His counsellors are addressed as 'Brother', followed by their last names.

Initiation Ceremony

Baptism follows the biblical example of immersion and is for the remission of one's sins. Since young children are incapable of sin, they are not baptised until the age of eight, which is considered the age of moral accountability. The baptismal ceremony may be for an individual child or for a group of children or for an adult convert. The baptism service lasts about thirty to sixty minutes.

The individual is 'confirmed' as a member of the Church by the laying on of hands by a member of the lay priesthood.

Before the ceremony

Are guests usually invited by a formal invitation? Invitations are usually issued verbally.

If not stated explicitly, should one assume that children are invited? Yes.

If one cannot attend, what should one do? RSVP with regrets.

Appropriate attire

Men: A suit or jacket and tie. No head covering required.

Women: A dress or a skirt and blouse. No head covering required, but the overall fashion statement should be conservative and dignified. Open-toed shoes and modest jewellery are permissible.

Modest and dignified clothing is appreciated.

Gifts

Is a gift customarily expected? No.

Should gifts be brought to the ceremony? See above.

The Ceremony

Where will the ceremony take place? There is a service in the chapel or in the baptismal font room of the church, then guests, family and the child proceed to the baptistery for the baptism itself.

When should guests arrive and where should they sit? Arrive at the time for which the ceremony has been called and sit wherever you wish.

If arriving late, are there times when a guest should not enter the ceremony? Do not enter during the baptism unless absolutely necessary.

Are there times when a guest should not leave the ceremony? Do not leave during the baptism unless absolutely necessary.

Who are the major officiants, leaders or participants at the ceremony and what do they do?

A presiding officer, usually (but not necessarily) a bishop, who presides over the service.
The father or a lay priest, who performs the baptismal immersion.
Other lay members, who deliver the invocation and benediction and deliver a brief talk.

What books are used? No texts are distributed, although speakers may refer to the Scriptures.

To indicate the order of the ceremony: A programme may be distributed.

Will a guest who is not a Latter-day Saint be expected to do anything other than sit? No.

Are there any parts of the ceremony in which a guest who is not a Latter-day Saint should not participate? No.

If not disruptive to the ceremony, is it OK to:

Take pictures? No.
Use a flash? No.
Use video recording equipment? No.
Use audio recording equipment? No.

Will contributions to the church be collected at the ceremony? No.

After the ceremony

Is there usually a reception after the ceremony? Depending on the family, there may be a reception at their home or elsewhere. If so, light food may be served, but no alcoholic drinks.

Would it be considered impolite to neither eat nor drink? No.

Is there a grace or benediction before eating or drinking? Possibly.

Tradition calls for a prayer of thanks for the food.

Is there a grace or benediction after eating or drinking? No.

Is there a traditional greeting for the family? Just offer your congratulations.

Is there a traditional form of address for clergy who may be at the reception? A bishop is referred to as 'Bishop', followed by his last name. Other officiants are addressed as 'Brother', followed by their last names.

Is it OK to leave early? Yes.

Marriage Ceremony

Reflecting the Church's emphasis on strong family solidarity and the potential for eternal family relationships, Latter-day Saints believe that marriage performed in a Church temple need not end at death, but, instead, has the potential of continuing for ever. Also reflecting Church interpretations of the 'strict morality' taught by Jesus are proscriptions against adultery and prescriptions for absolute fidelity during marriage.

Before the ceremony

Are guests usually invited by a formal invitation? Yes.

If not stated explicitly, should one assume that children are invited? Children do not attend a marriage ceremony performed in the temples, but they may be invited to a ceremony performed in a church or a civil ceremony performed elsewhere.

If one cannot attend, what should one do? RSVP with regrets.

Appropriate attire

Men: A suit or jacket and tie. No head covering required.

Women: A dress or a skirt and blouse. No head covering required, but the overall fashion statement should be conservative and dignified. Hems should be near the knees. Open-toed shoes and modest jewellery are permissible.

Modest and dignified clothing is appreciated.

Gifts

Is a gift customarily expected? The option to present a gift (and the nature of the gift) is left to the invited individual.

Should gifts be brought to the ceremony? Gifts are traditionally presented at postnuptial receptions.

The ceremony

Where will the ceremony take place? Members of the Church are encouraged to be married in one of its temples, which are located around the world. A temple, which is different from a local church building where worship services are conducted, is closed on Sundays, but open every other day of the week for marriages and other sacred ordinances.

In the UK, an initial marriage service will typically take place in a Latter-day Saint chapel and will be open to all. Following the service, a reception will be held, then the couple will go to a temple on the same day. Only faithful members of the Church may enter a temple. Guests invited to the temple marriage ceremony must present a 'temple recommend' issued by their bishop to indicate that they are, indeed, faithful members.

A couple may also choose to be married in a local church meeting house, a home or another location.

When should guests arrive and where should they sit? Arrive at the time for which the service is called and sit wherever you wish.

If arriving late, are there times when a guest should not enter the ceremony? No.

Are there times when a guest should not leave the ceremony? Leaving early is discouraged.

*Who are the major officiants, leaders or participants at the
ceremony and what do they do?* Authorised clergy perform the ceremony.

What books are used? Possibly Scriptures.

*Will a guest who is not a Latter-day Saint be expected to do
anything other than sit?* No.

*Are there any parts of the ceremony in which a guest who is not
a Latter-day Saint should not participate?* All guests only observe
the ceremony.

If not disruptive to the ceremony, is it OK to:

Take pictures? No.
Use a flash? No.
Use video recording equipment? No.
Use audio recording equipment? No.

Will contributions to the church be collected at the ceremony? No.

After the ceremony

Is there usually a reception after the ceremony? There is usually
a reception, but where it is held and what is done there are the
personal choice of the bride and groom.

Would it be considered impolite to neither eat nor drink? No.

Is there a grace or benediction before eating or drinking? Usually.
This is the choice of the hosts.

Is there a grace or benediction after eating or drinking? No.

Is there a traditional greeting for the family? No. Just offer your
congratulations.

*Is there a traditional form of address for clergy who may be at
the reception?* A bishop is referred to as 'Bishop', followed by his
last name. His counsellors are addressed as 'Brother', followed by
their last names.

Is it OK to leave early? Yes, since at the traditional open-house type of reception guests stay as long as they feel is appropriate.

.·彩·.

Funerals and Mourning

Latter-day Saints believe that all who have ever lived on earth are literally the spiritual children of God and resided with him in a pre-mortal existence. The same with those who will ever live on earth. Through the resurrection of Jesus, all will be resurrected and through atonement and obedience to his gospel, all have the opportunity for salvation.

A Latter-day Saint funeral is a service in itself. The length of the service varies according to the programme outlined by the family, but it usually lasts about sixty to ninety minutes.

Before the ceremony

How soon after the death does the funeral usually take place? There is no set limit, although typically it occurs within one to two weeks after the death. The timing of the funeral is solely the choice of the immediate family and depends on circumstances.

What should someone who is not a Latter-day Saint do upon hearing of the death of a member of that faith? Visit, telephone or write to the family, expressing your condolences and offering your assistance, if needed.

Appropriate attire

Men: A suit or jacket and tie. No head covering required.

Women: A dress, suit or a skirt and blouse. No head covering required, but the overall fashion statement should be conservative and digni-fied. Hems should be near the knees. Open-toed shoes and modest jewellery are permissible.

Modest and dignified clothing is appreciated.

Gifts

Is it appropriate to send flowers or make a contribution? It is appropriate to send flowers. These may be sent before the funeral, to the funeral directors.

Is it appropriate to send food? Food for the bereaved family members is usually prepared by the women's organisation of the local congregation.

The ceremony

Where will the ceremony take place? Either in a church or funeral home, or near the graveside.

When should guests arrive and where should they sit? Arrive at the time for which the service has been called. Sit wherever you wish.

If arriving late, are there times when a guest should not enter the ceremony? No.

Will the bereaved family be present at the church or the funeral home before the ceremony? Sometimes.

Is there a traditional greeting for the family? No. Just offer your condolences.

Will there be an open coffin? Rarely. This is done at the choice of the family.

Is a guest expected to view the body? Viewing is entirely optional.

What is appropriate behaviour upon viewing the body? Observe it with dignity and reverence.

Who are the major officiants at the ceremony and what do they do?

The officer of the church, who conducts the service. This person is chosen by the family, but is typically the bishop of the congregation to which the deceased belonged.

Speakers, who deliver eulogies.

What books are used? Speakers will use Scriptures. Hymn books may be used by the congregation.

To indicate the order of the ceremony: A programme may be distributed.

Will a guest who is not a Latter-day Saint be expected to do anything other than sit? No.

Are there any parts of the ceremony in which a guest who is not a Latter-day Saint should not participate? No.

If not disruptive to the ceremony, is it OK to:

Take pictures? No.
Use a flash? No.
Use video recording equipment? No.
Use audio recording equipment? Possibly, if it can be done with discretion.

Will contributions to the church be collected at the ceremony? No.

The interment

Should guests attend the interment? Yes, unless it is a private interment, which is rare. If the burial is private, attendance is only by invitation.

Whom should one ask for directions? The director of the funeral home or the person who officiated at the service may give directions from the pulpit. Also, the printed programme may have directions.

What happens at the graveside? The grave is dedicated in a prayer offered by a lay priest, who is usually (but not necessarily) a member of the family of the deceased. Then the deceased is buried.

Do guests who are not Latter-day Saints participate at the graveside ceremony? No, they are simply present.

Comforting the bereaved

Is it appropriate to visit the home of the bereaved after the funeral? Yes, if one wishes to do so.

Will there be a religious service at the home of the bereaved? No.

Will food be served? There may be light food, but no alcoholic drinks. At the choice of the hosts, a grace or benediction may be said before eating.

How soon after the funeral will a mourner usually return to a normal work schedule? There is no set time. Absence from work is at the discretion of the mourner.

How soon after the funeral will a mourner usually return to a normal social schedule? There is no set time. Absence from social events is at the discretion of the mourner.

Are there mourning customs to which a friend who is not a Latter-day Saint should be sensitive? No.

Are there rituals for observing the anniversary of the death? No.

5. HOME CELEBRATIONS

Latter-day Saints observe a Family Home Evening one night each week. This is usually held on Mondays, but may be held on any other day. The intention is to cement family ties and cohesion. Usually attending are family members, but occasionally guests may be invited.

While there are no set activities, a Family Home Evening may include conversation, reading and singing together, taking walks or engaging in other recreational pursuits, playing games or praying together.

14

Muslim

Islam

1. HISTORY AND BELIEFS

The Arabic word *islam* means 'submission', and Islam is the religion of submission to the will of God ('Allah' in Arabic).

Muhammad, who is regarded as the last and final prophet of Allah, was born in Mecca (in present-day Saudi Arabia) in approximately AD 570. As a young man, he sought solitude in a cave on the outskirts of Mecca, where, according to Muslim belief, he received revelation from God. The basic creed that Muhammad taught is that the one God in heaven demands morality and monotheistic devotion from those he has created.

Initially, Muhammad's message was widely rejected, especially by Mecca's elite, who felt threatened by its egalitarian teachings. But by the time he died in AD 632, most of Arabia had embraced Islam.

Muslims revere the Qur'an, their holy book, as the earthly cornerstone of their faith.

Islam teaches that the Hebrew Bible and the New Testament were also authentic revelations from God and recognises as prophets all those prophets who were mentioned in these Scriptures, including Abraham, Moses, David and Jesus.

With about 1 billion Muslims around the globe, Islam is the fastest-growing religion in the world, and the second largest. Every country in the world has at least a small Muslim community.

UK Islamic mosques: over 1,500
UK membership: over 2 million

For more information, contact:

The Muslim Council of Britain
PO Box 57330
London
E1 2WJ
Tel: 0845 2626 786
Email: admin@mcb.org.uk

2. THE BASIC SERVICE

While Muslims are required to pray five times a day – daybreak, noon, mid-afternoon, sunset and evening – this can be done either in a mosque or wherever individual Muslims may be. Prayer, which is in Arabic, is preceded with *wadu* ('WAH-doo'), washing with water that cleanses the body (hands, mouth, face and feet) and spirit. Congregants then face Mecca and, depending on the time of day, do two to four prostrations (*raka'ah*, pronounced 'RA-kah'). Each *raka'ah* begins with the declaration 'God is most great', and consists of bows, prostrations and the recitation of fixed prayers. At the end of prayer, the *taslim* ('tahs-lihm'), or 'peace greeting', 'Peace be upon all of you and the mercy and the blessings of God', is repeated twice.

On Friday, *jumma* ('JUM-ma'), the noon prayer, is a congregational prayer and is recited at almost every mosque. In a mosque, men and women form separate lines for prayer, extending from one side of the mosque's main sanctuary to the other. The tight ranks symbolise unity and equality within the Muslim community. Each gender has its own line to maintain modesty and concentration during the physical movements of standing, bowing and prostration. Their separation does not indicate relative superiority or inferiority.

Appropriate Attire

Men: Casual shirt and trousers. Head covering is not required.

Women: A dress or skirt and blouse are recommended. Clothing should cover arms and hems should reach below the knees. A scarf is required to cover the head. Women may wear open-toed shoes and/or modest jewellery.

There are no rules regarding colours of clothing, but openly wearing crosses, Stars of David, jewellery with the signs of the zodiac and pendants with faces or heads of animals or people is discouraged.

~

The Sanctuary

What are the major sections of the mosque?

The entrance: Where shoes are removed, since they are not worn inside a mosque.

A musallah ('muh-SAL-ah'), or prayer room: Where prayers are recited. Every musallah is oriented towards Mecca, which Muslims face during prayers. The prayer room is open and uncluttered to accommodate lines of worshippers who stand and bow in unison. There are no pews or chairs. Members of the congregation sit on the floor. Some mosques have a balcony in the musallah reserved for women. Other mosques accommodate men and women in the same musallah, or they may have totally separate areas for men and women.

The qiblah ('KIHB-lah'): The direction to which the imam, or prayer leader, faces while praying.

A mihrab ('MEE-rahb'), or niche, that indicates which wall of the mosque faces towards Mecca: The *mihrab* is often decorated with Arabic calligraphy. Its curved shape helps reflect the voice of the imam, the prayer leader, back towards the congregation.

Facilities to perform wadu ('WAH-doo'), or washings with water of the hands, face and feet: These are done prior to prayers as a way to purify oneself before standing in front of God. *Wadu* facilities range from washbasins to specially designed areas with built-in benches, floor drains and taps.

A multi-purpose room: Used for seminars and lectures.

.ﷺ.

The Service

When should guests arrive and where should they sit? Arrive early.
Some congregants arrive as much as thirty to sixty minutes before
the service starts. Like the rest of the worshippers in the mosque,
guests sit on the prayer rug on the floor.

*If arriving late, are there times when a guest should not enter the
service?* No.

Are there times when a guest should not leave the service?
Do not leave when congregational prayer is being conducted.

A congregational prayer is offered in a group. Muslims are encouraged to pray in groups in mosques, although many pray as individuals and families at home.

*Who are the major officiants, leaders or participants and what do
they do?*
An imam ('EE-mahm'), who leads the prayers and delivers a sermon.
A muazzin ('MOO-ah-zin'), who calls the faithful to prayer.

What are the major ritual objects of the service? None.

What books are used? None, since prayers are memorised. (This
means that praying individually requires learning the proper rituals
in advance. Newcomers to the faith pray in groups and follow the
lead of the imam.)

To indicate the order of the service: Periodic announcements are
made by a *muazzin*, who calls the *Adhan* ('AHD-han') and the *Iqamah*
('IK-ah-mah'). The *Adhan*, which is aired through public loudspeakers,
alerts people that the time of prayer has started. The *Iqamah* is
intended to alert mosque worshippers that congregational prayer is
about to begin.

༺༺

Guest Behaviour during the Service

Will a guest who is not a Muslim be expected to do anything other than sit? No.

Are there any parts of the service in which a guest who is not a Muslim should not participate? No.

If not disruptive to the service, is it OK to:

Take pictures? No.
Use a flash? No.
Use video recording equipment? No.
Use audio recording equipment? Yes.

(Note: Different Islamic centres have different policies regarding such matters as cameras and tape recorders. If you wish to use such equipment during the service, check in advance with an official of the mosque or centre.)

Will contributions to the mosque be collected at the service? Some mosque leaders pass boxes to collect donations; others mount boxes in mosques for voluntary contributions. Non-Muslims are not expected to make a contribution, since that would be perceived as having imposed an obligation upon guests and, thus, would violate the traditional generosity shown towards guests in Islamic culture.

How much is it customary to contribute? This is entirely at the discretion of each person. A few pennies would be fine.

༺༺

After the Service

Is there usually a reception after the service? No.

Is there a traditional form of address for clergy whom a guest may meet? An imam may be directly addressed by the title of 'Imam' or by his name.

Is it OK to leave early? Yes.

✿

General Guidelines and Advice

Guests will observe Muslims making two *raka'ah* of prayer upon entering the mosque. This is a way to 'greet' and honour the mosque. A full *raka'ah* consists of recitations during one standing, one bowing and two prostrating motions (separated by a short sitting). Each prayer time requires a specific number of *raka'ah*. For example, dawn prayer consists of two *raka'ah*, noon consists of four and sunset of three. Visiting non-Muslims should not perform *raka'ah*, since the ritual is reserved for Muslims.

Worshippers and guests must not talk when the imam delivers a sermon.

Women should cover their hair with a scarf before entering *musallah*, or the prayer area of a mosque. Some mosques have a separate area for women. When there is no separate room for women, they pray behind the men.

✿

Special Vocabulary

Key words or phrases that it might be helpful for a visitor to know:

Salat ('SA-laht'): 'Prayer'.

As salaam alaikum ('as SA-lam ah-LAI-ikoom'): 'Peace be upon you'. A common greeting between Muslims.

Wa alaikum salaam ('wa a-LAI-ikoom SA-lam'): 'And upon you the peace'. A common response to the above greeting.

Salla allahu alayhi wa salaam ('SAH-lah ah-LAH-hoo ah-LAY-hee wah SAH-lahm'): 'May the peace and blessings of Allah be upon him'. This is said when any prophet of God is mentioned.

Allah subhana wa tala ('AH-lah SOOB-hah-nah wah TAH-lah'): 'God, Who is highly glorified and honoured'.

Raka'ah ('RA-kah'): A unit of prayer ritual that consists of motions and verbal recitations.

Some Basic Beliefs

Muslims believe:

One becomes a Muslim by saying and believing the *shahadah* ('SHAH-hah-dah'): 'There is no god but God and Muhammad is the messenger of God.'

A Muslim prays five times a day. The prayers take five to ten minutes. Muslims pray communally at around noon on Friday. Muslims face Mecca during their prayers as a sign of unity. But they do not 'pray' to Mecca; they pray to God.

A tax on assets is gathered by the community and distributed according to need. Called the *zakat*, it is generally 2.5 per cent of one's income.

Muslims abstain from food, drink and sexual activity from sunrise to sunset during the lunar month of Ramadan.

A Muslim must make the *hajj* ('hahj'), or pilgrimage to Mecca, at least once in his or her lifetime if physically and financially able. The hajj symbolises unity and equality. Muslims of different races, wealth, status and gender gather in Mecca for hajj, and all are equal before God.

Some basic books to which a guest can refer to learn more about Islam:

Islam: A Short History, by Karen Armstrong (Phoenix, 2000).

Islam: The Straight Path, by John L. Esposito (Oxford University Press, 2009).

The Qur'an ('koo-RAHN'), of which there are several English translations. A good translation is by Yusuf Ali, or by Abdul Haleem, a professor at SOAS University. These can be found in mosques and many bookshops.

What You Will See Inside a Mosque, by Aisha Karen Khan, with photographs by Aaron Pepis (SkyLight Paths Publishing, 2008).

3. HOLY DAYS AND FESTIVALS

Ramadan ('RAH-mah-dahn'): Occurs during all of Ramadan, the ninth month of the Islamic calendar. (Since Muslims follow the lunar calendar, Ramadan starts about ten days earlier in the solar calendar every year.) From dawn to sunset, all adult Muslims whose health permits are to abstain from food, drink, smoking and sexual activity. Ramadan is a time for reflection and spiritual discipline, to express gratitude for God's guidance and to atone for past sins. It is recommended that each Muslim read the entire Qur'an during this month. The traditional greeting for this holiday is *'Ramadan mubarak'* ('RAH-mah-dahn moo-BAR-ahk'), meaning, 'May God give you a blessed month'. The traditional response is *'Ramadan karim'* ('RAH-mah-dahn KAH-reem'), meaning, 'May God give you a generous month'.

Idal-Fitr ('id AHL-fih-ter'): The Feast of the Breaking of the Fast, which is celebrated at the end of Ramadan to mark the completion of fasting. The holiday lasts for one day, during which family members gather to feast and exchange presents. In many Muslim countries, it is a national holiday. It is also a time for attending mosque and paying the special alms for the poor, *zakat al-fitr*, required by Islamic law. The traditional greeting for this holiday is *'Id mubarak'* ('id moo-BAR-ahk'), which means '[May God make it a] blessed feast'. The response is *'Id karim'* ('id KAH-reem'), which means '[May God make it a] kind feast'.

Idal-Adha ('id uhl-AHD-hah'): Occurs two to three months after Ramadan and commemorates Abraham's obedience to God when he told him to sacrifice his son, Ishmael, and Ishmael's submission to the sacrifice. The holiday lasts for three days and is marked by slaughtering animals to feed the poor. The traditional greeting for this holiday is *'Id mubarak'* ('id moo-BAR-ahk'), which means '[May God make it] a blessed feast'.

Lailat ul-Qadr ('LIE-laht ul-KAH-dur'): The last ten days of Ramadan, during which special prayers are offered. This commemorates the 'Night of Power' when the Prophet Muhammad first received God's revelation. Although the revelation occurred upon one particular night, it is celebrated during ten days since the exact night is unknown. All that is known is that the revelation occurred during the last ten days of Ramadan. During *Lailat ul-Qadr*, Muslims sometimes seclude themselves in their mosque, leaving only when necessary. There is no traditional greeting for these days.

al-Isra Wal Miraj ('al-IZ-rah wahl MEE-rahj'): 'The Night Journey and the Ascension', which is observed on the twenty-seventh day of Rajab, which is the seventh month of the Muslim lunar calendar. The holiday commemorates the night when the Prophet Muhammad is believed to have made a miraculous journey from Mecca to the Aqsa Mosque in Jerusalem, where he then travelled to the heavens, where God commanded him to initiate prayers five times each day. There is no traditional greeting for this holiday.

4. LIFE CYCLE EVENTS

Birth Ceremony

The ceremony is called an *akikah* ('ah-KEE-kah'). A ceremony in itself, it usually lasts about thirty to sixty minutes. An *akikah* is very informal and is not universally practised by Muslims. What transpires at it varies from culture to culture and, often, from home to home. Generally, it is simply a way to welcome a newborn infant.

Before the ceremony

Are guests usually invited by a formal invitation? Non-Muslims will usually receive an oral or written invitation. For Muslims, the time and place of the event are usually posted in the mosque or announced after Friday prayers.

If not stated explicitly, should one assume that children are invited? Yes.

If one cannot attend, what should one do? RSVP with regrets and send a gift. Usually cash is appropriate. While the range of the cash given as presents is wide, Muslims are taught to be generous.

Appropriate attire

Men: Casual shirt and trousers. Head covering is not required.

Women: A dress or skirt and blouse are recommended. Clothing should cover the arms and hems should reach below the knees. A scarf is required to cover the head. Women may wear open-toed shoes and/or modest jewellery.

For both men and women, there are no rules regarding colours of clothing, but openly wearing crosses, Stars of David, jewellery with the signs of the zodiac and pendants with faces or heads of animals or people is discouraged.

Gifts

Is a gift customarily expected? Yes. Usually cash is appropriate. While the range of the cash given as presents is wide, Muslims are taught to be generous.

Should gifts be brought to the ceremony? They can either be sent to the home of the parents or be brought to the ceremony. If cash is given, it is usually presented in an envelope, along with a card.

The ceremony

Where will the ceremony take place? Either in the home of the parents of the child or in the general purpose room of their mosque.

When should guests arrive and where should they sit? Arrive at the time called for the ceremony to begin. Sit wherever you wish. Men and women will sit in different parts of the room. Guests should enquire about where women go and where men go.

If arriving late, are there times when a guest should not enter the ceremony? No.

Are there times when a guest should not leave the ceremony? No.

Who are the major officiants, leaders or participants at the ceremony and what do they do? Possibly a family member, who may say some informal words about the newborn.

What books are used? None.

To indicate the order of the ceremony: An *akikah* is brief and informal. There is no need to indicate the order of the event.

Will a guest who is not a Muslim be expected to do anything other than sit? No.

Are there any parts of the ceremony in which a guest who is not a Muslim should not participate? No.

If not disruptive to the ceremony, is it OK to:

Take pictures? No.
Use a flash? No.
Use video recording equipment? No.
Use audio recording equipment? Yes.

(Note: Different Islamic centres have different policies regarding such matters as cameras and tape recorders. If you wish to use such equipment during the ceremony, check in advance with an official of the mosque or centre.)

Will contributions to the mosque be collected at the ceremony? Some mosque leaders pass boxes to collect donations; others mount boxes in mosques for voluntary contributions. Non-Muslims are not expected to make a contribution, since that would be perceived as having imposed an obligation upon guests and, thus, would violate the traditional generosity shown towards guests in Islamic culture.

How much is it customary to contribute? This is entirely at the discretion of each person. A few pennies would be fine.

After the ceremony

Is there usually a reception after the ceremony? There may be a reception. Such traditions differ from culture to culture and from mosque to mosque. If so, light food and drinks will be served, but no alcoholic drinks and any meat would be halal. There may be dancing and/or music, again depending on the particular mosque and the culture in which it is set.

Would it be considered impolite to neither eat nor drink? No.

Is there a grace or benediction before eating or drinking? Usually '*Bismillah*' is said, which means 'In the name of Allah'.

Is there a grace or benediction after eating or drinking? Usually '*Alhamdulilla*' is said, which means 'Praise be to God'.

Is there a traditional greeting for the family? Yes. It is '*Mabrook*' ('MAH-brook'). This means 'Congratulations'.

Is there a traditional form of address for clergy who may be at the reception? An imam may be directly addressed by the title of 'Imam' or by his name.

Is it OK to leave early? Yes.

Initiation Ceremony

At the *shahada* ('SHAH-hah-dah') or 'witnessing', a Muslim repeats the Islamic declaration of faith: 'There is no deity but God, and Muhammad is the messenger of God.' 'Taking *shahada*', as the ritual is called, is a ceremony in itself. It is usually done at any age from the mid-teens upwards. It must be witnessed by two male Muslims. The *shahada* may last between fifteen and thirty minutes.

Before the ceremony

Are guests usually invited by a formal invitation? The individual making the *shahada* will invite friends or family, either in person, by phone or by written invitation. Often an announcement is made that certain individuals will make *shahada* at the end of a particular service.

If not stated explicitly, should one assume that children are invited? Yes.

If one cannot attend, what should one do? RSVP with regrets. No gift is expected.

Appropriate attire

Men: Casual shirt and trousers. Head covering is not required.

Women: A dress or skirt and blouse are recommended. Clothing should cover the arms and hems should reach below the knees. A scarf is required to cover the head. Women may wear open-toed shoes and/or modest jewellery.

For both men and women, there are no rules regarding colours of clothing, but openly wearing crosses, Stars of David, jewellery with the signs of the zodiac and pendants with faces or heads of animals or people is discouraged.

Gifts

Is a gift customarily expected? No.

Should gifts be brought to the ceremony? See above.

The ceremony

Where will the ceremony take place? Often in the main sanctuary or in a special room of a mosque or at the home of the person making the *shahada*. However, a *shahada* can take place anywhere.

When should guests arrive and where should they sit? Arrive early. Someone will advise guests where to sit.

If arriving late, are there times when a guest should not enter the ceremony? No.

Are there times when a guest should not leave the ceremony? No.

Who are the major officiants, leaders or participants at the ceremony and what do they do?

An imam, who leads the prayers and delivers a sermon.
A muazzin, who calls the faithful to prayer.

What books are used? None, since prayers are memorised. (This means that praying individually requires learning the proper rituals in advance. Newcomers to the faith pray in groups and follow the lead of the imam.)

To indicate the order of the ceremony: A *shahada* is brief and informal. No need to indicate the order of the event.

Will a guest who is not a Muslim be expected to do anything other than sit? No.

Are there any parts of the ceremony in which a guest who is not a Muslim should not participate? No.

If not disruptive to the ceremony, is it OK to:

Take pictures? Yes.
Use a flash? No.
Use video recording equipment? Yes.
Use audio recording equipment? Yes.

(Note: Different Islamic centres have different policies regarding such matters as cameras and tape recorders. If you wish to use such equipment during the ceremony, check in advance with an official of the mosque or centre.)

If the shahada *is held in a mosque, will contributions to the mosque be collected at the service?* There will not be a collection, but in some mosques, boxes are mounted on the wall for voluntary contributions. Non-Muslims are not expected to make a contribution, since that would be perceived as having imposed an obligation upon guests and, thus, would violate the traditional generosity shown towards guests in Islamic culture.

How much is it customary to contribute? This is entirely at the discretion of each person. A few pennies would be fine.

After the ceremony

Is there usually a reception after the ceremony? No.

Is there a traditional greeting for the family? Yes. It is '*Mabrook*' ('MAH-brook'). This means 'Congratulations'.

Is there a traditional form of address for clergy whom a guest may meet? An imam may be directly addressed by the title of 'Imam' or by his name.

Marriage Ceremony

Marriage is incumbent on every Muslim man and woman unless they are financially or physically unable to be married. It is regarded as the norm for all and essential to the growth and stability of the family, which is the basic unit of society. Marriage is regarded as a sacred contract or covenant, not a sacrament, that legalises sexual intercourse and the procreation of children.

The marriage ceremony usually lasts about thirty minutes, but can last more than one hour. It is a ceremony in itself.

Before the ceremony

Are guests usually invited by a formal invitation? Non-Muslims are usually invited by written invitation. For Muslims, invitations may be posted in a mosque or announced after the noon prayers on Friday.

If not stated explicitly, should one assume that children are invited? Yes.

If one cannot attend, what should one do? RSVP with regrets and send a gift, either money or whatever items one deems appropriate for the needs of the newlyweds.

Appropriate attire

Men: Casual shirt and trousers. Head covering is not required.

Women: A dress or skirt and blouse are recommended. Clothing should cover the arms and hems should reach below the knees. A scarf is required to cover the head. Women may wear open-toed shoes and/or jewellery.

For both men and women, there are no rules regarding colours of clothing, but openly wearing crosses, Stars of David, jewellery with the signs of the zodiac and pendants with faces or heads of animals or people is discouraged.

Gifts

Is a gift customarily expected? Yes, either money or whatever items one deems appropriate for the needs of the newlyweds.

Should gifts be brought to the ceremony? They can either be sent to the home of the newlyweds or be brought to the ceremony.

The ceremony

Where will the ceremony take place? Often in a mosque, but it can take place anywhere.

When should guests arrive and where should they sit? Arrive at the time called for the wedding to start. Sit wherever you wish.

If arriving late, are there times when a guest should not enter the ceremony? No.

Are there times when a guest should not leave the ceremony? No.

Who are the major officiants, leaders or participants at the ceremony and what do they do?

An imam, or Islamic prayer leader, who usually delivers a sermon about marriage. This may be in Arabic if the newlyweds are Arabic-speaking, or in English if they are English-speaking. Or it may be a mixture of both languages.

Two witnesses, who witness the oral and written contract entered into by the bride and groom.

The groom, who offers marriage to the bride.

The bride, who accepts the offer.

What books are used? None.

To indicate the order of the ceremony: Weddings are brief and informal. There is no need to indicate the order of the event.

Will a guest who is not a Muslim be expected to do anything other than sit? No.

Are there any parts of the ceremony in which a guest who is not a Muslim should not participate? No.

If not disruptive to the ceremony, is it OK to:

Take pictures? Yes.
Use a flash? Yes.
Use video recording equipment? Yes.
Use audio recording equipment? Yes.

(Note: Different Islamic centres have different policies regarding such matters as cameras and tape recorders. If you wish to use such equipment during the ceremony, check in advance with an official of the mosque or centre.)

Will contributions to the mosque be collected at the ceremony? There will not be a collection, but in some mosques, boxes are mounted on the wall for voluntary contributions. Non-Muslims are not expected to make a contribution, since that would be perceived as having imposed an obligation upon guests and, thus, would violate the traditional generosity shown towards guests in Islamic culture.

How much is it customary to contribute? This is entirely at the discretion of each person. A few pennies would be fine.

After the ceremony

Is there usually a reception after the ceremony? Yes. This is called a *waleemah* ('wah-leeh-mah'). It may last two hours or more and can be held anywhere: in the mosque, a home, a catering hall or any other site. Drinks and such food as meat, rice, fruit and sweets will be served. There will be no alcoholic drinks. There may be dancing and/or music, but not if the *waleemah* is held in a mosque.

Would it be considered impolite to neither eat nor drink? No.

Is there a grace or benediction before eating or drinking? Usually '*Bismillah*' is said, which means 'In the name of Allah'.

Is there a grace or benediction after eating or drinking? Usually '*Alhamdulilla*' is said, which means 'Praise be to God'.

Is there a traditional greeting for the family? '*Mabrook alaik*' ('MAH-brook ah-LAYK'), 'Congratulations', if addressing a male. '*Mabrook alaiki*' ('MAH-brook ah-LAYK-ee'), 'Congratulations', if addressing a female.

Is there a traditional form of address for clergy who may be at the reception? An imam may be directly addressed by the title of 'Imam' or by his name.

Is it OK to leave early? Yes.

꙳

Funerals and Mourning

The Muslim view of the afterlife includes a universal belief in a final Day of Reckoning, when all people will be called upon to give account for their actions. The Qur'an describes the pleasures of heaven enjoyed by the righteous – as well as the torments of hell – in vivid, physical detail. Individual Muslims hold a range of differing opinions about how literally those descriptions are to be taken.

An Islamic funeral is a service in itself and usually lasts about thirty to sixty minutes. In some cases, it may last more than an hour.

Before the ceremony

How soon after the death does the funeral usually take place? As soon as possible, sometimes even on the same day.

What should a non-Muslim do upon hearing of the death of a member of that faith? Call or visit the bereaved. If one visits, shake hands or hug and kiss the family members of the same gender, sit and talk quietly and offer some quiet prayer.

Appropriate attire

Men: Casual shirt and trousers. Head covering is not required.

Women: A dress is recommended. Clothing should cover the arms and hems should reach below the knees. A scarf is required to cover the head.

For both men and women, there are no rules regarding colours of clothing, but openly wearing crosses, Stars of David, jewellery with the signs of the zodiac and pendants with faces or heads of animals or people is discouraged.

Dark, sombre colours are advised.

Gifts

Is it appropriate to send flowers or make a contribution? Send flowers after the funeral to the home of the bereaved.

Is it appropriate to send food? Yes, but any food should be halal (including no gelatine), and do not include any alcoholic drinks.

The ceremony

Where will the ceremony take place? At a funeral home or in the general purpose room of the mosque.

When should guests arrive and where should they sit? Arrive at the time set for the funeral. An usher will advise guests on where to sit.

If arriving late, are there times when a guest should not enter the ceremony? No.

Will the bereaved family be present at the funeral home before the ceremony? No.

Is there a traditional greeting for the family? No. Just offer your condolences.

Will there be an open coffin? No.

Who are the major officiants at the ceremony and what do they do?

An imam, who presides.

What books are used? The Qur'an.

To indicate the order of the ceremony: No directions are given during the service, which is intended to be as simple as possible.

Will a guest who is not a Muslim be expected to do anything other than sit? No.

Are there any parts of the ceremony in which a guest who is not a Muslim should not participate? No.

If not disruptive to the ceremony, is it OK to:

Take pictures? No.
Use a flash? No.
Use video recording equipment? No.
Use audio recording equipment? No.

Will contributions to the mosque be collected at the ceremony? No.

The interment

Should guests attend the interment? Yes.

Whom should one ask for directions? An imam.

What happens at the graveside? The *Janazah* prayers ('jah-NAH-zah') for the dead are recited and the deceased is buried. Muslims are never cremated.

Do guests who are not Muslims participate at the graveside ceremony? No, they are simply present.

Comforting the bereaved

Is it appropriate to visit the home of the bereaved after the funeral? Yes. Visit any time during the days of mourning, which are religiously mandated not to exceed forty days. The number of mourning days that one actually observes is individually set and can be determined by telephoning the home of the bereaved. When visiting the home of a mourner, talk quietly with the bereaved and other visitors. Often, visitors and mourners sit in silence while someone reads aloud from the Qur'an or a tape of a reading from the Qur'an is played.

Will there be a religious service at the home of the bereaved? No.

Will food be served? Possibly. Often, women in the local Muslim community prepare food for mourners and their guests.

How soon after the funeral will a mourner usually return to a normal work schedule? After four days.

How soon after the funeral will a mourner usually return to a normal social schedule? There are no prescriptions in Islam about such matters. This is more culturally determined than religiously determined. Usually, women do not engage in normal social activities until forty days after the death of a member of their immediate family. There are no norms for men, but for a woman whose husband dies there is a waiting period of three months, called *Iddah*, before she can remarry.

Are there mourning customs to which a friend who is not a Muslim should be sensitive? Bereaved usually wear black, although this is a cultural norm and not a religious prescription.

Are there rituals for observing the anniversary of the death? No.

5. HOME CELEBRATIONS

Not applicable for Islam.

15
Orthodox

1. HISTORY AND BELIEFS

The term *Orthodox* is used to reflect Orthodox Christians' belief that they believe and worship God correctly. Essentially, adherents consider their beliefs to be similar to those of other Christian traditions, and that the balance and integrity of the teachings of Jesus' twelve apostles have been preserved inviolate by their Church.

Orthodoxy holds that the eternal truths of God's saving revelation in Jesus Christ are preserved in the living tradition of the Church under the guidance and inspiration of the Holy Spirit, which is the empowering Spirit of God and the particular endowment of the Church. While the Holy Scriptures are the written testimony of God's revelation, Holy Tradition is the all-encompassing experience of the Church under the guidance and direction of the Holy Spirit.

The global family of churches and Christian communities commonly defined as 'Orthodox' may be grouped into three main branches, all of which are represented by churches in the UK.

The existence of the *Holy Apostolic Catholic Assyrian Church of the East* (which includes traditions sometimes referred to as Assyrian, Nestorian and East Syrian; and Chaldean, which refers to a part of the Assyrian Church that has communion with Rome while retaining its own rites and traditions) as a distinct body of Christian tradition dates back to the Council of Ephesus in AD 431. It was here that the views of Nestorius, Bishop of Constantinople, concerning the nature of Christ were denounced (he held that Christ has two separate natures, human and divine), leading to the separation of two major bodies of Christendom. Churches within this tradition do not refer to themselves as 'Orthodox', although they are sometimes classified as such by outsiders.

The existence of the *Oriental Orthodox* or *Non-Chalcedonian Churches* (which include the Syrian Churches of Antioch and India, the Coptic Church in Egypt, the Armenian Church and Ethiopian Church) as a distinct body of Christian tradition dates back to the Council of Chalcedon in AD 451. Here the nature of Christ was further disputed, the Council concluding that he has two natures in one person. Those churches now known as Oriental Orthodox rejected this teaching, holding that Christ's divinity and humanity are united as one unseparated nature.

Orthodoxy's third branch, and the most widely represented in Britain today, is best known as the *Eastern Orthodox Church*, which is commonly dated from the 'Great Schism' of AD 1054. Churches in the eastern regions of the Roman Empire refused to accept supreme authority in the Pope. Another significant dispute between Christians on both sides of this division was the inclusion of the statement in the Nicene Creed that the Holy Spirit proceeds 'from the Son' as well as the Father. Eastern Orthodox Christians objected to the insertion of this statement by the Western half of the Church without a consensus of affirmation.

The Eastern Orthodox Church now comprises four ancient churches (or *patriarchates*): those of Constantinople, Alexandria, Antioch and Jerusalem, together with a number of other autocephalous churches (governed by their own national synods) of more recent foundation, including those of Russia, Serbia, Romania, Bulgaria, Georgia, Cyprus, Greece, Poland and Albania. Each of these churches is presided over by its own senior bishop, some of whom also bear the title of 'Patriarch', and exists in communion with other Eastern Orthodox churches. When the patriarchs meet, they are presided over by the Patriarch of Constantinople (present-day Istanbul), who is considered to be the 'first among equals'.

While the majority of these churches carry a national title, this indicates their cultural tradition more than their geographical boundaries. Although generally unified on matters of faith, the diversity of cultural traditions across the Orthodox spectrum makes it difficult to provide a definitive guide to practice, dress and etiquette in a single chapter. Even within a single church parish there are likely to be differences in approach between individual worshippers.

What follows should therefore be considered an overview of Orthodox worship and practice, with significant variations noted where requested by representatives of the most prevalent traditions in the UK. If you have been invited to a ceremony in an Orthodox church, and have unanswered questions about what to expect, it is recommended that you ask the person who issued the invitation.

UK churches: approximately 220
UK membership: approximately 300,000

2. THE BASIC SERVICE

In Orthodox churches, the purpose of worship and theology is mystical union with God. The Liturgy is not a private performance by a priest, since he cannot perform the Liturgy alone, but a joint act of laity and clergy. The language of prayer alludes to the majesty and transcendence of God, while also conveying God's presence.

Eucharistic services, sometimes known as the Divine (or Holy) Liturgy, take place every Sunday and on major feast days. They usually last from one and a half to two hours.

❧

Appropriate Attire

There is no official dress code for men or women, although it is worth asking in advance whether the particular church you are visiting has a preference. It is recommended that you dress smartly but without ostentation. Women may wear open-toed shoes and modest jewellery.

In some more conservative churches it is expected that women will wear a head covering, such as a hat or headscarf.

There are no rules regarding colours of clothing.

❧

The Sanctuary

What are the major sections of the church?

The narthex: The main entrance.
The altar: Where the priest or bishop stands.
The nave: Where one worships and participates in the service.

Many Orthodox churches do not have pews, and the expectation in these instances is that congregants will stand for most of the Liturgy but sit when they feel the need to. Do not cross your legs when sitting down.

❧

The Service

When should guests arrive and where should they sit? It is polite to arrive either early or at the time for which the service has been called. In some more conservative churches it is customary for men to stand or sit on the right-hand side of the nave as one enters, and women on the left. If uncertain, it would be worth asking what the church's custom is before arrival.

If arriving late, are there times when a guest should not enter the service? Do not enter during Scripture readings and priestly blessings.

Are there times when a guest should not leave the service? No.

Who are the major officiants, leaders or participants and what do they do?

A priest, who is usually the chief celebrant, unless a bishop is present, in which case the bishop will be chief celebrant and the priest will assist him.
The deacon, subdeacon and altar servers, all of whom, when present, assist the bishop or priest.

What are the major ritual objects of the service?

Icons, two-dimensional artistic images of Christ, the Virgin Mary and other saints, or of significant events in the Bible or Church history.

A gold-covered book containing the four Gospels from the New Testament.

Censer, an incense holder. Smoke from the incense represents prayers being carried to heaven.

Chalice, a gold cup, containing the Holy Eucharist (the bread and wine, which, having been consecrated by the Holy Spirit at the prayers of the bishop or priest, are mystically changed into the body and blood of Christ, and are offered to the people in Communion).

To indicate the order of the service: An order of service or Liturgy service book may be provided. If not, most texts are freely available, both online and in hard copy. It would be worth enquiring in advance if you are interested in following the service.

Guest Behaviour during the Service

Will a guest who is not a member of an Orthodox church be expected to do anything other than just be present? Yes, try to follow the lead of the rest of the congregation. There are certain elements of the Liturgy for which all are expected to stand: the Entrances (the Little Entrance, being a procession with the Gospel, and the Great Entrance, being a procession with the paten and chalice), when being censed, during the reading of the Gospel, during the prayer of consecration and during the communion of the people. Reading prayers aloud and singing with the congregants are optional.

Are there any parts of the service in which a guest who is not a member of an Orthodox church should not participate? Do not participate in Holy Communion. This is the high point of the service. It occurs after the priest or deacon advances towards the congregation from the altar, holds up the chalice and says, 'With fear of God, with faith and with love, draw near.' Congregants who are members of an Orthodox church will then go forward to receive Communion; remain seated if you are not Orthodox.

If not disruptive to the service, is it OK to:

Take pictures? Only with prior permission of a church official.
Use a flash? Only with prior permission of a church official.
Use video recording equipment? Only with prior permission of a church official.
Use audio recording equipment? If disruptive, then only with prior permission of a church official.

Will contributions to the church be collected at the service? Sometimes, in which case a plate will be passed through the congregation. Another way of contributing to the upkeep of the church is by the purchase of candles, which are usually on sale in some part of the church, and are lit by individuals as part of their prayer. In many Orthodox churches visitors will be welcome to light candles.

How much is it customary to contribute? While the amount of the contribution is at the discretion of congregants or visitors, and the various Orthodox churches do not feel comfortable recommending specific amounts to guests, contributions between £1 and £5 are common.

After the Service

Is there usually a reception after the service? A thirty- to sixty-minute reception is usually held in a room or hall adjoining the church. Food is usually served. Alcoholic drinks are not ordinarily served at this reception in Orthodox churches (although alcohol may be served on special occasions, such as major feasts, birthdays or other celebrations).

In the Russian Orthodox Church, there will be a prayer of blessing before eating or drinking.

Is there a traditional form of address for clergy who may be at the reception? Yes. It is 'Father'.

Is it OK to leave early? Yes.

꧁

Special Vocabulary

Key words or phrases that it might be helpful for a visitor to know:

Theotokos ('Thee-oh-TOH-kohs'): 'Mother of God'.

Prokimenon ('Proh-KEE-min-non'): 'Verses from a Psalm intoned before the reading of the Epistle'.

Proskomen ('PROS-koh-men'): 'Let us attend'.

꧁

Some Basic Beliefs

Members of Orthodox churches believe:

In the Holy Trinity (the Father, the Son and the Holy Spirit).

That after consecration, the bread and wine of the Holy Communion (the ritual meal that forms the heart of the Liturgy) become the body and blood of Christ. This is in contrast to some Christian denominations that consider the Eucharist to be symbolic.

That the final authority for the Church is not vested in the Pope.

Some basic books to which a guest can refer to learn more about Orthodox churches:

The Orthodox Church, by Timothy Ware (Penguin Books, 1993).

The Orthodox Way, by Bishop Kallistos Ware (St Vladimir's Seminary Press, 1982).

3. HOLY DAYS AND FESTIVALS

A selection of holy days and festivals:

Exaltation of the Cross: Observed on 14 September. Marks the finding of the true cross by the Empress Helena, the mother of Emperor Constantine, in the fourth century. This is a strict fast day. There is no traditional greeting for this holiday.

Nativity of Christ: A one-week celebration that begins on 25 December. Marks the birth of Jesus Christ. Non-Orthodox can greet church members with 'Merry Christmas!'

Theophany of Our Lord: A one-week celebration beginning on 6 January. Marks the baptism of Jesus Christ. Non-Orthodox can greet members with a smile and a handshake, or the common greeting, 'Happy Feast!'

Annunciation: 25 March. Marks the conception of Jesus Christ within the Virgin Mary. There are no traditional greetings for this holiday. Although this holiday usually occurs during Lent, a forty-day fast during which one abstains from eating fish, meat and dairy products, church members may eat fish on this day.

Palm Sunday: Date of observance varies, although it usually occurs in April and is always the Sunday before Easter. Marks the entrance of Jesus Christ into Jerusalem. Although Palm Sunday occurs during Lent, a forty-day fast during which one abstains from eating fish, meat and dairy products, members of Orthodox churches may eat fish on this day.

Easter, also called Pascha ('PAS-ka'): Date of observance varies, but it usually occurs in April. Observes the resurrection of Jesus Christ after his crucifixion. The traditional greeting among church members is 'Christ is risen!' The response to this is 'He is risen indeed!' Those who do not belong to the Orthodox Church can also greet Church members with 'Happy Easter'.

Note that some Orthodox churches follow the Julian Calendar, which is now thirteen days behind the 'New Calendar'. So, for example, these churches would celebrate the Exaltation of the Cross on their 14 September, which would be 27 September on the conventional British calendar.

4. LIFE CYCLE EVENTS

Birth and Initiation Ceremony

The ceremony marking the birth of a child is the same for a male and a female infant. It marks initiation into the Church, forgiveness of sins and the beginning of the Christian life. Through baptism, one dies with Christ so one may rise with Christ.

The baptism is followed immediately by *Chrismation* (known in other Christian denominations as 'confirmation') and sometimes by First Communion. During the baptism, the child is fully immersed three times in a baptismal font, and then anointed (or 'chrismated') with oil on the forehead, chest, hands, neck, back and feet.

The First Communion, which is sometimes given at the next suitable celebration of the Liturgy rather than on the same day as baptism, emphasises the fullness of participation in the sacramental life of the Church. During it, the child is given the Holy Eucharist (bread and wine, which, having been consecrated by the Holy Spirit at the prayers of the bishop or priest, are mystically changed into the body and blood of Christ).

In most cases baptism followed by Chrismation is a ceremony in itself, but sometimes it may be incorporated within a celebration of the Divine Liturgy.

Before the ceremony

Are guests usually invited by a formal invitation? Yes, usually either by a written invitation or over the telephone.

If not stated explicitly, should one assume that children are invited? Yes.

If one cannot attend, what should one do? Telephone your regrets to the family, send a gift and visit the family soon after the ceremony.

Appropriate attire

There is no official dress code for men or women, although it is worth asking in advance whether the particular church you are visiting has a preference. It is recommended that you dress smartly but without ostentation. Women may wear open-toed shoes and modest jewellery.

In some more conservative churches it is expected that women will wear a head covering, such as a hat or headscarf.

There are no rules regarding colours of clothing.

Gifts

Is a gift customarily expected? Yes. If one chooses to give a gift, either cash or baby clothes are appropriate.

Should gifts be brought to the ceremony? Yes.

The ceremony

Where will the ceremony take place? Most often in the parents' house of worship.

When should guests arrive and where should they sit? It is polite to arrive either early or at the time for which the service has been called. In some more conservative churches it is customary for men to stand or sit on the right-hand side of the nave as one enters, and women on the left. If uncertain, it would be worth asking what the church's custom is before arrival.

If arriving late, are there times when a guest should not enter the ceremony? Do not enter during Scripture readings and priestly blessings.

Are there times when a guest should not leave the ceremony? No.

Who are the major officiants, leaders or participants at the ceremony and what do they do?

A priest, who is usually the chief celebrant, unless a bishop is present, in which case the bishop will be chief celebrant and the priest will assist him.

The deacon, subdeacon and altar servers, all of whom, if present, assist the bishop or priest.

To indicate the order of the service: An order of service or Liturgy service book may be provided. If not, most texts are freely available, both online and in hard copy. It would be worth enquiring in advance if you are interested in following the service.

Will a guest who is not a member of an Orthodox church be expected to do anything other than just be present? Yes, try to follow the lead of the rest of the congregation. There are certain elements of the Liturgy for which all are expected to stand: the Entrances (the Little Entrance, being a procession with the Gospel, and the Great Entrance, being a procession with the paten and chalice), when being censed, during the reading of the Gospel, during the prayer of consecration and during the communion of the people. Reading prayers aloud and singing with the congregants are optional.

Are there any parts of the service in which a guest who is not a member of an Orthodox church should not participate? Do not participate in Holy Communion. This is the high point of the service. It occurs after the priest or deacon advances towards the congregation from the altar, holds up the chalice and says, 'With fear of God, with faith and with love, draw near.' Congregants who are members of an Orthodox church will then go forward to receive Communion; remain seated if you are not Orthodox.

If not disruptive to the service, is it OK to:

Take pictures? Only with prior permission of a church official.
Use a flash? Only with prior permission of a church official.
Use video recording equipment? Only with prior permission of a church official.
Use audio recording equipment? If disruptive, then only with prior permission of a church official.

Will contributions to the church be collected at the service? Sometimes, in which case a plate will be passed through the congregation. Another way of contributing to the upkeep of the church is by the purchase of candles, which are usually on sale in some part of the church, and are lit by individuals as part of their prayer. In many Orthodox churches visitors will be welcome to light candles.

How much is it customary to contribute? While the amount of the contribution is at the discretion of congregants or visitors, and the various Orthodox churches do not feel comfortable recommending specific amounts to guests, contributions between £1 and £5 are common.

After the ceremony

Is there usually a reception after the ceremony? Yes. This may last from thirty minutes to two hours and may be held in the same building as the ceremony, at the parents' home or at a catering hall. A meal will be served, often accompanied by alcoholic drinks.

Would it be considered impolite to neither eat nor drink? No.

Is there a grace or benediction before eating or drinking? Usually. An invocation is recited to bless the food.

Is there a grace or benediction after eating or drinking? Sometimes.

Is there a traditional greeting for the family? Guests who are not members of an Orthodox church can just offer their congratulations. Parents who belong to the Antiochian Orthodox Church are often greeted with the phrase 'A blessed Churching' or 'A blessed baptism', although the traditional greeting for all occasions in the Church is '*Mabbrook*' ('MAB-brook'), which means 'Blessings'. For other Orthodox churches, there is no traditional greeting.

Is there a traditional form of address for clergy who may be at the reception? Yes. It is 'Father'.

Is it OK to leave early? Yes.

Marriage Ceremony

To Orthodox Christians, marriage is a sacrament of union between man and woman, who enter it to be mutually complemented and to propagate the human race. In the Orthodox churches, rings are blessed and the bride and groom each wear a crown during the ceremony to symbolise sacrifices made in marriage, the priestly nature of marriage and the fact that the bride and groom are now rulers, under God, of their household, which is to be an earthly image of the kingdom of God. In some traditions these crowns are not worn but held over their heads by friends of the couple, known as 'crown bearers'.

The forty-five- to sixty-minute marriage ceremony is usually a service in itself, but is sometimes incorporated into a celebration of the Divine Liturgy.

Before the ceremony

Are guests usually invited by a formal invitation? Yes.

If not stated explicitly, should one assume that children are invited? No.

If one cannot attend, what should one do? RSVP with regrets and send a gift.

Appropriate attire

There is no official dress code for men or women, although it is worth asking in advance whether the particular church you are visiting has a preference. It is recommended that you dress smartly but without ostentation. Women may wear open-toed shoes and modest jewellery.

In some more conservative churches it is expected that women will wear a head covering, such as a hat or headscarf.

There are no rules regarding colours of clothing.

Gifts

Is a gift customarily expected? Yes. Customarily, this may be cash or household goods.

Should gifts be brought to the ceremony? Bring the gift to the ceremony or the reception or send it to the home of the newlyweds.

The ceremony

Where will the ceremony take place? In the main sanctuary of the church chosen by the celebrants and their family.

When should guests arrive and where should they sit? It is polite to arrive either early or at the time for which the service has been called. In some more conservative churches it is customary for men to stand or sit on the right-hand side of the nave as one enters, and women on the left. If uncertain, it would be worth asking what the church's custom is before arrival.

If arriving late, are there times when a guest should not enter the ceremony? Do not enter during Scripture readings and priestly blessings.

Are there times when a guest should not leave the ceremony? No.

Who are the major officiants, leaders or participants at the ceremony and what do they do?

A priest, who is usually the chief celebrant, unless a bishop is present, in which case the bishop will be chief celebrant and the priest will assist him.

The deacon, subdeacon and altar servers, all of whom, if present, assist the bishop or priest.

The bride and groom.

To indicate the order of the service: An order of service or Liturgy service book may be provided. If not, most texts are freely available, both online and in hard copy. It would be worth enquiring in advance if you are interested in following the service.

Will a guest who is not a member of an Orthodox church be expected to do anything other than just be present? Yes, try to follow the lead of the rest of the congregation. If the marriage service is part of a Divine Liturgy, then there will be certain elements of the service for which all are expected to stand: the Entrances (the Little Entrance, being a procession with the Gospel, and the Great Entrance, being a procession with the paten and chalice), when being censed, during the reading of the Gospel, during the prayer of consecration and during the communion of the people. Reading prayers aloud and singing with the congregants are optional.

Are there any parts of the service in which a guest who is not a member of an Orthodox church should not participate? Do not participate in Holy Communion, if such occurs. This is the high point of the service. It occurs after the priest or deacon advances towards the congregation from the altar, holds up the chalice and says, 'With fear of God, with faith and with love, draw near.' Congregants who are members of an Orthodox church will then go forward to receive Communion; remain seated if you are not Orthodox.

If not disruptive to the service, is it OK to:

Take pictures? Only with prior permission of a church official.
Use a flash? Only with prior permission of a church official.
Use video recording equipment? Only with prior permission of a church official.
Use audio recording equipment? If disruptive, then only with prior permission of a church official.

Will contributions to the church be collected at the service? Sometimes, if the ceremony is part of a Divine Liturgy, in which case a plate will be passed through the congregation. Another way of contributing to the upkeep of the church is by the purchase of candles, which are usually on sale in some part of the church, and are lit by individuals as part of their prayer. In many Orthodox churches visitors will be welcome to light candles.

How much is it customary to contribute? While the amount of the contribution is at the discretion of congregants or visitors, and the various Orthodox churches do not feel comfortable recommending specific amounts to guests, contributions between £1 and £5 are common.

After the ceremony

Is there usually a reception after the ceremony? Yes. This may last from one to four hours and may be held in the same building as the ceremony, at a catering hall or at the bride's parents' home. A meal will be served, often accompanied by alcoholic drinks.

Would it be considered impolite to neither eat nor drink? No.

Is there a grace or benediction before eating or drinking? Usually. An invocation is recited to bless the food.

Is there a grace or benediction after eating or drinking? Sometimes.

Is there a traditional greeting for the family? In the Antiochian Orthodox Church, the traditional greeting for all occasions is '*Mabbrook*' ('MAB-brook'), which means 'Blessings'.

In the Romanian Orthodox Church, the traditional greeting is '*La multi ani!*' ('Lah MOOLTZ AH-nee'), which means 'Many years!'

In the Greek Orthodox Church, the traditional greeting is '*Khronia Polla!*' (HRON-ee-ah poll-AH), which also means 'Many years!'

In all Orthodox churches, 'Congratulations!' is appropriate.

Is there a traditional form of address for clergy who may be at the reception? 'Father'.

Is it OK to leave early? Yes.

Funerals and Mourning

Orthodox churches believe that death is the separation of the soul (the spiritual dimension of each human being) from the body (the physical dimension of each human being). Upon death, we immediately begin to experience a foretaste of heaven and hell. This experience, known as the partial judgement, is based on the general character of our lives regarding behaviour, character and communion with God.

At some unknown time in the future, the churches teach, Jesus Christ will return and inaugurate a new era in which his kingdom will be established. The souls of the departed will be reunited with their bodies and the final judgement will then occur. In our resurrected existence, we will either live eternally in heaven in communion with God, or live eternally in hell, in continual rejection of the love of God.

The funeral ceremony normally lasts about an hour, and is not generally part of a larger service, although in some cases the Eucharistic Liturgy (essentially the Sunday morning worship service) is often celebrated before the funeral service. This may cause the entire ceremony to last up to ninety minutes.

Before the ceremony

How soon after the death does the funeral usually take place?
Usually about a week.

What should a non-Orthodox do upon hearing of the death of a member of that faith? It is appropriate to visit or telephone the bereaved at their home before the funeral to express condolences and recall the life of the deceased. When visiting a bereaved family before the service, a traditional greeting is 'May his (or her) memory be eternal'.

Appropriate attire

Smart clothes in sombre, dark colours are recommended for both men and women.

Gifts

Is it appropriate to send flowers or make a contribution? It is appropriate to send flowers to the funeral home before the funeral. It is also appropriate to make a contribution in memory of the deceased either to his or her church or to a fund or charity designated by the family of the deceased.

Is it appropriate to send food? Not unless requested.

The ceremony

Where will the ceremony take place? Usually at the church of the deceased.

When should guests arrive and where should they sit? It is polite to arrive either early or at the time for which the service has been called. In some more conservative churches it is customary for men to stand or sit on the right-hand side of the nave as one enters, and women on the left. If uncertain, it would be worth asking what the church's custom is before arrival.

Are there times when a guest should not leave the ceremony? No.

Will the bereaved family be present at the church or funeral home before the ceremony? Yes.

Is there a traditional greeting for the family? A traditional greeting is 'May God give you the strength to bear your loss', but simply expressing your condolences is fine.

Will there be an open coffin? Traditionally, yes, usually in the centre of the church.

Is a guest expected to view the body? This is optional for non-Orthodox guests.

What is appropriate behaviour upon viewing the body? Stand briefly in front of the coffin and offer a silent prayer. It is usual for Orthodox Christians as they arrive at the church to make the sign of the cross and to kiss either the face of the departed or the icon or cross held in the hands of the departed or placed on the coffin. Towards the end of the service comes the 'last kiss', the moment at which people make their farewell to the departed by kissing their face or the cross or icon. After this the lid is placed on the coffin, and the deceased conveyed to the place of burial.

Who are the major officiants at the ceremony and what do they do?

A priest, who is usually the chief celebrant, unless a bishop is present, in which case the bishop will be chief celebrant and the priest will assist him.

The deacon, subdeacon and altar servers, all of whom, when present, assist the bishop or priest.

To indicate the order of the ceremony: An order of service may be distributed.

Will a guest who is not a member of an Orthodox church be expected to do anything other than just be present? Yes, try to follow the lead of the rest of the congregation. If the funeral is preceded by a Divine Liturgy, then there will be certain elements of the service for which all are expected to stand: the Entrances (the Little Entrance, being a procession with the Gospel, and the Great Entrance, being a procession with the paten and chalice), when being censed, during the reading of the Gospel, during the prayer of consecration and during the communion of the people. Reading prayers aloud and singing with the congregants are optional.

Are there any parts of the service in which a guest who is not a member of an Orthodox church should not participate? Do not participate in Holy Communion, if such occurs. This is the high point of the service. It occurs after the priest or deacon advances towards the congregation from the altar, holds up the chalice and says, 'With fear of God, with faith and with love, draw near.' Congregants who are members of an Orthodox church will then go forward to receive Communion; remain seated if you are not Orthodox.

If not disruptive to the service, is it OK to:

Take pictures? Only with prior permission of a church official.
Use a flash? Only with prior permission of a church official.
Use video recording equipment? Only with prior permission of a church official.
Use audio recording equipment? If disruptive, then only with prior permission of a church official.

Will contributions to the church be collected at the ceremony? No.

The interment

Should guests attend the interment? This is entirely optional.

Whom should one ask for directions? Ask the funeral director or a family member.

What happens at the graveside? There will be a brief prayer ceremony, followed by the officiating priest or bishop usually scattering soil on top of the coffin so it forms the shape of a cross, and then each person present placing one flower on the coffin or spreading soil on the coffin. The flowers usually come from those sent to the church for the funeral and then conveyed to the cemetery with the coffin. Cremation is not usually permitted in the Orthodox tradition.

Do guests who are not members of an Orthodox church participate at the graveside ceremony?

No. They are simply present.

Comforting the bereaved

Is it appropriate to visit the home of the bereaved after the funeral? Yes. Religious objects that a visitor may see at such a visit are icons, a lighted candle and burning incense.

Will there be a religious service at the home of the bereaved? No.

Will food be served? A Meal of Mercy is often given in the church hall, a restaurant or the home of the deceased shortly after the burial.

How soon after the funeral will a mourner usually return to a normal work schedule? The bereaved usually stays home from work for one week.

How soon after the funeral will a mourner usually return to a normal social schedule? The bereaved usually avoids social gatherings for two months. In some cases, especially that of widows, the bereaved may avoid such occasions for a full year after the loss of the deceased. Mourning attire, such as black clothing, is generally worn for this entire period.

Are there rituals for observing the anniversary of the death? A memorial service is held on the third, ninth and the Sunday closest to the fortieth day after the death. Subsequent memorial services are held, either at the church or at the graveside, three, six and nine months after the death, and on the annual anniversary of the death.

5. HOME CELEBRATIONS

The Home Blessing

When does it occur? Either annually during the week following 6 January, the feast of Theophany, or shortly after moving into a new home.

What is its significance? Holy water, which is sprinkled in each room, is used to sanctify the home, just as Jesus' baptism sanctified the waters of the River Jordan and all creation.

What is the proper greeting to the celebrants? 'Congratulations' or 'May God grant you many years!'

Before the ceremony

Are guests usually invited by a formal invitation? Either by telephone or by a written invitation.

If not stated explicitly, should one assume children are invited? Yes.

If one cannot attend, what should one do? Telephone the celebrants with your regrets.

Appropriate attire

Men: A jacket and tie or more casual clothing is appropriate.

Women: A dress or a skirt and blouse or trousers.

There are no rules regarding colours of clothing.

Gifts

Is a gift customarily expected? This is entirely optional.

If one decides to give a gift, is a certain type of gift appropriate? The usual sort of housewarming gift, which should be brought to the house when you arrive.

The ceremony

The home blessing ceremony lasts between fifteen and thirty minutes. The major officiant is the priest, who blesses the home.

What are the major ritual objects of the ceremony?

The cross, which represents Christ's victory over death through his resurrection.

Water, which is a vehicle for sanctification.

A sprig of greenery (often basil), which is used to sprinkle water in the air in the configuration of a cross in each room throughout the house as the priest recites blessings.

A candle, which symbolises that Christ is the Light of the world.

Incense, representing the fragrance of prayer.

Will a guest who is not a member of an Orthodox church be expected to do anything other than sit? Stand when the celebrants rise.

Are there any parts of the ceremony in which a guest who is not a member of an Orthodox church should not participate? No.

If not disruptive to the service, is it OK to:

Take pictures? Only with prior permission of the celebrants.

Use a flash? Only with prior permission of the celebrants.

Use video recording equipment? Only with prior permission of the celebrants.

Use audio recording equipment? Only with prior permission of the celebrants.

Eating and drinking

Is a meal part of the celebration? Possibly. If so, it is served after the ceremony.

Will there be alcoholic drinks? Possibly.

Would it be considered impolite to neither eat nor drink? No.

Is there a grace or benediction before eating or drinking? Usually. An invocation is recited to bless the food.

Is there a grace or benediction after eating or drinking? Sometimes.

At the meal, will a guest be asked to say or do anything? No.

Will there be:

Dancing? No.

Music? No.

16

Pentecostal

1. HISTORY AND BELIEFS

Pentecostalism is the name of a movement within Christianity rather than a particular church or denomination. In the UK, there are several networks of churches commonly described as Pentecostal, such as Assemblies of God, Elim Pentecostal and Hillsong Churches, and also independent congregations in the Pentecostal tradition. It has been cited as the fastest-growing group of Christians in the UK, and the third largest behind Catholics and Anglicans.

Pentecostal Christians tend to place great importance on the literal and infallible authority of the Bible, and seek to live a life of faith modelled closely on that of the earliest Christians as recorded in Scripture. Their faith is also strongly experiential, rather than something that is found through ritual or intellectualism. Pentecostals emphasise the work of the Holy Spirit and direct encounter with God. A true conversion, according to most Pentecostals, will involve 'baptism in the Spirit', by which a person is filled with the Holy Spirit. As well as equipping that person with the strength and ability to live the Christian life, the Holy Spirit will also bless that person with 'gifts of the Spirit', such as prophecy, healing and 'speaking in tongues' – the ability to speak in a language previously unknown to the speaker. The term 'Pentecostal' is derived from the account of Pentecost recorded in the Bible: the day on which a gathering of Jesus' first disciples experienced a violent wind from heaven, followed by the corporate ability to speak in tongues.

Pentecostal worship is typically more emotionally and physically expressive than that of most other Christian traditions.

The first Pentecostal church in the UK was founded in 1908 by William Oliver Hutchinson at the Emmanuel Mission Hall, Bournemouth. It became the headquarters of a network of Pentecostal churches which would later be known as the Apostolic Faith Church. Another early British Pentecostal denomination was the Elim Pentecostal Church, which was founded in 1915 in Ireland by a Welshman, George Jeffreys.

Traditions and practices may vary slightly between individual Pentecostal churches and networks, so the following chapter should be treated as a rough guide only. Its primary source for information has been the Elim Pentecostal Church, which has over 500 congregations throughout the UK.

UK churches: unknown
UK membership: approximately 1 million

For more information, contact:

Apostolic Faith Church
95 Fenham Road
Peckham
London
SE15 1AE
Tel: 020 7639 8897
Email: worship@apostolicfaith.org.uk

Elim International Centre
De Walden Road
West Malvern
Worcestershire
WR14 4DF
Tel: 0845 302 6750
Email: info@elimhq.net

Hillsong Church London
PO Box 29971

London
SW6 2WX
Tel: 020 7384 9200

2. THE BASIC SERVICE

The basic service of Christian celebration in Pentecostal churches generally takes place on a Sunday morning, although some churches will also hold a Sunday evening service. The service, the dual purpose of which is to build up, challenge and encourage believers and to present unbelievers with the challenge of faith, will comprise worship, praise, a presentation from the Bible (often the Gospel – the good news of Jesus Christ) and sometimes Communion (partaking of bread and wine representing the body and blood of Christ).

Pentecostal services are open for anybody to attend with or without an invitation. A service will typically last about one hour.

Appropriate Attire

There is no dress code for men or women, and casual clothing is generally worn by all.

The Sanctuary

While most Pentecostal churches will have their own building in which to meet for worship, some will hire premises for the purpose, such as a public hall or a school hall.

What are the major sections of the church or hall?

Open meeting room: Where the main service takes place.
Ancillary rooms: There may be smaller rooms to which children will be taken for crèche and Sunday school while the main service takes place.

꧂

The Service

When should guests arrive and where should they sit? Try to arrive early. While there is no particular order to the seating, there will often be a steward on hand to help you find an available seat.

If arriving late, are there times when a guest should not enter the service? No.

Are there times when a guest should not leave the service? No.

Who are the major officiants, leaders or participants and what do they do?

A minister or pastor, who will preach, lead the service and administer Communion.

A worship leader, who will lead the congregation, singers and musicians in praise and worship.

What are the major ritual objects of the service?

The Communion tray, which may be used to distribute the bread and wine throughout the congregation.

What books are used? A Bible and sometimes a song book, although more often the words of songs will be projected onto a screen.

To indicate the order of the service: Whoever is leading the service will make periodic announcements.

꧂

Guest Behaviour during the Service

Will a guest who is not a member of the Pentecostal church be expected to do anything other than sit? It is acceptable to stand and sing along with other members of the congregation, if this does not compromise your personal beliefs.

Are there any parts of the service in which a guest who is not a member of the Pentecostal church should not participate? You should not take Communion if you are not a believer.

If not disruptive to the service, is it OK to:

Take pictures? Yes.

Use a flash? No.

Use video recording equipment? No.

Use audio recording equipment? Not unless specifically authorised (most churches record the sermon).

Will contributions to the church be collected at the service? Yes, although guests are not expected to contribute unless they so wish.

How much is it customary to contribute? Church members often tithe a percentage of their income, but this is not compulsory and would not be expected of a guest. If you wish to contribute, the amount is entirely at your own discretion.

After the Service

Is there usually a reception after the ceremony? There is usually a short, informal reception after the service, held in the church itself or an adjoining room or hall. It will be announced during or at the end of the service. Coffee and biscuits are usually served. Occasionally a longer reception may be held, with buffet-style food. There would not be any alcoholic drinks.

Would it be considered impolite to neither eat nor drink? No.

Is there a ritual before eating or drinking? A grace would normally be said if there was a meal, but not if the only food is biscuits.

Is there a grace or benediction after eating or drinking? No.

Is there a traditional form of address for clergy who may be at the reception? 'Pastor'.

Is it OK to leave early? Yes.

✻

Some Basic Beliefs

Pentecostals believe:

That the Bible is the fully inspired and infallible Word of God and the supreme and final authority in all matters of faith and conduct.

That the Godhead exists co-equally and co-eternally in three persons, Father, Son and Holy Spirit.

That through repentance towards God and faith in Jesus Christ, all sinners may be pardoned and accepted as righteous in God's sight.

That through baptism in the Holy Spirit, believers are empowered for fuller participation in the ministry of the Church, its worship, evangelism and service.

Some basic resources to which a guest can refer to learn more about the Pentecostal faith:

The Elim Pentecostal movement has a national magazine called *Direction*, which includes a visitors' guide and a brief history of Elim.

3. HOLY DAYS AND FESTIVALS

Christmas: Always falls on 25 December. Celebrates the birth of Jesus Christ. The traditional greeting is 'Merry Christmas'.

Easter: Always falls on the Sunday after the first full moon that occurs on or after the spring equinox of 21 March. Celebrates the resurrection of Jesus. The traditional greeting is 'Happy Easter'.

Pentecost: Occurs fifty days after Easter because this is when the Holy Spirit descended on Jesus' apostles. Celebrates the power of the Holy Spirit and its manifestation in the early Christian church. There is no traditional greeting for this holiday.

Ash Wednesday: Occurs forty days before Easter. Commemorates the beginning of Lent, which is a season for preparation and penitence before Easter itself. There is no traditional greeting for this holiday.

Maundy Thursday: Falls four days before Easter. Commemorates the institution of the Eucharist (also known as Communion) and Jesus' subsequent arrest and trial. There is no traditional greeting.

Good Friday: Three days before Easter. Commemorates the crucifixion, death and burial of Jesus.

Christmas, Easter and Pentecost are joyful celebrations. Ash Wednesday, Maundy Thursday and Good Friday are sombre, penitential commemorations. During the services for these latter three holidays, decorum and discretion are of great importance.

4. LIFE CYCLE EVENTS

Birth Ceremony

Most Pentecostal churches will hold a service of dedication for a child born to members of their church. The service witnesses the parents' commitment to bring up the child by Christian principles, and dedicates him or her to God.

The dedication ceremony is generally held as a short segment of the normal Sunday worship service.

Before the ceremony

Are guests usually invited by a formal invitation? Normally by verbal invitation.

If not stated explicitly, should one assume that children are invited? Yes.

If one cannot attend, what should one do? This is at the discretion of the individual. A polite and prompt reply, expressing regret, is recommended.

Appropriate attire

There is no dress code for men or women, but smart casual clothing is recommended for a dedication ceremony.

Gifts

Is a gift customarily expected? No.

The service

When should guests arrive and where should they sit? Try to arrive early. While there is no particular order to the seating, there will often be a steward on hand to help you find an available seat.

If arriving late, are there times when a guest should not enter the service? No.

Are there times when a guest should not leave the service? It would be preferable not to leave during the actual dedication.

Who are the major officiants, leaders or participants and what do they do?

A minister or pastor, who will preach, lead the service and administer Communion.

A worship leader, who will lead the congregation, singers and musicians in praise and worship.

Parents, who will offer the child for dedication.

What are the major ritual objects of the service?

The Communion tray, which may be used to distribute the bread and wine throughout the congregation.

What books are used? A Bible and sometimes a song book, although more often the words of songs will be projected onto a screen.

To indicate the order of the service: Whoever is leading the service will make periodic announcements.

Guest Behaviour during the Service

Will a guest who is not a member of the Pentecostal church be expected to do anything other than sit? It is acceptable to stand and sing along with other members of the congregation, if this does not compromise your personal beliefs.

Are there any parts of the service in which a guest who is not a member of the Pentecostal church should not participate? You should not take Communion if you are not a believer.

If not disruptive to the service, is it OK to:

Take pictures? Yes.
Use a flash? No.
Use video recording equipment? Yes.
Use audio recording equipment? Yes.

Will contributions to the church be collected at the service? Yes, although guests are not expected to contribute unless they so wish.

How much is it customary to contribute? Church members often tithe a percentage of their income, but this is not compulsory and would not be expected of a guest. If you wish to contribute, the amount is entirely at your own discretion.

After the ceremony

Is there usually a reception after the ceremony? There may be an informal reception as described above under 'The Basic Service'. The parents of the dedicated child may also hold a reception at their own house.

Would it be considered impolite to neither eat nor drink? No.

Is there a ritual before eating or drinking? A grace may be said if there is a meal.

Is there a grace or benediction after eating or drinking? No.

Is there a traditional form of address for clergy who may be at the reception? 'Pastor'.

Is it OK to leave early? Yes.

꧁

Initiation Ceremony

A baptism ceremony will be held for believers following their having made a commitment of faith in Jesus Christ. This is applicable to adults as well as children, although it is rare that a child less than twelve years old will be baptised. During the baptism, the individual will be completely immersed in baptismal waters, a public witness of their faith. Most Pentecostal churches will have their own baptismal pool or tank, while others may hire the public swimming pool for the baptism. If the ceremony takes place in the church, it will commonly be part of the basic Sunday worship service.

Before the ceremony

Are guests usually invited by a formal invitation? Normally by verbal invitation.

If not stated explicitly, should one assume that children are invited? Yes.

If one cannot attend, what should one do? This is at the discretion of the individual. A polite and prompt reply, expressing regret, is recommended.

Appropriate attire

There is no dress code for men or women, and casual clothing is generally worn by all.

Gifts

Is a gift customarily expected? No.

The service

When should guests arrive and where should they sit? Try to arrive early. While there is no particular order to the seating, there will often be a steward on hand to help you find an available seat.

If arriving late, are there times when a guest should not enter the service? No.

Are there times when a guest should not leave the service? There are no rules governing this, but it would be preferable not to leave during the baptism part of the ceremony.

Who are the major officiants, leaders or participants and what do they do?

A minister or pastor, who will preach, lead the service, administer Communion and perform the baptism.

Assistant, who will assist the minister with the baptism.

A worship leader, who will lead the congregation, singers and musicians in praise and worship.

What are the major ritual objects of the service?

Baptismal pool or tank, in which the baptism will be performed.

The Communion tray, which may be used to distribute the bread and wine throughout the congregation.

What books are used? A Bible and sometimes a song book, although more often the words of songs will be projected onto a screen.

To indicate the order of the service: Whoever is leading the service will make periodic announcements.

Guest behaviour during the service

Will a guest who is not a member of the Pentecostal church be expected to do anything other than sit? It is acceptable to stand and sing along with other members of the congregation, if this does not compromise your personal beliefs.

Are there any parts of the service in which a guest who is not a member of the Pentecostal church should not participate? You should not take Communion if you are not a believer.

If not disruptive to the service, is it OK to:

Take pictures? Yes.

Use a flash? Yes, with prior permission.
Use video recording equipment? Yes.
Use audio recording equipment? Yes.

Will contributions to the church be collected at the service? Yes, although guests are not expected to contribute unless they so wish.

How much is it customary to contribute? Church members often tithe a percentage of their income, but this is not compulsory and would not be expected of a guest. If you wish to contribute, the amount is entirely at your own discretion.

Is there usually a reception after the ceremony? Not particular to the baptism, although there may be a short informal reception as described under 'The Basic Service' above.

Some basic beliefs

Guests should be aware that only believers are baptised in a Pentecostal church, as a witness of their faith. Most Pentecostal churches do not practise infant baptism.

Marriage Ceremony

Pentecostal Christians believe that, through marriage, God joins together man and woman in physical and spiritual union.

The marriage ceremony is most commonly a service in itself lasting between thirty and sixty minutes, and will be held at the local Pentecostal church.

Before the ceremony

Are guests usually invited by a formal invitation? Yes.

If not stated explicitly, should one assume that children are invited? No.

If one cannot attend, what should one do? Send a polite and prompt reply, and send a gift if possible.

Appropriate attire

There is no dress code for men or women, but smart casual clothing is recommended.

Gifts

Is a gift customarily expected? Yes. Details of a gift list are often included with the wedding invitation. If not, then the nature of the gift is at the discretion of the individual.

Should gifts be brought to the ceremony? This depends on the wishes of the bride and groom.

The ceremony

When should guests arrive and where should they sit? Arrive early. Ushers will be on hand to show guests where to sit.

If arriving late, are there times when a guest should not enter the ceremony? Yes, try not to enter during the marriage vows.

Are there times when a guest should not leave the ceremony? Yes, try not to leave during the marriage vows.

Who are the major officiants, leaders or participants at the ceremony and what do they do?

A minister or pastor, who will preach, lead the service and administer Communion.
A registrar, who will record the wedding for legal purposes.
A worship leader, who will lead the congregation, singers and musicians in praise and worship.

What books are used? A Bible and a printed order of service.

Guest behaviour during the service

Will a guest who is not a member of the Pentecostal church be expected to do anything other than sit? It is acceptable to stand

and sing along with other members of the congregation, if this does not compromise your personal beliefs.

Are there any parts of the service in which a guest who is not a member of the Pentecostal church should not participate? You should not take Communion (if it is taken as part of the service) if you are not a believer.

If not disruptive to the service, is it OK to:

Take pictures? Yes.
Use a flash? Yes, with prior permission.
Use video recording equipment? Yes.
Use audio recording equipment? Yes.

Will contributions to the church be collected at the service? No.

After the ceremony

Is there usually a reception after the ceremony? There will usually be a formal reception after the service, which may be held at the church, a hotel or other hired venue, or wherever the bride and groom choose. A meal will usually be provided for all guests, there will be speeches and a cutting the cake ceremony. There may be alcoholic drinks, but not if the ceremony is held on church premises. The reception will most likely last for a few hours.

Would it be considered impolite to neither eat nor drink? No.

Is there a ritual before eating? A grace will usually be said before people start to eat.

Is there a ritual after eating? No.

Is there a traditional form of address for clergy who may be at the reception? 'Pastor'.

Funerals and Mourning

Most Pentecostals believe that those who accept Jesus Christ as their personal Saviour are assured of eternal life in heaven.

A funeral service will precede either burial or cremation of the deceased's body. It will be held at the local Pentecostal church and will usually last between thirty and sixty minutes.

Before the ceremony

How soon after the death does the funeral usually take place? Usually within one week.

What should someone who is not a member of the Pentecostal church do upon hearing of the death of a member of that faith? A personal visit to a member of the family of, or close friend of, the deceased would be appropriate if you know them well. Allow the bereaved to express their emotions and to talk about their loved one. Assure them of your love, support and prayers.

Gifts

Is it appropriate to send flowers or make a contribution? Flowers are appropriate, unless there has been a specific request for none. A contribution to a specific cause is appropriate if requested by the bereaved.

Appropriate attire

There is no dress code for men or women, but smart clothing such as a jacket and tie for men, and a dress or skirt and blouse for women, is recommended.

The ceremony

When should guests arrive and where should they sit? Arrive early. Ushers will be on hand to show guests where to sit.

If arriving late, are there times when a guest should not enter the ceremony? No.

Are there times when a guest should not leave the ceremony? No.

Who are the major officiants, leaders or participants at the ceremony and what do they do?

A minister or pastor, who will preach, lead the service and administer Communion.

Family or friends of the bereaved, who may have been requested to pay a tribute.

Will the bereaved family be present at the church or funeral home before the service? Not usually.

Is there a traditional greeting for the family? No.

Will there be an open coffin? No.

What books are used? A Bible.

To indicate the order of the service: A printed order of service may be provided, and the minister will make periodic announcements.

Guest behaviour during the service

Will a guest who is not a member of the Pentecostal church be expected to do anything other than sit? It is acceptable to stand and sing along with other members of the congregation, if this does not compromise your personal beliefs.

Are there any parts of the service in which a guest who is not a member of the Pentecostal church should not participate? No.

If not disruptive to the service, is it OK to:

Take pictures? Only with permission of bereaved.
Use a flash? Only with permission of bereaved.
Use video recording equipment? Only with permission of bereaved.
Use audio recording equipment? Only with permission of bereaved.

Will contributions to the church be collected at the service? No.

The interment

Should guests attend the interment? Yes, if requested.

Whom should one ask for directions? The funeral director.

What happens at the graveside of a burial? There may be a reading from Scripture, a short spoken tribute, a hymn or song and finally the committal of the body. Guests are required simply to be present.

What happens at a cremation? There may be a reading from Scripture, a short spoken tribute, a hymn or song and finally the committal of the body. Guests are required simply to be present.

Comforting the bereaved

Is it appropriate to visit the home of the bereaved after the funeral? Yes.

How soon after the funeral will a mourner usually return to a normal work schedule? This varies, depending on the individual.

How soon after the funeral will a mourner usually return to a normal social schedule? This varies, depending on the individual.

5. HOME CELEBRATIONS

House Group

When does it occur? Weekly or monthly.

What is its significance? Members of the church meet together in small groups for prayer, Bible study and fellowship. This follows the biblical tradition of members of the early church meeting 'from house to house' (Acts 2:46).

Before the ceremony

Are guests usually invited by a formal invitation? No, more likely by informal conversation.

If not stated explicitly, should one assume children are invited? No.

If one cannot attend, what should one do? Visit at another time.

Appropriate attire

There is no dress code for men or women, and casual clothing is generally worn by all.

Gifts

Is a gift customarily expected? No.

The meeting

When should guests arrive and where should they sit? Arrive at the time called. The group will normally be in the living area of the host's house, and just sit in one of the chairs provided or on the floor.

If arriving late, are there times when a guest should not enter the meeting? No.

Are there times when a guest should not leave the meeting? No.

Who are the major officiants, leaders or participants at the meeting and what do they do?

A house group leader, who will lead the meeting.

What books are used? A Bible.

Guest behaviour during the meeting

Will a guest who is not a member of the Pentecostal church be expected to do anything other than sit? No, but you will be free to join in the conversation as you wish.

Are there any parts of the meeting in which a guest who is not a member of the Pentecostal church should not participate? You should not take Communion (if it is taken as part of the group) if you are not a believer.

If not disruptive to the meeting, is it OK to:

Take pictures? Not without the host's permission.
Use a flash? Not without the host's permission.
Use video recording equipment? Not without the host's permission.
Use audio recording equipment? Not without the host's permission.

Will contributions to the church be collected at the meeting? No.

Eating and drinking

Is a meal part of the meeting? Tea, coffee and biscuits will usually be provided. Occasionally there will be a buffet or meal.

Will there be alcoholic drinks? Not usually.

Would it be considered impolite to neither eat nor drink? No.

Is there a grace or benediction before eating or drinking? A grace may be said before eating a meal.

Is there a grace or benediction after eating or drinking? No.

Will there be:

Dancing? No.

Music? There may be gospel music played.

General guidelines and advice

The home group meetings are generally informal. Simply behave as you normally would in somebody else's house.

17

Quaker

1. HISTORY AND BELIEFS

The name 'Quakers' was originally a nickname for the followers of a movement founded by George Fox in the mid-seventeenth century. Fox was critical of the established churches of the day, and many Christians' way of life, which did not seem consistent with what the faith taught. He aimed to inspire people to hear and obey the voice of God for themselves, and become a community 'renewed up again in God's image' by living the principles of their faith. Members of the group were said to tremble or quake with religious zeal, and the nickname stuck. In time, they came to be known simply as 'Friends'.

The central Quaker conviction is that every person has an inner light (part of God's Spirit) inside them, so there is a unity between all human beings. The movement has Christian origins and some Quakers still affirm their acceptance of Jesus as their personal Saviour. Others conceive of the inward guide as a universal spirit that was in Jesus in abundant nature and is in everyone to some degree. Most agree that spiritual truth can only be known through direct revelation from God, who continues to 'talk' to people today.

This reliance on the spirit within and an individual's direct encounter with God was a direct challenge to religions that relied on outward authority, such as Catholicism or mainstream Protestantism. Largely because of this, Quakers were persecuted from the time they were founded in England in the 1650s. This tapered off about four decades later, and the English Quakers continued to grow and establish Quaker meetings, or congregations, in many parts of the world.

Quakers do not have ordained ministers and do not celebrate outward Christian sacraments. They seek, instead, an inward reality and contend that all life is sacramental.

Belief in the 'inner light' present in every person also accounts for the distinctive nature of Quaker worship, in which the congregation is silent except when individuals are moved to speak. This conviction also motivates Quaker confidence in working for the kingdom of God in this world and their emphasis over the years on non-violence and peace, abolishing slavery, relieving suffering, improving housing, educational and employment opportunities, reforming prisons, and eliminating prejudice and discrimination against minorities and the underprivileged.

Quakers are strongly opposed to war and conscription and seek to remove the causes of war and conflict; many declare themselves to be conscientious objectors.

UK meetings, or congregations: approximately 400
UK membership: approximately 17,000

For more information, contact:

Friends House
173 Euston Road
London
NW1 2BJ
Tel: 020 7663 1000
Email: enquiries@quaker.org.uk

2. THE BASIC MEETING

A Quaker meeting for worship happens when two or more people feel the need to be still together, expecting to experience God's presence. A Quaker meeting creates a space of gathered stillness. Quaker meetings are based on stillness: a silence of waiting and listening for the promptings of truth and love in the hearts of those gathered. There may be silence for quite some time, perhaps half an hour or more, combined with spoken contributions if someone feels moved to offer something to the meeting.

Quaker meetings are open for anybody to attend and, while they often take place on Sunday mornings, they can be on any day of the week and at any time. They normally take place in a Quaker meeting house, rented rooms or sometimes in Quakers' houses.

❦

Appropriate Attire

There are no rules for what people should wear. Some will come dressed smartly, and others in casual clothes.

❦

The Sanctuary

What are the major sections of the meeting house?

Meeting room, a simple room with a (normally) circular arrangement of chairs for participants to sit in.

❦

The Meeting

When should guests arrive and where should they sit? Arrive early or at the time called. Sit anywhere – there is no fixed seating in a Quaker meeting for worship.

If arriving late, are there times when a guest should not enter the meeting? Most meetings will admit latecomers all together, normally after ten or fifteen minutes of the meeting. Others allow people to enter whenever they arrive. The Quaker welcoming you at the door will be able to say what local practice is. In any case, it is normal not to enter when somebody is speaking, but to wait until they have finished and sat down.

Are there times when a guest should not leave the meeting? It is normal not to leave when somebody is speaking. Most people will stay all the way through the meeting.

Who are the major officiants, leaders or participants and what do they do? There are no particular leaders of worship within a Quaker meeting for worship; all those present are equal and can take a full part. One or two Quakers will have been appointed to signal the end of the meeting, often by shaking hands.

The other roles within the meeting (outside of worship) are undertaken by Quakers who are asked to serve for specific periods. There are no ordained or professional clergy in Britain.

What are the major ritual objects of the meeting?

Central table, which has no ritual significance, but normally holds religious books including the Bible and *Quaker Faith and Practice* (a book of organisation and an anthology of Quaker writings). There would typically also be a vase of flowers. Some meetings have drinking water available.

What books are used? Sometimes none; at other times, the Bible, *Quaker Faith and Practice* or another book may be referred to.

To indicate the order of the meeting: In most meetings, no announcements are made or programmes provided. The 'order' of the meeting is spontaneous and determined by who is present and what, if anything, they are moved to say. The leaflet *Your First Time in a Quaker Meeting* will normally be available, which describes what happens in a meeting.

Guest Behaviour during the Meeting

Will a guest who is not a Quaker be expected to do anything other than sit? Listen with an open mind to any spoken contributions. It is also customary to shake hands with neighbours at the end of the meeting.

Are there any parts of the meeting in which a guest who is not a Quaker should not participate? No.

If not disruptive to the meeting, is it OK to:

Take pictures? No.

Use a flash? No.

Use video recording equipment? No.

Use audio recording equipment? No.

Will contributions to the meeting be collected at the meeting? A collection bowl is normally available in the meeting house; donations are not collected publicly during a meeting for worship. Collections are normally either for the expenses of the meeting, or to support Quaker or non-Quaker peace or social witness work.

How much is it customary to contribute? Contributions are strictly voluntary; there is no recommended amount.

After the Meeting

Is there usually a reception after the meeting? Yes, usually somewhere in the meeting building. It will usually last less than thirty minutes, tea and coffee will be served and there will be an opportunity to chat to the other people present. Sometimes there may be a simple lunch, particularly if there is an event that the meeting is holding in the afternoon.

Would it be considered impolite to neither eat nor drink? No.

Is there a ritual before eating or drinking? Not usually, although sometimes a moment of silence is enjoyed during food, but this will be announced and people can start eating beforehand.

Is there a grace or benediction after eating or drinking? No.

Is there a traditional form of address for clergy who may be at the reception? There are no members of the clergy. It is customary to address Quakers by their given names, rather than by any titles including 'Ms', 'Mr' or 'Mrs'. This is because Quakers believe that everybody is equal. If addressing a group of people in a Quaker setting, then the generic 'Friends' is normally used, rather than 'Ladies and gentlemen'.

Is it OK to leave early? Yes.

※

General Guidelines and Advice

If anyone is moved to offer vocal ministry, they should first consider their motivation for speaking. Those who speak should be mindful about how long they speak and respect the need for an interval of time for worshippers to receive and consider the previous contribution from another worshipper.

Do not speak unless deeply moved and certain that your message is one that needs to be shared with those present, and speaking more than once in a single meeting is exceptionally rare. The messages offered at Quaker worship are not a discussion. Do not feel that you need to respond to a previous message.

※

Special Vocabulary

Friend: A traditional way for Quakers to refer to each other.
Vocal ministry: Feeling called to make a spoken contribution to a meeting for worship.

※

Some Basic Beliefs

Quakers believe:

Quakers share a way of life rather than a set of beliefs. They seek to experience God directly, within themselves and in their relationships with others and the world around them.

The Quaker way has its roots in Christianity and finds inspiration in the Bible and the life and teachings of Jesus. Quakers also find meaning and value in the teachings of other faiths; they acknowledge that theirs is not the only way. Their focus is on experience rather than written statements of belief. Their sense of community does not depend on professing identical beliefs, but on worshipping, sharing and working together.

They place a special value on truth, equality, simplicity and peace.

These testimonies, as they are known, lead Quakers to translate their faith into action by working locally and globally for social justice, to support peacemakers and care for the environment.

Some basic books to which a guest can refer to learn more about Quakers:

The Quaker website at http://www.quaker.org.uk/you has a good deal of introductory material.

A free information pack is available, including the book *A Light that is Shining*, by Harvey Gillman, an introduction to Quakers. Contact: 0808 109 1651 or outreach@quaker.org.uk

Another good introductory book is *New Light: Twelve Quaker Voices*, edited by Jennifer Kavanagh, which offers a range of diverse Quaker viewpoints. This, and many other books on Quakers, are available from the Quaker Bookshop: http://www.quaker.org.uk/bookshop, 020 7663 1030, or in person in the Quaker Centre at Friends House, opposite Euston Station in London.

For those wanting a lot of detail on Quaker organisation and spiritual understanding, the book *Quaker Faith and Practice* is available, either in print from the Quaker Bookshop (details above) or online at http://qfp.quakerweb.org.uk/

3. HOLY DAYS AND FESTIVALS

Quakers believe that every day is a holy day and that no one day is to be celebrated more than any other. Nevertheless, some Christmas and Easter celebrations do occasionally occur among Quakers through the influence of other Christian denominations. As with those denominations, Christmas, which always falls on 25 December, celebrates the birth of Christ; and Easter, which usually occurs in April, commemorates the death and resurrection of Jesus. Easter always falls on the Sunday after the first full moon that occurs on or after the spring equinox of 21 March.

As with other Christian faiths, the traditional greetings among Quakers for these holidays are 'Merry Christmas' and 'Happy Easter'.

4. LIFE CYCLE EVENTS

꧁꧂

Birth and Initiation Ceremonies

Quakers have no special birth or initiation ceremonies. Some meetings informally introduce new babies to the meeting when they first attend.

꧁꧂

Marriage Ceremony

Quakers believe that marriage is a binding relationship entered into in the presence of God and of witnessing friends. There is no priest or other clergy person involved in the ceremony.

A couple wishing to have a Quaker wedding must make an application to the registering officer at the Quakers' regular meeting. This must be received about six weeks before the date of the intended wedding. The couple must state that they are members of the Quakers when giving notice of marriage. If only one partner is a member, the other will be asked to state that they are in sympathy with the nature of the marriage and they must provide letters of recommendation from two other members.

A Quaker marriage ceremony has the form of a regular meeting, or worship meeting, but during it the bride and groom exchange vows and sign a marriage certificate. The certificate, which is a religious document, is read aloud, and then the meeting continues.

The marriage ceremony may last thirty to sixty minutes and is similar to a normal meeting for worship, but specifically focused on the couple and their marriage.

Before the ceremony

Are guests usually invited by a formal invitation? Yes.

If not stated explicitly, should one assume that children are invited? No – check with the couple.

If one cannot attend, what should one do? RSVP with your regrets. Possibly send a gift.

Appropriate attire

There are no rules for what people should wear. However, smart or smart casual clothes are recommended.

Gifts

Is a gift customarily expected? Yes. The couple will normally give guidance as to whether they have a gift list, or sometimes a chosen charity. Otherwise, use your best judgement.

Should gifts be brought to the ceremony? Usually they are sent to the home or brought to the reception.

The ceremony

Where will the ceremony take place? Depending on the wishes of the bride and groom, it may be in their meeting house or another house or building regularly used for Quaker worship.

When should guests arrive and where should they sit? Arrive early. Sit wherever you choose, but bear in mind that it is normal for the couple to sit near the table and for close family to sit by them. If in doubt, ask the Quaker welcomer.

If arriving late, are there times when a guest should not enter the meeting? Most meetings will admit latecomers all together, normally after ten or fifteen minutes of the meeting. Others allow people to enter whenever they arrive. The Quaker welcoming you at the door will be able to say what local practice is. In any case, it is normal not to enter when somebody is speaking, but to wait until they have finished and sat down.

Are there times when a guest should not leave the meeting? It is normal not to leave when somebody is speaking. Most people will stay all the way through the meeting.

Who are the major officiants, leaders or participants and what do they do?

Registering officer, a member of the meeting, who has been appointed to handle the record-keeping and registration of the wedding. They will ensure that the certificate is properly signed and may help to organise the meeting. They have no sacramental role.

What are the major ritual objects of the meeting?

Certificate of marriage, which is a formal (not a civil) record of the wedding, giving the names of the two people getting married, the fact that the marriage has been approved by Quakers in the area, and having the declarations (promises) made by the couple to each other recorded. This is signed by the couple during the wedding and by two or three people during the worship itself. After the worship, everyone who is present is asked to sign it. The certificate is a reminder that marriage is a public act of commitment.

What books are used? Sometimes none; at other times, the Bible, *Quaker Faith and Practice* or another book may be referred to.

To indicate the order of the ceremony: There will be no order of service, but the leaflet *A Quaker Wedding* will normally be available, which gives an indication of what will take place. A Quaker may introduce the meeting at the beginning.

Will a guest who is not a Quaker be expected to do anything other than sit? No, but guests are welcome to speak if moved to do so. At the end of the meeting, it is normal for all present, including children and non-Quaker guests, to sign the marriage certificate.

Are there any parts of the ceremony in which a guest who is not a Quaker should not participate? No.

If not disruptive to the ceremony, is it OK to:

Take pictures? No.
Use a flash? No.
Use video recording equipment? No.
Use audio recording equipment? No.

Will contributions to the meeting be collected at the ceremony?
No.

After the ceremony

Is there usually a reception after the ceremony? There will usually
be a private reception after the service, which will be organised by
the wedding couple, and details will be provided with the wedding
invitation. It may take place at the meeting house or at a private
venue, and could last through the rest of the day and evening.
Depending on the wishes of the wedding couple, food and drink may
be served and there may be speeches, the cutting of a wedding cake,
dancing and music.

Would it be considered impolite to neither eat nor drink? No.

Is there a grace or benediction before eating or drinking? No.

Is there a grace or benediction after eating or drinking? No.

Is it OK to leave early? Yes, but usually only after the wedding cake
is cut and served.

General guidelines and advice

It is normal for the meeting to gather in silence until the couple stand
up to make their promises to each other. After this has been done,
and the couple have sat down, other people present can offer vocal
ministry, if they feel called to do so.

Quakers in Britain decided at their Yearly Meeting in 2009 to celebrate same-sex marriages, and to push for these to be legally recognised in law as opposite-sex Quaker marriages are.

Funerals and Mourning

There is no particular Quaker etiquette or fixed practices for mourning,
although they do hold funerals and memorial meetings. These will
normally be held at the meeting house, or at a graveside or crematorium. They will generally be similar in form to an ordinary meeting

for worship, but vocal ministry will often be focused on the life of the deceased and the grace of God shown through it.

In funeral meetings, Quakers seek to experience a deep sense of communion with God and with one another, which they hope will comfort and strengthen those who mourn. There are at least two aims in their worship: to give thanks to God for the life that has been lived, and to help the mourners to feel a deep sense of God's presence.

Quakers have a diversity of views on death and the afterlife; there is no agreed view about what happens after death.

Before the ceremony

How soon after death does the funeral usually take place? Whenever arranged by the family or friends of the deceased.

What should a non-Quaker do upon hearing of the death of a member of that faith? Telephone, visit or send letters of sympathy to the bereaved. There is no specific 'ritual' for calling or expressing sympathy to someone who is mourning.

Appropriate attire

There are no rules for what people should wear. However, smart or smart casual clothes are recommended, unless the family has indicated in advance that casual clothes are acceptable or preferred.

Gifts

Is it appropriate to send flowers or make a contribution? Both are appropriate. When an announcement of a death, funeral or memorial service is made, then it may be stated that donations may be made to one or more charities in memory of the deceased. Never give more than you can afford.

The ceremony

When should guests arrive and where should they sit? Arrive early. There is normally no reserved seating, but check with the Quaker welcoming you at the door if you want to be sure.

If arriving late, are there times when a guest should not enter the ceremony? You should take advice from the Quaker welcoming you at the door.

Are there times when a guest should not leave the ceremony? It is normal to stay for the whole meeting. If you need to leave, you should not do so while somebody is speaking. It is polite to let the welcomer know that you may have to leave early.

Will the bereaved family be present at the meeting house or funeral home before the ceremony? There is no particular Quaker practice for this.

Is there a traditional greeting for the family? No.

Will there be an open coffin? There is no particular Quaker practice for this.

Who are the major officiants, leaders or participants and what do they do? There are no particular leaders of worship within a Quaker meeting for worship; all those present are equal and can take a full part. One or two Quakers will have been appointed to signal the end of the meeting, often by shaking hands.

The other roles within the meeting (outside of worship) are undertaken by Quakers who are asked to serve for specific periods. There are no ordained or professional clergy in Britain.

What are the major ritual objects of the meeting?

Central table, which has no ritual significance, but normally holds religious books including the Bible and *Quaker Faith and Practice* (a book of organisation and an anthology of Quaker writings). There would typically also be a vase of flowers. Some meetings have drinking water available.

What books are used? Sometimes none; at other times, the Bible, *Quaker Faith and Practice* or another book may be referred to.

To indicate the order of the ceremony: There is likely to be no order of service, but copies of the leaflet *Quaker Funerals* are likely to be available, explaining the process of Quaker funerals and memorial meetings. A Friend may introduce the meeting for worship.

Will a guest who is not a Quaker be expected to do anything other than sit? No.

Are there any parts of the ceremony in which a guest who is not a Quaker should not participate? No.

If not disruptive to the ceremony, is it OK to:

Take pictures? No.
Use a flash? No.
Use video recording equipment? No.
Use audio recording equipment? No.

Will contributions to the meeting be collected at the ceremony? No.

The interment

Should guests attend the interment? Yes if invited to do so. Sometimes a memorial meeting is held separately, with the interment or cremation limited to family and close friends.

What happens at the graveside? There is no particular Quaker burial ceremony. A meeting for worship may be held at the graveside or crematorium.

Do guests who are not Quakers participate at the graveside ceremony? No. They are simply present.

Comforting the bereaved

Is it appropriate to visit the home of the bereaved after the funeral? Yes, although there is no specific 'ritual' for calling or expressing sympathy to someone who is mourning. Nor is there a 'ritual' that guides the behaviour of the mourners.

Are there rituals for observing the anniversary of the death? No.

5. HOME CELEBRATIONS

Not applicable to Quakers.

18

Roman Catholic

1. HISTORY AND BELIEFS

The term *catholic* was first applied around AD 100 to the Christian Church, which was then one entity. It meant being geographically universal, continuous with the Christian past and transcending language, race and nation. The test of catholicity was communion with the universal Church and with the See of Rome.

After the Eastern and Western wings of the Church divided in 1054, *catholic* was more usually used to refer to the Church in the West under the spiritual leadership of the Bishop of Rome, living at the Vatican. Since the sixteenth century, 'Roman Catholic' has meant the religious body that acknowledges the Pope's authority and the Vatican as the centre of ecclesiastical unity.

In the nineteenth century, the Church became increasingly centralised in Rome. In 1870, the First Vatican Council declared that the Pope had jurisdictional primacy over the entire Church, and that under certain circumstances he was infallible in proclaiming doctrines of faith and morals.

In Roman Catholic teaching, revelation is summed up in Jesus Christ, who commanded his apostles to preach the gospel. To preserve the living gospel, the apostles appointed bishops as their successors. Roman Catholics believe in the unity of God, who is understood as God the Father, God (Jesus Christ) the Son, and God the Holy Spirit. Catholicism teaches that original sin – Adam and Eve's expulsion from the Garden of Eden for disobeying God – alienated humanity from God, but did not totally corrupt man and woman, and that grace through the death and resurrection of Jesus Christ can fully make a sinner just.

Catholics especially venerate Mary, the mother of Jesus. Catholics believe that Mary was conceived without original sin, and that she was a virgin when Jesus was conceived.

Roman Catholicism has about 900 million members in 2,000 dioceses around the world.

UK churches: approximately 4,200
UK membership: 5.6 million

For more information, contact:

The Bishops' Conference of England and Wales
39 Ecclestone Square
London
SW1V 1BX
Tel: 020 7630 8220
www.catholic-ew.org.uk

The Bishops' Conference of Scotland
General Secretariat
64 Aitken Street
Airdrie
ML6 6LT
Tel: 01236 764061
www.bpsconfscot.com

2. THE BASIC SERVICE

Sunday Mass lasts about thirty to sixty minutes. It consists of two principal divisions called the 'Liturgy of the Word', which features the proclamation of the Word of God, and the 'Liturgy of the Eucharist', which focuses on Jesus' sacrifice on behalf of humanity through the crucifixion.

During the Liturgy of the Word, passages from the Bible are read.

On a Sunday there are three readings: the first is usually from the Hebrew Scriptures (the Old Testament), the second and the third from the New Testament. Also, the presiding priest gives a homily, an explanation of some point in the readings and teaching in the faith. He and the congregation together recite 'the creed', a profession of their faith, and 'the prayers of the faithful', which are prayers of petition concerning the needs of the Church, the salvation of the world, public figures, individuals in need, and the local community.

During the Liturgy of the Eucharist, bread and wine are transubstantiated through consecration into the body and blood of Jesus Christ, and the priest administers Communion (portions of the consecrated bread and wine) to the congregation.

Appropriate Attire

Men: Jacket and tie or smart casual. No head covering required.

Women: Dress or a skirt and blouse or trousers. Jewellery and open-toed shoes are acceptable. Clothing should be modest, depending on the fashion and the locale. No head covering required.

There are no rules regarding colours of clothing.

The Sanctuary

What are the major sections of the church?

The sanctuary: The part of the church where the altar is located and from where the priest leads the congregation in prayer. It is set off from the body of the church by a distinctive structural feature, such as an elevation above the floor level, or by ornamentation. It is usually at the front of the church, but may be centrally located.

The lectern or ambo: The stand at which scriptural lessons and psalm responses are read and the Word of God is preached.

Seating for congregation: Benches with kneelers, usually in front and/or to the side of the altar.

Statues: Images of Jesus, the Virgin Mary, Catholic saints and persons from the Old Testament. Generally, there is only one statue of any individual saint in a church.

Baptistery: The place for administering baptism. Some churches have baptisteries adjoining or near their entrance. This position indicates that through baptism, one is initiated into, or 'enters', the church. Contemporary practice favours placing the baptistery near the sanctuary and altar, or using a portable font in the same position. This emphasises the relationship of baptism to the Eucharist, and the celebration of the death and resurrection of Jesus Christ.

The reconciliation room: A box-like structure in which priests hear confession of sins from penitents. There are separate compartments for each, and a grating or screen between them. Since the Second Vatican Council in the mid-1960s, there has been a trend to replace or supplement confessional boxes with small reconciliation rooms that are arranged so priest and penitent can converse face to face.

Holy water fonts: Receptacles, usually at a church's entrance, containing holy water for Roman Catholics to use. It is customary for them, upon entering a church, to dip their first two fingers into a font and with them to make a sign of the cross. (Guests need not do this.)

Sanctuary lamp: A lamp that is kept burning continuously before a tabernacle in which the blessed sacrament is reserved, as a sign of the presence of Christ.

The Service

When should guests arrive and where should they sit? It is customary to arrive a few minutes before the beginning of Mass. Once you enter the church, sit wherever you like.

If arriving late, are there times when a guest should not enter the service? No.

Are there times when a guest should not leave the service? Unless it is an emergency, do not leave the service until it is over.

Who are the major officiants, leaders or participants and what do they do?

The priest, who reads the Gospel, comments upon it and offers the sacrifice, also known as the Eucharist, or Communion.

A deacon, who can read the Gospel and preach as well as assisting the priest at the service. A deacon can preside at baptisms, funerals and weddings in the absence of a priest. A deacon cannot celebrate Mass.

The lector, who reads the first two readings from the Scriptures to the congregation. They can also lead the Bidding Prayers.

What are the major ritual objects of the service?

Bread and wine, which are transubstantiated through consecration into the body and blood of Jesus Christ.

The paten and chalice, which, respectively, hold the consecrated bread and wine. Gold coating is required of the interior parts of sacred vessels.

Candles, used for symbolic purposes. They represent Christ, the light and life of grace, at liturgical functions. Made of a high percentage of beeswax.

What books are used? The New Jerusalem Bible translation is used in the lectionary that contains selections from the Bible, and a prayer book, which is also called a missal. Members of the congregation would usually be given a prayer book with the words of the Mass and the readings contained in it, along with a hymn book.

To indicate the order of the service: Periodic announcements may be made by the lector or priest. Hymns may be announced by a display located near the front of the sanctuary.

Guest Behaviour during the Service

Will a guest who is not a Catholic be expected to do anything other than sit? Guests are expected to stand and kneel with the congregation. It is optional for them to read prayers aloud and sing with the congregation.

Are there any parts of the service in which a guest who is not a Catholic should not participate? Such guests should not receive Communion or say any prayers contradictory to the beliefs of their own faith.

If not disruptive to the service, is it OK to:

Take pictures? Only with prior permission from the priest.
Use a flash? Only with prior permission from the priest.
Use video recording equipment? Only with prior permission from the priest and the music group or organist if there is one.
Use audio recording equipment? Only with prior permission from the priest and the music group or organist if there is one.

Will contributions to the church be collected at the service? Yes, but guests are not expected to contribute unless they wish to.

How much is it customary to contribute? From £1 upwards.

After the Service

Is there usually a reception after the service? Sometimes there is tea and coffee available in a room or hall next door to the church.

Is there a traditional form of address for clergy who may be at the reception? 'Father' if greeting a priest. 'Bishop' if greeting a bishop. 'Your Eminence' if greeting a cardinal.

Is it OK to leave early? Yes.

Some Basic Beliefs

Roman Catholics believe:

Worship is directed towards God alone.

All revelation is summed up in Jesus Christ, who was both human and divine and commanded his twelve apostles to preach the gospel.

The Pope has primacy of jurisdiction over the Church. He and the body of bishops have infallibility when addressing religious issues of faith or morals.

The Eucharist (or Communion) is the centre of church life. The Mass is considered to make present Christ's one sacrifice of death and resurrection. During it, Christ is said to be present through the transubstantiation of the bread and wine of the Eucharist.

Some basic books to which a guest can refer to learn more about the Roman Catholic Church:

The Catechism of the Catholic Church (USCCB Publishing, 2000).
What You Will See Inside a Catholic Church, by Michael Keane (SkyLight Paths, 2003).

3. HOLY DAYS AND FESTIVALS

Christmas: Always falls on 25 December. Celebrates the birth of Christ.

Easter: Commemorates the death and resurrection of Jesus. Always falls on the Sunday after the first full moon that occurs on or after the spring equinox of 21 March.

Pentecost: Occurs fifty days after Easter because this is when the Holy Ghost (the Spirit of Jesus) descended on his apostles. Celebrates the power of the Holy Spirit and its manifestation in the early Christian church.

Ash Wednesday: Occurs forty days before Easter. Commemorates the beginning of Lent, which is a season for preparation and penitence before Easter itself.

Maundy/Holy Thursday: Falls four days before Easter. Commemorates the institution of the Eucharist (also known as Communion) and Jesus' subsequent arrest and trial.

Good Friday: Three days before Easter. Commemorates the crucifixion, death and burial of Jesus.

4. LIFE CYCLE EVENTS

Birth Ceremony

Baptism is the sacrament of spiritual regeneration by which a person, usually a six- to eight-week-old infant, is incorporated into Christ and made a member of his Mystical Body, given grace and cleansed of original sin. The virtues of faith, hope and charity are given with grace. The sacrament confers a character on the soul and can only be received once.

The thirty-minute baptismal ceremony is sometimes part of a larger service, usually a Sunday Mass. During the ceremony, a bishop, priest or deacon pours water on the forehead of the person being baptised and says, 'I baptise you in the name of the Father and of the Son and of the Holy Spirit.'

Catholics must first be baptised before they can receive other sacraments from their church.

Before the ceremony

Are guests usually invited by a formal invitation? Yes.

If not stated explicitly, should one assume that children are invited? Yes.

If one cannot attend, what should one do? RSVP with regrets and send a gift.

Appropriate attire

Men: Jacket and tie or more relaxed clothing. No head covering required.

Women: Dress or a skirt and blouse or trousers. Jewellery and open-toed shoes are acceptable. Clothing should be modest, depending on the fashion and the locale. No head covering required.

There are no rules regarding colours of clothing.

Gifts

Is a gift customarily expected? Yes, the value of which depends solely on your socio-economic level.

Should gifts be brought to the ceremony? Bring them to the reception afterwards.

The ceremony

Where will the ceremony take place? In the baptistery, which is usually near or adjoins the church entrance. Contemporary practice favours placing the baptistery near the sanctuary and altar, or using a portable font in the same position. This emphasises the relationship of baptism to Communion and, thus, to the celebration of the death and resurrection of Jesus Christ.

When should guests arrive and where should they sit? Arrive on time. Once you enter the church, sit wherever you like.

If arriving late, are there times when a guest should not enter the ceremony? No.

Are there times when a guest should not leave the ceremony? Unless it is an emergency, do not leave the service until it is over.

Who are the major officiants, leaders or participants at the ceremony and what do they do?
A priest or a deacon, who will baptise the child.

What books are used? The New Jerusalem Bible translation is used in the lectionary that contains selections from the Bible, and a prayer book, which is also called a missal. Members of the congregation would usually be given a prayer book with the words of the Mass and the readings contained in it, along with a hymn book.

To indicate the order of the service: Periodic announcements may be made by the lector or priest. Also, the basic outline of the service is usually provided in a printed programme, and hymns and prayers may be announced by a display located near the front of the sanctuary.

Will a guest who is not a Catholic be expected to do anything other than sit? Guests are expected to stand and kneel with the congregation. It is optional for them to read prayers aloud and sing with the congregation.

Are there any parts of the ceremony in which a guest who is not a Catholic should not participate? Such guests should not receive Communion or say any prayers contradictory to the beliefs of their own faith.

If not disruptive to the service, is it OK to:

Take pictures? Only with prior permission from the priest or usher.

Use a flash? Only with prior permission from the priest or usher.

Use video recording equipment? Only with prior permission from the priest or usher and the music group or organist if there is one.

Use audio recording equipment? Only with prior permission from the priest or usher and the music group or organist if there is one.

Will contributions to the church be collected at the ceremony? No.

After the ceremony

Is there usually a reception after the ceremony? Yes, usually at the home of the baptised child. Food will be served. Alcoholic drinks may be served. There may be music and dancing. The reception may last at least one or two hours.

Would it be considered impolite to neither eat nor drink? No.

Is there a grace or benediction before eating or drinking? Sometimes.

Is there a grace or benediction after eating or drinking? Sometimes.

Is there a traditional greeting for the family? No, just offer your congratulations.

Is there a traditional form of address for clergy who may be at the reception? 'Father' if greeting a priest. 'Bishop' if greeting a bishop. 'Your Eminence' if greeting a cardinal.

Is it OK to leave early? Yes.

꧁

Initiation Ceremony

Confirmation is the sacrament by which a baptised early adolescent is endowed with the fullness of baptismal grace, is united more intimately with the Church, is enriched with the special power of the Holy Spirit, and is committed to be an authentic witness to Christ in word and action.

Those being confirmed often receive the sacrament with their entire confirmation class. The ceremony is sometimes part of a larger service. It will last slightly more than one hour.

Confirmation may occur between the ages of seven and eighteen, depending on the policy of the local diocese.

Before the ceremony

Are guests usually invited by a formal invitation? Yes.

If not stated explicitly, should one assume that children are invited? Yes.

If one cannot attend, what should one do? RSVP with regrets and send a gift.

Appropriate attire

Men: Jacket and tie or more relaxed clothing. No head covering required.

Women: Dress or a skirt and blouse or trousers. Jewellery and open-toed shoes are acceptable. Clothing should be modest, depending on the fashion and the locale. No head covering required.

There are no rules regarding colours of clothing.

Gifts

Is a gift customarily expected? Yes. Often money is appropriate. The exact amount is totally discretionary.

Should gifts be brought to the ceremony? Bring them to the reception afterwards.

The ceremony

Where will the ceremony take place? In the main sanctuary of the confirmation candidate's church.

When should guests arrive and where should they sit? It is customary to arrive at the time called. Sit wherever you wish.

If arriving late, are there times when a guest should not enter the ceremony? No.

Are there times when a guest should not leave the ceremony? Guests should remain until the ceremony ends.

Who are the major officiants, leaders or participants at the ceremony and what do they do?

The bishop, who anoints each confirmation candidate with oil on the forehead.

What books are used? The New Jerusalem Bible translation is used in the lectionary that contains selections from the Bible, and a prayer book, which is also called a missal. Members of the congregation would usually be given a prayer book with the words of the Mass and the readings contained in it, along with a hymn book.

To indicate the order of the service: Periodic announcements may be made by the lector or priest. Also, the basic outline of the service is usually provided in a printed programme, and hymns and prayers may be announced by a display located near the front of the sanctuary.

Will a guest who is not a Catholic be expected to do anything other than sit? Guests are expected to stand and kneel with the congregation. It is optional for them to read prayers aloud and sing with the congregation.

Are there any parts of the ceremony in which a guest who is not a Catholic should not participate? Such guests should not receive Communion or say any prayers contradictory to the beliefs of their own faith.

If not disruptive to the service, is it OK to:

Take pictures? Only with prior permission from the priest or usher.
Use a flash? Only with prior permission from the priest or usher.
Use video recording equipment? Only with prior permission from the priest or usher and the music group or organist if there is one.
Use audio recording equipment? Only with prior permission from the priest or usher and the music group or organist if there is one.

Will contributions to the church be collected at the ceremony? No.

After the ceremony

Is there usually a reception after the ceremony? There is a reception, usually at the home of the confirmation candidate. Food and soft drinks will be served. Alcoholic drinks may be served. The reception may last at least one or two hours.

Would it be considered impolite to neither eat nor drink? No.

Is there a grace or benediction before eating or drinking? No.

Is there a grace or benediction after eating or drinking? No.

Is there a traditional greeting for the family? Just offer your congratulations.

Is there a traditional form of address for clergy who may be at the reception? 'Father' if greeting a priest. 'Bishop' if greeting a bishop. 'Your Eminence' if greeting a cardinal.

Is it OK to leave early? Yes.

❦

Marriage Ceremony

Catholics consider married life, which was created by God, to have a decisive bearing on the continuation of the human race, on the personal development and eternal destiny of individual members of a family, and on the dignity, stability, peace and prosperity of families and society.

Love, the Church teaches, is uniquely expressed and perfected through marriage. Children are the 'gift of marriage', although marriage is not instituted solely for procreation. Rather, its essential nature as an unbreakable compact between man and wife and for the welfare of the children that come out of it both demand that the love of the respective spouses be embodied in a manner that grows, thrives and ripens.

The wedding may be a ceremony in itself and not part of a larger service or it may be part of a Sunday Mass. It may last between thirty and sixty minutes to more than one hour.

Before the ceremony

Are guests usually invited by a formal invitation? Yes.

If not stated explicitly, should one assume that children are invited? Yes.

If one cannot attend, what should one do? RSVP with regrets and send a gift.

Appropriate attire

Men: Jacket and tie or more relaxed clothing. No head covering required.

Women: Dress or a skirt and blouse or trousers. Jewellery and open-toed shoes are acceptable. Clothing should be modest, depending on the fashion and the locale. No head covering required.

There are no rules regarding colours of clothing.

Gifts

Is a gift customarily expected? Details of a gift list are often included with the wedding invitation. If not, then the nature of the gift is at the discretion of the individual.

Should gifts be brought to the ceremony? Gifts should be sent to the home or brought to the reception.

The ceremony

Where will the ceremony take place? In the main sanctuary of the church.

When should guests arrive and where should they sit? Arrive on time. An usher will show guests where to sit.

If arriving late, are there times when a guest should not enter the ceremony? Ushers may guide latecomers. Do not enter as the wedding party processes into the sanctuary.

Are there times when a guest should not leave the service? Do not leave until it ends.

Who are the major officiants, leaders or participants at the ceremony and what do they do?
The priest or deacon, who witnesses the vows.

What books are used? The New Jerusalem Bible translation is used in the lectionary that contains selections from the Bible, and a prayer book, which is also called a missal. Members of the congregation would usually be given a prayer book with the words of the Mass and the readings contained in it, along with a hymn book.

To indicate the order of the ceremony: There will be a printed order of service.

Will a guest who is not a Catholic be expected to do anything other than sit? Guests are expected to stand and kneel with the congregation. It is optional for them to read prayers aloud and sing with the congregation.

Are there any parts of the ceremony in which a guest who is not a Catholic should not participate? Such guests should not receive Communion or say any prayers contradictory to the beliefs of their own faith.

If not disruptive to the service, is it OK to:

Take pictures? Only with prior permission from the priest or usher.
Use a flash? Only with prior permission from the priest or usher.
Use video recording equipment? Only with prior permission from the priest or usher and the music group or organist if there is one.
Use audio recording equipment? Only with prior permission from the priest or usher and the music group or organist if there is one.

Will contributions to the church be collected at the ceremony? No.

After the ceremony

Is there usually a reception after the ceremony? There is a reception that may last more than two hours. It is usually at a hotel, where food and drinks will be served and there will be dancing and music.

Would it be considered impolite to neither eat nor drink? No.

Is there a grace or benediction before eating or drinking? Yes, the blessing before the meal.

Is there a grace or benediction after eating or drinking? Usually not.

Is there a traditional greeting for the family? Just offer your congratulations.

Is there a traditional form of address for clergy who may be at the reception? 'Father' if greeting a priest. 'Bishop' if greeting a bishop. 'Your Eminence' if greeting a cardinal.

Is it OK to leave early? Yes.

꧁

Funerals and Mourning

Roman Catholicism deeply believes in immortality. Each human being does not face utter spiritual dissolution, since God loves him or her. Not only does all love desire immortality, but God's love *is* immortality. On the 'last day', when the Messiah has arrived, one's physical body will join the spirit in the beatific vision of heaven or the damnation of hell.

A Catholic funeral may be part of a larger service or a ceremony in itself. If it is part of a service, that will be a Mass.

Before the ceremony

How soon after the death does the funeral usually take place? Sometimes as much as one week later (although in Ireland it is generally within two or three days).

What should a non-Catholic do upon hearing of the death of a member of that faith? Telephone the bereaved at home to express condolences.

Appropriate attire

Men: Jacket and black tie. No head covering required.

Women: Dress or a skirt and blouse or trousers. Jewellery and open-toed shoes are acceptable. Clothing should be modest, depending on the fashion and the locale. No head covering required.

Black or equally sober colours are recommended.

Gifts

Is it appropriate to send flowers or make a contribution? Flowers of any kind are appreciated. They may be sent upon hearing the news of the death or shortly thereafter. They may be sent to the home of the deceased before or after the funeral or to the funeral home before the funeral.

Contributions are not customary unless the family indicates they are appropriate.

Is it appropriate to send food? Yes, if there is to be a reception at the home of the deceased after the funeral.

The ceremony

Where will the ceremony take place? At a church, cemetery or crematorium.

When should guests arrive and where should they sit? Arrive on time. Sit wherever you like.

If arriving late, are there times when a guest should not enter the ceremony? No.

Will the bereaved family be present at the church or funeral home before the ceremony? Yes.

Is there a traditional greeting for the family? Offer your condolences.

Will there be an open coffin? Not usually.

Is a guest expected to view the body? No.

Who are the major officiants at the ceremony and what do they do?

The priest, who says the Mass and the prayers at graveside.

What books are used? The New Jerusalem Bible translation is used in the lectionary that contains selections from the Bible, and a prayer book, which is also called a missal. Members of the congregation would usually be given a prayer book with the words of the Mass and the readings contained in it, along with a hymn book.

To indicate the order of the ceremony: There will usually be a printed order of service.

Will a guest who is not a Catholic be expected to do anything other than sit? Guests are expected to stand and kneel with the congregation. It is optional for them to read prayers aloud and sing with the congregation.

Are there any parts of the ceremony in which a guest who is not a Catholic should not participate? Such guests should not receive Communion or say any prayers contradictory to the beliefs of their own faith.

If not disruptive to the service, is it OK to:

Take pictures? Only with prior permission from the priest.
Use a flash? Only with prior permission from the priest.
Use video recording equipment? Only with prior permission from the priest and the music group or organist if there is one.
Use audio recording equipment? Only with prior permission from the priest and the music group or organist if there is one.

Will contributions to the church be collected at the ceremony? No.

The interment

Should guests attend the interment? Not always – sometimes this is a private family affair.

Whom should one ask for directions? The funeral director.

What happens at the graveside? The priest or deacon leads prayers for the deceased.

Do guests who are not Catholics participate at the graveside ceremony? No. They are simply present.

Comforting the bereaved

Is it appropriate to visit the home of the bereaved after the funeral? Yes, briefly.

Will there be a religious service at the home of the bereaved? No.

Will food be served? Possibly. Given the broad ethnic mixture of Catholicism, some Catholics may have a gathering at which food (and often drink) is served.

How soon after the funeral will a mourner usually return to a normal work schedule? Perhaps a week.

How soon after the funeral will a mourner usually return to a normal social schedule? Perhaps a week.

Are there mourning customs to which a friend who is not a Catholic should be sensitive? No.

Are there rituals for observing the anniversary of the death? Often there is a month's mind Mass one month after the death and a Mass on the annual anniversary of the death.

5. HOME CELEBRATIONS

Not applicable to Roman Catholicism.

19

Salvation Army

1. HISTORY AND BELIEFS

The international Christian movement now known as the Salvation Army was founded by an Englishman, William Booth, in 1865. Once a Methodist minister, Booth felt a conviction that he was not doing enough to reach the poor, destitute and hungry of society with both the spiritual and physical salvation offered by the gospel of Jesus Christ. Following a successful series of meetings held for the poor of London's East End, Booth formed a new movement, originally known as the Christian Mission.

In 1878, the movement changed its name to the Salvation Army, adopting the imagery of an army fighting sin in God's name. This vision captured the imagination of many, and the movement began to grow in size, influence and impact, attracting many new members committed to the Salvation Army's aims of demonstrating the gospel in both word and action – to all people, regardless of sex, colour, class or creed – and spreading throughout the UK and abroad.

By the time of Booth's death in 1912, the Army was at work in fifty-eight countries. It now has over 1.6 million members and is established in 109 countries around the world.

Salvation Army officers are ordained ministers of religion, and wear a uniform that reflects the military influence of its foundation. Salvation Army halls are registered places of worship, and the organisation is divided into parishes (known as *corps*). It is particularly well known for its social work, including working with people who are homeless, addicted to drugs and alcohol, imprisoned, the elderly, and its campaigning for social justice, all underpinned by Christian conviction.

UK corps: over 800
UK membership: over 54,000

For more information, contact:

The Salvation Army
Territorial Headquarters
101 Newington Causeway
London
SE1 6BN
Tel: 0845 634 0101
Email: info@salvationarmy.org.uk

2. THE BASIC SERVICE

Salvationists meet regularly for times of Christian worship, usually on Sunday mornings and evenings, although the times of meetings can vary. The meeting will usually take place at the local Salvation Army hall, and is open to anybody, regardless of faith or denomination. Readings from the Bible and music – often performed by a Salvation Army band or choir – are very important elements of the worship meeting, which will probably last for about an hour.

Appropriate Attire

There is no official dress code for men or women. Salvation Army officers will wear their uniforms, but guests may come as they wish.

The Service

When should guests arrive and where should they sit? Try to arrive early, and there are no rules on where to sit. Guests should take a seat wherever they feel most comfortable.

If arriving late, are there times when a guest should not enter the service? No.

Are there times when a guest should not leave the service? No.

Who are the major officiants, leaders or participants and what do they do?

A Salvation Army officer, who will lead the meeting and give the address or sermon. Other people may also join in, however, reading from the Bible or giving their 'testimony' (the story of their personal experience of God).

What are the major ritual objects of the service?

The Bible, from which the Gospel, which records the life and ministry of Jesus, and other scriptural readings are read.

The Salvation Army flag, which symbolises God the Father, God the Son (Jesus) and God the Holy Spirit.

The Mercy Seat, a bench at the front of the hall on which people can choose to kneel as a symbolic act of faith before God, such as a public demonstration of an inner commitment of faith or a simple act of worship.

What books are used? A Bible and a book of hymns.

To indicate the order of the service: A printed order of service may be provided, and the Salvation Army officer will make periodic announcements.

Guest Behaviour during the Service

Will a guest who is not a Salvationist be expected to do anything other than sit? It is acceptable to stand with the congregation, read prayers aloud and sing with congregants, if this does not compromise your personal beliefs.

Are there any parts of the service in which a guest who is not a Salvationist should not participate? No.

If not disruptive to the service, is it OK to:

Take pictures? Yes.

Use a flash? Yes.

Use video recording equipment? Yes.

Use audio recording equipment? Yes.

Will contributions to the church be collected at the service? Yes, although guests are not expected to contribute unless they so wish.

꧁꧂

After the Service

Is there usually a reception after the ceremony? No.

Is there a traditional form of address for Salvation Army officers who may be at the service? Officers are officially addressed by rank, such as 'Sergeant' or 'Major', but many will request that they are addressed simply by their first name.

꧁꧂

Some Basic Beliefs

The Salvation Army has eleven core articles of faith:

That the Scriptures of the Old and New Testaments were given by inspiration of God: and that only they constitute the divine rule of Christian faith and practice.

That there is only one God, who is infinitely perfect, the Creator, Preserver and Governor of all things, and who is the only proper object of religious worship.

That there are three persons in the Godhead – the Father, the Son and the Holy Ghost – undivided in essence and co-equal in power and glory.

That in the person of Jesus Christ the divine and human natures are united, so that he is truly and properly God and truly and properly man.

That our first parents were created in a state of innocency, but by their disobedience they lost their purity and happiness; and that in consequence of their fall all men have become sinners, totally depraved, and as such are justly exposed to the wrath of God.

That the Lord Jesus Christ has, by his suffering and death, made an atonement for the whole world so that whosoever will may be saved.

That repentance towards God, faith in our Lord Jesus Christ and regeneration by the Holy Spirit are necessary to salvation.

That we are justified by grace, through faith in our Lord Jesus Christ; and that he that believeth hath the witness in himself.

That continuance in a state of salvation depends upon continued obedient faith in Christ.

That it is the privilege of all believers to be wholly sanctified, and that their whole spirit and soul and body may be preserved blameless unto the coming of our Lord Jesus Christ.

A belief in the immortality of the soul; in the resurrection of the body; in the general judgement at the end of the world; in the eternal happiness of the righteous; and in the endless punishment of the wicked.

Some basic resources to which a guest can refer to learn more about the Salvation Army faith:

www.salvationarmy.org
www.salvationarmy.org.uk

3. HOLY DAYS AND FESTIVALS

Christmas: Always falls on 25 December. Celebrates the birth of Jesus Christ. The traditional greeting is 'Merry Christmas'.

Easter: Always falls on the Sunday after the first full moon that occurs on or after the spring equinox of 21 March. Celebrates the resurrection of Jesus. The traditional greeting is 'Happy Easter'.

Pentecost: Occurs fifty days after Easter because this is when the Holy Spirit descended on Jesus' apostles. Celebrates the power of the Holy Spirit and its manifestation in the early Christian church. There is no traditional greeting for this holiday.

Ash Wednesday: Occurs forty days before Easter. Commemorates the beginning of Lent, which is a season for preparation and penitence before Easter itself. There is no traditional greeting for this holiday.

Maundy Thursday: Falls four days before Easter. Commemorates the institution of the Eucharist (also known as Communion) and Jesus' subsequent arrest and trial. There is no traditional greeting.

Good Friday: Three days before Easter. Commemorates the crucifixion, death and burial of Jesus.

Christmas, Easter and Pentecost are joyful celebrations. Ash Wednesday, Maundy Thursday and Good Friday are sombre, penitential commemorations. During the services for these latter three holidays, decorum and discretion are of great importance.

4. LIFE CYCLE EVENTS

Birth Ceremony

The Salvation Army holds a dedication or thanksgiving ceremony for recently born children, in which thanks are given for the child and its parents commit to giving it a Christian upbringing. This is not considered to 'make' the child a Christian or Salvationist – the child will make its own decision on its faith when it is able to.

The dedication ceremony is held as part of a normal Sunday worship service.

Before the ceremony

Are guests usually invited by a formal invitation? Normally by verbal invitation.

If not stated explicitly, should one assume that children are invited? No.

If one cannot attend, what should one do? This is at the discretion of the individual. A polite and prompt reply, expressing regret, is recommended.

Appropriate attire

There is no official dress code for men or women. Salvation Army officers will wear their uniforms, but guests may come as they wish.

Gifts

Is a gift customarily expected? No.

The service

When should guests arrive and where should they sit? Try to arrive early, and there are no rules on where to sit. Guests should take a seat wherever they feel most comfortable.

If arriving late, are there times when a guest should not enter the service? No.

Are there times when a guest should not leave the service? No.

Who are the major officiants, leaders or participants and what do they do?

A Salvation Army officer, who will lead the meeting and give the address or sermon. Other people may also join in, however, reading from the Bible or giving their 'testimony' (the story of their personal experience of God).

What are the major ritual objects of the service?

The Bible, from which the Gospel, which records the life and ministry of Jesus, and other scriptural readings are read.

The Salvation Army flag, which symbolises God the Father, God the Son (Jesus) and God the Holy Spirit.

What books are used? A Bible and a book of hymns.

To indicate the order of the service: A printed order of service may be provided, and the Salvation Army officer will make periodic announcements.

Guest behaviour during the service

Will a guest who is not a Salvationist be expected to do anything other than sit? It is acceptable to stand with the congregation, read prayers aloud and sing with congregants, if this does not compromise your personal beliefs.

Are there any parts of the service in which a guest who is not a Salvationist should not participate? No.

If not disruptive to the service, is it OK to:

Take pictures? Yes.
Use a flash? Yes.
Use video recording equipment? Yes.
Use audio recording equipment? Yes.

Will contributions to the church be collected at the service? Yes, although guests are not expected to contribute unless they so wish.

Is there usually a reception after the ceremony? No.

Initiation Ceremony

From the age of seven, children in the Salvation Army have the opportunity to become a Junior Soldier. At a simple ceremony as part of the regular Sunday worship service, they will publicly affirm their faith and be given a badge and certificate.

From the age of fifteen, men and women have the opportunity to become a Senior Soldier. At a ceremony which will also be part of the regular Sunday worship service, they will stand under the Salvation Army flag, publicly confess their salvation from sin and commit to living by the Army's Articles of War. Prayers will then be said for the person.

Before the ceremony

Are guests usually invited by a formal invitation? Normally by verbal invitation.

If not stated explicitly, should one assume that children are invited?
Yes.

If one cannot attend, what should one do? This is at the discretion of the individual. A polite and prompt reply, expressing regret, is recommended.

Appropriate attire

There is no official dress code for men or women. Salvation Army officers will wear their uniforms, but guests may come as they wish.

Gifts

Is a gift customarily expected? No.

The service

When should guests arrive and where should they sit? Try to arrive early, and there are no rules on where to sit. Guests should take a seat wherever they feel most comfortable.

If arriving late, are there times when a guest should not enter the service? No.

Are there times when a guest should not leave the service? No.

Who are the major officiants, leaders or participants and what do they do?

A Salvation Army officer, who will lead the meeting and give the address or sermon. Other people may also join in, however, reading from the Bible or giving their 'testimony' (the story of their personal experience of God).

What are the major ritual objects of the service?

The Bible, from which the Gospel, which records the life and ministry of Jesus, and other scriptural readings are read.

The Salvation Army flag, which symbolises God the Father, God the Son (Jesus) and God the Holy Spirit.

What books are used? A Bible and a book of hymns.

To indicate the order of the service: A printed order of service may be provided, and the Salvation Army officer will make periodic announcements.

Guest behaviour during the service

Will a guest who is not a Salvationist be expected to do anything other than sit? It is acceptable to stand with the congregation, read prayers aloud and sing with congregants, if this does not compromise your personal beliefs.

Are there any parts of the service in which a guest who is not a Salvationist should not participate? No.

If not disruptive to the service, is it OK to:

Take pictures? Yes.
Use a flash? Yes.
Use video recording equipment? Yes.
Use audio recording equipment? Yes.

Will contributions to the church be collected at the service? Yes, although guests are not expected to contribute unless they so wish.

Is there usually a reception after the ceremony? No.

Marriage Ceremony

Salvationists believe that, through marriage, God joins together man and woman in physical and spiritual union.

The marriage ceremony is most commonly a service in itself lasting between thirty and sixty minutes, and will be held at the local Salvation Army hall. The Salvation Army flag will be prominently displayed, indicating that marriage includes a spiritual commitment.

Before the ceremony

Are guests usually invited by a formal invitation? Yes.

If not stated explicitly, should one assume that children are invited? No.

If one cannot attend, what should one do? Send a polite and prompt reply, and send a gift if possible.

Appropriate attire

There is no official dress code for men or women. Salvation Army officers will wear their uniforms, while guests may come as they wish, but it is recommended that you dress smartly.

Gifts

Is a gift customarily expected? Yes. Details of a gift list are often included with the wedding invitation. If not, then the nature of the gift is at the discretion of the individual.

Should gifts be brought to the ceremony? Yes, and then given to the couple at the formal reception.

The ceremony

When should guests arrive and where should they sit? Arrive early. Ushers will be on hand to show guests where to sit.

If arriving late, are there times when a guest should not enter the ceremony? No.

Are there times when a guest should not leave the ceremony? No.

Who are the major officiants, leaders or participants at the ceremony and what do they do?

A Salvation Army officer, who will lead the meeting and lead the couple in their wedding vows and the Articles of Marriage – promises made by Salvation Army soldiers.

What books are used? A Bible and a book of hymns. A specially printed order of service containing the prayers, readings and the words of the hymns or songs is usually provided by the wedding couple.

Guest behaviour during the service

Will a guest who is not a Salvationist be expected to do anything other than sit? It is acceptable to stand with the congregation, read prayers aloud and sing with congregants, if this does not compromise your personal beliefs.

Are there any parts of the service in which a guest who is not a Salvationist should not participate? No.

If not disruptive to the service, is it OK to:

Take pictures? Yes.
Use a flash? Yes.
Use video recording equipment? Yes.
Use audio recording equipment? Yes.

Will contributions to the church be collected at the service? No.

After the ceremony

Is there usually a reception after the ceremony? There will usually be a formal reception after the service, which will be held at a hotel or meeting hall. There will be speeches and a meal will be provided for all guests. There are unlikely to be alcoholic drinks, as Salvationists do not drink alcohol. The reception will most likely last for a few hours.

Would it be considered impolite to neither eat nor drink? Yes, unless there are special circumstances, and it is advisable to inform the wedding couple of any special dietary requirements before the day.

Is there a ritual before eating? A grace will usually be said before people start to eat.

Is there a ritual after eating? No.

Is there a traditional form of address for Salvation Army officers who may be at the reception? Officers are officially addressed by rank, such as 'Sergeant' or 'Major', but many will request that they are addressed simply by their first name.

❄

Funerals and Mourning

Salvationists believe that the resurrection of Jesus Christ was a victory for good over evil, and life over death, making eternal life available to us all. Those who are believers will, following death, proceed to an afterlife in the nearer presence of God – Salvationists often use the term 'Promotion to Glory'.

A funeral service will precede either burial or cremation of the deceased's body. It will be held at the local Salvation Army hall and will usually last between thirty and sixty minutes.

Before the ceremony

How soon after the death does the funeral usually take place? It can be within a week of the death, but may take longer if medical or legal reasons dictate.

What should someone who is not a Salvationist do upon hearing of the death of a member of that faith? Telephone or visit the bereaved, or send a card expressing your sympathy.

Gifts

Is it appropriate to send flowers or make a contribution? Only send flowers if the family have requested them. Some families ask for the gift of money to charity.

Appropriate attire

There is no official dress code for men or women. Salvation Army officers will wear their uniforms, while guests may come as they wish, but it is recommended that you dress respectfully, in black or white.

The ceremony

When should guests arrive and where should they sit? Arrive early and sit wherever you choose.

If arriving late, are there times when a guest should not enter the ceremony? No.

Will the bereaved family be present at the church or funeral home before the service? No.

Is there a traditional greeting for the family? No.

Will there be an open coffin? No.

Who are the major officiants at the ceremony and what do they do?

A Salvation Army officer, who will conduct the service.

What are the major ritual objects of the service?

The Bible, from which the Gospel, which records the life and ministry of Jesus, and other scriptural readings are read.

The Salvation Army flag, which symbolises God the Father, God the Son (Jesus) and God the Holy Spirit.

What books are used? A Bible and a book of hymns.

To indicate the order of the service: A printed order of service may be provided, and the Salvation Army officer will make periodic announcements.

Guest behaviour during the service

Will a guest who is not a Salvationist be expected to do anything other than sit? It is acceptable to stand with the congregation, read prayers aloud and sing with congregants, if this does not compromise your personal beliefs.

Are there any parts of the service in which a guest who is not a Salvationist should not participate? No.

If not disruptive to the service, is it OK to:

Take pictures? No.
Use a flash? No.
Use video recording equipment? No.

Use audio recording equipment? No.

Will contributions to the church be collected at the service? No.

The interment

Should guests attend the interment? Yes.

Whom should one ask for directions? The funeral director or another guest.

What happens at the graveside of a burial? There will be a Bible reading, prayers and sometimes a hymn will be sung, after which the coffin will be lowered into the ground. Guests are required simply to be present.

What happens at a cremation? There will be a Bible reading, prayers and sometimes a hymn will be sung, after which the coffin will be transported away to be burned. Guests are required simply to be present.

Comforting the bereaved

Is it appropriate to visit the home of the bereaved after the funeral? This is at your personal discretion. There is no specific tradition governing this, although visits are usually appreciated.

How soon after the funeral will a mourner usually return to a normal work schedule? This varies, depending on the individual.

How soon after the funeral will a mourner usually return to a normal social schedule? This is entirely at the discretion of the individual.

5. HOME CELEBRATIONS

Not applicable for Salvation Army churches.

20

Seventh-day Adventist

1. HISTORY AND BELIEFS

The Seventh-day Adventist Church stemmed from a worldwide religious revival in the mid-1800s when people of many faiths fervently believed biblical prophecies that they interpreted as meaning that Jesus Christ's second coming, or 'advent', was imminent.

When Christ did not come in the 1840s, a group of these disappointed Adventists in the United States concluded that they had misinterpreted prophetic events, and that the second coming was still in the future. This same group later became known as Seventh-day Adventists, which organised formally as a denomination in 1863.

Adventists anticipate and prepare for the world's end in conjunction with the second coming of Jesus Christ. They believe that the end of the world is near and that eternal hell for the wicked is not consistent with the concept of a 'loving Father'. Instead, they believe in eventual annihilation of the wicked and eternal bliss for the saved. After a thousand-year reign of the saints with Christ in heaven, the wicked will be raised and, along with Satan, annihilated. Out of the chaos of the old earth will emerge a new earth, which the redeemed will inherit as their everlasting home.

Worldwide, there are about 11 million Seventh-day Adventists. The movement grows by about 6 per cent annually and has more than 48,000 congregations in over 204 countries.

In addition to a mission programme, the Church has the largest worldwide Protestant parochial school system, with over 1 million elementary to college students in more than 6,000 schools. It also operates medical schools and hospitals.

UK churches: 281
UK membership: 29,331

For more information, contact:

British Union Conference of Seventh-day Adventists
Stanborough Park
Watford
Herts
WD25 9JZ
Tel: 01923 672251
www.adventist.org.uk

2. THE BASIC SERVICE

The Adventists' basic religious service is held on Saturday mornings and lasts about sixty minutes. The service is strong on fellowship. About half of it is devoted to readings and teachings from the Old and New Testaments.

Appropriate Attire

Men: Jacket and tie or more relaxed clothing. No head covering required.

Women: Suit, dress, skirt and blouse or conservative trouser suit are acceptable. No head covering required. Clothing usually covers the arms and hems are below the knee, but neither is obligatory.

Although Adventists do not ordinarily wear jewellery, guests should feel comfortable wearing it.

There are no rules regarding colours of clothing.

❧

The Sanctuary

What are the major sections of the church?

The sanctuary: Where congregants sit.
The speakers' platform: A slightly elevated section for speakers and, at times, the choir.

❧

The Service

When should guests arrive and where should they sit? It is customary to arrive at the time the service is scheduled. There will usually be someone to help you find a seat; if not, take any open seat.

If arriving late, are there times when a guest should not enter the service? If arriving late, do not enter during prayer.

Are there times when a guest should not leave the service? Do not leave during prayer.

Who are the major officiants, leaders or participants and what do they do?

The elders, who are elected lay leaders in charge of individual congregations. They are usually elected for one year.
An ordained pastor, although not every congregation has one. Adventists ordain only men.

What are the major ritual objects of the service? There are no specific ritual objects.

What books are used? A hymnal and the Old and New Testaments.

To indicate the order of the service: A programme will be distributed to congregants and guests.

꧁ ꧂

Guest Behaviour during the Service

Will a guest who is not a Seventh-day Adventist be expected to do anything other than sit? It is optional for guests to stand, kneel and sing with the congregation. It is also optional for them to join in the washing of feet during the quarterly Communion service. During this ritual, men and women will leave the sanctuary and go to rooms reserved, for the sake of modesty, for the separate genders. Guests may remain in the sanctuary, during which time the organist will be playing. The entire ritual may take about ten minutes. The ritual is based on a passage in the New Testament (John 13:14–15) in which Jesus first washes the feet of his disciples at the Last Supper, then instructs them that they should do the same to one another.

Are there any parts of the service in which a guest who is not a Seventh-day Adventist should not participate? Guests can participate in all aspects of the service, unless their own faith forbids it.

If not disruptive to the service, is it OK to:

Take pictures? Yes.
Use a flash? Yes.
Use video recording equipment? Yes.
Use audio recording equipment? Yes.

Will contributions to the church be collected at the service? An offering plate will be passed through the congregation. Donations by guests are optional.

How much is it customary to contribute? Contributions from £1 to £5 are customary.

꧁ ꧂

After the Service

Is there usually a reception after the service? Often, yes, lasting thirty to sixty minutes. A variety of foods may be served. Often, a pot-luck luncheon is provided for members and guests, in an activity room. There is usually a benediction or prayer before eating. There will be no alcoholic drinks.

It is not considered impolite to neither eat nor drink, especially if one has dietary restrictions.

Is there a traditional form of address for clergy who may be at the reception? 'Elder' or 'Pastor'.

Is it OK to leave early? Yes.

❧

Special Vocabulary

Key words or phrases that it might be helpful for a visitor to know:

Sabbath School: The study service preceding the worship service.
Prayer Meeting: The midweek service, usually held on Wednesday evenings.

❧

Some Basic Beliefs

Seventh-day Adventists believe:

The Scriptures of both the Old and New Testaments are the final authority. The Saturday service focuses on the study of these Scriptures and their exposition. (No specific translation of the Bible is used.)

A basic book to which a guest can refer to learn more about the Seventh-day Adventist Church:

Seventh-day Adventists Believe (Ministerial Association, General Conference of Seventh-day Adventists).
www.adventist.org.uk

3. HOLY DAYS AND FESTIVALS

Seventh-day Adventists' only holy day is the Sabbath, which occurs each Saturday. This is Seventh-day Adventists' central day of worship, on which they avoid labour and secular activities.

The faith recognises no other holy days because the Sabbath is the only universal holy day mentioned in the Scriptures.

4. LIFE CYCLE EVENTS

Baptism Ceremony

Baptism initiates an adolescent or adult into the Church. During the ceremony, which usually lasts less than thirty minutes, the person to be baptised enters a baptismal pool with a pastor or elder and is fully and briefly immersed under the water. The baptism is part of a public service, usually the basic Sabbath worship service.

Baptism is a sign of remission of sin and spiritual rebirth by symbolically participating in Christ's death, burial and resurrection.

Before the ceremony

Are guests usually invited by a formal invitation? There will be no formal invitation.

If not stated explicitly, should one assume that children are invited? Yes.

If one cannot attend, what should one do? One may offer best wishes to the family.

Appropriate attire

Men: Jacket and tie or more relaxed clothing. No head covering required.

Women: Dress, skirt and blouse or conservative trouser suit are acceptable. No head covering required. Clothing usually covers the arms and hems are below the knee, but neither is obligatory.

Although Adventists do not ordinarily wear jewellery, guests should feel comfortable wearing it.

There are no rules regarding colours of clothing.

Gifts

Is a gift customarily expected? A gift is neither customary nor expected.

Should gifts be brought to the ceremony? See above.

The ceremony

Where will the ceremony take place? Generally, in the main sanctuary of the church. Sometimes, the baptismal immersion will be at an outdoor site, such as a lake, a stream or even the ocean.

When should guests arrive and where should they sit? It is customary to arrive at the time the service is called. There will usually be someone to help you find a seat; if not, you can take any open seat.

If arriving late, are there times when a guest should not enter the ceremony? If arriving late, do not enter during prayer.

Are there times when a guest should not leave the ceremony? Do not leave during prayer.

Who are the major officiants, leaders or participants at the ceremony and what do they do?
The elder or pastor, who performs the baptism by immersion.

What books are used? None.

To indicate the order of the ceremony: There may be a programme.

Will a guest who is not a Seventh-day Adventist be expected to do anything other than sit? It is optional for guests to stand, kneel and sing with the congregation.

Are there any parts of the ceremony in which a guest who is not a Seventh-day Adventist should not participate? Guests can participate in all aspects of the service, unless their own faith forbids it.

If not disruptive to the ceremony, is it OK to:

Take pictures? Yes.
Use a flash? Yes.
Use video recording equipment? Yes.
Use audio recording equipment? Yes.

Will contributions to the church be collected at the ceremony? Normally baptism is a part of the regular worship service, during which an offering plate is passed through the congregation. No special offering will be taken in connection with the baptism itself. Donations by guests are optional.

How much is it customary to contribute? Contributions from £1 to £5 are customary.

After the ceremony

Is there usually a reception after the ceremony? No.

Is there a traditional greeting for the family? No.

Is there a traditional form of address for clergy whom a guest may meet? 'Elder' or 'Pastor'.

Marriage Ceremony

Seventh-day Adventists believe that marriage was divinely established in Eden. To accomplish this most important part of creation, God performed a miracle and brought forth Eve from the side of Adam, and gave her to Adam as his wife. Jesus later affirmed marriage to be a lifelong union between a man and a woman in loving companionship.

A marriage commitment is to God, as well as to the spouse. Marriage should be entered into only between partners who share a common religious faith. Mutual love, honour, respect and responsibility are the fabric of this relationship.

The marriage ceremony usually lasts between thirty and sixty minutes.

Before the ceremony

Are guests usually invited by a formal invitation? Yes. Occasionally, there will be a general invitation in the local church bulletin.

If not stated explicity, should one assume that children are invited? Yes.

If one cannot attend, what should one do? RSVP with your regrets and send a gift to the bride and groom.

Appropriate attire

Men: Jacket and tie. No head covering required.

Women: Dress or skirt and blouse. No head covering required. Clothing should cover the arms and hems should reach below the knee.

Although Adventists do not ordinarily wear jewellery, guests should feel comfortable wearing it.

There are no rules regarding colours of clothing.

Gifts

Is a gift customarily expected? Only if the celebrants are close friends or relatives. Money and other gifts are appropriate.

Should gifts be brought to the ceremony? Gifts may be sent to the home before or after the wedding ceremony or brought to the ceremony and placed in the reception area.

The ceremony

Where will the ceremony take place? In the church sanctuary.

When should guests arrive and where should they sit? Arrive shortly before the ceremony is scheduled to start.

If arriving late, are there times when a guest should not enter the ceremony? Latecomers should not enter during the bride's entry.

Are there times when a guest should not leave the ceremony? Do not leave during prayer.

Who are the major officiants, leaders or participants at the ceremony and what do they do?

The pastor, who will deliver a few comments.

What books are used? Only the clergyman uses a Bible.

To indicate the order of the ceremony: A programme will be distributed.

Will a guest who is not a Seventh-day Adventist be expected to do anything other than sit? It is optional for guests to stand, kneel and sing with the congregation.

Are there any parts of the ceremony in which a guest who is not a Seventh-day Adventist should not participate? Guests who belong to other faiths can participate in all aspects of the service, unless restricted from doing so by their own faith.

If not disruptive to the ceremony, is it OK to:

Take photographs? Seek prior permission.
Use a flash? Seek prior permission.
Use video recording equipment? Seek prior permission.
Use audio recording equipment? Seek prior permission.

Will contributions to the church be collected at the ceremony? No.

After the ceremony

Is there usually a reception after the ceremony? There is usually a reception which will last at least two hours. The location varies, but will be announced in advance. Guests greet the participants, visit with other guests and enjoy the food. Sometimes, there is a sit-down meal. There will be no alcoholic drinks.

Would it be considered impolite to neither eat or drink? No, especially if a guest has dietary restrictions.

Is there a grace or benediction before eating or drinking? Wait for a brief prayer of thanks for the food before eating.

Is there a grace or benediction after eating or drinking? No.

Is there a traditional greeting for the family? Just offer your congratulations.

Is there a traditional form of address for clergy who may be at the reception? 'Pastor'.

Is it OK to leave early? Yes.

Funerals and Mourning

Seventh-day Adventists believe that the deceased sleep until the resurrection of Jesus. A Seventh-day Adventist funeral usually lasts about thirty to sixty minutes.

Before the ceremony

How soon after the death does the funeral usually take place? Within one week of the death.

What should someone who is not a Seventh-day Adventist do upon hearing of the death of a member of that faith? Telephone or visit to express sorrow. Express such words of comfort as 'I sense your grief and share it with you.' When speaking with each other, Adventists usually follow this phrase with, 'We look for the coming resurrection.' One should not consign the deceased to heaven or hell.

Appropriate attire

Men: Jacket and tie. No head covering required.

Women: Dress or skirt and blouse. No head covering required. Clothing should cover the arms, and hems should be below the knee.

No jewellery should be worn.

Sombre colours are recommended.

Gifts

Is it appropriate to send flowers or make a contribution? The family will often request that donations are made to a favourite charity.

Is it appropriate to send food? No.

The ceremony

Where will the ceremony take place? Either in a church or in a funeral chapel or crematorium.

When should guests arrive and where should they sit? It is customary to arrive early. If there is no usher, sit in any seat.

If arriving late, are there times when a guest should not enter the ceremony? Do not enter during prayer.

Will the bereaved family be present at the church or funeral home before the ceremony? Often.

Is there a traditional greeting for the family? It is appropriate to offer the family a brief word of encouragement before the funeral.

Will there be an open coffin? Occasionally.

Is a guest expected to view the body? This is optional.

What is appropriate behaviour upon viewing the body? Simply stand in silent observation.

Who are the major officiants at the ceremony and what do they do?
A clergyman, who leads the service; possibly also an associate clergy or lay person and musician(s).
Close friends and family often make a contribution.

What books are used? The clergy alone uses the Bible.

To indicate the order of the ceremony: A programme will be distributed.

Will a guest who is not a Seventh-day Adventist be expected to do anything other than sit? You are not expected to do anything other than sit respectfully.

Are there any parts of the ceremony in which a guest who is not a Seventh-day Adventist should not participate? No.

If not disruptive to the service, is it OK to:

Take pictures? No.
Use a flash? No.
Use video recording equipment? No.
Use audio recording equipment? No.

Will contributions to the church be collected at the ceremony? No.

The interment

Should guests attend the interment? This is optional.

Whom should one ask for directions? The funeral director.

What happens at the graveside? There will be a brief message of encouragement and prayer from the clergyman. There may be singing of hymns while the grave is filled.

Do guests who are not Seventh-day Adventists participate at the graveside ceremony? No. They are simply present.

Comforting the bereaved

Is it appropriate to visit the home of the bereaved after the funeral? Yes, especially during the first few days after the funeral. More than once is appropriate. One should visit briefly, perhaps for ten minutes, to express words of encouragement or to offer to help with any difficulties the bereaved may encounter.

Will there be a religious service at the home of the bereaved?
There are no special customs or religious services at the home.

Will food be served? No.

How soon after the funeral will a mourner usually return to a normal work schedule? This is left entirely to the discretion of individual mourners, since the Bible does not mandate specific periods for mourning. Probably within days of the funeral.

How soon after the funeral will a mourner usually return to a normal social schedule? Probably within days of the funeral.

Are there rituals for observing the anniversary of the death? No, since the Bible does not mandate such rituals.

5. HOME CELEBRATIONS

Not applicable to Seventh-day Adventists.

21
Sikh

1. HISTORY AND BELIEFS

The Sikh faith originated in India in the late fifteenth century through the life and teachings of Guru Nanak (1469–1539), the first Sikh guru. At a time of great religious conflict, he taught that all creation is a part of the One Creator. After Guru Nanak's life, he passed his 'light' on successively to nine other gurus who further evolved his teachings, based on universal welfare and universal brotherhood. Each guru denounced India's caste system and the oppression of anyone based on class, creed, colour or sex.

In 1699, the tenth and last human guru, Guru Gobind Singh, initiated his followers as the *Khalsa*, which means 'King's Own'. He instructed the *Khalsa* to keep the five symbols (*Panj Kakar*) which are outward signs of a disciple's discipline and strength of faith: *kachha* (special underwear, symbolising readiness and chastity), *kara* (a stainless-steel bracelet, showing restraint and loyalty to the guru), *kirpan* (a sword, symbolising compassion and one's task to defend the truth), *kes* (unshorn hair) and *kanga* (a small comb, which ensured the disciple's hair would remain in the image of the Creator, *Waheguru*, 'Wonderful Teacher' – the term used most often to refer to the supreme Being, or Creator of all); to be monogamous; and to live righteously. Before his soul passed back to the Creator in 1708, Guru Gobind Singh 'gave' the guruship to the Sikh scriptures known as the *Siri Guru Granth Sahib*. These scriptures were compiled by the fifth guru, Arjan Dev, and contain sacred writings by some Sikh gurus and several Hindu and Muslim saints. Since then, Sikhs have bowed before the *Siri Guru Granth Sahib*, consulted it as their only guru and treated it with reverence.

Today, there are 20 million Sikhs throughout the world. Sikhism is a path of discipleship, concerned with living a pure and moral life, for the benefit of one's family, community and the whole of humanity, which is seen as a brotherhood under one God. A devout Sikh respects the adherents of all other faiths irrespective of the differences of creed and ways of worship.

UK temples/gurdwaras: approximately 300
UK membership: approximately 430,000

For more information, contact:

Sikh Missionary Society UK
10 Featherstone Road
Southall
Middlesex
UB2 5AA
Tel: 020 8574 1902
Email: info@sikhmissionarysociety.org

2. THE BASIC SERVICE

A Sikh service takes place in a *gurdwara*, which literally means 'Gate to the Guru' and is an environment that has been especially readied for uplifting one's consciousness. The service may take place in someone's home, in a rented hall, or in a special place built for the purpose. The main focus of any Sikh *gurdwara* is the *Siri Guru Granth Sahib*, a compilation of sacred writings that is covered in cloth and is usually at the centre of the room. Sikhs bow to the *Siri Guru Granth Sahib*, which symbolises the Infinite Word of God, as an act of humility and to acknowledge that an Infinite Power pervades all.

Everyone attending the *gurdwara* sits on the floor as an act of humility, equality and respect. They also sit in a cross-legged position, which is conducive to meditation. If helpful to their comfort, guests do not have to sit with their legs crossed.

The Sikh service consists of *kirtan* (songs of praise to God), an *ardas* (community prayer led by any one person) and a *hukamama* (the 'Guru's Instructions'), which is read from the *Siri Guru Granth Sahib*. The *hukamama*, which is a portion of the *Siri Guru Granth Sahib* chosen randomly by the reader, is first read in the original Gurmukhi language and then translated into English (or the main language of the congregation).

Often guest speakers address the *sangat*, or congregation, on spiritual topics. Many *sangats* hold services every Sunday morning that last more than two hours.

Appropriate Attire

Men: A jacket and tie or more casual, modest clothing. Shoes are always removed before entering the *gurdwara*, and the head must always be covered while in the *gurdwara*. Guests may wear any hat, cap or scarf that covers the top of the head.

Women: A modest dress or trousers. It is best if the legs are covered enough so one can comfortably sit cross-legged. Shoes are always removed before entering the *gurdwara*, and the head must always be covered with a scarf that covers the top of the head while in the *gurdwara*. Sikh women are forbidden from wearing caps. Modest jewellery is permissible.

There are no rules regarding colours of clothing.

The Sanctuary

What are the major sections of the gurdwara? *Gurdwaras* can range from a room or house converted for the purpose of worship to magnificent buildings inlaid with gold and marble. However, many *gurdwaras* have the following sections:

The entry room: Has shelves where shoes can be left before entering the main room. Often the entry room has bowls or sinks for washing one's hands and feet. If there is no entry room, shoes should be left outside the *gurdwara*.

The main room (the dardar): Congregants sit on the covered floor in this area. In some *gurdwaras*, the men sit on the left and the women sit on the right.

The front or central area: Where the Sikh scriptures, the *Siri Guru Granth Sahib*, presides under a canopy and is elevated above the congregation. To the right or left of the *Siri Guru Granth Sahib* is an area for *kirtanis*, musicians who lead congregants in song.

The Service

When should guests arrive and where should they sit? Because of the length of the ordinary worship service, it is not required to arrive at the time designated for the start of worship. Guests should sit anywhere in the main area with the men on the left and women on the right, although this may not apply in some *gurdwaras*. Everyone, including guests, must always face the *Siri Guru Granth Sahib*, which is at the front (or central location) of the room.

Before entering the *gurdwara*, remove your shoes and cover your head. It is optional to wash your hands and feet. If desired, the guest may offer money or a gift, such as flowers or fruit, to the *Siri Guru Granth Sahib* and then bow before it. Money may be placed in a box with a slot in it or on an offering plate. Either will be in front of the *Siri Guru Granth Sahib*. Other gifts may be placed in front of the *Siri Guru Granth Sahib*.

Next, guests should sit on the floor facing the front. The feet of all present face away from the *Siri Guru Granth Sahib* as a sign of respect. It is important to refrain from eating, drinking or unnecessary conversation in the *gurdwara*.

If arriving late, are there times when a guest should not enter the service? It is best to enter during the *kirtan*, or songs. Do not enter during the *ardas*, or community prayer, when everyone is standing.

Are there times when a guest should not leave the service? A guest may leave at any time. However, it is recommended not to leave during the *ardas* (community prayer) or *hukam*, the reading from the

Siri Guru Granth Sahib. It may be advisable for guests to sit near the door if they plan on leaving the service early.

Who are the major officiants, leaders or participants and what do they do?

The granthi or giani ji, who reads the *hukam* from the *Siri Guru Granth Sahib*, and will also announce guest speakers and the order of the service.

Attendants, several people who sit behind the *Siri Guru Granth Sahib* and attend to it by frequently waving a long-handled brush made of long horsehair called a *chori sahib* above the *Siri Guru Granth Sahib*, or take out or put away the scriptures. The attendants also serve *prasad*, or sweet pudding, at the end of the service; read the *hukam* translation in English; and assist in the *gurdwara* as needed. Many people from the *sangat*, the congregation, participate in these functions.

Kirtanis, musicians who lead the *sangat* in *kirtan*, songs of praise to God.

What are the major ritual objects of the service?

The manji sahib, the 'bed' or platform for the *Siri Guru Granth Sahib*. It is covered by ornate cloths called *ramalas*.

The chandoa, the canopy hanging over the *Siri Guru Granth Sahib*.

The adi shakti or khanda, a symbol shaped like a circle surrounded by two swords and cut through by one double-edged sword. It symbolises the primal, creative energy of the universe. The sword cutting through the circle represents the breaking of the cycle of birth and death.

The kirpana, a sword used to bless *langar* ('sacred food') and *prasad* (sweet pudding) during the *ardas* (community prayer).

The chori sahib, a long-handled brush made of long horsehair. It is identical to brushes used in ancient India that were waved over royalty to show their state of sovereignty. It is waved over the *Siri Guru Granth Sahib* to symbolise its sovereignty and to show its status as a living guru.

What books are used?

Booklets or sheets containing transliterations and translations of the *kirtan* (songs of praise to God) to be sung may be available, depending on the *gurdwara*. Effort should be made not to put them on the floor. Since Sikhs respect the written word of God, anything containing it should not be stepped upon or marred in any way.
If these booklets are available, they are often found at the front of the *gurdwara*.

To indicate the order of the service: There may be a written programme and/or the master of ceremonies may make periodic announcements.

Guest Behaviour during the Service

Will a guest who is not a Sikh be expected to do anything other than sit? A guest will be expected to stand and sit at the same time as everyone else. It is entirely optional for the guest to sing or bow to the *Siri Guru Granth Sahib*. Guests are expected to accept *prasad* (sweet pudding), which is considered a blessing from the *Siri Guru Granth Sahib*.

Customarily, *prasad* is placed into one's hands, which are placed together with the palms up. One does not have to be a Sikh to eat the *prasad*.

Are there any parts of the service in which a guest who is not a Sikh should not participate? Only Sikhs will be asked to serve *prasad*, read from the *Siri Guru Granth Sahib*, do the *ardas* (prayer) and serve in any way needed. A guest will not be expected to perform any of these functions. Other than this, a guest may participate in every part of the service as desired.

If not disruptive to the service, is it OK to:

Take pictures? Yes, but only if intended solely for personal use.
Use a flash? Yes, but only if intended solely for personal use.
Use video recording equipment? Yes, but only if intended solely for personal use.

Use audio recording equipment? Yes, but only if intended solely for personal use.

Will contributions to the gurdwara *be collected at the service?* Donations collected at each service help fund the *langar* (the food provided after the service), *prasad* (sweet pudding) and the general maintenance and administration of the *gurdwara*. No collection plate is passed through the congregation. Instead, money, flowers or fruit may be offered to the *Siri Guru Granth Sahib*, if one chooses to bow to it, which is optional. Money may be placed in a box with a slot in it or on an offering plate. Either will be in front of the *Siri Guru Granth Sahib*. Other gifts may be placed in front of the *Siri Guru Granth Sahib*.

How much is it customary to contribute? There is no expectation: guests are free to contribute as much as they wish or nothing at all.

After the Service

Is there usually a reception after the service? Langar, or sacred food, is served after (and often during) each service. It is available to all. *Langar* may be served in the *gurdwara* itself, outside, or in a special hall built for the purpose.

Also, a vegetarian meal is usually provided and often consists of East Indian cuisine. Since alcohol is prohibited to Sikhs, it will not be served. Guests with dietary restrictions may politely decline food. It is not considered impolite if they decline the offered food for this reason. Smoking is also strictly prohibited within the precincts and no one should have tobacco or cigarettes on his or her person. The reception may last anywhere from half an hour to several hours.

Is there a traditional form of address for clergy who may be at the reception? 'Granthi' and then the first name, or 'Giani Ji'.

Is it OK to leave early? Yes.

༄

General Guidelines and Advice

Many *gurdwaras* do not designate specific people to help guests, but feel free to ask any Sikh to help you or to explain any part of the service you may not understand.

Remember always to face the *Siri Guru Granth Sahib* and to have your head covered throughout the service. Also, shoes are never worn within the *gurdwara*, even when a service is not taking place.

༄

Special Vocabulary

Key words or phrases that it might be helpful for a visitor to know:

Siri Guru Granth Sahib ('See-ree GOO-roo GRANTH SAH-heeb'): Scriptures compiled by the fifth Sikh guru, Arjan Dev, that contain sacred writings by some Sikh gurus and several Hindu and Muslim saints. Sikhs bow before the *Siri Guru Granth Sahib*, consult it as their only guru, and treat it with reverence.

Prasad ('prah-SAHD'): The sweet pudding served towards the end of the service. It consists of water, honey, wheat flour and clarified butter. *Prasad* is considered to be a blessing from the *Siri Guru Granth Sahib* that everyone can eat.

Ardas ('AHR-das'): Community prayer led by one person in the *gurdwara* service. Blessings for special occasions or events may be requested during the *ardas*.

Sangat ('SAHN-gaht'): The congregation of Sikhs and guests who come together for a worship service.

Langar ('LAHN-gahr'): The vegetarian meal prepared in a prayerful environment and served as an offering after or throughout the worship service to the *sangat*, including guests.

Sat Nam ('SAHT NAHM'): A common phrase and greeting among Sikhs that means 'True Name' and acknowledges the God in all.

Wahe Guruji ka khalsa. Wahe Guruji ki fateh ('WAH-heh GOO-ROO-ji kah KAHL-sah. WAH-heh GOO-ROO-ji kee FAH-the'): A common greeting or phrase that means 'The Pure Ones belong to God. Victory be to God!'

꒲

Some Basic Beliefs

Sikhs believe:

While one God pervades everyone and everything, there are many ways to worship God.

The body is a temple that can serve the spirit.

Women may fully participate in all *gurdwara* services and in any positions of leadership and ministry.

The *Siri Guru Granth Sahib* is the only guru in a Sikh's life. Sikhs are encouraged to learn guru script so that they can read and recite the words within *Siri Guru Granth Sahib*, and by doing so they can achieve the same consciousness as did the gurus who wrote them. Sikhs will never bow to any man or woman, only to the *Siri Guru Granth Sahib*.

Some basic books to which a guest can refer to learn more about Sikhism:

Philosophy and Faith of Sikhism, by K. S. Duggal (Himalayan Publishers, 1973).

The Sikh Religion, 6 vols, by Arthur Macauliffe (Golden Temple Enterprises, 1990).

Victory and Virtue Ceremonies and Code of Conduct of Sikh Dharma, by Bhai Sahiba Dr Inderjit Kaur (Golden Temple Enterprises, 1995).

The websites of Shiromani Gurdwara Parbandhak Committee, also known as the Parliament of the Sikh Nation, www.sgpc.net, and the Sikh Missionary Society UK, www.gurmat.info, contain useful explanations of key aspects of Sikhism.

3. HOLY DAYS AND FESTIVALS

Sikhs used to observe a lunar calendar, so the dates for holidays could not be accurately correlated to the solar calendar in use in the West. They now observe a solar calendar, so dates for holidays are fixed.

The birthdays of the ten Sikh gurus are celebrated throughout the year:

Guru Gobind Singh ('GOH-beend SING'): Celebrated 5 January.

Guru Har Rai ('hahr rye'): Celebrated 31 January.

Guru Teg Bahadur ('TEHG BAH-hah-door'): Celebrated 18 April.

Guru Angad ('Ahn-GAHD'): Celebrated 18 April.

Guru Arjan ('AHR-jahn'): Celebrated 2 May.

Guru Amar Das ('Ah-MAR DAHS'): Celebrated 23 May.

Guru Hargobind ('Hahr-GOH-beend'): Celebrated 5 July.

Guru Har Krishnan ('HAHR KRISH-nan'): Celebrated 23 July.

Guru Ram Das ('rahm dahs'): Celebrated 9 October.

Guru Nanak ('Nah-NAHK'): Celebrated 23 November.

There are no traditional greetings for the above holidays.

Other important religious celebrations include:

Bhaisaki ('BHAY-soo-ki'): When the *Khalsa* (the Pure Ones) was formed in 1699. This usually occurs in the middle of April. There is no traditional greeting for this holiday.

Guru Gaddi Day ('GOO-ROO GAHD-dee'): Commemorates the *Siri Guru Granth Sahib* proclamation as the Living Guru. This usually occurs in November. There is no traditional greeting for this holiday.

To obtain a list of the exact days on which these holidays fall, consult with a Sikh centre in your area.

These celebrations take place through the same *gurdwara* service as described earlier. Behaviour and expectations for guests at these celebrations are the same as for the typical Sikh service.

4. LIFE CYCLE EVENTS

Marriage Ceremony

A couple is considered to come together in a Sikh marriage to help each other on the spiritual path. The merging of two identities that takes place in a marriage is an earthly symbol for the more infinite merger between the soul and God.

A wedding can take place as part of the regular *gurdwara* service, but it may be a service in itself. One or more couples may be married at the same time. A minister addresses the *sangat* (the congregation), then explains to the couple the Sikh concept of marriage and commitment. The bride and groom will be called to sit in front of the *Siri Guru Granth Sahib*. The *kirtanis* (musicians) will be seated on one side and the minister on the other side at the front of the *gurdwara*.

A short prayer called an *ardas* is recited to bless the wedding. Only parents and the wedding couple stand at this time. A *hukam*, or 'Guru's command', for the wedding is then read from the *Siri Guru Granth Sahib*. Next, a special shawl is placed on the shoulder of the groom and in the hands of the bride. The shawl links the couple throughout the wedding ceremony.

The couple is considered to be married when they have circled the *Siri Guru Granth Sahib* four times after reciting four 'marriage rounds', which are special verses from the *Siri Guru Granth Sahib*, in Gurmukhi and then in English (or the primary language of the *sangat*, the congregation). The rounds are then sung by the *kirtanis*. These marriage rounds were written by the fourth Sikh, Guru Ramdass Sahib. They include special instructions for married life. In some *gurdwaras*, as the couple finishes the last round, the congregation may shower the couple with flower petals to show joy and congratulations. At this point, the couple is officially considered to be married and the minister may then make a legal pronouncement of marriage.

If the wedding ceremony is part of a full worship service, the couple and their family and friends now rejoin the *sangat* and the service proceeds as usual.

The wedding itself usually lasts about one hour.

Before the ceremony

Are guests usually invited by a formal invitation? Possibly, but not always. Sikh weddings are open to everyone.

If not stated explicitly, should one assume that children are invited?
Yes.

If one cannot attend, what should one do? Respond in writing or call, and send a gift if you desire to do so.

Appropriate attire

Men: A jacket and tie or more casual, modest clothing. Shoes are always removed before entering the *gurdwara*, and the head must always be covered while in the *gurdwara*. Guests may wear any hat, cap or scarf that covers the top of the head.

Women: A modest dress or trousers. It is best if the legs are covered enough so one can comfortably sit cross-legged. Shoes are always removed before entering the *gurdwara*, and the head must always be covered with a scarf. Sikh women are forbidden from wearing caps. Modest jewellery is permissible.

There are no rules regarding colours of clothing.

Gifts

Is a gift customarily expected? There is no Sikh tradition dictating gift-giving for weddings. If one wishes to present a gift, appropriate gifts may include household items (such as sheets, kitchenware or small appliances), a special, inspirational gift or money.

Should gifts be brought to the ceremony? Gifts may either be left in the entry room or brought to a later reception.

The ceremony

Where will the ceremony take place? In the main in a *gurdwara*.

When should guests arrive and where should they sit? Arrive shortly before the time for which the ceremony has been called, although some *gurdwaras* with primarily Eastern Indian congregants begin weddings much later than the time indicated on an invitation, so it is best to enquire of your host beforehand when the ceremony will actually start.

As with all *gurdwara* services, everyone sits facing the *Siri Guru Granth Sahib*, sometimes with the men on the left and women on the right.

If arriving late, are there times when a guest should not enter the ceremony? A guest may enter at any time during the service, except during the *ardas* (community prayer), which is the point during the service when everyone is standing. One should wait at the entrance to the main worship room until these prayers have ended.

Are there times when a guest should not leave the ceremony? It is advised not to leave during the *ardas* (prayer), *hukam* (the reading from the *Siri Guru Granth Sahib*) or the 'wedding rounds', which are special verses from the *Siri Guru Granth Sahib* recited by the couple in Gurmukhi and then in English (or the primary language of the *sangat*, the congregation).

Guests may wish to sit near the door if they plan on leaving the ceremony early.

Who are the major officiants, leaders or participants at the ceremony and what do they do?

The granthi or giani ji, the person reading the *hukam*, or portion, from the *Siri Guru Granth Sahib*. He or she also reads the four wedding rounds.

The minister, the person who officiates at the wedding ceremony.

The bride and groom and their wedding party.

Kirtanis, musicians who lead the *sangat*, or congregation, in *kirtan* (songs of praise to God).

What books are used? Booklets or sheets containing transliterations and translations of the *kirtan* to be sung may be available, depending on the *gurdwara*. These are often found at the front of the *gurdwara* and in front of the *Siri Guru Granth Sahib*. Effort should be made not to place these booklets on the floor. Since Sikhs respect the written word of God, anything containing it should not be stepped upon or marred in any way.

To indicate the order of the ceremony: There may be a written programme and/or the master of ceremonies may make periodic announcements.

Will a guest who is not a Sikh be expected to do anything other than sit? A guest is expected to stand and sit at the same time as everyone else, but it is optional to sing or bow to the *Siri Guru Granth Sahib*. Family and close friends wishing to stand behind the *Siri Guru Granth Sahib* to offer support to the couple may do so at the time indicated by the minister.

Are there any parts of the ceremony in which a guest who is not a Sikh should not participate? No.

If not disruptive to the ceremony, is it OK to:

Take pictures? Yes, but only if intended solely for personal use.
Use a flash? Yes, but only if intended solely for personal use.
Use video recording equipment? Yes, but only if intended solely for personal use.
Use audio recording equipment? Yes, but only if intended solely for personal use.

Will contributions to the gurdwara be collected at the ceremony? Money or flowers may be offered to the *Siri Guru Granth Sahib* if one chooses to bow to it, which is optional. Money may be placed in a box with a slot in it or on an offering plate. Either will be in front of the *Siri Guru Granth Sahib*. Other gifts may be placed in front of the *Siri Guru Granth Sahib*.

How much is it customary to contribute? There is no expectation: guests are free to contribute as much as they wish or nothing at all.

After the ceremony

Is there usually a reception after the ceremony? *Langar*, or sacred food, may be served after (and sometimes during) the ceremony. *Langar* may be served inside or outside the *gurdwara* or in a special hall built for the purpose. An additional reception at another location may take place after the *langar*, where a vegetarian meal is provided. This often consists of East Indian cuisine. Since alcoholic drinks are prohibited to Sikhs, they will not be served. The reception may last anywhere from half an hour to several hours.

Would it be considered impolite to neither eat nor drink? No.

Is there a grace or benediction before eating or drinking? No.

Is there a grace or benediction after eating or drinking? No.

Is there a traditional greeting for the family? Just offer your congratulations.

Is there a traditional form of address for clergy who may be at the reception? 'Granthi' and then the first name, or 'Giani Ji'.

Is it OK to leave early? Yes.

❀

Funerals and Mourning

Sikhs believe that the soul itself is not subject to death. Death is only the progression of the soul on its journey from God, through the created universe, and back to God again. Because the soul never dies, there is no mourning at the death of a Sikh.

After death, Sikhs prepare the body for the funeral with a bath while reciting prayers. Next the body is dressed in new clothes and, if the person is baptised, the five symbols (*Khalsa* – see above) stay with the body rather than being removed.

A short ceremony takes place at the funeral home before the cremation. An *ardas*, or community prayer, is recited to begin the service. A minister may be present to offer prayers and say a few words, but this is optional. One of the Sikh daily prayers, *Kirtan Sohila*, is recited, and the cremation begins. Although these prayers may be continuously recited throughout the cremation, the basic funeral service ends at this time, and guests may leave. This service usually lasts about thirty to sixty minutes. Afterwards there may be another service at the *gurdwara*, but this is optional. Traditionally, the word *akal*, which means 'undying', is chanted at this service to help release the soul to return to the Infinite. This second ceremony, which is a service in itself, lasts about one hour.

Before the ceremony

What should a non-Sikh do upon hearing of the death of a member of that faith? It is fine to call the family of the deceased to express your love and concern and offer help or support they may need. In calling or writing, it is best not to focus on loss or sadness, but rather to help the family and friends remember the joy of the soul returning to its true home with God.

Appropriate attire

Men: A jacket and tie or more casual, modest clothing. Any colour is fine. Shoes may be worn inside a funeral home, but not in a *gurdwara* service. The head should be covered with a hat, cap or scarf.

Women: A modest dress or trousers. It is best if the legs are covered enough to sit comfortably cross-legged. Shoes may be worn inside a funeral home, but not at a *gurdwara* service. The head should be covered with a scarf. Sikh women are forbidden from wearing caps. Open-toed shoes (which may be worn only in the funeral home, not in the *gurdwara*) and modest jewellery are permissible.

There are no rules regarding colours of clothing.

Gifts

Is it appropriate to send flowers or make a contribution? Flowers, food or contributions to a charity chosen by the family of the deceased may be given, but are not expected.

Is it appropriate to send food? Yes, but do not send food that contains meat, fish, eggs or alcohol.

The ceremony

Where will the ceremony take place? The pre-cremation ceremony will take place at a funeral home. The optional, post-cremation ceremony will be at the *gurdwara*.

When should guests arrive and where should they sit?

It is best to arrive early enough to be seated before the funeral service begins. At a funeral home, one may sit wherever one wishes, but the family of the deceased will sit in the front. For *gurdwara* services, everyone sits on the floor facing the *Siri Guru Granth Sahib*, sometimes with the men on the left and women on the right.

If arriving late, are there times when a guest should not enter the ceremony? One can enter the ceremony in the funeral home and quietly sit anywhere.

Wait at the entrance to the *gurdwara* until the *ardas*, or community prayer, ends and everyone has again been seated.

Will the bereaved family be present at the funeral home before the ceremony? Depending on the customs of a particular Sikh community, the body of the deceased may be displayed at a visitation before the funeral. If this is not the case, the family of the deceased will most likely arrive at the time of the ceremony and not before.

Is there a traditional greeting for the family? Just offer your condolences.

Will there be an open coffin? Possibly, depending on the customs of a particular Sikh community.

Is a guest expected to view the body? No.

What is appropriate behaviour upon viewing the body? Silently say a short prayer for the soul of the deceased as you pass by the coffin.

Who are the major officiants at the ceremony and what do they do?

One person, usually a close family member, officiates at the ceremony at the funeral home and leads the prayers recited there.

Officiating at the service in the gurdwara are:

The granthi or giani ji, the person reading the *hukam* from the *Siri Guru Granth Sahib*. The *hukam*, which is a portion of the *Siri Guru Granth Sahib* chosen randomly by the reader, is first read in the original Gurmukhi language and then translated into English (or the main language of the congregation).

Attendants, several people who sit behind the *Siri Guru Granth Sahib* and attend to it by frequently waving a long-handled brush made of long horsehair called a *chori sahib* above the *Siri Guru Granth Sahib*, or who take out or put away the scriptures. The attendants also serve *prasad*, or sweet pudding, at the end of the service; read the *hukam* translation in English; and assist in the *gurdwara* in any way. Many people from the *sangat*, the congregation, participate in these functions.

Kirtanis, musicians who lead the *sangat* in *kirtan*, songs of praise to God.

The master of ceremonies, the person announcing guest speakers and the order of the service. This role is often fulfilled by the *gurdwara* secretary or *granthi*.

What books are used? A *Nit Nem*, or daily prayer book of the Sikhs is used to recite the prayers before cremation. Since all prayers are read in Gurmukhi (the original language of the gurus), it is not expected for guests to also recite these. If desired, however, a *Nit Nam* with a transliteration may be available upon request.

To indicate the order of the ceremony: In the funeral home, no one indicates the order of the ceremony that is held there. For the *gurdwara* service, there may be a written programme and/or the master of ceremonies may make periodic announcements.

Will a guest who is not a Sikh be expected to do anything other than sit? There are no expectations for guests attending the ceremony in the funeral home. Those guests attending the *gurdwara* ceremony will be expected to stand and sit at the same time as everyone else. It is entirely optional for guests to sing or bow to the *Siri Guru Granth Sahib*, although they are expected to accept *prasad* (sweet pudding), which is considered a blessing from the *Siri Guru Granth Sahib*. Customarily, one receives *prasad* with both hands together, palms up. One does not have to be a Sikh to eat the *prasad*.

Are there any parts of the ceremony in which a guest who is not a Sikh should not participate? Guests may participate in all aspects of the ceremony in the funeral home. In the *gurdwara* ceremony, only Sikhs will be asked to serve *prasad*, read from the *Siri Guru Granth Sahib*, do the *ardas* (prayer) and to serve in any way needed. Other than this, guests may participate in every part of the *gurdwara* ceremony as desired.

If not disruptive to the ceremony, is it OK to:

Take pictures? Only with prior permission of the family of the deceased and if intended solely for personal use.

Use a flash? Only with prior permission of the family of the deceased and if intended solely for personal use.

Use video recording equipment? Only with prior permission of the family of the deceased and if intended solely for personal use.

Use audio recording equipment? Only with prior permission of the family of the deceased and if intended solely for personal use.

Will contributions to the local Sikh temple be collected at the service? No contributions will be collected at a funeral home service. At *gurdwara* services, money or flowers may be offered to the *Siri Guru Granth Sahib* at the time of bowing, but this is optional. Money may be placed in a box with a slot in it or on an offering plate. Either will be in front of the *Siri Guru Granth Sahib*. Other gifts may be placed in front of the *Siri Guru Granth Sahib*.

How much is it customary to contribute? The customary contribution is £1 to £5.

The cremation

It is common for Sikh bodies to be cremated, although not essential. As the soul has passed from the body there is no necessity for it to be disposed of by a specific method.

Should guests attend the cremation? Usually only close family members remain for the cremation, since it lasts several hours.

Whom should one ask for directions? Friends or the family of the deceased.

What happens at the cremation? An *ardas*, or community prayer, is recited to begin the service. A minister may offer prayers and say a few words, but this is optional. A Sikh daily prayer, *Kirtan Sohila*, is recited, and the cremation begins.

Do guests who are not Sikhs participate at the cremation ceremony? Not usually, unless they are invited by the family to do so.

Comforting the bereaved

Is it appropriate to visit the home of the bereaved after the funeral ceremony? This is optional, though not really expected.

Will there be a religious service at the home of the bereaved? Memorial services are often held at home, especially when the funeral ceremony has taken place in another city. Sometimes, the family of the deceased sponsors an *Akhand Path* (unbroken) or other reading of the *Siri Guru Granth Sahib*. This may take place at their home, at the *gurdwara*, or elsewhere. During the *Akhand Path* service, the entire *Siri Guru Granth Sahib* is read in forty-eight hours in the Gurmukhi language or in seventy-two hours in English. People take turns reading the text.

Will food be served? Possibly. Since Sikhs are prohibited from drinking alcoholic drinks, none will be offered.

How soon after the funeral will a mourner usually return to a normal work schedule? Usually one returns to a normal work routine anywhere from a few days to a few weeks after the funeral. This is at the personal discretion of each individual.

How soon after the funeral will a mourner usually return to a normal social schedule? Usually one returns to a normal social routine anywhere from a few days to a few weeks after the funeral. This is at the personal discretion of each individual.

Are there mourning customs to which a friend who is not a Sikh should be sensitive? When visiting, it is best not to focus on loss or sadness, but rather to help the family and friends remember the joy of the soul returning to its true home with God.

Are there rituals for observing the anniversary of the death? No, although some Sikhs may choose to remember a deceased loved one in prayer during a *gurdwara* service on the anniversary of a death. Some Sikhs also choose to hold a special *gurdwara* and *langar* at the anniversary.

5. HOME CELEBRATIONS

The Home or Business Blessing

When does it occur? Often before occupying a new house or apartment or launching a new venture or business, although there are no rules to govern this.

What is its significance? To bless a new home or enterprise with success and happiness. Many Sikhs may hold a *gurdwara* service called an *Akhand Path*, during which the entire *Siri Guru Granth Sahib* is read in forty-eight hours in the Gurmukhi language or in seventy-two hours in English. People take turns reading the text. Other Sikhs may choose to serve *langar*, or sacred food, in the new home or business location.

What is the proper greeting to the celebrants? 'Congratulations', or anything expressing similar sentiments.

Before the ceremony

Are guests usually invited by a formal invitation? Yes.

If not stated explicitly, should one assume children are invited? Yes.

If one cannot attend, what should one do? Politely decline by note or a telephone call. A housewarming gift is appropriate for a new dwelling, but this is entirely optional.

Appropriate attire

Men: A jacket and tie or more casual, modest clothing. Shoes are always removed before entering the *gurdwara*, and the head must always be covered while in the *gurdwara*. Guests may wear any hat, cap or scarf that covers the top of the head.

Women: A modest dress, skirt and blouse, or trouser suit. It is best if the legs are covered enough so one can comfortably sit cross-legged. Shoes are always removed before entering the *gurdwara*, and the head must always be covered with a scarf that covers the top of the head while in the *gurdwara*. Sikh women are forbidden from wearing caps. Modest jewellery is permissible.

There are no rules regarding colours of clothing.

Gifts

Is a gift customarily expected? No. This is optional.

If one decides to give a gift, is a certain type of gift appropriate? Anything for a new home or business.

The ceremony

If the hosts choose to have an *Akhand Path* (see above), it is preceded by a one-hour *gurdwara* service at which the following officiate:

The granthi or giani ji, the person reading the *hukam* from the *Siri Guru Granth Sahib*.

Attendants, several people who sit behind the *Siri Guru Granth Sahib* and attend to it by frequently waving a long-handled brush made of long horsehair called a *chori sahib* above the *Siri Guru Granth Sahib*, or take out or put away the scriptures. The attendants also serve *prasad*, or sweet pudding, at the end of the service; read the *hukam* translation in English; and assist in the *gurdwara* in any way. Many people from the *sangat*, the congregation, participate in these functions.

Kirtanis, musicians who lead those present in *kirtan*, songs of praise to God.

It is customary to arrive for the service at the time for which it has been called.

What are the major ritual objects of the ceremony?

If there is an *Akhand Path*, the following are used:

The manji sahib, the 'bed' or platform for the *Siri Guru Granth Sahib*. It is covered by ornate cloths called *ramalas*.

The chandoa, the canopy hanging over the *Siri Guru Granth Sahib*.

The adi shakti or khanda, a symbol shaped like a circle surrounded by two swords and cut through by one double-edged sword. It symbolises the primal, creative energy of the universe. The sword cutting through the circle represents the breaking of the cycle of birth and death.

The kirpan, a special knife used to bless *langar* ('sacred food') and *prasad* (sweet pudding) during the *ardas* (community prayer).

The chori sahib, a long-handled brush made of long horsehair. It is identical to brushes used in ancient India that were waved over royalty to show their state of sovereignty. It is waved over the *Siri Guru Granth Sahib* to symbolise its sovereignty, to purify the energy around it, and to show its status as a living guru.

What books are used? Booklets or sheets containing transliterations and translations of the *kirtan* (songs of praise to God) to be sung may be available. Effort should be made not to put them on the floor. Since Sikhs respect the written word of God, anything containing it should not be stepped upon or marred in any way.

Will a guest who is not a Sikh be expected to do anything other than sit? A guest will be expected to stand and sit at the same time as everyone else. It is entirely optional for the guest to sing or bow to the *Siri Guru Granth Sahib*. Guests are expected to accept *prasad* (sweet pudding), which is considered a blessing from the *Siri Guru Granth Sahib*.

Customarily, one receives *prasad* with both hands together, palms up. One does not have to be a Sikh to eat the *prasad*.

Are there any parts of the ceremony in which a guest who is not a Sikh should not participate? Only Sikhs will be asked to serve *prasad*, read from the *Siri Guru Granth Sahib*, do the *ardas* (prayer) and to serve in any way needed. Other than this, a guest may participate in every part of the service as desired.

If not disruptive to the ceremony, is it OK to:

Take pictures? Yes, but only if intended solely for personal use.
Use a flash? Yes, but only if intended solely for personal use.
Use video recording equipment? Yes, but only if intended solely for personal use.
Use audio recording equipment? Yes, but only if intended solely for personal use.

Eating and drinking

Is a meal part of the celebration? Possibly.

Will there be alcoholic drinks? No.

Would it be considered impolite to neither eat nor drink? No.

Is there a grace or benediction before eating or drinking? No.

Is there a grace or benediction after eating or drinking? No.

At the meal, will a guest be asked to say or do anything? No.

Will there be:

Dancing? No.

Music? Only *kirtan*, songs of praise to God.

22

Spiritualist

1. HISTORY AND BELIEFS

The Spiritualist Church is a multi-denominational movement with adherents around the world, being particularly strong in the UK and North America. It recognises an intelligent, single force which created the universe and all life – called God by many – and that a spirit world, to which our souls or 'spirit bodies' progress after death, is an integral part of creation. Spiritualism is founded upon the scientifically verified discovery that it is possible for us to communicate with spirits that occupy the spirit world, and that we can seek guidance and inspiration from them that will help us live a better life in the physical world.

The belief in, and practice of communication with, spirits has taken place in almost all cultures throughout recorded history, and Spiritualists often claim that the Christian faith has its roots in spiritual practices. The Bible records various instances of spiritual phenonema, such as the miracles of Jesus and the first apostles, angelic visitations and prophecies, spirits both speaking and inspiring people and other instances of spiritual gifts. The Christian Church has also denounced mediums and others involved in spiritual practices, with such force that several periods of history have seen such people suffer suspicion and extreme, often fatal, persecution.

Most Spiritualists cite the events at a family house in New York State, USA, in 1848 as the birth of the modern Spiritualist movement. The Fox family reported continual occurrences of unexplained physical sensations, loud raps (described as 'knockings') and apparitions and, as the phenomena increased, the three daughters of the household discovered a means of communicating with the supposed spirit. A code was devised whereby the girls would snap their fingers and the spirit would respond with the same number of raps, and so a basis of two-way communication was developed. Investigative committees were formed to verify the events, which attracted international attention and encouraged thousands of other people to experiment in mediumship. A formal movement was born.

The first Spiritualist Church in Britain was founded in 1853 in Keighley, Yorkshire, and by the 1870s there were numerous Spiritualist churches and societies across the country. Today, the Spiritualist Church aims to offer all people the opportunity to witness spirit communication and learn the practice for themselves, both to learn from the wisdom and guidance of those who have gone before, and to stimulate people's spiritual growth, understanding of God and preparation for their own eventual existence in the spirit world.

UK congregations: approximately 400
UK membership: approximately 16,000

For more information, contact:

Spiritualists National Union
Redwoods
Stansted Hall
Stansted
CM24 8UD
Tel: 01279 816363
www.snu.org.uk

2. THE BASIC SERVICE

Most Spiritualist churches hold at least one service a week to which guests and visitors are welcome. These usually take place on a Sunday, with an evening start at around 6 or 6.30 p.m., or occasionally in the morning at around 11 a.m., and generally last between one and a quarter and one and a half hours. It is sometimes called a Divine

Service, and sometimes simply a Sunday Service. Some churches also hold a weekday service.

The purpose of the meetings is to show reverence to the divine through prayer and hymns, to learn about communication with spirits through a visiting medium who will demonstrate the practice and sometimes give a talk on the subject. There is often a time in which the medium will pass on messages from the spirit world to members of the congregation.

Appropriate Attire

There are no rules regarding clothing. Wear what feels most comfortable and reasonable, using common sense.

The Service

When should guests arrive and where should they sit? Arrive shortly before the time that the service has been called for, and sit in any spare seat that you choose.

If arriving late, are there times when a guest should not enter the service? Yes, when a prayer is being said.

Are there times when a guest should not leave the service? No.

Who are the major officiants, leaders or participants and what do they do?

The chairperson, who controls the service.
The medium, who conducts the service.
Stewards, who assist members of the congregation and take the collection.

What books are used? A hymn book.

To indicate the order of the service: A programme or order of service will be provided. The chairperson will also make announcements to the congregation.

✧

Guest Behaviour during the Service

Will a guest who is not a Spiritualist be expected to do anything other than sit? No.

Are there any parts of the service in which a guest who is not a member of the Spiritualist Church should not participate? No.

If not disruptive to the service, is it OK to:

Take pictures? No, unless by prior arrangement.
Use a flash? No, unless by prior arrangement.
Use video recording equipment? No, unless by prior arrangement.
Use audio recording equipment? No, unless by prior arrangement.

Will contributions to the church be collected at the service? Yes, stewards will bring collecting boxes around all members of the congregation.

How much is it customary to contribute? This is entirely down to personal discretion.

✧

After the Service

Is there usually a reception after the service? Not a formal reception, but refreshments are usually provided after the service and there will be an opportunity to stay to chat to other members of the congregation.

Is it OK to leave early? Yes.

✧

Special Vocabulary

Discarnate spirit: A spirit living in the spirit world.
Incarnate spirit: A spirit living in the physical world.

❧

Some Basic Beliefs

Spiritualists believe:

There is a creative force in the universe. This force created the whole universe and life itself in its many forms. It manifests in all things and as we are part of the Life created by God, we acknowledge God as our Father.

We are all part of the universal creative force, one large human family in God. Spiritualists try to understand the needs of others and aim to help all people materially, emotionally and spiritually.

There are people in the spirit world who are dedicated to the welfare and service of mankind, some bring inspiration and guidance while others help with healing.

After death the spirit continues in a different dimension, that we call the 'spirit world'. In the spirit world we have a spirit body which, until we progress far enough, is a replica of our earthly body. We have the same personality and characteristics and we change and grow, as we would on earth, by experience and as a result of our own efforts.

Responsibility for wrongful thoughts and actions, in every aspect of life, lies with the individual. No other person or influence can put right our wrongdoings. No one can interfere with our spiritual development unless we allow this.

If someone is cruel and vindictive towards others, then in some way retribution will follow; if someone gives love and kindness, then compensation follows. This law operates now, on earth as well as in the spirit world.

All who want to walk the path that leads to perfection are able to progress in mental and spiritual understanding. By doing our best in earthly life and by following our inward intuitions we shall find progress comes on earth and in spirit.

Some basic books and pamphlets to which a guest can refer to learn more about Spiritualism:

The History of Spiritualism, by Sir Arthur Conan Doyle (The Echo Library, 2006).

This Is Spiritualism, by Maurice Barbanell (Spiritual Truth Press, 2001).

The University of Spiritualism, by Harry Boddington (Spiritualist Press, 1974).

Any of the Silver Birch Books available from Psychic News.

3. HOLY DAYS AND FESTIVALS

Hydesville Day: On 31 March every year, Spiritualists celebrate the anniversary of the day that the Fox sisters established two-way communication with the spirit world. Special services are held, and these sometimes include a dramatic re-enactment of the events, and people dressing up in costumes from the time.

4. LIFE CYCLE EVENTS

Birth Ceremony

Spiritualists will often hold a naming ceremony for a newborn child. Lasting between fifteen and thirty minutes, it is a service in its own right, rather than a part of the regular Divine Service, and a medium will channel a 'spirit name' for the child. It may take place directly after the Divine Service, so that members of the initial congregation can stay on.

Spiritualists do not use water in the same way that it is used in Christian ceremonies (i.e. as a symbol of cleansing a baptismal candidate of their sins), as they believe that when children enter our world they are pure. Flowers or flower petals are often given to the child.

Naming ceremonies are also sometimes held for adults.

Before the ceremony

Are guests usually invited by a formal invitation? Yes.

If not stated explicitly, should one assume that children are invited? Yes.

If one cannot attend, what should one do? This is down to individual discretion.

Appropriate attire

There are no rules regarding clothing. Wear what feels most comfortable and reasonable, using common sense.

Gifts

Is a gift customarily expected? This is down to individual discretion.

The ceremony

Where will the ceremony take place? It will often take place at the regular place of worship, but it is a ceremony that can be conducted in any room or building.

When should guests arrive and where should they sit? Arrive shortly before the time that the service has been called for, and sit in any spare seat that you choose.

If arriving late, are there times when a guest should not enter the service? No.

Are there times when a guest should not leave the service? No.

Who are the major officiants, leaders or participants and what do they do?

The minister or official, who conducts the service.
Sponsors, who are chosen, like godparents, to help and guide the child through life.

What books are used? A hymn book or Spiritualist lyceum manual.

To indicate the order of the service: A programme or order of service will be provided. The minister will also make announcements to the congregation.

Will a guest who is not a Spiritualist be expected to do anything other than sit? Yes, it is common for all members of the congregation to give the child a flower.

Are there any parts of the service in which a guest who is not a member of the Spiritualist Church should not participate? No.

If not disruptive to the service, is it OK to:

Take pictures? Only by prior arrangement.
Use a flash? Only by prior arrangement.
Use video recording equipment? Only by prior arrangement.
Use audio recording equipment? Only by prior arrangement.

Will contributions to the church be collected at the service? Yes, stewards will bring collecting boxes around all members of the congregation.

How much is it customary to contribute? This is entirely down to personal discretion.

After the ceremony

Is there usually a reception after the ceremony? The parents may often arrange a reception after the ceremony, sometimes held at the church. It will normally last between thirty and sixty minutes. There is likely to be food and drink served, although not usually alcoholic drinks.

Would it be considered impolite to neither eat nor drink? No.

Is there a grace or benediction before eating or drinking? No.

Is there a grace or benediction after eating or drinking? No.

Is there a traditional greeting for the family? Just offer your congratulations.

Is there a traditional form of address for clergy who may be at the reception? Yes, 'Minister'.

Is it OK to leave early? Yes, whenever you wish.

༄

Initiation Ceremony

When a person is accepted into full membership of the Spiritualist Church, a special service is held to welcome them. It is normally a service in its own right, rather than a part of the regular Divine Service, and will last between fifteen and thirty minutes. There is not normally a reception after the service.

Before the ceremony

Are guests usually invited by a formal invitation? No, it is more likely to be an informal invitation by word of mouth.

If not stated explicitly, should one assume that children are invited? Yes.

If one cannot attend, what should one do? This is down to individual discretion.

Appropriate attire

There are no rules regarding clothing. Wear what feels most comfortable and reasonable, using common sense.

Gifts

Is a gift customarily expected? No.

The ceremony

Where will the ceremony take place? It will usually take place at the regular place of worship.

When should guests arrive and where should they sit? Arrive shortly before the time that the service has been called for, and sit in any spare seat that you choose.

If arriving late, are there times when a guest should not enter the service? No.

Are there times when a guest should not leave the service? No.

Who are the major officiants, leaders or participants and what do they do?

The minister or official, who conducts the service.

To indicate the order of the service: A programme or order of service will be provided. The minister will also make announcements to the congregation.

Will a guest who is not a Spiritualist be expected to do anything other than sit? No.

Are there any parts of the service in which a guest who is not a member of the Spiritualist Church should not participate? No.

If not disruptive to the service, is it OK to:

Take pictures? Only by prior arrangement.
Use a flash? Only by prior arrangement.
Use video recording equipment? Only by prior arrangement.
Use audio recording equipment? Only by prior arrangement.

Will contributions to the church be collected at the service? No.

Marriage Ceremony

Spiritualist churches conduct a wedding service for a man and woman to be married, celebrating their love for each other and commitment to live together in partnership, providing comfort, support and understanding for each other. The service is a ceremony in its own right and takes place at the Spiritualist place of worship, and usually lasts between thirty and sixty minutes.

Before the ceremony

Are guests usually invited by a formal invitation? Anybody is free to attend the ceremony, although the parents of the bride and groom will also send out invitations.

If not stated explicitly, should one assume that children are invited? Yes.

If one cannot attend, what should one do? This is down to individual discretion.

Appropriate attire

There are no rules regarding clothing. Wear what feels most comfortable and reasonable, using common sense.

Gifts

Is a gift customarily expected? This is down to individual discretion. There is no particular Spiritualist custom or requirement, but treat the wedding as you would if going to one in any other faith or denomination.

The ceremony

Where will the ceremony take place? It will usually take place at the regular place of worship.

When should guests arrive and where should they sit? Arrive shortly before the time that the service has been called for, and a steward will normally be on hand to show you where to sit.

If arriving late, are there times when a guest should not enter the service? No.

Are there times when a guest should not leave the service? No.

Who are the major officiants, leaders or participants and what do they do?
The minister, who conducts the service.
A registrar, to register the marriage.
Stewards, who will assist guests.

To indicate the order of the service: A programme or order of service will be provided. The minister will also make announcements to the congregation.

Will a guest who is not a Spiritualist be expected to do anything other than sit? No.

Are there any parts of the service in which a guest who is not a member of the Spiritualist Church should not participate? No.

If not disruptive to the service, is it OK to:

Take pictures? Only by prior arrangement.
Use a flash? Only by prior arrangement.
Use video recording equipment? Only by prior arrangement.
Use audio recording equipment? Only by prior arrangement.

Will contributions to the church be collected at the service? Yes, there will usually be a collecting box on a table at the back of the hall.

How much is it customary to contribute? This is entirely down to personal discretion.

After the ceremony

Is there usually a reception after the ceremony? A reception will usually be arranged by the wedding couple, in a hotel or other hired venue. Its format will be at their own discretion, but it is possible that there will be a communal meal, speeches and toasts, and often music and dancing. The reception will usually last at least two hours.

Would it be considered impolite to neither eat nor drink? Not if there are good reasons.

Is there a grace or benediction before eating or drinking? At the discretion of the wedding couple.

Is there a grace or benediction after eating or drinking? At the discretion of the wedding couple.

Is there a traditional greeting for the family? Just offer your congratulations.

Is there a traditional form of address for clergy who may be at the reception? Yes, 'Minister'.

Is it OK to leave early? Yes.

◌

Funerals and Mourning

Spiritualists believe that, after death, the spirit continues in a different dimension, the 'spirit world'. In the spirit world we have a spirit body which, until we progress far enough, is a replica of our earthly body. We have the same personality and characteristics and we change and grow, as we would on earth, by experience and as a result of our own efforts.

A Spiritualist funeral service is designed to pay tribute to the life of a loved one who has progressed to the spirit world, and to acknowledge that we will eventually join them there.

The ceremony, which normally lasts between fifteen and thirty minutes, is a service in its own right and usually takes place at the Spiritualist place of worship, sometimes followed by another short service at the funeral parlour.

Before the ceremony

How soon after the death does the memorial service usually take place? Usually within one week, subject to legal or medical requirements.

What should someone who is not a Spiritualist do upon hearing of the death of a member of that faith? This is down to individual discretion, although visiting the bereaved is usually appropriate.

Appropriate attire

There are no rules regarding clothing. Wear what feels most comfortable and reasonable, using common sense.

Gifts

Is it appropriate to send flowers or make a contribution? Flowers or a donation to a charity favoured by the deceased are usually welcome. Specific requests are sometimes made by the bereaved.

Is it appropriate to send food? No.

The ceremony

When should guests arrive and where should they sit? Arrive shortly before the time that the service has been called for. Stewards may be present to advise guests where to sit. If not, sit wherever you wish.

If arriving late, are there times when a guest should not enter the ceremony? No.

Are there times when a guest should not leave the service? Yes, when the family of the deceased are leaving.

Will the bereaved family be present at the funeral home or church before the ceremony? No.

Is there a traditional greeting for the family? No.

Will there be an open coffin? Not normally, although some families may choose otherwise. If yes, there is no requirement for guests to view the body if they would prefer not to.

Who are the major officiants, leaders or participants and what do they do?
The minister, who conducts the service.
The stewards, who will will assist guests.

What books are used? A hymn book.

To indicate the order of the service: A printed order of service will usually be provided.

Will a guest who is not a Spiritualist be expected to do anything other than sit? No.

Are there any parts of the service in which a guest who is not a member of the Spiritualist Church should not participate? No.

If not disruptive to the service, is it OK to:

Take pictures? Only by prior arrangement.
Use a flash? Only by prior arrangement.
Use video recording equipment? Only by prior arrangement.
Use audio recording equipment? Only by prior arrangement.

Will contributions to the church be collected at the service? Yes, there will usually be a collecting box on a table at the back of the hall.

How much is it customary to contribute? This is entirely down to personal discretion.

The interment

Should guests attend the interment? This is entirely optional, unless it is requested that only close family attend.

Whom should one ask for directions? A member of the family, or the minister.

What happens at the graveside? A short burial service takes place.

Do guests who are not Spiritualists participate at the graveside ceremony? No. They are simply present.

What happens at the cremation ceremony? A short cremation service takes place.

Do guests who are not Spiritualists participate at the cremation? No. They are simply present.

Comforting the bereaved

Is it appropriate to visit the home of the bereaved after the memorial service? This is left to your own discretion.

How soon after the memorial service will a mourner usually return to a normal work schedule? This is left to the discretion of the mourner.

How soon after the memorial service will a mourner usually return to a normal social schedule? This is left to the discretion of the mourner.

Are there mourning customs to which a friend who is not a Spiritualist should be sensitive? No.

Are there rituals for observing the anniversary of the death? No.

5. HOME CELEBRATIONS

Not applicable to Spiritualists.

23

Unitarian

1. HISTORY AND BELIEFS

The historic roots of the Unitarian movement can be traced back to
the European Reformation of the Christian Church in the sixteenth
century, a time at which people across the continent started finding
the courage to read and interpret the Bible themselves, and to understand that relationship with God was not necessarily dependent on
mediation through a priest or church. Against this backdrop of religious and philosophical upheaval, the belief that God is single-personed
(as opposed to three-personed, or trinitarian, as held by orthodox
Christian doctrine) became more formalised in small groups across
Europe, notably in Italy, Poland and Transylvania.

In England, this Unitarian view of God began to gain a foothold
through the seventeenth century, particularly in the writing and
preaching of John Biddle, who was imprisoned for his views. Others
were martyred for their beliefs. In 1774, the first Unitarian congregation met in London, led by Theophilus Lindsey, a former Church
of England priest. By the first decade of the nineteenth century,
twenty Unitarian churches had been established in England.

Today, Unitarians around the world aim to be a spiritual community which encourages individuals to think for themselves. Central to
their belief system is that everybody has the right to seek truth for
themselves, on the basis of their own life experiences, personal reflection and the prompting of their own intuition and conscience. They
seek inspiration from the insights of other people, sacred writings of
all traditions and the products of both art and science. Unitarians

are generally known to be tolerant and respectful of other faith traditions, claiming no exclusive divine revelation or status for themselves.

The movement's name is now generally considered to refer more to the importance Unitarians ascribe to the unity of humankind and creation, than to the theological disputes from which it first arose. They believe that values such as reason and honesty, tolerance, peace, compassion, justice and respect for the natural world form a more effective foundation for true community than insistence on uniformity of doctrine.

UK congregations: approximately 200
UK membership: approximately 5,000

For more information, contact:

The General Assembly of Unitarian and Free Christian Churches
(Great Britain)
Essex Hall
1–6 Essex Street
London
WC2R 3HY
Tel: 020 7240 2384
Email: info@unitarian.org.uk

2. THE BASIC SERVICE

Worship is at the heart of Unitarianism, and – while there are many differences in the worship style and detail of different congregations – almost all will meet regularly on Sundays, coming together in community to celebrate and worship God, 'the holy' or that which gives life its meaning and value.

Services can be held in a variety of buildings, from traditional church buildings to rented rooms or sometimes in people's homes. Unitarians have professionally trained clergy, although they believe that no special authority enables one person to conduct worship, so it is possible that parts or all of a service may also be led by a lay member of the congregation. The worship of a congregation reflects what a particular community regards as being of supreme worth, whether this be worship of the divine, celebration of life or affirmation of shared values.

Some congregations may hold a service of Communion, in which thanks are given for Jesus, the bounty of the earth and human solidarity, but it is unlikely to be similar to the Christian ritual of Communion that involves bread and wine. An increasingly popular alternative in some Unitarian churches is the Flower Communion, in which congregants each bring a flower and place it in a communal vase at the start of the service, then, at the end, each takes a different flower from the vase home with them.

❧

Appropriate Attire

There are no rules regarding clothing. Wear what feels most comfortable and reasonable, using common sense.

❧

The Service

When should guests arrive and where should they sit? Arrive shortly before the time for which the service has been called. Stewards may be present to advise guests where to sit. If not, sit wherever you wish.

If arriving late, are there times when a guest should not enter the service? Do not enter during prayers or quiet meditation.

Are there times when a guest should not leave the service? Try not to leave at a time that might disturb others, such as during prayers.

Who are the major officiants, leaders or participants and what do they do?

The minister or lay preacher, who conducts the service.
The organist or pianist, who will lead the music and hymns.

What books are used? A hymn book.

To indicate the order of the service: Some congregations use a printed order of service. In others, the minister or lay preacher will make periodic announcements.

Guest Behaviour during the Service

Will a guest who is not a Unitarian be expected to do anything other than sit? It is expected for guests to stand with congregants when they rise for songs. It is optional for guests to sing and read prayers aloud with congregants if this does not violate their own religious beliefs.

Are there any parts of the service in which a guest who is not a member of the Unitarian Church should not participate? No.

If not disruptive to the service, is it OK to:
Take pictures? No, unless by arrangement.
Use a flash? No, unless by arrangement.
Use video recording equipment? No, unless by arrangement.
Use audio recording equipment? No, unless by arrangement.

Will contributions to the church be collected at the service? Yes, a collection is normally taken during the service.

How much is it customary to contribute? It is entirely optional for guests to contribute. If they choose to do so, a contribution between £1 and £5 is appropriate.

After the Service

Is there usually a reception after the service? Yes. An informal reception is usually held and may consist of coffee, tea and biscuits. There is no grace or benediction before or after eating or drinking. The reception may last about thirty to sixty minutes.

Is it OK to leave early? Yes.

Some Basic Beliefs

Unitarians believe:

Personal experience, conscience and reason should be the final authorities in religion. Religious authority lies not in a book or a person or an institution, but in ourselves.

One cannot be bound by a statement of belief. Unitarianism does not ask anyone to subscribe to a creed.

Religious wisdom is ever changing, and human understanding of life and death, the world and its mysteries is never final, and revelation is continuous.

All men and women have worth. Differences in opinion and lifestyle should be honoured.

One should act as a moral force in the world, and ethical living is the supreme witness of religion. The here and now and the effects that our actions will have on future generations are of great concern. Relations with each other, with other peoples, nations and races should be governed by justice, equity and compassion.

Some basic books and pamphlets to which a guest can refer to learn more about Unitarianism:

Unitarian? What's That?, by Cliff Reed (Lindsey Press, 1999).
The Unitarian Life, by Stephen Lingwood (Lindsey Press, 2008).
The Elements of Unitarianism, by George Chryssides (Element Books, 1998).

3. HOLY DAYS AND FESTIVALS

Unitarians usually mark the feasts and fasts of the Christian year, such as Lent, Easter and Christmas, and will often hold services or make special mention of the changing seasons and cycles of the earth, secular events such as Human Rights Day and World AIDS Day and anniversaries of lives and events that have a special place in human history and spiritual development.

4. LIFE CYCLE EVENTS

Birth Ceremony

Depending on the specific congregation, this may be called a 'christening', 'naming service', 'dedication' or 'welcoming'. 'Christening' means 'to make Christian' and emphasises the importance of a faith community to nurture and sustain individuals and families in times of joy and sorrow. 'Naming' signifies that each child is a unique individual whose name is a powerful symbol of their individuality. 'Dedication' may include these meanings, as well as underscore a covenant with God, the Church and the family, in which parents dedicate themselves to raise their child lovingly in a home that will promote the fullest growth of the child's body, mind and spirit.

The ceremony is usually devised by the parents of the child, in consultation with the minister, according to their individual needs and wishes. There are no traditional rules or customs.

The fifteen- to thirty-minute ceremony is often part of a Sunday worship service, but sometimes a ceremony in its own right.

Before the ceremony

Are guests usually invited by a formal invitation? Sometimes.

If not stated explicitly, should one assume that children are invited? Yes.

If one cannot attend, what should one do? Send apologies.

Appropriate attire

There are no rules regarding clothing, although it would be preferable to dress smartly out of respect for the occasion.

Gifts

Is a gift customarily expected? Sometimes from close family, but generally not from other guests.

The ceremony

Where will the ceremony take place? Depending on the choice of the parents, this might be at the local Unitarian building, or in their home or garden.

When should guests arrive and where should they sit? Arrive shortly before the time for which the service has been called. Stewards may be present to advise guests where to sit. If not, sit wherever you wish.

If arriving late, are there times when a guest should not enter the service? Do not enter during prayers or quiet meditation.

Are there times when a guest should not leave the service? Try not to leave at a time that might disturb others, such as during prayers.

Who are the major officiants, leaders or participants and what do they do?

The minister or lay preacher, who conducts the service.
The organist or pianist, who will lead the music and hymns.

What books are used? A hymn book.

To indicate the order of the service: Some congregations use a printed order of service. In others, the minister or lay preacher will make periodic announcements.

Will a guest who is not a Unitarian be expected to do anything other than sit? It is expected for guests to stand with congregants when they rise for songs. It is optional for guests to sing and read prayers aloud with congregants if this does not violate their own religious beliefs.

Are there any parts of the service in which a guest who is not a member of the Unitarian Church should not participate? No.

If not disruptive to the service, is it OK to:

Take pictures? No, unless by arrangement.
Use a flash? No, unless by arrangement.

Use video recording equipment? No, unless by arrangement.
Use audio recording equipment? No, unless by arrangement.

Will contributions to the church be collected at the service? Yes, if the birth ceremony is part of a main Unitarian service.

How much is it customary to contribute? It is entirely optional for guests to contribute. If they choose to do so, a contribution between £1 and £5 is appropriate.

After the ceremony

Is there usually a reception after the ceremony? Possibly, although this depends entirely on the wishes of the parents.

Would it be considered impolite to neither eat nor drink? No.

Is there a grace or benediction before eating or drinking? Sometimes.

Is there a grace or benediction after eating or drinking? Sometimes.

Is there a traditional greeting for the family? Just offer your congratulations.

Is there a traditional form of address for clergy who may be at the reception? 'Mr', 'Mrs', 'Ms', 'Dr', 'Reverend', or simply call the clergyperson by his or her first name.

Is it OK to leave early? Yes, whenever one wishes.

Initiation Ceremony

There is no initiation ceremony as such for Unitarians, although guests may be invited to a regular service at which new members of the congregation are welcomed. The service would not differ radically from the main service described above, however.

❀

Marriage Ceremony

Unitarians view marriage as the committed joining of two lives as witnessed by the community, rather than an act of conformity to religious codes. Many people who feel unable to be married in other religious venues, but still wish to have a spiritual dimension in their wedding ceremony, choose to be married in a Unitarian church. Unitarianism supports same-sex marriages, a stance that reflects the faith's long-time call for lesbians and gays to be fully included in the religious community and in society at large.

The wedding ceremony is nearly always a service in itself, and will usually last about thirty to sixty minutes.

Before the ceremony

Are guests usually invited by a formal invitation? Yes.

If not stated explicitly, should one assume that children are invited? No.

If one cannot attend, what should one do? Send written apologies and a gift.

Appropriate attire

Men: A jacket and tie.

Women: A dress, skirt and blouse or trouser suit.

There are no rules regarding colours of clothing.

Gifts

Is a gift customarily expected? Yes. Details of a gift list are often included with the wedding invitation. If not, then the nature of the gift is at the discretion of the individual.

Should gifts be brought to the ceremony? Gifts are usually brought to the ceremony and given to the couple at the reception.

The ceremony

Where will the ceremony take place? In England and Wales there is a legal requirement for the marriage to take place in a registered location, so it will need to be at a registered Unitarian church.

When should guests arrive and where should they sit? Arrive shortly before the time that the service has been called for. Stewards will be present to advise guests where to sit.

If arriving late, are there times when a guest should not enter the service? Do not enter during prayers or quiet meditation.

Are there times when a guest should not leave the service? Try not to leave at a time that might disturb others, such as during prayers.

Who are the major officiants, leaders or participants and what do they do?
The minister or lay preacher, who conducts the service.
The organist or pianist, who will lead the music and hymns.

What books are used? A hymn book.

To indicate the order of the service: A printed order of service will usually be provided.

Will a guest who is not a Unitarian be expected to do anything other than sit? It is expected for guests to stand with congregants when they rise for songs. It is optional for guests to sing and read prayers aloud with congregants if this does not violate their own religious beliefs.

Are there any parts of the service in which a guest who is not a member of the Unitarian Church should not participate? No.

If not disruptive to the service, is it OK to:

Take pictures? No, unless by arrangement.
Use a flash? No, unless by arrangement.
Use video recording equipment? No, unless by arrangement.

Use audio recording equipment? No, unless by arrangement.

Will contributions to the church be collected at the service? No.

After the ceremony

Is there usually a reception after the ceremony? A reception will usually be arranged by the wedding couple, in a hotel or other hired venue. There will be a communal meal, speeches and toasts, and often music and dancing. The reception will usually last at least two hours.

Would it be considered impolite to neither eat nor drink? Not if there are good reasons.

Is there a grace or benediction before eating or drinking? Usually.

Is there a grace or benediction after eating or drinking? Sometimes.

Is there a traditional greeting for the family? Just offer your congratulations.

Is there a traditional form of address for clergy who may be at the reception? 'Mr', 'Mrs', 'Ms', 'Dr', 'Reverend', or simply call the clergyperson by his or her first name.

Is it OK to leave early? Yes, but only after the wedding cake has been cut and served.

Funerals and Mourning

There is no specific Unitarian doctrine about afterlife. Some Unitarians believe in an afterlife; some doubt that there is one. Most Unitarian officiants will tailor the format of the service to fit the wishes of the deceased and bereaved, and will be happy to exclude traditional religious language.

The funeral service is a ceremony in itself and may last about thirty to sixty minutes.

Before the ceremony

How soon after the death does the memorial service usually take place? Usually within one week, subject to legal or medical requirements.

What should someone who is not a Unitarian do upon hearing of the death of a member of that faith? Visit the bereaved, telephone or send a card to express your condolences and share your memories of the deceased.

Appropriate attire

There are no rules regarding clothing, although it would be preferable to dress smartly and sombrely, respecting the deceased's close family.

Gifts

Is it appropriate to send flowers or make a contribution? Flowers or a donation to a charity favoured by the deceased are usually welcome. Specific requests are sometimes made by the bereaved.

Is it appropriate to send food? No.

The ceremony

Where will the ceremony take place? Usually at the Unitarian place of worship, or sometimes at a crematorium.

When should guests arrive and where should they sit? Arrive shortly before the time for which the service has been called. Stewards may be present to advise guests where to sit. If not, sit wherever you wish.

If arriving late, are there times when a guest should not enter the ceremony? No.

Will the bereaved family be present at the funeral home or church before the ceremony? No.

Is there a traditional greeting for the family? Express your condolences. Such comments as 'I am so very sorry for your loss' are appropriate.

Will there be an open coffin? No.

Who are the major officiants, leaders or participants and what do they do?
The minister or lay preacher, who conducts the service.
The organist or pianist, who will lead the music and hymns.

What books are used? A hymn book.

To indicate the order of the service: A printed order of service will usually be provided.

Will a guest who is not a Unitarian be expected to do anything other than sit? It is expected for guests to stand with congregants when they rise for songs. It is optional for guests to sing and read prayers aloud with congregants if this does not violate their own religious beliefs.

Are there any parts of the service in which a guest who is not a member of the Unitarian Church should not participate? No.

If not disruptive to the service, is it OK to:
Take pictures? No, unless by arrangement.
Use a flash? No, unless by arrangement.
Use video recording equipment? No, unless by arrangement.
Use audio recording equipment? No, unless by arrangement.

Will contributions to the church be collected at the service? No.

The interment

Should guests attend the interment? This is entirely optional, unless it is requested that only close family attend.

Whom should one ask for directions? A member of the family, or the minister.

What happens at the graveside? There are no set rituals, but it is normal for a prayer and one or two appropriate readings to be said.

Do guests who are not Unitarians participate at the graveside ceremony? No. They are simply present.

What happens at the cremation ceremony? The deceased's life and contribution are acknowledged, sometimes with a short talk by a family member. Appropriate readings and prayers may be said, and hymns sung.

Do guests who are not Unitarians participate at the cremation? No. They are simply present.

Comforting the bereaved

Is it appropriate to visit the home of the bereaved after the memorial service? Yes. The length of the visit depends on one's relationship with the bereaved and with the deceased. When visiting, express your sympathy to the bereaved and offer specific help to them. Fond memories of the deceased are especially appreciated.

How soon after the memorial service will a mourner usually return to a normal work schedule? This is left to the discretion of the mourner.

How soon after the memorial service will a mourner usually return to a normal social schedule? This is left to the discretion of the mourner.

Are there mourning customs to which a friend who is not a Unitarian should be sensitive? No.

Are there rituals for observing the anniversary of the death? No.

5. HOME CELEBRATIONS

Not applicable to Unitarianism.

24

United Reformed Church

1. HISTORY AND BELIEFS

The United Reformed Church is a Christian denomination whose theological roots stretch back to the Reformation of the sixteenth century and the Bible-based teaching of Calvinism. It places a particular emphasis on the Trinity – the three-personed nature of God (Father, Son and Holy Spirit) – and recognition of God's Word as revealed in the Bible, discerned under the guidance of the Holy Spirit, as the highest authority for how we live today.

The United Reformed Church was formed in 1972 as a union between the Presbyterian Church in England and the majority of churches in the Congregational Church in England and Wales. It has subsequently also made union with the Reformed Association of Churches in Christ, in 1981, and the Congregational Union of Scotland, in 2000. It is part of the worldwide family of Reformed Churches, which has a total membership of around 70 million people.

United Reformed Churches set high value on individual conscience and the ability of their members to reach a common understanding. Individual churches are governed by a group of elected elders, and regular church meetings of all members. The Church is also typified by its commitment to ecumenism and partnership with local churches of other Christian denominations.

UK United Reformed Church churches: approximately 1,600
UK United Reformed Church membership: approximately 100,000

For more information, contact:

The United Reformed Church
Church House
86 Tavistock Place
London
WC1H 9RT
Tel: 020 7916 2020
Email: urc@urc.org.uk

2. THE BASIC SERVICE

The United Reformed Church holds regular meetings of Morning and Evening Worship on Sundays, the purpose of which are to offer worship and praise to God, to build Christian community, to help people to grow in understanding of their faith and to equip them for Christian service during the week. These services take place in the main sanctuary area or main hall of the local United Reformed Church building, and are open for anybody to attend, with or without an official invitation. Most services last for about an hour, although occasionally some might last for two to three hours, particularly if there is a charismatic or Afro-Caribbean congregation.

Appropriate Attire

There is no official dress code for men or women, although it is worth asking in advance whether the particular church you are visiting has a preference. Open-toed shoes and jewellery are fine for women.

The Sanctuary

What are the major sections of the church?

Front: The front of the church will contain a pulpit and/or lectern
for the reading and preaching of the Word, a Communion table,

a font and possibly an area for a choir or musical worship group.
Main: The main section of the church is where the congregation will
sit, facing the front.

✵

The Service

When should guests arrive and where should they sit? Depending
on the nature of the congregation, the time of arrival will vary. For
the majority of congregations it would be customary to arrive a
few minutes before the stated time of the service. For some congregations, arrival can be within the first half hour after the start of
the service. You are usually free to sit anywhere, unless specifically
told.

*If arriving late, are there times when a guest should not enter the
service?* No.

Are there times when a guest should not leave the service? No,
although it is normally anticipated that people will stay from beginning to end.

*Who are the major officiants, leaders or participants and what do
they do?*

A minister, or lay preacher, who leads the service.
Readers, who will read from the Scriptures.
Prayer leaders, who will lead the prayers of intercession.
Elders, who share in presiding at Holy Communion.
A church secretary, who will announce the notices.

What are the major ritual objects of the service?

The Bible, containing God's Word.
The baptismal font, from which a person may be baptised through
the sprinkling of water. Some churches will have a *baptismal pool*
in which a person may be baptised by full body immersion.
Holy Communion table, for the celebration of the sacrament of
Holy Communion.

What books are used? A Bible and a hymn book or song sheet, both of which should be provided for you upon entering the church, or laid out by the chairs or pews.

To indicate the order of the service: A printed order of service will be provided in the majority of churches. Increasing numbers of churches will have a projected screen display. The minister or lay preacher will make periodic announcements.

Guest Behaviour during the Service

Will a guest who is not a member of the United Reformed Church be expected to do anything other than sit? It is expected that you would stand and sing at the same time as the rest of the congregation, but it is acceptable not to if you so wish.

Are there any parts of the service in which a guest who is not a member of the United Reformed Church should not participate? Holy Communion is normally open to those who are baptised members of the United Reformed Church, although an open invitation is often extended to all people present. In such cases the decision to receive Communion is left to the individual's discretion.

If not disruptive to the service, is it OK to:

Take pictures? Possibly, but ask permission beforehand.
Use a flash? Possibly, but ask permission beforehand.
Use video recording equipment? Possibly, but ask permission beforehand.
Use audio recording equipment? Possibly, but ask permission beforehand.

Will contributions to the church be collected at the service? Yes, a collection will be announced during the service and will be made by the passing of a plate or small bag around the congregation.

How much is it customary to contribute? Members of the church may give up to a tenth of their weekly income as their offering, and visitors normally give pocket change. It is optional to contribute, but generally expected that most people will.

⁂

After the Service

Is there usually a reception after the ceremony? Tea and coffee and biscuits will normally be served at an informal reception after the service, usually in a different room.

Would it be considered impolite to neither eat nor drink? No.

Is there a ritual before eating or drinking? No.

Is there a grace or benediction after eating or drinking? No.

Is there a traditional form of address for clergy who may be at the reception? This varies between churches and, while there is no harm in enquiring what form of address is appropriate, it is unlikely that you would cause offence by using the wrong one. Clergy can be called 'Reverend' or 'Minister', or by their first name.

Is it OK to leave early? The reception will normally last between half an hour and an hour, but it is fine to leave whenever you need to.

⁂

General Guidelines

In some churches there may be a time of quiet before the service, during which people pray. It would be inappropriate to talk in a way that would be distracting during this time. It would also be inappropriate to talk during the service itself, unless there is a particular invitation to greet other people in the congregation.

Some basic books to which a guest can refer to learn more about the United Reformed Church:

Worship: from the United Reformed Church, the basic book of services.

Under God's Good Hand, by David Cornick (United Reformed Church).

Reforming Theology, by David Peel (United Reformed Church).

Reformed Ministry, by Tony Tucker (United Reformed Church).

Daughters of Dissent, by Elaine Kaye, Janet Lees and Kirsty Thorpe (United Reformed Church).

Stating the Gospel, by David Thompson (Continuum, 1997).

3. HOLY DAYS AND FESTIVALS

Advent: Occurs four weeks before Christmas. Its purpose is to begin preparing for Christmas and to focus on Christ. There is no traditional greeting for this holiday.

Christmas: Occurs on the evening of 24 December and the day of 25 December. Marks the birth and the incarnation of God as a man. The traditional greeting is 'Merry Christmas'.

Lent: Begins on Ash Wednesday, which occurs six weeks before Easter. The purpose is to prepare for Easter. There is no traditional greeting for Lent. Often, there are midweek worship services.

Easter: Always falls on the Sunday after the first full moon that occurs on or after the spring equinox on 21 March. Celebrates the resurrection of Jesus Christ. The traditional greeting is 'Happy Easter!'

Pentecost Sunday: The seventh Sunday after Easter. Celebrates the coming of the Holy Spirit, which is the empowering Spirit of God in human life. This is often considered the birth of the Christian Church. There is no traditional greeting for this holiday.

4. LIFE CYCLE EVENTS

Birth Ceremony

Baptism – which marks both a person's dying and rising with Christ and their reception into the family of the United Reformed Church

– can take place in infancy or in adulthood. The baptismal candidate will be sprinkled with, or immersed in, water, signifying death to their old life and birth to new life in Christ.

Baptism normally takes place as part of a regular service of morning worship, but is occasionally a brief, separate occasion, depending on circumstances.

If a family does not believe infant baptism is appropriate, then the church will offer a service of thanksgiving and/or dedication to mark the birth of their child. Baptism will then take place when the child has grown to an age of understanding about the Christian faith and can affirm that faith for him- or herself.

Before the ceremony

Are guests usually invited by a formal invitation? Yes, or by verbal invitation.

If not stated explicitly, should one assume that children are invited? Yes.

If one cannot attend, what should one do? This is at the discretion of the individual. A polite and prompt reply, expressing regret, is recommended.

Appropriate attire

There is no official dress code for men or women, although it is worth asking the person who invited you whether the particular church you are visiting has a preference. Open-toed shoes and jewellery are fine for women.

Gifts

Is a gift customarily expected? No, although it is a nice gesture to bring a small gift – perhaps a children's book or Bible, or a suitable item for a baby – if the baptismal candidate is a child.

Should gifts be brought to the ceremony? They are normally brought to the ceremony and given to the family after the ceremony is over.

The ceremony

Where will the ceremony take place? In the main sanctuary of the church. The actual baptism part of the service will take place around the font or baptismal pool.

When should guests arrive and where should they sit? It is customary to arrive at the time called. There will usually be someone to tell you where to sit. If not, try to sit close to the family of the baptismal candidate.

If arriving late, are there times when a guest should not enter the service? No.

Are there times when a guest should not leave the service? It would be preferable to stay for the whole service.

Who are the major officiants, leaders or participants in the ceremony and what do they do?
As under 'The Basic Service'.
The minister or a local leader will baptise the baby.

What are the major ritual objects of the service?

The font: A receptacle containing water, signifying new birth in Christ.
A candle: A candle will be given to the family of the baby, symbolising the light of Christ.

What books are used? A Bible and a hymn book or song sheet, both of which should be provided for you upon entering the church, or laid out by the chairs or pews.

To indicate the order of the service: A printed order of service will be provided in the majority of churches. Increasing numbers of churches will have a projected screen display. The minister or lay preacher will make periodic announcements.

Will a guest who is not a member of the United Reformed Church be expected to do anything other than sit? It is expected that you would stand and sing at the same time as the rest of the congregation, but it is acceptable not to if you so wish.

Are there any parts of the service in which a guest who is not a member of the United Reformed Church should not participate? During the actual baptism, the minister will ask the congregation to make promises concerning bringing the candidate up in the Christian faith; if you are not Christian it would be inappropriate to join in these promises.

If not disruptive to the service, is it OK to:

Take pictures? Possibly, but ask permission beforehand.

Use a flash? Possibly, but ask permission beforehand.

Use video recording equipment? Possibly, but ask permission beforehand.

Use audio recording equipment? Possibly, but ask permission beforehand.

Will contributions to the church be collected at the service? Yes, a collection will be announced during the service and will be made by the passing of a plate or small bag around the congregation.

How much is it customary to contribute? Members of the church may give up to a tenth of their weekly income as their offering, and visitors normally give pocket change. It is optional to contribute, but generally expected that most people will.

After the ceremony

Is there usually a reception after the ceremony? There will sometimes be tea, coffee and biscuits offered in the church after the ceremony, while in other cases a full meal will be served. The family of the baptismal candidate may extend an invitation to their own house for refreshments after the ceremony, or to a local restaurant for a meal.

Would it be considered impolite to neither eat nor drink? No.

Is there a ritual before eating or drinking? In the event of a full meal, it is possible that a grace or prayer of thanksgiving will be said before eating starts.

Is there a grace or benediction after eating or drinking? No.

Is there a traditional form of address for clergy who may be at the reception? This varies between churches and, while there is no harm in enquiring what form of address is appropriate, it is unlikely that you would cause offence by using the wrong one. Clergy can be called 'Reverend' or 'Minister', or by their first name.

Is it OK to leave early? It is fine to leave whenever you need to.

Initiation Ceremony

The ceremony of confirmation, or believer's baptism, which marks the confirmation by the Holy Spirit of what took place during infant baptism, takes place when an individual feels ready to make a firm commitment of faith and to be received into full church membership. Sometimes local churches have policies on the age they feel it is appropriate for a child to be confirmed, but more often it depends on the individual.

The ceremony will occasionally be a service in its own right, but usually takes place as a part of the regular service of morning worship. It will sometimes involve a group of confirmation candidates rather than just one.

Before the ceremony

Are guests usually invited by a formal invitation? Yes, or by verbal invitation.

If not stated explicitly, should one assume that children are invited? Yes.

If one cannot attend, what should one do? This is at the discretion of the individual. A polite and prompt reply, expressing regret, is recommended.

Appropriate attire

There is no official dress code for men or women, although it is worth asking the person who invited you whether the particular church you are visiting has a preference. Open-toed shoes and jewellery are fine for women.

Gifts

Is a gift customarily expected? No, although it is a nice gesture to bring a small gift – perhaps a book of prayers, a CD of Christian music, a small cross or some other symbol of the Christian faith.

Should gifts be brought to the ceremony? They are normally brought to the ceremony and given to the candidate after the ceremony is over.

The ceremony

Where will the ceremony take place? In the main sanctuary of the church.

When should guests arrive and where should they sit? It is customary to arrive at the time called. There will usually be someone to tell you where to sit. If not, try to sit close to the family of the confirmation candidate.

If arriving late, are there times when a guest should not enter the service? No.

Are there times when a guest should not leave the service? It would be preferable to stay for the whole service.

Who are the major officiants, leaders or participants in the ceremony and what do they do? [As under 'The Basic Service'.]

Elders may assist with the laying on of hands and a 'right hand of fellowship' as a welcome to those who have been confirmed and become members.

What books are used? A Bible and a hymn book or song sheet, both of which should be provided for you upon entering the church, or laid out by the chairs or pews.

To indicate the order of the service: A printed order of service will be provided in the majority of churches. Increasing numbers of churches will have a projected screen display. The minister or lay preacher will make periodic announcements.

Will a guest who is not a member of the United Reformed Church be expected to do anything other than sit? It is expected that you would stand and sing at the same time as the rest of the congregation, but it is acceptable not to if you so wish.

Are there any parts of the service in which a guest who is not a member of the United Reformed Church should not participate? During the actual baptism, the minister will ask the congregation to make promises of their commitment to support the person being confirmed; if you are not Christian it would be inappropriate to join in these promises.

Holy Communion is usually a part of this service and is normally open to those who are baptised members of the United Reformed Church, although an open invitation is often extended to all people present. In such cases the decision to receive Communion is left to the individual's discretion.

If not disruptive to the service, is it OK to:

Take pictures? Possibly, but ask permission beforehand.
Use a flash? Possibly, but ask permission beforehand.
Use video recording equipment? Possibly, but ask permission beforehand.
Use audio recording equipment? Possibly, but ask permission beforehand.

Will contributions to the church be collected at the service? Yes, a collection will be announced during the service and will be made by the passing of a plate or small bag around the congregation.

How much is it customary to contribute? Members of the church may give up to a tenth of their weekly income as their offering, and visitors normally give pocket change. It is optional to contribute, but generally expected that most people will.

After the ceremony

Is there usually a reception after the ceremony? There will some-times be tea, coffee and biscuits offered in the church after the ceremony, while in other cases a full meal will be served. The confirmation candidate may extend an invitation to their own house for refreshments after the ceremony, or to a local restaurant for a meal.

Would it be considered impolite to neither eat nor drink? No.

Is there a ritual before eating or drinking? In the event of a full meal, it is possible that a grace or prayer of thanksgiving will be said before eating starts.

Is there a grace or benediction after eating or drinking? No.

Is there a traditional form of address for clergy who may be at the reception? This varies between churches and, while there is no harm in enquiring what form of address is appropriate, it is unlikely that you would cause offence by using the wrong one. Clergy can be called 'Reverend' or 'Minister', or by their first name.

Is it OK to leave early? It is fine to leave whenever you need to.

Marriage Ceremony

Christians believe that man and woman are given to each other in marriage as a gift of God for their mutual fulfilment and for the nurturing of children.

The wedding service will be a ceremony unto itself with its own order of service comprising readings, prayers and a short talk, and will focus on the making of promises and the exchange of rings. It will usually last between half an hour and an hour, depending on how much music and singing there is, and the length of the talk.

Before the ceremony

Are guests usually invited by a formal invitation? Yes.

If not stated explicitly, should one assume that children are invited? No. If you are unsure, it is worth asking rather than just bringing the children.

If one cannot attend, what should one do? Send a polite and prompt reply, and send a gift if possible.

Appropriate attire

Men: Jacket and tie or smart casual is the normal custom, but it is worth enquiring beforehand if unsure.

Women: Dress or a skirt and blouse or a trouser suit. Open-toed shoes and jewellery are permissible. A hat is acceptable.

Gifts

Is a gift customarily expected? Yes. The couple will often have a 'wedding list' from which family and friends can choose an appropriate gift to buy.

Should gifts be brought to the ceremony? Usually given to the couple to be placed on a table at the reception after the ceremony.

The ceremony

Where will the ceremony take place? In the main sanctuary of the church. The wedding couple will be at the front of the congregation throughout the service.

When should guests arrive and where should they sit? Arrive at the time called. There will usually be stewards or ushers on hand who will show you where to sit. Traditionally, this will be the right-hand side for the bride's family and friends and the left-hand side for the groom's family and friends.

If arriving late, are there times when a guest should not enter the ceremony? No.

Are there times when a guest should not leave the ceremony? It would be preferable to stay for the whole service.

Who are the major officiants, leaders or participants at the ceremony and what do they do?

As under 'The Basic Service'. And:

An 'authorised person', who will take the couple through the signing of the registers after the ceremony.

The bride's father, who will traditionally 'give away' the bride. However, other people can take on this role, depending on the age and circumstance of the bride.

The best man, who will support the groom throughout the service.

What books are used? A Bible and a hymn book or song sheet, both of which should be provided for you upon entering the church, or laid out by the chairs or pews.

To indicate the order of the service: A printed order of service will be provided in the majority of churches. Increasing numbers of churches will have a projected screen display. The minister or lay preacher will make periodic announcements.

Will a guest who is not a member of the United Reformed Church be expected to do anything other than sit? It is expected that you would stand and sing at the same time as the rest of the congregation, but it is acceptable not to if you so wish.

Are there any parts of the service in which a guest who is not a member of the United Reformed Church should not participate? No.

If not disruptive to the service, is it OK to:

Take pictures? Possibly, but ask permission beforehand.

Use a flash? Possibly, but ask permission beforehand.

Use video recording equipment? Possibly, but ask permission beforehand.

Use audio recording equipment? Possibly, but ask permission beforehand.

Will contributions to the church be collected at the service? Occasionally, a collection will be announced during the service and will be made by the passing of a plate or small bag around the congregation, although this is not so common at weddings.

How much is it customary to contribute? Most people contribute pocket change. It is optional to contribute, but generally expected that most people will.

After the ceremony

Is there usually a reception after the ceremony? There will usually be a private reception after the service, which will be organised by the wedding couple, and details will be provided with the wedding invitation. It will take place at a private venue, and could last through the rest of the day and evening. Depending on the wishes of the wedding couple, food and drink may be served and there may be speeches, the cutting of a wedding cake, dancing and music.

Would it be considered impolite to neither eat nor drink? Yes, unless there are special circumstances, and it is advisable to inform the wedding couple of any special dietary requirements before the day.

Is there a ritual before eating or drinking? After all the guests are seated, it is common for everyone to wait for the official entry of the bride and groom to the dining hall. There may be a grace said before people start to eat.

Is there a ritual after eating or drinking? There may be an official departure of the bride and groom from the dining hall.

Is there a traditional greeting for the family? It is common for the wedding couple, their parents, best man and bridesmaids to meet all guests in an official line before the meal. Offer your congratulations and best wishes.

Is there a traditional form of address for clergy who may be at the reception? This varies between churches and, while there is no harm in enquiring what form of address is appropriate, it is unlikely that you would cause offence by using the wrong one. Clergy can be called 'Reverend' or 'Minister', or by their first name.

Is it OK to leave early? It is fine to leave whenever you need to.

Some basic beliefs

In the United Reformed Church, in contrast to some other Christian denominations, it is acknowledged that marriages can fail. It is possible, trusting in God's forgiveness and the renewing power of the Holy Spirit, for a couple to get remarried in church, when one or both have been previously divorced (depending on the circumstances of the divorce).

Funerals and Mourning

A funeral service in the United Reformed Church is likely to contain elements of grieving for the person who has died, thanksgiving for his or her life and for the faith that Christians share and a proclamation of that faith in words and scripture. It will also celebrate the new life that Jesus Christ promised in his own resurrection.

A funeral is usually a ceremony in its own right, and will last between half an hour and an hour.

Before the ceremony

How soon after the death does the funeral usually take place? It can be within one week, but occasionally takes a little longer depending on arrangements with the local funeral director and the graveyard or crematorium.

What should someone who is not a member of the United Reformed Church do upon hearing of the death of a member of that faith? Telephone or visit the bereaved, or send a card expressing your sympathy.

Gifts

Is it appropriate to send flowers or make a contribution? Yes, flowers may be sent upon hearing the news of the person's death or after the funeral, either to the bereaved person's house or to the funeral itself. It may also be appropriate to make a donation to a favoured charity of the deceased person.

Appropriate attire

Men: Jacket and tie.

Women: A dress, skirt and blouse or trouser suit. Open-toed shoes and modest jewellery are permissible.

Dark colours are usually appropriate, although sometimes the family of the deceased request that people wear brighter colours out of thanksgiving for his or her life.

The ceremony

Where will the ceremony take place? At a church within the main sanctuary, to be either followed or preceded by a service at the crematorium or cemetery. The ceremony at the crematorium or cemetery is sometimes a ceremony only for the family, depending on their own wishes.

When should guests arrive and where should they sit? Arrive at the time called. There will normally be a steward at the door to show you where to sit. If not, you are free to sit where you like, while reserving the first few rows of seats or pews for the family of the deceased.

If arriving late, are there times when a guest should not enter the ceremony? No.

Will there be an open coffin? Rarely.

Is a guest expected to view the body? In the event of an open coffin, it would be considered appropriate to view the body.

What is appropriate behaviour upon viewing the body? Pausing for a few moments to offer a prayer.

Who are the major officiants at the ceremony and what do they do?

A minister, lay leader or local preacher will preside at the service. Members of the deceased's family, colleagues and friends may contribute by giving a short talk about the deceased or reciting a reading.

What books are used? A Bible and a hymn book or song sheet, both of which should be provided for you upon entering the church, or laid out by the chairs or pews.

To indicate the order of the service: A printed order of service will be provided in the majority of churches. The minister or lay preacher will make periodic announcements.

Will a guest who is not a member of the United Reformed Church be expected to do anything other than sit? It is expected that you would stand and sing at the same time as the rest of the congregation, but it is acceptable not to if you so wish.

Are there any parts of the service in which a guest who is not a member of the United Reformed Church should not participate? No.

If not disruptive to the service, is it OK to:

Take pictures? Possibly, but ask permission beforehand.
Use a flash? Possibly, but ask permission beforehand.
Use video recording equipment? Possibly, but ask permission beforehand.
Use audio recording equipment? Possibly, but ask permission beforehand.

Will contributions to the church be collected at the service? There will often be a collection for a particular church, charity or area of concern that was close to the deceased. Money can be given in cash or cheque.

How much is it customary to contribute? This can vary from pocket change to a substantial donation, depending on the judgement of the individual.

The interment

Should guests attend the interment? Yes, unless the family have asked for it to be private.

Whom should one ask for directions? Directions will normally be given out at the church, or in advance if the interment is to take place before the ceremony in the church.

What happens at the graveside of a burial? The mourners will gather around the graveside and listen to the words and prayers of the presiding minister as the coffin is lowered into the ground. It is sometimes appropriate to offer a flower to go into the grave, or to put a handful of earth into the grave. Otherwise, mourners are expected simply to be present.

What happens at a cremation? The mourners will enter the crematorium at the same time as the family and other guests, and sit and listen to the service led by the presiding minister. There will be a moment of commendation, at which point the congregation will stand, then curtains will close around the coffin which will be removed out of sight. Otherwise, mourners are expected simply to be present.

After the funeral

Is it appropriate to visit the home of the bereaved after the funeral? After the funeral there will usually be refreshments served at the church, in the home, or in a local hall or hotel. After that, visiting the bereaved depends on the closeness of your relationship with them or the deceased. If you had a close relationship, it would be appropriate to visit the bereaved more than once.

How soon after the funeral will a mourner usually return to a normal work schedule? This varies, depending on the individual.

How soon after the funeral will a mourner usually return to a normal social schedule? This is entirely at the discretion of the individual.

5. HOME CELEBRATIONS

Not applicable for United Reformed Churches.

Glossary of Common
Religious Terms and Names

'Abdu'l-Bahá ('Ab-DOOL-bah-HAH'): Son of Bahá'u'lláh, the founder of the Bahá'í faith. His name means 'Servant of Baha'.

Adhan ('AHD-han'): In Islam, and announcement made by a *muazzin*, and aired through public loudspeakers, alerting people that the time of prayer has started.

Aliyah ('ah-lee-YAH'): [Hebrew] Literally translated as 'going up', it is the honour of being called to participate in the reading of the Torah in a synagogue/temple.

Allah'u'Abhá ('Ah-lah-oo-ab-HAH'): [Arabic] A Bahá'í phrase that means 'God is most glorious'.

Alleluia (Hallelujah): A common pronouncement in Christian worship, from the Hebrew for: 'Praise ye the Lord!'.

Amidah ('ah-mee-DAH'): A series of praises, thanks and petitions to God in Jewish worship. Recited by the entire congregation while standing, they are the central part of the prayer service.

Apostles' Creed: The most widely used creed, or declaratory affirmation, in the Christian church in the West. Based on a creed used in Rome in the third century and given its present form in France in the sixth or seventh century.

Ardas ('AHR-das'): [Gurmukhi] Community prayer led by one person in a Sikh *gurdwara* service. Blessings for special occasions or events may be requested during the *ardas*.

Ayyám-i-há ('Ah-yah-mee-HAH'): [Arabic] 'Days of Ha', which Bahá'ís celebrate from 26 February TO 1 March. The holiday is devoted to hospitality, charity and gift-giving and to spiritually preparing oneself for the annual fast that lasts for all 19 days of the last month in the Bahá'í calendar.

The Báb ('Bob'): [Arabic] Literally means 'Gate' or 'Door' and is used in the Bahá'í faith to refer to Mírzá 'Ali-Muhammad, a direct descendent of the Prophet Muhammad, who announced in mid-19th-century Persia that he was the forerunner of the Universal Messenger of God.

450

Bahá'í ('Ba-HIGH'): [Arabic] A follower of Bahá'u'lláh, founder of the Bahá'í faith.

Bahá'u'lláh ('Bah-HAH-oo-LAH'): Prophet. The founder of the Bahá'í faith, whose name means 'Glory of God'.

Baptism: In Christianity, a ritual washing for initiation; a sign of remission of sin and of spiritual rebirth by symbolically participating in Christ's death, burial and resurrection. Depending on the specific Christian denomination, baptism may occur at birth, during the preteen or teen years or as an adult.

Bar mitzvah ('bahr MITS-vah'): Jewish initiation ceremony for boys. Occurs upon reaching the age of 13, when, according to Jewish tradition, males are liable for their own transgressions and their fathers no longer bear this responsibility.

Bat mitzvah ('baht MITS-vah'): Jewish initiation ceremony for girls. Occurs at the age of 12 or 13. According to Jewish law, females attain religious adulthood and responsibility upon reaching 12 years and one day.

Benedict XVI, Pope: Elected in 2005, known for his conservative approach to doctrine.

Bhagavad Gita ('BAHG-ah-vahd GEE-tah'): [Sanskrit] The epic Hindu poem in which Krishna, god in human form, expounds the nature of reality.

Bible: As used by Judaism, applies to the Hebrew Scriptures and ascribes primary authority to the Torah (the first five books of the Bible); secondary authority to the Books of the Prophets; and tertiary authority to the Kethubim, whose thirteen books include Psalms, Proverbs and Daniel. As used by Christianity, *Bible* refers to the Hebrew and Christian Scriptures known as the Old and New Testaments.

Bimah ('BEE-mah'): [Hebrew] The part of the sanctuary in a Jewish synagogue or temple from which the service is led and where the rabbi and cantor stand and sit. It is usually raised above the level where congregants sit and is at the front or in the middle of the sanctuary.

Book of Mormon: Joseph Smith's translation of God's revelations. First published in 1830.

Booth, William: (1829–1912) Founder of the Salvation Army.

Brahman ('BRAH-mahn'): [Sanskrit] In Hinduism, the One, All-Encompassing soul.

Brit ('breet'): [Hebrew] The Jewish birth ceremony. The term literally means 'covenant'. For boys, the *brit milah* ('breet mee-LAH'), or the 'covenant of circumcision', occurs on the eighth day of a male child's life. The *brit bat* or *brit hayyim* ('breet baht' or 'breet hy-YEEM'), the 'covenant of a daughter' or the 'covenant of life', is a naming ceremony for a girl.

Calvin, John: (1509–1564) Christian reformer considered to be the father of Presbyterianism.

Censer: An incense burner holder. Smoke from the incense represents prayers being carried to heaven. Used in Greek Orthodox churches.

Chalice: In Christianity, a cup, sometimes covered with gold and often with a tall stem. Held by a priest or other clergy and contains the holy wine, which, depending on the Christian denomination, either symbolises the blood of Christ or is believed to have become transubstantiated into the actual blood of Christ.

Chrismation: Term used in Orthodox churches for the confirmation (or first Communion) of a child. During baptism, the child is fully immersed three times in a baptismal font, and then anointed (or 'chrismated') with oil on the forehead, chest, hands, neck, back and feet.

Christian Greek Scriptures: The term Jehovah's Witnesses use for the Scriptures written in the time of the early Christian church; see 'New Testament'.

Chanukah ('HAH-noo-kah'): In the Jewish calendar, the Festival of Lights, which commemorates the victory in about 163 BC of the Maccabees over the Syrians, who tried to eradicate Judaism.

Chumash ('KOOH-mahsh'): [Hebrew] The first five books of the Torah, also known as the Five Books of Moses. These are the biblical books of Genesis, Exodus, Leviticus, Numbers and Deuteronomy. It also contains the traditional sections from Prophets that are associated with each Torah section and are read after the Torah reading.

Communion: A rite through which Christians believe they receive either the symbolic or the real body and blood of Christ as assurance that God has forgiven their sins; also known as the Eucharist.

Confirmation: A church rite in which one who was previously baptised expresses his or her faith in Jesus Christ.

Creed: A statement of belief. Christian churches generally use one of the early Christian creeds, either the Apostles' Creed or the Nicene Creed.

Dedication: The term used in some Christian churches for a ceremony for infants or young children during which the child's parents publicly commit themselves to raise the child in the teachings of Jesus.

Discarnate spirit: Spiritualist term for a spirit living in the spirit world.

Eddy, Mary Baker: (1821–1910) Founder of the Church of Christ, Scientist.

Epistles: Generally refers to the letters of St Paul or another New Testament writer.

Error: The Christian Science term for 'evil'.

Eucharist: The most widely accepted name for Communion, the central act of Christian worship, in which Christians believe they receive either the symbolic or the real body and blood of Christ as assurance that God has forgiven their sins.

Feast days: Days set aside in Roman Catholic and liturgical churches to commemorate significant events in the life of Jesus Christ, the saints, or the Christian people.

Festival of Ridván ('RIZ-von'): [Arabic] A twelve-day Bahá'í holiday celebrated from 21 April to 2 May; it commemorates the 12 days in 1863 when Bahá'u'lláh, the prophet-founder of the Bahá'í faith, publicly proclaimed in a garden in Baghdad his mission as God's messenger for this age.

First Reader: The man or woman who conducts a Christian Science service. The Second Reader shares the platform with the First Reader and presides in the absence of the First Reader.

Fox, George: (1624–1691) Founder of the Quaker movement.

Friend: a traditional way for Quakers to refer to each other.

Ghanta: The name of a bell used in a Hindu worship ceremony.

Gospel: The New Testament Books of Matthew, Mark, Luke and John, which record the life and ministry of Jesus. *Gospel* literally means 'good news'. For Christians, the 'good news' is that the Son of God became a man in the person of Jesus and suffered for the sins of humanity so people will not have to undergo that suffering.

Grace: A Christian term for the loving mercy that God shows people through Jesus Christ.

Gurdwara: Place in which a Sikh service of worship takes place. It literally means 'Gate to the Guru' and is an environment that has been especially readied for uplifting one's consciousness.

Guru Nanak: (1469–1539) The first Sikh guru, from whose life and teachings the Sikh faith grew.

Haftarah ('hahf-TOH-rah'): [Hebrew] In Judaism, the Torah reading during a service in a synagogue or temple.

Haggadah ('hah-GAH-dah'): [Hebrew] The Jewish text, usually in Hebrew and English, that tells the Passover story and its meaning for each generation. Read at the Passover *seder*.

Hajj ('hahj'): [Arabic] A pilgrimage to Mecca that a Muslim must make at least once in his or her lifetime if physically and financially able.

Healing: In Christian Science, a realisation of God's goodness and the perfection of man made in his image; regeneration of thought reflected on the body.

Hebrew Scriptures: Name used by Jehovah's Witnesses for the scriptures known to Christians as the Old Testament.

Holy Communion: Also called the Lord's Supper. A rite through which Christians believe they receive either the symbolic or the real body and blood of Christ as assurance that God has forgiven their sins.

Holy Spirit: In Christianity, the empowering spirit of God; the third person of the Triune God.

Huppah ('hoo-PAH'): [Hebrew] The canopy under which a Jewish wedding ceremony takes place. Symbolises the canopy of the heavens under which all life transpires.

Icons: Two-dimensional artistic images of saints. Found primarily in Orthodox churches.

Imam ('EE-mahm'): [Arabic] In Islam, the person who leads prayers and delivers a sermon.

Incarnate spirit: Spiritualist term for a spirit living in the physical world.

Jehovah: According to Jehovah's Witnesses, the one true name for God.

John XXIII, Pope: (1881–1963) Known for his role in the Second Vatican Council.

John Paul II, Pope: (1920–2005) Known for his international, interfaith efforts.

Jumma ('JUH-mah'): [Arabic] In Islam, noon prayer on Friday. This congregational prayer is recited at a central mosque designated for that purpose.

Kaddish ('KAH-dish'): [Hebrew] The Jewish prayer for the dead.

Karma: In Hindu belief, the term for the consequences of one's actions, which determine one's lot in a future reincarnation from one lifetime to another.

Khalsa: Meaning 'King's Own'; followers of the Sikh faith.

Kiddush Cup ('kee-DOOSH'): [Hebrew] Used to drink ritual wine at certain Jewish ritual events, such as the *shabbat* meal or by the bridal couple during a wedding ceremony.

Kingdom Halls: The name of Jehovah's Witnesses' meeting halls.

Kosher ('KOH-sher'): [Hebrew] Food deemed fit for consumption according to Jewish dietary laws, which prohibit such foods as pork or shellfish and the mixing of dairy and meat products at the same meal or within several hours after eating either one of these dishes.

Langar ('LAHN-gahr'): [Gurmukhi] The vegetarian meal prepared in a prayerful environment and served as an offering after or throughout a Sikh worship service to the *sangat,* or community of worshippers.

Lectio divina: The ancient Christian practice of spiritual reading, once only the practice of monks, now commonly practised by laypeople.

Luther, Martin: (1483–1546) Christian reformer whose objections to doctrines and practices of the Roman Catholic Church were one of the most significant factors causing the Reformation.

Mantra: A sacred word of syllable. In Hinduism, the most sacred sound, often used as a mantra, is OM. (OM is also a symbol of God, or Brahman.)

Mazal tov ('MAH-zahl tohv'): A Jewish term, literally meaning 'Good luck', but used as 'congratulations'. Especially used at the occasion of a *simcha.*

Meeting: The Quaker term for worship service.

Menorah ('min-OHR-ah'): [Hebrew] A seven-branched candelabra, which has become a central motif in the consciousness of the Jewish people. Often placed on the *bima,* or pulpit, in a synagogue or temple.

Mohel ('MOH-hail'): [Hebrew] A specially trained male who performs a ritual Jewish circumcision. The *mohel* may also be a rabbi or physician.

Mortal Mind A Christian Science term for error or evil; the belief in a mind or life separate from God.

Muazzin ('MOO-ah-zin'): [Arabic] In Islam, the person who calls Muslims to prayer.

Musallah ('muh-SAL-ah'): In Islam, a room in a mosque in which prayers are recited. Every *musallah* is oriented toward Mecca, which Muslims face during prayers.

Naw-Rúz ('Naw-ROOZ'): [Arabic] The Bahá'í New Year's Day, which occurs on 21 March. The day is astronomically fixed so the new year commences on the first day of spring.

New Testament: Scriptures written in the time of the early Christian church. Comprises four Gospels, the Acts of the Apostles, 21 epistles, and the Apocalyptic revelations of John.

Nicene Creed: A declaratory affirmation in the Christian church that states the full deity of Jesus Christ.

Nineteen Day Feast: The centrepiece of the Bahá'í community, it is held every nineteen days and is the local community's regular worship gathering. 'Feast' does not imply that a large meal will be served, but that a 'spiritual feast' – worship, companionship and unity – will be available.

Offertory: The portion of a Christian service set apart for the collection from congregants.

Old Testament: The Christian name for the collection of writings sacred to Christians and Jews. Its thirty-nine books, beginning with Genesis and ending with Malachi, include history, law and poems.

Panj Kakar: The five symbols which are outward signs of a Sikh disciple's discipline and strength of faith. They are *kachha* (special underwear, symbolising readiness and chastity), *kara* (a stainless steel bracelet, showing restraint and loyalty to the Guru), *kirpan* (sword, symbolising compassion and one's task to defend the truth), *kes* (unshorn hair) and *kanga* (small comb, which ensured the disciple's hair would remain in the image of the creator).

Paten: Holds the consecrated bread or wafer of the Eucharist during a Christian service. Depending on the denomination, the wafer either symbolises the body of Christ or is believed to have been transubstantiated into the actual body of Christ.

Pesach ('PAY-sakh'): In the Jewish calendar, the Passover, which celebrates the Jewish people's freedom from slavery in Egypt.

Pooja ('POO-jah'): [Sanskrit] In Hinduism, a ritual worship held before a specific deity.

Prasad ('prah-SAHD'): [Gurmukhi] The sweet pudding served toward the end of a Sikh service that consists of water, honey, wheat flour, and clarified butter. Prasad is considered to be a blessing from the *Siri Guru Granth Sahib* that everyone can eat.

Prasad ('PRAH-sahd'): [Sanskrit] In Hinduism, sacramental food served to those present at certain rituals and ceremonies.

Prokimenon ('Proh-KEE-min-non'): [Greek] In Orthodox churches, the verses from a Psalm intoned before the reading of the Epistle.

Proskomen ('PROS-koh-men'): [Greek] Used in Orthodox churches; means 'Let us attend'.

Purim ('POO-rim'). In the Jewish calendar, a celebration of deliverance from destruction.

Qiblah ('KIHB-lah'): [Arabic] In Islam, the direction to which the imam, or prayer leader, faces while praying.

Qur'an ('koo-RAHN'): [Arabic] Islam's holy book, also known as *The Recitation*. Consists of 114 chapters or suras and a total of 6,000 verses. Divinely revealed to the Prophet Muhammad during the twenty-two years from AD 610 to 632.

Raka'ah ('RAH-kah'): [Arabic] In Islam, a way to 'greet' and honour the mosque upon entering it. A full *raka'ah* consists of recitations during which one first stands, then makes one bow, followed by two prostrating motions (separated by a short sitting). Each prayer time requires a specific number of *raka'ah*.

Ramadan: In the Muslim calendar, a time for reflection and spiritual discipline, to express gratitude for God's guidance and to atone for past sins. From dawn to sunset, all adult Muslims whose health permits are to abstain from food, drink, smoking and sexual activity.

Rapture: The 'catching away' of believers by the Lord upon the return of Jesus Christ.

Rosh Hashanah ('rohsh hah-SHAH-nah'). The Jewish religious New Year, which also commemorates the creation of the world, traditionally counted as being approximately 5,800 years ago.

Russell, Charles Taze: (1852–1916) Founder of the Jehovah's Witnesses faith.

Sabbath School: The study service preceding the Seventh-day Adventist worship service.

Sacrament Meeting: Mormons' term for their basic service.

Salat ('SA-laht'): Muslim term for 'prayer'.

Salvation: Also known as *saved* and *born again*. Different Christian terms for accepting Christ as one's saviour and his teachings as guiding principles.

Samsara ('SAHM-sah-rah'): [Sanskrit] In Buddhism and Hinduism, recurrent birth-and-death from which one is finally liberated.

Sangat ('SAHN-gaht'): [Gurmukhi] The congregation of Sikhs and guests who come together for a Sikh worship service.

Sat Nam ('SAHT NAHM'): [Gurmukhi] A common phrase and greeting among Sikhs that means 'True Name' and acknowledges the God in all.

Scriptures: A general term for holy writings.

Seder ('SAY-dihr'): [Hebrew] The festive dinner during the Jewish holiday of Passover during which the story of the Jewish people's liberation from slavery in Egypt is told. Rituals precede and follow the meal.

Sermon A talk, based on the Gospel text that is read during a Christian service.

Shabbat ('shah-BAHT'): [Hebrew] The Jewish word for 'Sabbath'. Commemorates the day on which God rested after creating the world during the previous six days. *Shabbat* begins at sunset on Friday and ends at nightfall on Saturday.

Shahadah ('SHAH-hah-dah'): [Arabic] The Islamic Declaration of Faith. One becomes a Muslim by saying and believing the *shahadah:* 'There is no god but God and Muhammad is the messenger of God'.

Shavuot ('shah-voo-OTE'): In the Jewish calendar, the Festival of Weeks. Commemorates the giving of the Torah at Mount Sinai, as well as the first fruits of the spring harvest.

Shiva ('SHIH-vah'): [Hebrew] The seven days immediately after the funeral of a family member during which Jews sit in mourning.

Sh'ma ('shih-MAH'): A central prayer of the Jewish worship service. Essentially a statement of faith that is derived from Deuteronomy, chapter 6: 'Hear O Israel, the Lord is our God, the Lord is One'.

Shoghi Effendi ('SHOW-gey Eh-FEN-dee'): Grandson of 'Abdu'l-Bahá, who was the founder of the Bahá'í faith. Shoghi Effendi was also called 'the Guardian'.

Shraddha ('SHRAD-dah'): [Sanskrit] A Hindu ceremony intended to liberate the soul of the deceased for its ascent to heaven.

Simcha ('SIHM-khah'): A Jewish term, meaning 'to rejoice'. May be used during a service to refer to a special happy event, such as a birth, a bar or bat mitzvah or a wedding.

Siri Guru Granth Sahib ('SEE-ree GOO-roo GRANTH-SAH-HEEB'): [Gurmukhi] Scriptures compiled by the fifth Sikh guru, Arjan Dev, which contain sacred writings by several Sikh gurus and Hindu and Muslim saints. Since then, Sikhs have bowed before the *Siri Guru Granth Sahib,* consulted it as their only guru, and treated it with reverence.

Smith, Joseph: (1805–1844) Founder of the Church of Jesus Christ of Latter-day Saints, also known as the Mormons.

Speaking in Tongues: Speaking in a language unknown to those speaking it, a phenomenon associated with the coming of the Holy

Spirit (the empowering quality of God) and common to Pentecostal faiths.

Sri: Literally, blessed, holy. A prefix commonly attached to the names of male religious leaders in India.

Sukkot ('soo-KOTE'). In the Jewish calendar, the Feast of Booths. A seven-day harvest holiday. This usually occurs in early or mid-October.

Taslim ('tahs-lihm'): In Islam, the peace greeting, 'Peace be upon all of you and the mercy and the blessings of God', which is repeated twice at the end of prayer.

Theotokos ('Thee-oh-TOH-kohs'): [Greek] Used in Orthodox church-. es; means 'Mother of God'.

Torah ('TOH-rah'): [Hebrew] Most commonly used to refer to the scroll of the Five Books of Moses, but its broader meaning includes the full body of rabbinic contributions to Judaism.

Upanishads: Hindu scriptures.

Vocal ministry: A spoken contribution to a Quaker meeting for worship.

Wadu ('WAH-doo'): [Arabic] In Islam, ablutions of the hands, face and feet performed before prayer.

Waheguru: Sikh term used most often to refer to the supreme being, or creator of all; the word means 'Wonderful Teacher'.

Williams, Rowan: (1950–) The current Archbishop of Canterbury, the symbolic head of the Church of England and the Anglican Communion.

Yahrzeit ('YAHR-tzite'): [Hebrew] In Judaism, the yearly anniversary of the death of a member of the immediate family. Upon the *yahrzeit*, a wife, husband and/or children attend services at synagogue and light a *yahrzeit* candle at home.

Yoga ('YOH-gah'): [Sanskrit] Specific disciplines in Hinduism to achieve enlightenment that address the intellect, emotions and labour and service to others.

Yom Kippur ('yohm kee-POOR'). In the Jewish calendar, the Day of Atonement, on which one engages in reflection and prayer and formally repents for sins committed during the previous Hebrew year.

Calendar of Religious Holidays and Festivals

The Gregorian calendar, in use throughout the world, was first introduced in 1582 by Pope Gregory XIII as a corrected form of the old Julian calendar.

The Hindu calendar is lunisolar and governs Hindu religious life and almost all Indian festivals.

The Jewish calendar is the official calendar of the Jewish religious community and is used to mark the dates of annual religious events and holidays.

The Muslim calendar is the official calendar in many Muslim countries, and is used throughout the Islamic world to mark religious events and festivals.

The following chart describes the basic structure of these calendars. Each list begins with the first month of the year.

GREGORIAN

The solar year of the Gregorian calendar consists of 365 days, except in a leap year – occurring every four years, in an even-numbered year – which has 366 days. (Centenary years are leap years only if they are evenly divisible by 400.)

Month	Number of Days
January	31
February	28
in leap year	29
March	31
April	30
May	31
June	30
July	31
August	31

September	30
October	31
November	30
December	31

HINDU

In the Hindu calendar, the solar year is divided into twelve lunar months in accordance with the successive entrances of the sun into the signs of the zodiac; the months vary in length from twenty-nine to thirty-two days. An intercalary month is inserted after every month in which two new moons occur (once in three years), and this intercalary month has the name of the month that precedes it. The months correspond approximately to the Gregorian months shown in parentheses in this chart.

Months
Chai (March–April)
Baisakh (April–May)
Jeth (May–June)
Asarh (June–July)
Sawan (July–August)
Bhadon (August–September)
Asin (September–October)
Kartik (October–November)
Aghan (November–December)
Pus (December–January)
Magh (January–February)
Phagun (February–March)

JEWISH

The Jewish calendar is based on both the solar and the lunar cycles. The lunar year, averaging 354 days, is adjusted to the solar year by periodic leap years, occurring approximately once every three years, which contain an intercalary month and ensure that the major religious holidays fall in the proper season. The months correspond approximately to the Gregorian months shown in parentheses in this chart.

Month	Number of Days
Tishrei (September–October)	30
Chesvan (October–November)	29
in some years	30
Kislev (November–December)	29
in some years	30
Tevet (December–January)	29
Shevat (January–February)	30
Adar (February–March)	29
in some years	30
Adar II	29
(intercalary month in leap year only)	
Nisan (March–April)	30
Iyar (April–May)	29
Sivan (May–June)	30
Tammuz (June–July)	29
Av (July–August)	30
Elul (August–September)	29

MUSLIM

The Muslim calendar is based on the lunar year. Each year consists of 354 days or 355 days (in leap years). The number of days per month is adjusted throughout the year, in accordance with each lunar cycle. The beginning of the Muslim year retrogresses through the solar year; it completes a full cycle every $32^{1}/_{2}$ years.

Month	Number of Days
Muharram	29 or 30
Safar	29 or 30
Rabi I	29 or 30
Rabi II	29 or 30
Jumada I	29 or 30
Jumada II	29 or 30
Rajab	29 or 30

Calendar of Religious Holidays and Festivals

Sha'ban	29 or 30
Ramadan	29 or 30
Shawwal	29 or 30
Dhu al-Qa'dah	29 or 30
Dhu al-Hijjah	29 or 30

Summary of Proper Forms for Addressing Leaders of Various Faiths

When you are introduced to the spiritual leader, member of the clergy or officiator of the religious ceremony that you are attending, what do you say after 'I am so pleased to meet you, . . .'? Most leaders of congregations or other religious groups are very understanding and sympathetic about visitors' confusion over what form of address to use, but checking this list will give you a head start.

Anglican: In churches of 'higher', catholic tradition, the clergy may be addressed as 'Father', whilst in churches of 'lower', evangelical tradition it is common to address the clergy by their first name. Some older people use the title 'vicar' or 'rector'.

Bahá'í: There are no clergy.

Baptist: 'Pastor' is the more formal address, but most would be happy being called 'Mr' or 'Mrs' followed by their surname, or even just by their Christian name.

Buddhist: There are many different conventions followed in the various Buddhist traditions.

Christadelphian: There is no conventional form of address.

Christian Science (Church of Christ, Scientist): There are no clergy.

Free Presbyterian: 'Mr' or 'Sir'.

Hindu: 'Swamiji' if a monk, 'Panditji' if a priest.

Jehovah's Witnesses: Either 'Brother' or 'Mr', followed by last name.

Jewish: 'Rabbi' or 'Cantor'.

Lutheran: When speaking English, usually 'Pastor' followed by the last name is appropriate; occasionally, clergy prefer being called 'Father', but this is quite unusual.

Methodist: 'Reverend' is a formal style of address; clergy will often prefer informality once introduced.

Mormon (Church of Jesus Christ of Latter-day Saints): The chief officiant is referred to as 'Bishop', followed by his last name. His counsellors are addressed as 'Brother', followed by their last names.

Muslim (Islam): An imam may be directly addressed by the title of 'Imam' or by his name.

Orthodox: 'Father'.

Pentecostal: 'Pastor'.

Quaker: There are no clergy.

Roman Catholic: 'Father' if greeting a priest. 'Bishop' if greeting a bishop. 'Your Eminence' if greeting a cardinal.

Salvation Army: Officers are officially addressed by rank, such as 'Sergeant' or 'Major', but many will request that they are addressed simply by their first name.

Seventh-day Adventist: 'Elder' or 'Pastor'.

Sikh: 'Granthi' and then the first name, or 'Giani Ji'.

Spiritualist: 'Minister'.

Unitarian: 'Mr', 'Mrs', 'Ms', 'Dr', 'Reverend' or their first name.

United Reformed Church: 'Reverend' or 'Minister', or by their first name.